BIBLIOTECA DELL' «ARCHIVUM ROMANICUM»
Serie I: Storia, Letteratura, Paleografia

508

GIADA GUASSARDO

THE ITALIAN LOVE POETRY OF LUDOVICO ARIOSTO

Court Culture and Classicism

Preface by
LINA BOLZONI

LEO S. OLSCHKI EDITORE
MMXXI

Casa Editrice Leo S. Olschki
Viuzzo del Pozzetto, 8
50126 Firenze
www.olschki.it

Published with the contribution of
Balliol College (University of Oxford)

ISBN 978 88 222 6731 3

PREFACE

There are sometimes aspects of the production of a classic that for various reasons have been neglected or have remained at the margins of scholarly attention. This has been the case with Ariosto's love poems, which Giada Guassardo here explores through a careful and often compelling analysis, through the critical tools she developed during her undergraduate years at the Scuola Normale of Pisa and during her PhD at Oxford.

The book opens with a description of the complex and somewhat dubious state of the texts: an – as yet unpublished – critical edition by Maria Finazzi exists, but the poems' destination remains uncertain as the 'canzoniere' discovered by Cesare Bozzetti in 1985, which only includes a part of the *rime*, was never meant to be published by Ariosto, despite a vogue for the *libro di poesia* in the early decades of the sixteenth century. Guassardo's careful analysis defines a precise context for Ariosto's lyrics, indicating their debt towards tradition as well as their specific characteristics, the poet's personal negotiations with this tradition. While Quattrocento court poetry certainly constitutes the background to Ariosto's lyric production, the poems, as this book demonstrates, are also marked by an intense dialogue with classical poetry and by autobiographical elements. Moreover, Guassardo's foregrounding of the textual features which the *rime* share with the *Satire* and the *Orlando furioso*, on the one hand lends new interest to these texts, and on the other usefully complicates our understanding of Ariosto's process of self-fashioning. Especially interesting, one feels, in relation to the *Furioso*, is the book's examination of themes such as error, madness, faithfulness, jealousy, reciprocity and recompense in the love relationship, and the tension between desire and duty. In light of these, the complex matter of Ariosto's involvement with the court, here intertwined with the problem of the *rime*'s ultimate destination, acquires new and interesting facets. To give an example, the capitolo *O vera o falsa che la fama suone* seems to recall an event in Ariosto's life, a visit the poet made to a bloodied battlefield, here used as a lens through which to view in a new light the old motif of love and death. Ariosto explains that he is seeking a remedy for the pains of love but now sees that these are greater even than those suffered by the soldiers, as to their pains death, at least, puts an end. Guassardo examines the way in which the text constructs its addressee: the name of the battle is not stated (perhaps it is the battle of Ravenna, which is also mentioned in the *Furioso*), but it does not have to be because the court readers to whom the poem is ideally addressed would have been aware of this fact. Indeed, as Guassardo suggests, we may be dealing with an elegiac transfiguration of a journey undertaken as a court duty. Examined through this critical lens, it is possible to fruitfully rethink the question of what sort of audience, whether public of private, Ariosto had in mind for his *rime*. Similarly, his relationship with Cardinal Ippolito is usefully complicated and nuanced by Guassardo's analysis of the capitolo *Del bel numero vostro havrete un manco*: in addition to the duty of service, often heavy and sometimes neglected, to the cardinal, what the poem stages is also a code of love shared by the two men, which points to a hitherto less than evident complicity.

Moving beyond a critical tradition that reads courtly poetry as well as most of sixteenth-century lyrics purely as a collection of *topoi*, this book infuses new life into these texts, allowing the erotic tension that underlies them to emerge, and giving just relevance to the pre-eminence they assign to the present over memory, the manner in which their 'life drawing' of the poet's feelings powerfully involves those who read his poems. Guassardo studies the way Ariosto utilises the rich tradition of mythological figures, and the symbology that had aggregated around the animal world, retracing the sophisticated erotic and intellectual game afforded by the interpretation of *imprese*. One of the main focuses of this book is the representation of the female figure, new facets of which are the position of equality enjoyed within the relationship of love, and a 'canon of beauties' that, while indebted to tradition, also lingers on the allure of the naked body, without, however, neglecting to touch on the inner world – through an appraisal, for example, of silence, which becomes the cipher of prudence and an understanding of the rules of society. Next to the *rime*'s relationship with classical tradition (especially Ovid, Tibullus and Catullus), this book explores their dialogue with contemporary treatises on love, women and on the theory of colours. In this context, Guassardo probes Ariosto's indebtedness to Bembo, but also brings into clearer light his relationship with Celio Calcagnini, the Ferrarese humanist whose encyclopaedic knowledge had already garnered interest from Ariosto scholars, but is here revealed as a truly significant interlocutor.

Ariosto will always intrigue and stimulate. This book places his poems on a carefully delineated geographical and cultural map, teasing out a complex portrait of their author; it is an invaluable guide for his readers.

LINA BOLZONI

ACKNOWLEDGEMENTS

This book evolved from my doctoral thesis in Medieval and Modern Languages, which I started to write at the University of Oxford (Balliol College) in 2016 and defended in 2020. A shorter version of Chapter III has been published separately as 'The Portrayals of Women in Ariosto's *Rime*', *Modern Language Review*, 115.3 (2020), pp. 538-572.

During my PhD years I was extremely fortunate in having truly exceptional *maestri* whose guidance was crucial, not only as regards this specific work but for my overall progress as a scholar. To them goes my deepest gratitude. The role played by Marco Dorigatti was certainly much greater than that normally associated with a supervisor. Not only did he believe in my project from the outset: he encouraged my own passion for Ariosto, offered me new ideas to think about and followed every step of my work with great care and attention to detail. Simon Gilson and Bernhard Huss in their role of examiners gave me feedback on the thesis and, later, were invaluable advisers in the thesis-to-book transition, generously helping me on my way through to its final form. Maria Cristina Cabani, as my former supervisor at the University of Pisa, was the first to encourage me to investigate this subject matter, and continued to provide insightful suggestions throughout my Oxford years. Extremely useful inputs also came from my tutors at the Scuola Normale Superiore, Lina Bolzoni and Alberto Casadei, whose Ariosto studies have always been constant orientation points for me. My sincere thanks also goes to Maria Finazzi for generously sharing with me her unpublished materials, which have been a fundamental informative basis for my own work.

Balliol College and the Arts and Humanities Research Council provided financial support for my period in Oxford: without them, this experience would not have materialised. I am also very grateful to the Fondation Barbier-Mueller of Geneva, which welcomed me at the final stage of my research, and in particular to Massimo Danzi, with whom I enjoyed illuminating conversations during my stay there.

Sylvia Greenup gave an invaluable contribution to my book by reviewing its language with unremitting attentiveness. She helped me make a qualitative leap in my command of English and in my sensitivity to its nuances.

The publishing house Olschki – in the persons of Daniele Olschki, Georgia Corbo, Erika Marchetti, Serena Ruffilli – has made the realisation of this book possible and offered impeccable editorial assistance. I feel honoured to have had the opportunity to work with them.

This book has benefited from the stimulating intellectual exchange with several scholars with whom I discussed details or parts of my work in progress: Simone Albonico, Gabriele Baldassari, Alessandro Basso, Ida Campeggiani, Giacomo Comiati, Anna Chiara Corradino, Marzia D'Amico, Barbara Distefano, Andrea Donnini, Nicola Gardini, Giovanni Grandi, Valentina Gritti, Stefano Jossa, Amelia Juri, Chiara Lastraioli, Federico Marchetti, Giorgio Masi, Martin McLaughlin, Maria Pavlova, Federica Pich, Emilio Russo, Anna Saroldi, Ela Tandello, Valentina Tibaldo, Antonia Tissoni Benvenuti, Paola Tomè (who sadly is no longer with us), Irene Torregrossa, Paola Ugolini, and Nicole Volta.

My parents, Giovanni and Luciana, and my family have always believed in this book. They have given me loving support throughout every stage of the writing process. I am glad that they too came to be curious and passionate about Ariosto. My friends, and especially Ambra, Elisa, Federica, Giacomo, Luca, Rishicca, Rubikha, have made its writing a pleasant chapter of my life. I will never be able to express adequately my gratitude to all of them.

The presence by my side of a deeply inspirational person is something I have in common with Ariosto. The book is dedicated 'a chi nel mar per tanta via m'ha scorto', that is to Mario, with love.

PRELIMINARY NOTE

The excerpts quoted from the *Orlando furioso* always include an indication of their collocation in the three editions of the poem, namely, that of 1516 (A), that of 1521 (B), and that of 1532 (C). The text of the lyric poems constituting Ariosto's provisional canzoniere is quoted from the unpublished critical edition by Maria Finazzi (FINAZZI 2002-2003), while the uncollected poems are quoted from Cesare Segre's edition, which in turn is based on Fatini's critical edition (ARIOSTO 1954). I explain this choice in Introduction, 6.

When I refer to manuscript or early printed testimonies of the lyrics, the abbreviations of their call numbers are also borrowed from Finazzi's edition. Here is the explanation of those most frequently used:

Cp = *LE RIME DI M. LO* | DOVICO ARIOSTO NON | *più uiste, & nuovamente stampate à in=* | *stantia di Iacopo Coppa Modanese, cio è* | | SONETTI. MADRIGALI. | CANZONI STANZE. | CAPITOLI, Venezia, [Giovanni Antonio e Pietro Nicolini da Sabbio], 1546.
F1 = Ferrara, Biblioteca Comunale Ariostea, Ms. I 64
F2 = Ferrara, Biblioteca Comunale Ariostea, Ms. I 365
L3 = Florence, Biblioteca Medicea Laurenziana, Ashb. 564
Mn = Mantua, Biblioteca Comunale, Ms. G II 14 (792)
Pc = Piacenza, Biblioteca Comunale Passerini Landi, Pallastrelli 230
Pd1 = Padua, Biblioteca del Seminario Vescovile, Ms. 91
Vb = Isola Bella (Stresa), Archivio Borromeo, ABIB, Scienze, lettere ed arti – Letteratura.Poesia [canz. Ariosto]
Vr = Città del Vaticano, Biblioteca Apostolica Vaticana, Rossiano 639

A complete list of bibliographical abbreviations can be found in the Bibliography.

INTRODUCTION

Preamble

The lyric poems of Ludovico Ariosto have always constituted for the modern reader the most elusive portion of his work, and have rarely been the subject of comprehensive studies. This is due to several difficulties that arise in their analysis. There is a stylistic dishomogeneity among the poems that is not found in his other works, and moreover, their philological status is not limpid, owing to the almost complete lack of autographs[1] and to the absence of any authorised printed edition. For a long period, the accepted critical position was to take the poems as sporadic and occasional products, and the only critical edition available was that by Giuseppe Fatini (Ariosto 1924), which was then improved by Cesare Segre (Ariosto 1954). This edition however does not follow a sound philological method.[2] In the mid-1980s, a significant shift took place in the perception of the *rime*, following Cesare Bozzetti's discovery that Ariosto had selected some of them in order to form a canzoniere (Bozzetti 1985), thereby proving the existence of an actual lyric project on Ariosto's part. This finding provoked a flurry of scholarly interest in this output, which resulted in a 1999 conference held in Gargnano sul Garda (whose proceedings are published in Berra 2000) aimed at re-examining Ariosto's 'brief' literary forms, i.e. the *Satire* and the

[1] The hypothesis of Finazzi 2002-2003, p. 105 that the two bifolios **Vb**, with the text of canzone 50, may have been authored by Ariosto has now become a certainty (I should like to thank Finazzi for offering me this update). So far this is the only known autograph of Ariosto's lyric poems.

[2] The corpus of this edition consisted of 5 canzoni, 41 sonnets, 12 madrigals, 27 capitoli, 2 eclogues. Following Segre's suggestions, two attempts were made at establishing a new critical edition, by Anna Carlini and Roberto Chittolina: the former stopped at a discussion of the stemmatic relationship between the testimonies known at the time (Carlini 1958), the latter completed the edition, which however remained unpublished (the scholar published a single article, Chittolina 1967, concerned exclusively with questions of attribution). As a consequence, the commentaries to the *rime* by Mario Santoro (Ariosto 1989) and Stefano Bianchi (Ariosto 1992) have continued to adopt the critical text established by Fatini.

lyrics themselves. Bozzetti's studies were also the basis for the most recent critical edition of the *rime* – more specifically, of the lyrics which Ariosto included in his selections –, compiled by Maria Finazzi and still unpublished (Finazzi 2002-2003). Despite the substantial steps forward this edition has made it possible to take, some major problems still remain – and will remain unless new documents are discovered – concerning the textual history of the poems, their chronology and the circumstances in which they were written. This fact has discouraged scholars from undertaking critical interpretations of the poems, which in recent years have been rare,[3] and restricted to the Italian academic scene.

The clear awareness we now have that Ariosto's lyric practice, far from being a marginal employment, formed the object of specific plans (albeit plans that remained somewhat open-ended), is only one of the reasons for which I believe that they now deserve to be the subject of a book-length study. Another reason is linked to the possibility that these poems can tell us something new not just about Ariosto himself, but also on the cultural context within which he moved. As a result, in undertaking this project, I have tried to maintain a two-sided approach: moving from a close reading of the poems (and from the identification of a number of thematic nuclei and stylistic traits), I examine Ariosto's poetic output with both an 'outward' and an 'inward' gaze, all the time keeping within the speculative range allowed by the lack of documentary data.

The first type of approach has led me to explore the literary environment closest to Ariosto, i.e. the cultural context of the courts of the Pianura Padana: not just poems, but also humanist and theoretical works that display points of contact with the ideas we find in the poems. The second methodological approach has led to a comparison between the way certain themes are used in the *rime* and in other works by Ariosto, in particular the *Satire* and the *Furioso*. In doing so I have sought to set aside, and indeed break through, all prejudice regarding the quality of these texts, and to dismantle the still strongly held conviction that the poems were merely a repository of literary materials waiting to be recycled in the so-called major works, by trying instead to identify (or confirm) certain traits peculiar to Ariosto. Sometimes, although these traits ostensibly diverge only very slightly from the tradition, they in fact reveal Ariosto's distinctive approach and open up a very different interpretive perspective.

---

3 A critical overview of the *rime* has nonetheless been included in recent monographs on Ariosto (Sangirardi 2006; Ferroni 2008; Jossa 2009). Other recent contributions will be mentioned where relevant.

1. The history of Ariosto's 'canzoniere'

While, as I mentioned, it is most often impossible to pinpoint an exact chronology for each of the lyrics (only for a few of them a *terminus ante quem* or *post quem* can be established), some more information is now at our disposal regarding the dynamics that drove Ariosto's selection of his poems with a view to forming a canzoniere.[4]

The oldest stage of this process is testified by an octavo codex, the Vaticano Rossiano 639 (**Vr**), which collects 48 poems, all by Ariosto. This manuscript was first studied by Bozzetti, who recognised in the ordering of the poems an authorial plan that followed the conventions of a love canzoniere, many of the poems having probably been composed specifically for this context. Bozzetti also began (but left unfinished) a commented edition of **Vr**, aimed at highlighting the 'narrativeness' created by its internal progression.[5] The scholar's belief, to which all later critics have subscribed, is that Ariosto himself ordered the manuscript to be transcribed, and that it should be dated to the mid-1520s.[6] Nothing is known, on the other hand, about its circulation, and it is indeed probable that this was non-existent. The elegant but incomplete decoration that features in the manuscript, and its fine calligraphy, suggest that **Vr** was intended as a presentation copy (whose addressee is unknown)[7] and that this project failed. This failure was certainly related to some mistakes made by the copyist, who, in addition to minor inaccuracies concerning the decoration of the initial letters and the layout of the poems, mixed up the text of two capitoli in terza rima. This fact suggests that he was copying from wrongly ordered quires, thus raising the question of what the authorial disposition of the poems was. After Bozzetti's and Finazzi's attempts, a new reconstruction of the archetype has recently been provided by Nicole Volta (Volta 2019), who has suggested that its central part looked substantially different from that of **Vr** – a point to which we shall return.

---

4 Even before the new philological findings, that Ariosto may have made a selection of his lyrics had been hypothesised by Bigi (1968 and 1975), who noted that the corpus of the main manuscript testimonies was almost identical to that of the *editio princeps*.

5 The surviving draft of Bozzetti's work, consisting in the text of the poems of **Vr** with a commentary to poems I-XX, was edited by Claudio Vela (Bozzetti – Vela 2000). On this codex, see Bozzetti 1985; Finazzi 2002-2003, pp. 66-69.

6 Note that in **Vr** there are some corrections which are not from the hand of the copyist. According to Vela (Bozzetti – Vela 2000, pp. 218-220), it is possible that they may have been authored by Ariosto.

7 At the centre of the lower margin of f. 1*r* there was originally a crest, later abraded (Finazzi 2002-2003, p. 67).

But even setting aside the material defects of the manuscripts, Ariosto was apparently not satisfied with the '**Vr** form' of his poems, and significantly, no other witness of this stage seems to exist. As a canzoniere it is fragile: its nature as an 'assembly' of texts of diverse origin, style and quality is easily perceivable, and has been duly noted by Cabani 2016. However, Ariosto continued to cultivate some sort of lyric project, also in later years. This is maybe what is hinted at in an octave added to the 1532 *Furioso*, where he expresses his wish to glorify his beloved lady:

> Pur vo' tanto cercar prima ch'io mora,
> anzi prima che 'l crin più mi s'imbianchi,
> che forse dirò un dì, che per me ancora
> alcuna sia che di sua fé non manchi.
> Se questo avvien (che di speranza fuora
> io non ne son), non fia mai ch'io mi stanchi
> di farla, a mia possanza, gloriosa
> con lingua e con inchiostro, e in verso e in prosa.
>
> (*Fur.*, XXVII 124 C)

A new stage in the author's selection of his poems is witnessed by manuscripts I 64 (**F1**) and I 365 (**F2**) from the Biblioteca Comunale Ariostea of Ferrara, which were copied from an antigraph which scholars have called **F**. Scholars agree that **F** derives from a 'dismantling' of the antigraph of **Vr**: copying the poems from the latter, the copyist would have divided them by metre instead of following the 'canzoniere' ordering. Most importantly, because in the antigraph several revisions had by then been carried out,[8] **F1** and **F2** transmit a later textual version of the poems which were already in **Vr**, adding, moreover, some new poems (and excluding one: the total number in **F** is fifty-six). Both codices have been dated to the early 1530s. It is impossible to establish a more specific dating, which would constitute a decisive piece of information as it would mean that the manuscripts could be placed either before or after Ariosto's death (1533). For the time being, scholars tend to consider **F1** as a clean copy ordered by the poet so as to carry out further corrections, perhaps with a view to reorganising them as a canzoniere, and **F2** – which contains the same poems as **F1** and in the same order, but is an elegant scribal copy – as a codex made after his death.[9]

---

[8] According to Bozzetti 1985, pp. 105-106, 'con ogni probabilità anche l'Ariosto lavorò [...] su copie in pulito che faceva eseguire delle sue rime in certe tappe del lavoro stesso, su basi, cioè, apografe sulle quali poi continuava ad operare con correzioni e varianti, aggiunte o sottrazioni'.

[9] See Bozzetti 1985, pp. 113-114; Finazzi 2002-2003, pp. 11-12. Clearly, if evidence were found that **F2** was instead also copied under Ariosto's supervision, its importance would in-

One further manuscript must be added to this philological framework: **Mn** (Mantova, Biblioteca Comunale Teresiana, G II 14 [792]). This was probably put together without Ariosto's control by a collector of rare poetic materials, who was compiling from the *archetipo in movimento* of **Vr** and **F** at an intermediate stage between the two. In **Mn** the poems are already divided by metre, but Ariosto was still to add the new poems (except one), and its textual readings are consistent at times with **Vr**, and at others with **F**.[10]

If, therefore, we speak of a 'canzoniere' by Ariosto, this is in fact a virtual one that was never accomplished. Most probably, only in its last stage did Ariosto decide to dedicate it to Alessandra Benucci, the woman he had been in love with since 1513. It is indeed only in the second selection that some poems arguably inspired by Alessandra appear – most evidently canzone 50, where the poet recalls the day he fell in love with her.[11] But in spite of the work carried out at this stage, Ariosto was still unsatisfied with his poems and was reluctant to circulate them. This is known from a letter written by Marco Pio to Guidubaldo Feltrio della Rovere, apparently after the latter's request for some poems by Ariosto (10 October 1532). Marco reports he has succeeded in gathering a few of them, but not from Ariosto himself. Indeed, the poet was unwilling and even ashamed that people should read works so inferior to what was expected from him:

> Cossì li mando queste poche rime dil ditto Areosto, le qualle contra sua voglia e con dificultate ho poste insieme; contra sua voglia, perché non voria che fossero viste, col dire che sono inchorette et che a lui è vergogna che siano viste, né mai da lui ho potuto havere cosa alcuna. Per questo dicho poi con dificultate, perché da più persone mi è stato forza rachorle insieme [...] in fatti son cose già da più tempo composte dal detto Areosto, né poi più mai reviste, che forsi non pareranno a V. Ex.tia di quel sappore che aspetta delle cose sue.[12]

The poems originally attached to the letter are not extant. According to Marco, these had been composed by Ariosto much earlier, and had nev-

---

crease accordingly: because it is a presentation copy, it would constitute an 'authorised' lyric sylloge, conceived for public circulation. Therefore, the division of the poems by metre should not be seen as provisional, but a structural choice for the sylloge itself. This scenario, however, is highly improbable because of some linguistic forms of **F2** which it is difficult to imagine would have been authorised by Ariosto. Note that just as **Vr**, **F2** apparently never circulated: it remained with the Ariosto family until the eighteenth century.

10 On **Mn**, which was not known to Bozzetti in 1985, see Finazzi 2002-2003, pp. 70-72.

11 Attempts to identify the lyrics inspired by Alessandra had been made by Salza 1914, pp. 44-68; Catalano 1930-1931, I, pp. 388-425; Fatini 1934, pp. 120-123.

12 Catalano 1930-1931, II, p. 325.

er been corrected since. He does not seem to be aware of anything that may be properly called lyric project on the part of Ariosto, which suggests that the poet did not wish to divulge it. We may suppose that his biggest concerns at this stage were linguistic, especially in the aftermath of the publication of Bembo's *Prose della volgar lingua* (1525) – which famously spurred Ariosto to make his final corrections to the *Furioso* – but also of the lyric collections by Bembo himself and Sannazaro, both published in 1530. The reconsideration of these sylloges (and of others from the same years, such as Trissino's *Rime*, 1529), moreover, must have convinced him of the 'old-fashionedness' of some stylistic and thematic features of his own poetry. I will return to this point in section 3.

That Ariosto never authorised his poems to be printed is all the more significant if we consider the boom of the printed *libro di poesia* in the first decades of the Cinquecento.[13] As may be expected, after his death the *rime* raised the interest and curiosity of the publishing market: from 1537 onward some of his poems were printed in clandestine editions of *cerretani* and within Gabriel Giolito's collections of *Rime diverse*.[14] As for the *editio princeps* proper of the 'selected' lyric poems, which is today called **Cp**, it was published in Venice in 1546 by the Modenese Jacopo Coppa, on the basis of autographs supplied by Ariosto's heirs.[15] The fact that these autographs had corrections in the margins means that in **Cp** the textual readings lack consistency and do not belong to a single phase of elaboration.[16] **Cp** is also structured as a 'macrotext'. In this case the ordering of the poems, however, was decided by the editor, who took as his model the canzonieri of that decade (as pointed out by Rabitti 2000).

Taking into account all these facts, in this work I shall refer to the sum of **Vr**, **Mn**, **F1**, **F2** and **Cp** as the 'main tradition'[17] of Ariosto's lyric poems.

---

13 Of use in reconstructing this context is Cannata Salamone 1989.

14 Vecchi Galli 2000, pp. 364-365; see also Segre's notes in Ariosto 1954, pp. 1171-1172.

15 *Le Rime di M. Lodovico Ariosto non più viste, & nuovamente stampate à instantia di Iacopo Modanese, cio è Sonetti Madrigali Canzoni Stanze Capitoli. In Vinegia con Privilegio del Sommo Pontefice, & del Eccelso Senato Veneto,* MDXLVI.

16 The edition has sixty-two poems, three of which are mistakenly attributed to Ariosto: these were probably found among his papers. On this point see Bozzetti 1985, pp. 86-87.

17 Bozzetti and Finazzi also considered ms. **Pc** (Piacenza, Biblioteca comunale Passerini Landi, Pallastrelli 230) as part of the main tradition. However, Finazzi herself has more recently demonstrated, again in an unpublished research, that it is a *descriptus* from **Cp**.

2. The *rime extravaganti*

If the history of Ariosto's 'canzoniere' is difficult to piece together and peppered with unanswered questions, the study of the *rime extravaganti*, i.e. of the uncollected poems that Ariosto did not include in his selections and which have reached us in miscellanies, is even more problematic. Some of these poems are weighted by doubts of attribution, and in several cases it is difficult to assess the reliability of the witness that transmitted them. Vecchi Galli 2000, in particular, has highlighted this problem. Furthermore, some specific cases have been the focus of studies by both Ariosto scholars[18] and scholars of those poets who have some claim to being themselves the authors. In her critical edition, Finazzi carried out a new count of the witnesses and reassessed the various hypotheses on attribution: the new estimate is of twenty-six *extravaganti*, plus twenty-seven apocryphal and eleven *dubbie*.[19] Finazzi, however, does not provide the text of the *extravaganti* – save for five poems which she herself discovered –, for which Segre's edition remains the most updated.

The reason for Ariosto's disregard of these poems was certainly related to their style. They display stylistic features that recall the lyric vogue popular among the authors of the Northern Italian courts (Ferrara, Milan, Mantua), belonging to the generation immediately following Boiardo but before the 'codification' of fully-fledged sixteenth-century Petrarchism. Among these authors I will mention Panfilo Sasso, Antonio Tebaldeo, Niccolò da Correggio, Timoteo Bendedei, Serafino Aquilano, Gaspare Visconti. Once viewed as a single undifferentiated bloc of work that served as a foil to Boiardo's much more accomplished and technically complex poetical output, the work of these authors has recently been more accurately distinguished and the individual traits of their style identified. Their artistic self-awareness, moreover (detectable, for example, in the way they set up their canzonieri), has come to the fore, as well as the influence exerted over them by various 'masters', including Boiardo, and their willingness to experiment with rhetorical tools. Taken together, all these aspects, to which we shall be returning, make a compelling case for applying the label

---

[18] Chittolina 1967 dwells extensively on problems of attribution. See moreover Vecchi Galli 2000 on capitolo XXVI ed. Fatini and Casadei 2004 on eclogue II and sonnet XLI ed. Fatini.

[19] Finazzi 2002-2003, pp. 26-30. To the last group the scholar also adds a set of twenty-three satirical sonnets (*In Cosmicum*) and fourteen allegedly Ariostean capitoli, whose *incipits* feature in a XIX century printing (their attribution to Ariosto is however highly improbable: *ibid.*, pp. 30-32).

of 'lirica volgare umanistica' to this tradition.[20] But despite this now critically recognised variety, it is still legitimate to view these writers as resorting to a poetical *koiné* that displays unmissable common features. Their works were, in most cases, destined for immediate fruition on the part of court gentlemen and ladies, and were publicly read or sung to the accompaniment of music (see the case of Serafino Aquilano, probably the most famous courtly poet of the time and a renowned *cantore*). They displayed a wide array of witticisms and drew extensively if superficially on Petrarch, often amplifying his most typical rhetorical figures such as the antithesis. These formal choices were paired with highly formalised love situations, whose main model was, in addition to Petrarch, the Latin classical poetry in elegiac couplets.[21] The figure who perhaps best represents this style was the Ferrarese Antonio Tebaldeo, who until 1513 (the year in which he moved to Rome) worked as a preceptor to Isabella d'Este and personal secretary to Lucrezia Borgia. An extraordinarily successful poet, and one Ariosto homaged in the *Furioso*,[22] Tebaldeo was nonetheless criticised for the superficiality of his style in a prose work by Vincenzo Calmeta, a court intellectual and theorist of Italian language and literature. As a matter of fact, while Calmeta's argument targets the 1498 edition of Tebaldeo's poems, it may in fact be seen as highlighting a general shortcoming of courtly occasional poetry. This may be very effective in the context of oral fruition, but on paper runs the risk of seeming stereotypical and repetitive:

> imperocché sentendo oggi d'un poeta qualche sonetto, elegia, stramotto o epigramma cantare o recitare, poi da qui a diece o quindeci giorni sentirne un altro, e da indi ad otto giorni un altro, e così discorrendo, facilmente la memoria di chi ascolta può essere defraudata, e con una sentenza detta per diversi modi potrà il poeta farsi bello per un anno [...]. Ma quando le opere insieme sono congiunte, chi legge può facilmente ogni alchimia discoprire [...]. E però, letta tutta questa opera del Tebaldeo, il giudico di grande ingegno, gravità nulla, elocuzione poca, per esser di sentenze non molto abondante [...].[23]

---

20 This phrase was adopted by Tania Basile and Jean-Jacques Marchand in the preface to their edition of Tebaldeo's poetry (Tebaldeo 1989-1992, I, p. 7). See also Malinverni 1998: the scholar was among the first to call attention to the need to exhaustively analyse these poets.

21 The features of this tradition are illustrated by Rossi 1980 (which focuses in particular on Serafino Aquilano); Tissoni Benvenuti 1976 and 1980; Vecchi Galli 1982, 1994 and 2003; Santagata – Carrai 1993; Malinverni 1998. Specifically on the reception of Petrarch in fifteenth-century Ferrarese court poetry, both in Latin and the vernacular, see Pantani 2002.

22 He is mentioned, together with Ercole Strozzi, as a celebrator of Lucrezia Borgia (*Fur.*, XXXVIII 80 7-8 A; XXXVIII 83 B; XLII C).

23 Calmeta 1959, p. 16 (the prose can be read in its entirety at pp. 15-19). On Calmeta's theory of language, see Mengaldo 1960.

In Ariosto's poetry, these features are well epitomised by five uncollected capitoli (XX-XV ed. Fatini), which exhibit fixed rhythmic and rhetorical patterns based on anaphorical repetitions and antitheses.[24] See the following example:

Tu festeggi in piacere, *ed io* tormento,
privo di te, che notte e dì ti chiamo:
però di ritornar non esser lento. [...]
Tu vivi lieto *ed in me* abbonda il pianto;
tu altri godi *ed io* te sol aspetto;
di bianco vesti, *ed io* di negro ho il manto.
(capitolo XXI ed. Fatini, ll. 10-18)[25]
(emphasis mine)

Although Ariosto discarded them, the uncollected poems are very interesting for the modern reader, both because they testify to the poet's engagement with his cultural milieu and because some original traits of his later work may be glimpsed in them. It appears clearly, therefore, how an analysis of the poems whose attribution to Ariosto is certain would usefully integrate the study of the 'canzoniere'.

3. General features of the lyric corpus

An element of outmodedness, however, is not an exclusive feature of the *rime extravaganti*, but rather appears to be recurring in Ariosto's poems. It is a feature that regards, for instance, the structure of **Vr**, to which we may now usefully return with the aid of some critical milestones on the canzoniere form, and in particular through the seminal work of Comboni – Zanato 2017.[26] This volume specifically examines the Quattrocento canzonieri, the word 'canzoniere' having been defined according to a set of parameters that are inherited from the critical tradition, but rendered more flexible, so as to do justice to the great variety of examples found. It

24 The stylistic immaturity of these and of two further capitoli (XLVI-XLVII of Finazzi's edition) had also been noted by Bigi (1968, pp. 30-35 and 1975), who distinguished between a first and a second manner in Ariosto's lyrics. On this point see also Tissoni Benvenuti 1976.

25 Among the numerous possible comparisons, see Sasso, capitolo II, ll. 55-60 (emphasis mine): '*Scio, che* levato ho tanto alto la mente / e che non potrò l'impresa seguitare / e che piacer non ha ch'al fin si pente. / *Scio, che* volendo sopra el ciel volare / caddero con ruina al basso fondo, / come Icar fece, e daro nome al mare'.

26 See moreover Santagata 1975; Longhi 1979; Gorni 1984 and 1989; Erspamer 1987; Zampese 2001; Albonico 2006.

features a detailed descriptive entry on each collection, thereby allowing us to understand the criteria that presided over the organisation of canzonieri in this period. Among the aspects examined are 'plot', themes, and the choice and distribution of the metrical forms; all these points are obviously analysed in relation to the main model, i.e. Petrarch's *Rerum vulgarium fragmenta*. The volume covers the work of authors that stood in the background of Ariosto's lyric development: among the canzonieri composed in Ferrara from 1460 onwards should be mentioned those of the Anonimo Costabili, Cornazano, Boiardo, Correggio, and Tebaldeo.[27]

If one tries to describe **Vr** according to the categories adopted by Comboni and Zanato, the following observations may be made:[28]

1) *Punto α*: a sonnet, characterised by the absence of any repentance, and by the persistence of the amorous sentiment. This sets it apart from *Rvf*, I, making it closer, instead, to several fifteenth-century *sonetti incipitari* (see the Preamble to Chapter II).

2) *Punto ω*: a sonnet addressed to God, as occurs in many Quattrocento canzonieri (see also point 8).

3) *Structural elements*: no rigid partitions are present in the structure of **Vr**. However, there are two recognisable blocks of capitoli ternari (XX-XXXI and XLII-XLVI). This probably harks back to a Quattrocento trend, as some canzonieri of that time – for instance, the third canzoniere by Cosmico and those by Ceresara, Liburnio, Sasso and Tebaldeo – group their poems by metre.[29] In other cases, such as Achillini's canzoniere, a series of capitoli interrupts a structure that is otherwise characterised by a regular alternation of metres (this case is closer to Ariosto's).[30]

4) *Sequences of poems sharing the same themes*: if Finazzi's reconstruction of the ordering of the poems in the antigraph of **Vr** is accepted, the following thematic nuclei may be mentioned:

II-VI: the poet's excessive boldness in love;

VII-X: the poet's fidelity, and his hope of receiving 'mercede';

XI-XIII: the poet's efforts to praise his beloved;

XVIII-XXII: expectation, satisfaction, or failure of the amorous encounter;

---

27 On this point, see Pantani 2002, pp. 358-404.

28 I will in particular be making comparisons with authors from the second half of the fifteenth century: this is in line with the two scholars' inclination to maintain a distinction between the first and the second part of the Quattrocento.

29 Comboni – Zanato 2017, XXVI and pp. 217, 257, 377, 538, 582.

30 *Ibid.*, p. 9.

XXIII-XXV: the lover laments the woman's coldness; she protests her constancy; he says he has reached the limit of his endurance;

XXVII-XXVIII: two moralistic capitoli voiced by a female speaker, against *multiloquium*;

XXIX-XXX: journeys which separate the speaker from his lady;

XXXVIII-XXXIX: his frustration for his unrequited love;

XLI-XLII: two poems describing sadness: the subject of the former, death, that of the latter, an illness (see below, point 10). The reconstruction of the antigraph by Volta establishes for the central capitoli (XX-XXXI) a very different ordering from that proposed by Bozzetti and Finazzi. This hypothesis leads to the disruption of the nucleus constituted by XVIII-XXII (thus, a clear transition towards the speaker's erotic accomplishment can no longer be recognised), while the other sequences I have singled out here are still valid. On this point see Chapter II, 1.

5) *Time frame of the love story*: not detectable.

6) *Poems on the anniversary of love*: absent.

7) *The lyric 'I'*: this coincides almost always with the poet himself, as one gathers from the fact that he refers to actual events of his life. Poems XXIV, XXVII, XXXVII and XLI adopt a female mouthpiece: this is again in keeping with a trend detectable in late-Quattrocento poems with elegiac connotations.[31]

8) *The lyric 'you'*: although several of the poems were arguably written when Ariosto was already in a relationship with Alessandra Benucci, nothing suggests that she is the dedicatee of the canzoniere. It is possible that Ariosto intentionally fashioned it as featuring more than one woman, something not unusual in the current poetic practice.[32] The only name that may be (indirectly) gathered is that of one Ginevra, praised in XII and identified through the juniper *senhal*:

> Uno arbuscel che 'n le solinghe rive
> all'aria spiega i rami horridi et hirti,
> et d'odor vince i pin', li abeti e i mirti
> et lieto al verde al caldo e al ghiaccio vive,
> il nome ha di colei che mi prescrive
> termine et legge a' travagliati spirti,
> da cui seguir non potrian Scille o Sirti
> ritrarmi, o le brumali hore o l'estive.

---

31 See LONGHI 1989.

32 The presence of multiple beloved ladies characterises several fifteenth-century canzonieri (COMBONI – ZANATO 2017, XXXIII).

Et se benigno influxo di pianeta,
lunghe vigilie, od amorosi sproni
son per condurmi ad honorata meta,
non voglio, et Phebo et Bacco mi perdoni,
che lor frondi mi mostrino poeta,
ma ch'un ginebro sia che mi coroni.

(*Rime del canzoniere*, XII)

As for the characterisation of the woman, in several poems it follows the model of the 'cruel lady' imposed by the Latin love elegy (see point 12), again in accordance with the lyric convention of the time. I should note, however, that Ariosto limits his accusations of betrayal and of 'perfidia' – which were instead popular with other authors –[33] and chooses to portray a more equal relationship with the lady (see Chapter II, 2). Other poems are instead celebrations, praising the woman's physical features as well as her *ingegno* (see Chapter II, 3, and Chapter III).

9) *Poems on religious repentance*: only XLVIII (the *punto* ω) may be qualified as such, though the spiritual afflatus it displays is quite unique: see Chapter II, 6. The entire or almost entire absence of religious repentance also characterises many Quattrocento canzonieri.[34]

10) *Poems featuring 'real' characters*: XLIII is addressed to Cardinal Ippolito d'Este; XXVI was written upon the illness of Lorenzo de' Medici, Duke of Urbino; in XLI, Philiberte of Savoy mourns the death of her husband Giuliano de' Medici. These poems however were included in **Vr** not as historical poems but on account of their amorous contents: in the latter two cases, Ariosto probably wanted their original meaning to be lost once included there.[35]

11) *Geographical references*: the river Po (XVII); the Garfagnana (XXIX); Florence and the river Po (XXX); Rome (XLI); the Furlo Pass (XLIII); Ravenna (XLV).

12) *Plot*: no clear progression can be identified in the plot. It may be stated that its first part, up to XVII, is more respectful of the Petrarchan tradition, while starting from XVIII one begins to detect a parallel presence of Petrarchan and classical themes. Accordingly, an unstable relationship between the poet and the woman (or women) is visible, and is marked by an alternation of satisfaction and frustration due to sudden moments of coldness on her part.

---

33 *Ibid.*, XXXIII-XXXIV.

34 *Ibid.*, XXIV-XXV.

35 On capitolo XXVI, see Guassardo 2020, where I particularly discuss the Medicean imagery it displays. On the 'camouflage' of these poems (and of XXV) in the context of **Vr**, see Bozzetti 1985, pp. 96-99.

13) *Intertextual connectors*: Bozzetti, and other critics after him, have examined the lexical or thematic internal links between the poems, substantially agreeing on their effectiveness.[36] My own position is closer to that of Cabani who, more cautiously, speaks of a 'forte ripetitività di motivi e forme' that 'rende persuasive, ma mai strettamente necessarie, altre forme di aggregazione dei testi'.[37]

14) *Poems on poetry*: XI, XII and XIII include metapoetic statements (see Chapter II, 4).

15) *Non-amorous contents*: capitoli XXVII e XXVIII deploy humanist themes. XLVII is an occasional poem written for a lady, who is not necessarily the poet's beloved. See Chapter III, 4.

The analytic tools provided by Comboni and Zanato therefore allow us to strengthen and confirm Bozzetti's interpretation of **Vr** as being characterised by 'fedeltà a quella cultura delle grandi corti lombarde che proprio in quel giro d'anni fu quasi irrimediabilmente travolta dalla storia insieme politica e letteraria'.[38] We shall not forget that several canzonieri were available to Ariosto as printed editions: that by Tebaldeo, for instance (*e.p.* 1498), as well as those by Sasso (*e.p.* 1500), Cornazano (*e.p.* 1502), and Liburnio (*e.p.* 1502).

But in addition to this line of tradition, a model whose prestige was certainly felt by Ariosto was Pietro Bembo. The influence of his poetry is perceivable in some lyrics: a clear example is the last poem of **Vr**, which is recognisably inspired by the final ballata of Bembo's canzoniere (see Chapter II, 6). This canzoniere, however, was first printed in 1530, and it is customarily assumed that **Vr** precedes this date.[39] As a matter of fact, however, Bembo's ballata had already been placed at the end of his first attempt at a canzoniere. This was dedicated to Elisabetta Gonzaga and included in the manuscript Marciano Italiano IX.143 (**VM**$_5$), compiled under the author's supervision in 1510-1511.[40] The manuscript testifies to multiple phases in the elaboration of the poems and includes corrections in Bembo's own hand whose dating is uncertain: according to Andrea Donnini 'non si può

36 Bozzetti – Vela 2000; Comboni 2000; Zampese 2000.

37 Cabani 2016, p. 100.

38 Bozzetti 1985, p. 95. Ariosto's indebtedness to the courtly poetry of the Po valley is also examined by Comboni 2000.

39 Its dating to the 1520s (capitolo XLV establishing a *terminus post quem* at 1522) is based on the copyist's handwriting and on the filigree: Bozzetti 1985, p. 90 (see also *ibid.*, p. 117).

40 On this canzoniere, see Vela 1988 (which also includes an edition of it) and Donnini's notes in Bembo 2008, II, pp. 760-772.

escludere che Bembo avesse con sé il ms. in tutti i suoi spostamenti e continuasse a tenerlo presente nell'elaborazione delle rime'.[41] It may even therefore be possible that Ariosto saw it.[42] As a matter of fact, if one compares the structure of **VM**$_5$ with that of **Vr**, some similarities may be noted. Bembo's canzoniere is only slightly longer than Ariosto's (59 vs. 48 poems). Both feature only two canzoni, and their collocation within the macrotext is similar: numbers 6 and 51 in Bembo, VI and XLI in Ariosto – furthermore, Ariosto's XLI is openly modelled on Bembo's 51 (*Alma cortese, che dal mondo errante*). Finally, the second-last poem of **Vr**, XLVII (*Non senza causa il giglio e l'amaranto*) describes the flowers which adorn the 'sacro manto' worn by a noble 'virgin', which signifies purity and constancy: if we accept the possibility that this lady might be about to enter a religious order,[43] this would be a further element in common with **VM**$_5$, whose penultimate sonnet (*Phrisio, che già da questa gente e quella*), which acts as a prelude to the spiritual closing of the canzoniere, is dedicated to Niccolò Frisio upon his taking the habit.

Even if we set aside **Vr**, the metrical preferences we see at work within Ariosto's corpus of lyric poems would appear to confirm his closeness to a style that continues to a great extent to look back to the Quattrocento. His predilection for the capitolo in terza rima is most definitely a stand-out feature: there are as many as seventeen capitoli in the 'canzoniere' (if the uncollected ones are added the number increases to twenty-five). The terza rima, on account of its being an open, eclectic form, was extremely popular in late-Quattrocento canzonieri,[44] and even if the capitoli by Ariosto that are included in the main tradition are clearly more mature in style than the uncollected ones, the poet's decision to deploy this metre was sufficient to classify his attempts of canzoniere as 'outdated'. Suffice it to say that Bembo himself, who in in his youth authored four capitoli, excluded all but one (*Le rime*, 38) from his canzoniere of 1530. As mentioned at

---

41 Bembo 2008, II, pp. 768-769.

42 It is on the other hand quite plausible that Ariosto had easy access to the individual texts, independently of their macrotextual context (Vela 2018, p. 55, notes that they circulated uncollected beyond the borders of Urbino) – without considering that some of these poems date to Bembo's years in Ferrara.

43 Salza 1914, p. 105. An alternative interpretation put forward by Fatini 1934, pp. 114-115, which follows sixteenth-century commentators Sansovino and Turchi (Ariosto 1730, II, p. 362), reads the poem as a the defence of a noblewoman whose honour had been stained.

44 Tissoni Benvenuti 1976, pp. 303-304: 'La massima diffusione della terza rima si ha [...] nel secondo Quattrocento, nel periodo aureo della letteratura cortigiana, quando il capitolo si specializza in diversi sottogeneri [...] e divide con il solo sonetto la presenza nei più importanti canzonieri'. On the history of this metre, see also Peirone 1990.

point 3 of the above scheme, the layout of the capitoli in **Vr**, which form two compact blocks, also harks back to a fifteenth-century fashion, while from a sixteenth-century perspective it probably disrupted the structural soundness of the canzoniere form.[45]

The scarceness of the canzone in Ariosto's lyrics, five in the entire corpus (one of which uncollected: canzone III ed. Fatini) also runs counter to the fully-fledged sixteenth-century Petrarchism in which this form was soon to gain the highest renown, once again thanks to Bembo.[46] As early as 1507, the association of this form with noble contents was boosted by his canzone *Alma cortese, che dal mondo errante*, an example of *stile grave* that remained extremely influential throughout the century. This poem also inspired Ariosto for his diptych of canzoni mourning Giuliano de' Medici, XLI and 49. Here his difficulty in mastering the canzone form, however, is evident.[47] Only the former is included in **Vr**; in his last selection, besides 49 Ariosto added the canzone on the day he fell in love, 50 (*Non so s'io potrò ben chiudere in rima*), and eliminated the more stereotyped VI.

The predominant form in Ariosto's lyric corpus is, as may be expected, the sonnet, which is adopted in as many as forty poems. Courtly patterns are deployed by Ariosto in this form, too: a typical example is the concentration of witticism and sententiousness in the last tercet, a technique in which the influence of the Latin epigram is clearly felt.[48] Conversely, the presence in this corpus of as many as six madrigals and six *ballate monostrofiche* may be seen as a distinctive feature, which may be attributed to sixteenth-century taste. These lyric forms were rarely included in the canzonieri in the previous century, and when they were, they rarely respected the 'metrical rules' set up by Petrarch becoming instead a subject of experimentation in a variey of guises (the most notable case of this is Boiardo).[49]

---

45 On this point, see Cabani 2016, pp. 98-100.

46 The privileged association between the canzone form and an elevated style was theorised, as is well known, also by Dante in *De vulgari eloquentia*, a work which, however, had fallen into oblivion until Trissino rediscovered it (which resulted in his translated edition, published in 1529).

47 *Ibid.*, pp. 110-111. The debts from Bembo in these canzoni are analysed by Vagni 2017, pp. 142-148.

48 This feature is analysed (with a focus on Serafino) in Rossi 1980, pp. 75-79. According to Cabani, Ariosto applies it in a manner similar to that of the last couplet of the octaves of the *Furioso*, which often constitutes 'un elemento di variazione o di rottura, un fattore di scarto e di sorpresa' (Cabani 2016, pp. 111-115, quotation at p. 111).

49 Note that in two ballate, VIII (*Amor, io non potrei*) and XVI (*Per gran vento che spire*), the last line of the *volta* does not rhyme with the last line of the *ripresa*, but with its first line. This structure was sometimes found in earlier poetry, and indeed, the borders between madrigal

Similarly, Ariosto eschews (even in the uncollected poems) other brief forms that are typically 'quattrocentesche' and non-Petrarchan, such as the *strambotto* or the *barzelletta*.

The style of Ariosto's poetry is, therefore, a hybridised one. But a similar hybridisation also invests the contents of his lyrical output, which derive from several cultural strands that he absorbed with equal ease. It seems necessary to introduce this point here by recalling his cultural background.

4. Between Latin and Italian: the cultural context

The cultural context in which Ariosto developed, late fifteenth-century Ferrara, was extremely lively and diversified. Two trends enjoyed particular popularity at the Este court, which fostered their development in equal measure, encouraging a keen interest, on the one hand, in romance and chivalric literature, on the other in classical literature and in the modes of its reuse. This second trend may ultimately be seen as stemming from the teachings of Guarino Veronese, whose presence in Ferrara from 1429 had boosted the activity of the Studio and promoted the knowledge of the classics at court. The classical legacy variously reverberated through court literature. In addition to a flourishing production of Latin poetry (see the cases of Boiardo, the two Strozzis, Tebaldeo and Sadoleto), a fashion for *volgarizzamenti* should be mentioned, as well as the birth of a classical-inspired theatre. Moreover, the classics also exerted their influence on Italian lyric poetry, the most accomplished case being the collection of poems by Boiardo – the *Amorum libri tres* –, which bears all the hallmarks of the author's humanist culture.

Ariosto's own youthful engagement with the classics, stimulated by this milieu, as well as his early studies undertaken under the guide of Gregorio da Spoleto, are recalled in satira VI, addressed to Pietro Bembo and written in 1524-1525, in the context of a wider reflection on humanist education. As we gather from the same satira (ll. 151-180), the poet never had the opportunity to study Greek; on the other hand, his extant output in Latin testifies to his accomplishment in this language and his command of

---

and ballata tended to be blurred until Bembo clearly illustrated their difference in his *Prose della volgar lingua*. On this point, see Castoldi 1993, pp. 253-254; on the freedom in the use of the two forms in the Quattrocento, see Comboni – Zanato 2017, XVI. Fatini and Segre had not distinguished between ballata and madrigal in their editions of Ariosto's *rime*.

several metres.[50] The dedications of these poems (to Timoteo Bendedei, Alberto Pio da Carpi, Ercole Strozzi, Pietro Bembo among others) allow us to grasp the climate of lively intellectual exchange and, at the same time, the social aim of this poetry, which constituted a means of identification in the literary community.[51] Because most of these poems may be dated between ca. 1494 and 1503, and because there is little evidence of such an early dating for his Italian lyrics, it is generally argued that Ariosto's activity as a Latin poet preceded that as a vernacular poet. On the other hand, in satira IV, in recalling his youthful years spent in Reggio, he claims to have been writing 'in più d'una lingua e in più d'un stile' (l. 127). Despite the lack of evidence suggesting his equally systematic involvement in vernacular poetry already in those years, I believe it is possible to hypothesise a relative bilingualism in his poetic activity (to some extent comparable to that of other writers, such as Tebaldeo), which paved the way to his final choice of Italian as his main language.

In recalling this point of transition, we must again highlight the role of Bembo (whose possible influence on the structure of **Vr** was suggested in the last section). Bembo's link with Ferrara began with his first visit in 1497, which was followed by others until he returned to Venice in 1503. After his love affair with Maria Savorgnan (1500-1501), he turned his interest to Lucrezia Borgia, who had recently married Alfonso d'Este. If the influence of court humanism was decisive for Bembo as a man of letters (since he hailed from an entirely different context, the Republic of Venice), his own contribution to this milieu was even more crucial. His activity in this period aimed, on the one hand, to recover the 'fathers' of Italian literature – through his groundbreaking editions, published by Aldus Manutius, of the works of Petrarch and Dante (1501 and 1502) –, and on the other, to the search for a new type of literature that focused on a reflection on the Petrarchan lesson and on the doctrine of love imposed by Neo-

---

[50] I shall refer the reader to the newest edition of Ariosto's Latin poetry (Ariosto 2017) and to its recent critical evaluation in Severi 2018. According to his son Virginio, 'Gli piaceva Virgilio; Tibullo nel suo dire; ma grandemente commendava Orazio e Catullo; ma non molto Properzio' (Ariosto 1954, p. 4). It should be noted that his alleged dislike for Propertius is contradicted by the debts themselves which are found even in his vernacular poetry, and which will be pointed out in the course of this study. Specifically on Ariosto's humanist upbringing and his background, Looney 2003, at least, should be mentioned. Still valid are the observations in Bigi 1968 on the cultural orientation of Ariosto's Latin poetry, which include a note on his Italian *rime*.

[51] In the words of Ferroni 2008, p. 27, 'La scrittura poetica latina valeva come manifestazione raffinata dell'essere sociale di un uomo di corte aspirante a riconoscere la propria dignità proprio nello spazio dello "studio umano"'.

platonic philosophy. The publication of the dialogue on love, *Asolani*, in 1505, eventually boosted his popularity. He and Ariosto were personally acquainted.[52] This is proved in the first instance by a Latin poetic exchange between them: Ariosto's poem in elegiac couplets *Ad Petrum Bembum* (VII), on the theme of jealousy, is a reply to Bembo's *Ad Melinum* (X), in which the author advised his addressee to show tolerance towards his beloved.[53] But their intellectual exchange also concerned vernacular literature. As observed by Vela, in that period the relationship between Bembo and Ariosto 'era già un rapporto a senso unico, non pacifico però'.[54] As a matter of fact, some echoes of the *Asolani* are detectable in the *Furioso* (whose first version was commenced in the first years of the century): these however were not passively absorbed, but testify to an ongoing debate on the theme of love.[55] Conversely, no influence of the *Furioso* may be found in Bembo's oeuvre. Already at that date, the essential difference between their 'major projects' was clear.[56] If, on the other hand, we examine their lyric corpora, some affinities may be found between them, which are in most cases more accurately explained as influences of Bembo on Ariosto rather than vice versa. These similarities will be pointed out further on in this study, but it may be useful here to recall Ariosto's participation in a vernacular *tenzone* of sonnets elaborated by the 'Compagnia degli Amici'. This was a Venetian society based on the intellectual affinity between a number of young *patrizi*, whose intellectual outlook was clearly influenced by Bembo himself. In this exchange, to which Gnocchi 1999 firstly called attention,

52 Ariosto may have been an intermediary in Bembo's relationship with Lucrezia Borgia, if we identify him as the 'Lodovico' that, Bembo writes to Lucrezia in 1503, had presented her with the manuscript of the *Asolani* and then reported back to him her reaction (Catalano 1930-1931, I, pp. 463-464).

53 This exchange develops under the sign of Propertius: Bembo's poem, also in elegiac couplets, imitates Propertius, II 18, which in turn, together with II 34, was also a source for Ariosto (Gnocchi 1999, p. 292).

54 Vela 2018, p. 50.

55 This is observed by Vela 2018, pp. 52-56, and these echoes are also usefully noted in the commentary to the 1516 *Furioso*, edited by Tina Matarrese and Marco Praloran (Ariosto 2016).

56 According to an anecdote reported by Giovan Battista Pigna, Bembo had discouraged Ariosto from writing in Italian, regarding his command of Latin as better: Ariosto replied that 'più tosto volea essere uno de' primi tra' scrittori toscani che appena il secondo tra' latini' (Pigna 1554, pp. 74-75). It is difficult to say whether there was true friendship between the two. While Ariosto would often pay homage to Bembo in later years, it looks as if Bembo made a point of hiding all evidence of their acquaintance, so much so that the 'silenzi del Bembo' (a phrase first used by Zanette) have become an established critical commonplace. A re-examination of this matter is in Procaccioli 2016.

the poets elaborated on a diptych of sonnets Bembo had composed during his Ferrarese period – something which explains Ariosto's involvement, but most importantly signals his determination to be part of this intellectual arena.[57] As a further proof of the charisma exerted by Bembo already in those years, I shall recall that it was probably his influence that determined, in 1508, the conversion to the use of Italian of the acclaimed Latin poet Ercole Strozzi. Bembo himself expressed his joy on this event in a strambotto (*Le rime*, 70), and, in later years, made Strozzi the addressee of his precepts for the reformed language in the *Prose della volgar lingua*.[58] Incidentally, as Ariosto had befriended Ercole, who belonged to the same generation,[59] the latter may be seen as constituting a further element in his cultural background and will on some occasions be mentioned again in this study. Likewise, the output of Ercole's father, Tito Vespasiano Strozzi, will also on occasion be considered. Unlike Ercole, he wrote exclusively in Latin and met with great success throughout the second half of the Quattrocento: in addition to a significant lyric-elegiac production and much celebratory poetry dedicated to the Estensi, he authored the earliest attempts at a Horatian satire.

A well-known testimony of Ariosto's 'fringe position' – marked by an engagement in the Ferrarese Neo-Latin milieu, but also by a search for his own path in the vernacular, which in fact led him, in this period, to begin the *Furioso* – is *Equitatio,* a dialogue by the court humanist Celio Calcagnini, datable to around 1507. Ariosto features among its interlocutors, who discuss various erudite subjects during a trip on horseback, and in particular is represented as lamenting the fact that he has abandoned higher subjects for the 'humble' chivalric poem.[60] This study will return to the figure of Calcagnini on account of his prominent role, at the time, in the intellectual world of Ferrara. An inveterate partisan of Latin (his portrayal of Ariosto also reveals that his sympathies were with Ariosto-the-humanist), he particularly distinguished himself as an author of erudite proses on the most

---

57 On this *tenzone* and on Ariosto's contribution to it, see also Chapter III, 1.

58 Only seven sonnets by Strozzi have survived: they are edited in Vagni 2011.

59 Strozzi and Ariosto probably studied together under Luca Ripa, and their friendship is also witnessed by the reciprocal mentions in their poetic works and by possible reciprocal influences in their Latin outputs. The most recent biographical account of Strozzi is Guassardo 2019, while in Guassardo 2018 I have attempted to reconstruct his relationship with Ariosto, touching on their vernacular as well as on their Latin outputs.

60 He adopts the expression 'Gallicanae […] ambubaiae', i.e. French courtesans, to indicate the Muses inspiring chivalric literature (this passage has been examined by Savarese 1984, pp. 15-37). The dialogue can be read in Calcagnini 1544, pp. 558-590. See also Curti 2016, a partial edition of the text with translation.

diverse subjects, in which he showed off his *vis rhetorica* and his encyclopaedic culture, as well as his fascination with philosophical questions and esoteric themes.[61] Scholars have already identified some excerpts of the *Furioso* that might have been influenced by his work. The most evident is the personification of Silence in *Fur.*, XIV C (XII AB): this has been linked to Calcagnini's pamphlet *Descriptio silentii*, which develops an *ekphrasis* on the god of silence Harpocrates.[62] Despite adopting different strategies in their portrayal, the two authors share the same tone, which bears the stamp of the principle of *spoudaiogeloion* ('serious play'). This technique was widely adopted by Ferrarese authors, as a result of the spread of the Lucianic tradition stimulated, in particular, by Leon Battista Alberti and also practiced by Leoniceno and Collenuccio:[63] the presence of this genre in the *Furioso* extends to other episodes, such as Astolfo's journey to the moon.[64] Ariosto's interest in this approach must in turn be seen as part of his more general fondness for philosophy and for the erudite subjects fashionable in the humanist milieu, which also led him to take an interest in Neoplatonism and to study the works of Marsilio Ficino, a copy of which he requested in a famous 1498 letter to Aldus Manutius.[65]

This lively and multifaceted mosaic of literary experiences, which it has only been possible here to touch upon, permeates Ariosto's poetry at various levels and will therefore be constantly in the background of my analysis of his work.

5. Ariosto as court poet?

The fact that the humanism of the Ferrarese court exerted a deep influence on Ariosto prompts a crucial question, namely, in what ways does his lyric output relate to the court patronage system? As is known, he served the Este family throughout his life, but his intellectual activity was not the

---

61 For a general overview on Calcagnini, see now Gardini 2017 and its bibliography. Other studies will be cited further on.

62 I will return to this point in Chapter III, 4.

63 On Alberti's influence on Ferrarese culture, see at least D'Ascia 1998 and Tissoni Benvenuti 2007 (p. 267: 'La cultura ferrarese sembra essere più di altre in consonanza con l'Alberti; o forse potremmo dire che è una cultura quasi predisposta a capirne e continuarne lo spirito').

64 This point has been examined in numerous seminal contributions: see Martelli 1964; Segre 1966, pp. 85-95; Pampaloni 1974; Ferroni 1975.

65 *Lettere*, 1. On Ariosto's Platonism, the most recent contributions are Dell'Aia 2013 and 2017.

reason for which he was employed. His court services obliged him to undertake a variety of tasks. During his service to Cardinal Ippolito (1503-1517), he had to carry out diplomatic missions, while when in the service of Duke Alfonso (which began in 1518) his journeys were on the whole less numerous; this phase however was marked by a three-year stay in the Garfagnana, in the role of ducal commissioner (1522-1525). These duties – which he resented, as famously recorded in the *Satire* – were nevertheless necessary, as, following his father's death in 1500, he had become responsible for the material support of his siblings.[66]

In close relation to the courtly environment must be placed the works Ariosto composed in the first decade of the Cinquecento. Among these should be mentioned the *Obizzeide* (ca. 1503), an unfinished epic experiment on the feats of Obizzo d'Este (an ancestor of the lords of Ferrara),[67] as well as several Latin poems, including the epithalamium on Alfonso d'Este's marriage to Lucrezia Borgia (1502), and the celebration of Ippolito's appointment as Bishop of Ferrara (1503 – these are poems LIII and LVII respectively). But what sanctioned his literary success were his comedies, which responded to the Este court's passion for the theatre: the staging of both *Cassaria* and *Suppositi* (1508 and 1509), promoted by Ippolito, was extremely successful – and, as is known, Ariosto also returned to theatre in later periods of his life.

Despite the very rare mention in his vernacular lyrics of dedicatees and interlocutors, and the lack of any other signal of his relationships with other court writers (a very different case from the poetry of other authors, such as Tebaldeo, and even from Ariosto's own Latin poems), it is likely that several of them were conceived for the court and were initially circulated there. An exordium of the *Furioso* may be significant in this respect. Here, the poet-narrator says that he has recorded his love sorrow on paper ('in vive carte') – a recognisable allusion to his own lyric poetry, most probably both that in Latin and that in the vernacular:[68]

> Gravi pene in amor si provan molte,
> di che patito io n'ho la maggior parte,
> e quelle in danno mio sì ben raccolte,

---

[66] On Ariosto's duties at court, see Catalano 1930-1931, I, pp. 204-206; pp. 476-478; pp. 535-546.

[67] I shall note here that, although the *Obizzeide* (written in terza rima) features in **F** and was included by Fatini in his edition of Ariosto's lyric poetry, I will not be touching on it in this study because it is not an example of the lyric genre. On this work I shall refer the reader to Casadei 1993, pp. 23-34.

[68] See Bigi's commentary in Ariosto 2012, p. 515, and Pich 2015, pp. 341-342.

ch'io ne posso parlar come per arte.
Però s'io dico e s'ho detto altre volte,
e quando in voce e quando in vive carte,
ch'un mal sia lieve, un altro acerbo e fiero,
date credenza al mio giudicio vero.

(*Fur.*, XIV 1 AB; XVI C)

Such an allusion implies the actual knowledge of these lyrics on the part of the privileged audience here addressed, the milieu of Ippolito d'Este. As a matter of fact, a certain diffusion of the lyrics is demonstrated, as mentioned above, by the presence of several of them in miscellanies (the 'uncollected' version of these poems is in some cases significantly different from the reworked version for the 'canzoniere'). Some of these testimonies are particularly notable in that they testify to the tastes of the courtly milieu.[69] Some especially popular poems, among those which Ariosto included in his selections, seem to have been the above-quoted sonnet to Ginevra and capitoli XXI and XXIII. In other cases, it is their very content that allows us to suppose their 'public' destination. Examples – which have already been mentioned in the last section – are capitolo XLIII, addressed to Ippolito, capitoli XXV and XXVII and sonnet XLVII, which describe *imprese*, capitolo XXVI, originally written for the Medici family and complaining the illness of Lorenzo, Duke of Urbino, and the two canzoni mourning the death of Giuliano de' Medici (XLI and 49). To these should be added some uncollected poems: a capitolo mourning the death of Eleonora d'Aragona in 1493, which in fact belongs to the *dubbie* (*Rime disposte a lamentarvi sempre*, capitolo I ed. Fatini),[70] a sonnet upon the elevation of Giuliano della Rovere as Pope Julius II in 1503 (*L'arbor ch'al viver prisco porse aita*, sonnet XXXVI ed. Fatini),[71] and, perhaps the most famous case, the dramatic eclogue *Dove vai*

---

[69] Examples are Padua, Biblioteca del Seminario Vescovile, ms. 91 (for which see Vecchi Galli 2000, p. 359); Ferrara, Biblioteca Comunale Ariostea, I 408 (Finazzi 2002-2003, pp. 90-91). On manuscript miscellanies at the court of Ferrara in the late Quattrocento and throughout the Cinquecento, see Tissoni Benvenuti 1989 and Vecchi Galli 1994.

[70] One of the two known testimonies of it is an autograph, but the author may have been Ariosto's namesake uncle according to Catalano 1930-1931, I, pp. 129-132; Chittolina 1967 argues instead in favour of Ariosto's authorship.

[71] This poem, documenting the festive atmosphere in the aftermath of Alexander VI's death, may be viewed in comparison to a Latin composition by Bembo, *Iulii secundi pontificatus maximus* (Bembo 2005, pp. 94-96). In both poems, the image of the oak representing the Pope (*rovere*) reaches the heavens where its fragrance is enjoyed by the gods. See ll. 1-4 of Ariosto's poem: 'L'arbor ch'al viver prisco porse aita [...] / or s'ha produtto un sì soave alloro / che la fragranza in fino al ciel n'è gita' and ll. 21-24 of Bembo's poem: 'Nec redit ad primos tantum bona quercus honores, / quos habuit mundi cum tener orbis erat: / sed provecta solo nitidis caput inserit astris, / quantum homines aluit, tantum alitura Deos'.

Melibeo, dove sì ratto (eclogue I ed. Fatini). The latter's subject, hidden under the poem's pastoral veil, is the plot hatched by Don Giulio and Don Ferrante d'Este against their brothers, Alfonso and Ippolito, which took place in 1506. The slanderous way in which the guilty party are described leads us to think that the poem was written after the plot, but before the convicts' punishment: that is, before Alfonso's 'moderate' ruling (life sentence for both) had made it inappropriate. It is probable that the piece was either commissioned by Ippolito or conceived as a personal homage to him. It seems, indeed, that Ariosto wanted to please the cardinal by endorsing his views – so much so that Riccardo Bacchelli, who analysed this poem and its historical context in great depth, saw it veined with an ante-litteram Machiavellism.[72] It is true, on the other hand, that some details are omitted which would have served to further glorify the cardinal, most notably, Ippolito's role in discovering the plot.[73] Nevertheless, the courtly destination of this poem is easy to see, being also suggested by the fact that the dramatic eclogue was a privileged form in the Este milieu.[74]

One final proof that Ariosto was part of the circuit of production and 'social' consumption of poetry at court is that at least one of his poems was set to music when he was alive (and was perhaps composed for this purpose). This is a capitolo which was included in a 1510 collection of music printed by Andrea Antico.[75] It is structured as a dialogue (a configuration typical of courtly poetry) between Love and a woman:

[D.] – Amor! [A.] – Che vòi? [D.] – Ragion. [A.] – Da cui la vòi?
[D.] – Da te. [A.] – Tu non l'harrai. [D.] – Perché la neghi?
[A.] – C'haver quel che non ho da me non pòi.
[D.] – Dammi consiglio ove rivolga i prieghi!
[A.] – Consiglio di fanciul saria legiero.
[D.] – Ah, Signor mio, per me pietà ti pieghi! (*Rime*, (1),1-6)

---

72 Bacchelli 1931, pp. 232-236.

73 Ariosto, however, does concede this merit to Ippolito in *Fur.*, XL 68 AB; XLVI 95 C. Another reference to the plot is in *Fur.*, III 60-62 ABC. Here, as noted by Bigi (Ariosto 2012, pp. 167-168), Ariosto's attitude towards Giulio and Ferrante has changed: he invokes Alfonso's mercy through the mouthpiece of Melissa.

74 Some contemporary examples are noted by Catalano 1930-1931, I, p. 242; another eclogue was written on the 1506 plot by Antonio Valtellino (on this see Dionisotti 1937).

75 *Canzoni nove con alcune scelte de varie libri di canto*, Roma, per Andrea Antiquo de Montona, 9 ottobre 1510, ff. 24-25. Einstein 1951, pp. 336-339 reproduces the soprano and tenor parts of this poem, also with a modern notation. The poem is otherwise testified only by manuscript **Pd1** (Padua, Biblioteca del Seminario Vescovile, ms. 91). The text of this poem was made available for the first time by Finazzi 2002-2003, pp. 319-322 (though Vecchi Galli 2000, pp. 359-360, had already called attention to it).

Rather than for the quality of the text, the poem must have distinguished itself precisely for its musical setting: the soprano-tenor score was composed by Bartolomeo Tromboncino, a musician much in demand at the courts of Ippolito d'Este, of Lucrezia Borgia and of Isabella d'Este between 1511 and 1513.[76]

These literary experiences, inextricably linked to Ariosto's life as a courtier, encourage a widening of the focus so as to include a broader subject, which has often been raised by Ariosto criticism: his relationship with those in power as it emerges from the statements he included throughout his oeuvre. As is known, the *Satire* record Ariosto's disillusionment with his service at court, where he felt as if he were in a 'cage';[77] they manifest deep disaffection towards the court environment, as well as more generally towards the political scene. The *Furioso* also voices a good deal of criticism against the greed, hypocrisy and ingratitude characterising the courtly dynamics. The image of Ariosto as an 'anti-courtier' that may be gathered from such passages coexists with the glorification of the Este dynasty in many passages of the *Furioso*. While this glorification has been taken by many scholars as a basis to argue in favour of Ariosto's essential conformity to the Ferrarese ideology, other critics[78] have foregrounded the conflictual aspects of his evaluation, which are evident, even if one considers the literary constraints imposed by the different poetic codes adopted. Giorgio Masi, in particular, has argued that 'there is present in Ariosto's work the idea of literature as a panegyrical instrument; at the same time its independence is clearly vindicated'. He also points out that Ariosto, while adhering to the political views of the court, did not adhere to the courtier's ethics, 'which was to identify with the judgements and moral laws that best reflected the interests of his own lord'.[79] Dennis Looney also recognised in Ariosto's output an 'atteggiamento tradizionalmente dicotomico' towards the court, which he probes more closely in relation to the Latin poetry and the *Furioso*.[80]

---

76 Tromboncino also set to music an octave from the *Furioso* (XXI 126 AB; XXIII C). On this point, see Dorigatti 2011, pp. 22-27 (who believes, on account of the slight differences between its version for music and that printed in the 1516 *Furioso*, that Tromboncino set to music an earlier authorial version of the octave) and Casadei 2016, pp. 138-139 (who suggests instead that Tromboncino himself adapted the octave to his musical needs). On music at the Ferrarese court, see Vela 1989; Prizer 1998; Cavicchi 2011.

77 In satira III he writes 'Mal può durar il rosignuolo in gabbia' (l. 37), obviously alluding to his own condition. In satira IV, because of his difficulty in familiarising with his new place in the Garfagnana he compares himself to an 'augel che muta gabbia' (l. 17).

78 See respectively Ferroni 1986; Larivaille 1990; Jossa 2003; Dorigatti 2017, and Baillet 1982; Masi 2003; Looney 2016.

79 Masi 2003, pp. 84-86.

80 Looney 2016 (the quotation is at p. 46).

Ariosto explicitly speaks of 'courtly poetry', endowing this concept with special ambiguity, in a passage from the lunar episode in the thirty-fifth canto of the *Furioso*. While describing the moon's landscape to Astolfo, St John the Evangelist voices a reflection on the condition of courtiers and especially of courtly writers. In this context he distinguishes between good and bad poets, the difference between them being qualitative rather than ethical.[81] The lords, St John says, should always choose their poets carefully, but also adequately reward them, since poets have the power to immortalise their lords for eternity in return. With regard to this, he criticises the 'ignorant' patrons, who do not understand the potential usefulness of literature in this sense. The whole speech pivots on the idea that poets resort constantly to mystification. The great figures of the past – St John argues – were different from their image as conveyed by writers (*Fur.*, XXXII 26,1-2 AB; XXXV C: 'Non fu sì santo né benigno Augusto / come la tuba di Virgilio suona').[82] At this point the reader can hardly not question the value of the *Furioso* itself, which would thus be exposed to the same charge of mystification. As a matter of fact, critics are divided as to the degree of seriousness that should be ascribed to St John's speech, and every different reading of this passage has in turn conditioned its author's interpretation of Ariosto's attitude towards poetry and towards the *Furioso* itself. Some scholars, such as David QUINT (1977), even came to the conclusion that the speech in fact debunks the encomiastic aim of the entire poem.[83] Rather than espousing such a radical reading, I would agree with Bigi that Ariosto is here aiming to 'ammonire, con tono tra serio e scherzoso, i principi (e magari lo stesso Ippolito)', while developing, at the same time, a more general reflection on poetry, based on his awareness of the difficulty of putting into effect the humanist idea which sees art as something that eternalises only those who are worth it.[84] Nevertheless, the adoption of the Lucianic strategy of *spoudaiogeloion* (which predicated the ultimate acceptability of its arguments on their overall ambiguity) is undoubtedly audacious here. Ariosto's choice of this strategy – it is here moreover that he adopts the im-

---

[81] This is noted by ZATTI 1990, p. 147.

[82] I will return to this passage in Chapter II, 4.

[83] An opposite position (that St John's speech should not be taken too seriously, and consequently that the 'epic' value of the poem should not be questioned) is put forward by DURLING 1965, pp. 148-150. The question on the meaning of the speech is also raised by ASCOLI 1987, pp. 275-278 and pp. 288-297; ZATTI 1990, pp. 127-148, and MAC CARTHY 2009, while other scholars, such as JOSSA 2013 and UGOLINI 2017, have rather taken this passage as a starting point to reflect on Ariosto's relationship to truth-telling.

[84] ARIOSTO 2012, pp. 1145-1146.

age of the 'burst cicadas' to symbolise precisely the laudatory verse[85] – sets him dramatically apart from other courtly writers such as Mario Equicola or Serafino Aquilano, whose works were most often stamped by a purely encomiastic register.[86] On the other hand, in satira I (1517) Ariosto says he would be ready to adopt this very register in praise of Ippolito, on condition that the cardinal pay him esclusively for his intellectual work, relieving him of all other duties.[87] He also alludes to courtly flattery in satira VI, saying (somewhat maliciously, but still in a context of praise) that it belongs to the skills of his addressee Pietro Bembo ('e far sovente / di false lode i principi satolli', ll. 53-54). In short, just as his concept of court, the idea of literary encomium that we gather from Ariosto's work is double-edged.

If we examine the *rime* in the light of these observations, it may be noted that both those contained in the 'canzoniere' (that is, the poems that he believed to be truly representative, albeit not definitively, of his lyric style), but to a great extent also the poems that he discarded, appear consistent with this framework. Very few concessions may be found there to the courtly panegyrical tones, or to any explicit reference to a specific occasion for the composition. Furthermore, almost no examples of *poesia politica* are found and love is, almost exclusively, the chosen theme. In other words, a tendency is observable towards what may be interpreted either as a vision of his lyric activity as less marked by 'social' factors than that of most of his contemporaries, or as an attempt to overcome the ephemerality that often characterised courtly poetry. With regard to this, it is interesting to note that the poems of the main tradition born in relation to some occasion may easily be read as straightforward love poems – hence their inclusion in the 'canzoniere'. As for the canzoni mourning Giuliano de' Medici, the presence of both in Ariosto's most recent selection appears justified by the attempt Ariosto made there to imitate Bembo's model.[88]

---

85 *Fur.*, XXXI 77,7-8 AB; XXXIV C: 'Di cicale scoppiate imagine hanno / versi ch'in laude dei signor si fanno'.

86 Stephen Kolsky's studies on their works have given a detailed account of the minutiae of the relationships between patrons and court intellectuals, and on the way the former influenced the latter's writings. On Equicola, see Kolsky 1986 and 1991. On Serafino's biography by Vincenzo Calmeta, a perfect vantage point from which to examine the relationships between patrons and poets, see Kolsky 1990.

87 *Sat.*, I 226-231: 'Il qual [= Ippolito] se vuol di calamo et inchiostro / di me servirsi, e non mi tòr da bomba, / digli: – Signore, il mio fratello è vostro. – / Io, stando qui, farò con chiara tromba / il suo nome sonar forse tanto alto / che tanto mai non si levò colomba'. Ludovico is here addressing his brother Alessandro, who was also employed at the cardinal's court.

88 I have purposely left these two canzoni out from this book, and propose to examine their unique and distinctive aspects in the context of Ariosto's lyric corpus in greater depth in a forthcoming work.

If all these factors are taken into account, a restricted definition of courtly poetry only partly reflects Ariosto's lyric project, even if a certain social fruition of this output took place at certain times, and even it maintains several of the stylistic features of the courtly manner.

To speak of 'poetry in its relation to the court' does not only mean, however, to examine a poet's contribution to the courtly milieu (i.e. the social and political task his work performed there). It also means to examine the reception of courtly culture on the part of the poet. As regards the latter point, Ariosto's position is much less ambiguous, and indeed it is absolutely clear that he was influenced by contemporary courtly discourse. The fact that nearly all poems by Ariosto have love as their subject must be duly weighed up in the balance as signalling his adhesion to a 'high' (and courtly) poetic tradition – as opposed to the 'comic' tradition, represented by Il Pistoia, which also enjoyed great popularity in Ferrara.[89] It seems therefore necessary, in the analysis of the poems that will be carried out in the following chapters, to also take into account those works that, in the same period, engaged with the courtly discourse and that therefore constitute a fundamental reference point for Ariosto. Among the key treatises that should be mentioned here are at least Equicola's *Libro de natura de amore* (defined by Quondam 'un vero e proprio repertorio topico, progettualmente funzionale alla consultazione e al riuso' of the amorous worldview),[90] Bembo's *Asolani* and Castiglione's *Cortegiano*. The key motifs in this debate – the nature of love, the role of the woman, social and courtly interaction – subtly imbue his poetical formula and must be seen as 'modern' elements that intertwine with much older and well-established love *topoi*.

6. Methodology

The three chapters of this study follow three thematic routes that I feel to be particularly useful in understanding the physiognomy of Ariosto's lyrics against the background of contemporary literary experiences. Chap-

---

[89] Vecchi Galli 1994, pp. 407-408 notes that in the years between the fifteenth and the sixteenth centuries the 'comic' tradition prevailed in Ferrara, while the leaders of the Petrarchist trend, Correggio and Tebaldeo, were active in Mantua, their work fostered by the powerful female presence of Isabella d'Este. According to Virginio's notes, in his youth Ariosto also authored 'baje', namely, comic poems (Catalano 1930-1931, I, pp. 98-100 – the reliability of Virginio's account, however, is questionable). If we look at Ariosto's extant output, the poems that may comply with this definition are sonnet XXIX ed. Fatini (*Magnifico fattor, Alfonso Trotto*) and, belonging to the *rime dubbie*, the twenty-three sonnets *In Cosmicum*.

[90] Quondam 1995, pp. 69-70.

ter I will scrutinise the theme of distance between lovers, focusing the lens in particular on the ways in which *topoi* of lyric poetry interact with the dimension of Ariosto's personal biography, intersecting the plane of 'courtly duties'. What emerges as regards the poet's self-fashioning as lover is then further explored in Chapter II, which will be concerned with the way in which the speaker is portrayed in the several possible declensions of the 'love relationship': it will be shown how Ariosto manages the influences inherited from a wide cultural horizon, featuring both classical and contemporary sources. Chapter III will shift the focus away from the lyric speaker and onto the female figure, whose discursive construction will be made to dialogue with contemporary formulations (both theoretical and poetical).

Because Finazzi's edition, although as yet unpublished, is the most recent critical edition, I have decided to use it as reference text for my quotations from the 'rime del canzoniere'. This will be, therefore, the text of **Vr**, except for the poems introduced in the new selection, for which Finazzi follows the text of **F1**. I will discuss, where relevant, some authorial variants and the different versions in which some poems are known. Also in the numbering of the poems I will be following Finazzi, to whose criteria some attention should here be dedicated: she indicates the forty-eight poems included in **Vr** (following the same ordering as the manuscript) with a Roman numeral; the poems only present in **Mn** / **F** continue this numbering starting from 49, but use Arabic numerals; finally, the poems that only feature in the *editio princeps* **Cp** are indicated with an Arabic numeral + asterisk. Given the restricted access to Finazzi's edition, at the end of this book I provide an appendix with a conversion from Fatini's to Finazzi's numbering.

The uncollected poems will instead be quoted from the edition by Fatini (with Segre's improvements) and will also respect its numbering. As Fatini divides the poems by metre, in these cases I will use the formulation 'poetic form + number + ed. Fatini' (e.g. sonnet I ed. Fatini).

Chapter I

BETWEEN LOVE AND DUTY: ARIOSTO'S ELEGIAC SELF-FASHIONING

Preamble

This study of Ariosto's lyrics will begin by examining some characteristics of the poetic 'I', or, to use Stephen Greenblatt's felicitous phrase (Greenblatt 1980), from the idea of 'self-fashioning'. This particular focus appears necessary, because even a superficial reading yields a strong sense that a number of poems use a systematic and coherent set of shared patterns in terms of the interaction between the lyric subject and the world that surrounds it. The label that may be attached to such patterns is, for the sake of convenience, that of 'autobiographism'.

A particularly suitable viewpoint for this phenomenon is offered by four poems – namely, *Rime del canzoniere*, XXIX, XXX, XLIII and XLV – which it seems to me possible to analyse as a group since they are linked to each other by the similarity of the situations presented: in each of them, the speaker-Ariosto refers to a real event and to his own involvement in it. To be more specific, in XLV the chronological reference is 1512, the year of the battle of Ravenna, whose effects the speaker says he witnessed; XLIII refers to an interrupted journey he made in 1514, when he was accompanying Cardinal Ippolito d'Este; in XXX he talks of having been sent to Florence; finally, in XXIX the lyric subject is travelling to the Garfagnana (the reference here is to his 1522 journey). These poems also share the same metrical form, the capitolo in terza rima – a form regarding which a premise should be made. The capitolo, which was extremely popular in the last decades of the fifteenth century (see Introduction, 3), had developed a strong link with the elegiac mood of the amorous lament. A 1504 letter to Isabella d'Este by Vincenzo Calmeta illustrates, within a wider discussion aimed at fixing the context in which the elegy could be used, how the link was made by one contemporary:

hanno li moderni poi e contemporanei nostri (o sia per la sonorità de la terza rima, o vero perché el terzetto più cum la musica abia conformitade) a li ternari

> l'officio de la elegia assignato. [...] Or, essendo a li moderni poeti piaciuto volere che 'l terzetto [...], secundo li elegi latini, flebili affetti e amorose lamentazioni esprimere, [...] doveriano da quello effetto che fanno el nome sortire, a ciò che li stili meno se venissero a confundere.[1]

Ariosto also embraces this association between the capitolo and the elegiac mode in several of his capitoli, which include those under examination here, and which are normally termed elegiac by critics. In this regard, it should be stated that the use of the term elegiac, when applied to the poetic output of both Ariosto and his contemporaries, raises some problems of definition and requires some qualifications. While in the Latin tradition the so-called love elegy – a genre defined by the use of the elegiac couplet – foregrounded situations of happy as well as unhappy love, in the vernacular tradition the word became more focused and came to indicate exclusively the grieving mood connected to the latter.[2] To use the term with this restricted meaning, is, however, somewhat problematic, both because the label was not at the time firmly established in the critical awareness of contemporary writers (with the exception of Calmeta),[3] and because it means disregarding one part of the legacy of Latin elegy, which is certainly not limited to this more sorrowful thread. Throughout this study, I will therefore use the word with a meaning closer to that which it carried in the classical period, in order to refer, that is, not merely to a plaintive mood but also to a set of contents and situations which are ultimately rooted in the Latin love elegy, and which are enthusiastically imported by the Italian tradition as part of a classicising poetics – including themes such as sensual love or *militia amoris*. This approach appears productive inasmuch as it provides further evidence

---

1 CALMETA 1959, pp. 52-54. Calmeta is here defining the elegiac capitolo as opposed to 'higher' poetic employments of the terza rima, which he simply calls 'capitolo': 'Altra cosa al capitulo e altra a la elegia, avvenga che ambi li stili siano in terzetti, se conviene. [...]' (*ibid.*). On Calmeta's codification of elegy, see also FLORIANI 1988*bis*, pp. 249-252; VECCHI GALLI 2003, pp. 68-76.

2 See Carrai's notes in COMBONI – DI RICCO 2003, VII.

3 As noted by VECCHI GALLI 2003, pp. 70-71, the authors rarely define their *ternari* as 'elegie', and prefer instead to use the names of their subgenres (*disperata*, *epistola*, ecc), despite the fact that in all these subgenres the convention that is commonly termed elegiac is recognisable. Ariosto's poems are no exception: no manuscript or early printed edition of them adopt the word *elegie*, opting instead for *capitoli* (*ibid.*, p. 77 – note, however, that Ariosto's capitoli are defined as 'elegies' by Pigna in his biography; see PIGNA 1554, p. 116: 'Trovò parimente la via delle volgari Elegie siccome nelle sue Rime si scorge [...]'). Reflecting this terminological uncertainty, modern criticism has also failed to adopt a single criterion; sometimes scholars have distinguished between the various subgenres, in other cases they have opted for the generic term 'elegie'.

to the link between Renaissance authors and their classical (and humanist) models. This is a link that, as will be seen, is also crucial for Ariosto.[4]

From the perspective outlined above, it is clear that in these capitoli two lines of influence converge, one highly stereotyped (elegiac), the other extremely private (autobiographical). In this chapter I will evaluate these two components and examine their interaction in order to understand the type of self-fashioning Ariosto here pursues. This analysis will be carried out against the background of contemporary examples of elegiac terza rima. In addition to this, however, a further point of reference will be Ariosto's *Satire*, which have never been systematically analysed in parallel with his capitoli. As is well known, Ariosto-the-satirist intertwines autobiographical facts with historical events and cultural issues. Through these multiple levels he weighs up his life at court, at the same time widening the horizon of his reflections to include contemporary society and the political scene. The literary convention that forms his framework of reference is moralistic: the *sermo cotidianus* of the *Satire* is clearly modelled after that of Horace, the choice of this source being probably prompted by Tito Vespasiano Strozzi's use of it in his *Sermones*.[5] Furthermore, as Alberto Godioli observes (Godioli 2010), Ariosto would have been able to take inspiration from the very popular contemporary tradition of sententious capitoli, and especially those by Niccolò da Correggio. We are therefore on very different literary territory from that of elegy.[6] Nevertheless, a parallel analysis may be justified for two main reasons. First, because a margin of continuity exists between the traditions of the 'moralistic' and the 'elegiac' capitolo in terms of the display of sententiousness. The second reason is that these four poems display autobiographical material far more than is normally found in the genre and seem to seek a balance between self-writing and convention, thus moving closer to the register of the *Satire*.[7] By examining in greater depth these similarities, the differences between the two codes will be clearer. Godioli has argued that Ariosto in the *Satire* develops 'la specificità del linguggio satirico', acquiring 'consapevolezza del confine fra i diversi generi e registri espressivi'.[8] On this point, it is worth dwelling fur-

---

4 An exploration of the elegiac themes in the Italian literary tradition may be found in the contributions gathered in Comboni – Di Ricco 2003 (on the Quattrocento repertoire, I once more refer the reader to Vecchi Galli 2003).

5 See Floriani 1988, pp. 73-77.

6 On the late-Quattrocento satirical genre (namely, the background for Ariosto's innovations), see also Galbiati 1987.

7 This feature was also noted, regarding capitolo XLIII, by Tissoni Benvenuti 1976, p. 309.

8 Godioli 2010, p. 120.

ther and investigating those aspects that allow us to understand Ariosto's perception of the borders dividing the different literary genres that could be pursued through terza rima –[9] and therefore between different forms of self-fashioning. Such a line of enquiry appears all the more justified if one considers the chronological overlap between these works. The arc of composition of the *Satire* is normally acknowledged to be 1517-1524, and their main testimony, the *manoscritto ferrarese*, has been placed by Segre at ca. 1525.[10] As for these capitoli, their composition took place in the years between 1512 and 1522, and 1522 is also the *terminus post quem* for their assembly in **Vr**. All these elements authorise us to presuppose a conscious reflection on Ariosto's part on the possibilities of the terza rima, carried out in a specific phase of his life.

It should be noted that the speaker of the *Satire* has recently been the subject of new critical readings, which have aimed to strike a balance between an interpretation of the work as a trustworthy biographical document and one that takes them as mostly 'fictional'.[11] My analysis of the lyrics will also attempt to integrate these two types of approach. In turn, the observations that will be made on this very limited corpus will provide useful points of orientation to understand certain dynamics that permeate the *rime* more extensively.

1. Ariosto and the tradition of the 'parting between two lovers'

In the four capitoli considered here, the lyric speaker, who is leaving Ferrara, suffers on account of his separation from his beloved. The theme of distance – resulting from either the poet's or the lady's departure, for reasons which include court duties or war – is a widespread legacy of the Latin love elegy in Quattrocento poetry, and in some canzonieri is actually an organising principle. For instance, one thinks of the Canzoniere Costabili, featuring several sequences of poems on the poet's departure, or that by Cornazano, where a clear dividing line may be drawn between the

9 Floriani 1988, p. 39, describes the *terza rima* as 'un genere-contenitore ancora indifferenziato nel primo Cinquecento, destinato nella fase successiva ad una fortuna mediocre in quanto forma dell'elegia, e ad una sorte migliore come forma della satira e del burlesco'.

10 Segre 1966, pp. 168-172.

11 Villa 2008, p. 513: 'L'opera stessa [the *Satire*] richiede al lettore di tenersi in un precario equilibrio tra la consapevolezza della finzione letteraria, della strategia dell'autorappresentazione, e la coscienza che le occasioni alle quali Ariosto reagisce sono reali'. I shall refer the reader to the most recent commentary to the *Satire* (Ariosto 2019) and to its bibliography. Specific contributions will be cited where relevant.

lyrics 'in presence' and those 'in absence' of the lady.[12] Although the distance theme could be modulated equally well in different metrical forms, its expression through the capitolo became regular at the turn of the century, and it came to constitute what may be regarded as a subgenre proper, the *dipartita*.[13] This is characterised by a high degree of formalisation: the speaker usually laments the difficulty of his journey, expresses his fears about his beloved's faithfulness during his absence, engages in long moral tirades against what he believes to be the original causes of the lovers' separation (e.g. warfare). These features are often combined with those of the *epistola* – therefore it may happen that the beloved person is also the addressee of the poem. And, in a further version of this genre, the speaker takes leave not from his beloved but from his lord. We shall consider, for example, the following excerpts by Tebaldeo and by Sasso; in the latter the speaker addresses Francesco and Isabella Gonzaga:

> Io me n'andrò: serà possibil questo?
> Se un dì da te non scio viver lontano,
> come vivrò se fuor più tempo io resto? [...]
> Ben fu crudel chi trovò prima l'arme,
> chi primo incominciò partir la terra,
> cagion che l'huom contra l'altro huomo se arme!
> (Tebaldeo, *Rime della vulgata*, 277,1-9)

> Partir convemme, e scio che solo el vaso
> del spirto portarò; che 'l spirto teco
> anci el partir, è già, signor, rimaso;
> Non essendo con te, non serò meco,
> che da te solo e non da me derivo,
> se 'l tuo lume non fosse, io seria cieco.
> (Sasso, capitolo XVIII, ll. 22-27)

On a stylistic level two elements must be highlighted. The first is that in most cases the poetic persona is not expanded into a well-rounded subject, and sometimes it does not even coincide with the author: the capitolo may be 'ghost written', as it were, in the persona of the lord or some other figure. The second thing to note regards narrative technique. Indeed, although the *dipartita* in some cases displays narrative sequences (the terza

12 See Baldassari's and Comboni's notes in Comboni – Zanato 2017, pp. 39-41 and p. 245 respectively.

13 On this tradition, see Tissoni Benvenuti 1976, p. 306 (the scholar examines it as a basis for analysing precisely Ariosto's case) and Gentili 2003, pp. 126-129 (who focuses on its application by Correggio).

rima was eminently suited to this use), its primary aim was to embody the voice of *pathos* and grief.[14] This holds true, in general, for all the manifestations of fifteenth-century elegy, whose speaker inherits the inwardness of its classical models, but without the psychological and narrative nuances that can be found in the latter. These characteristics later elicited the disapproval of Equicola, who, in his *Libro de natura de amore,* criticised the repetitive commonplaces of the genre (including the recurrence of the 'partenze') and opted to ignore them in his treatise on love.[15]

Although Tissoni Benvenuti regards XXIX as the only example of *dipartita* among Ariosto's lyrics,[16] arguably XXX, XLIII and XLV also appear to be influenced by this genre, as they pivot on the same themes: the distance of the beloved and the tension between the space 'of the affections' and the space 'of duty'. The way these motifs are fashioned in these capitoli, on a double level of adhesion and innovation, will be explored in the next sections, respecting the chronological order that critics have traditionally given these poems.

2. Love and warfare

In capitolo XLV (*O vera o falsa che la fama suone*), the lyric voice states that he has just visited a battlefield, without specifying its location but with a clear allusion to the involvement of the French (referred to as 'those who live between the Garonne and the Rhine'). Let us look first at the passage containing the historical reference:

  Io venni dove le campagne rosse
eran del sangue barbaro et latino,
che fiera stella dianzi a furor mosse;

---

14 To mention but one example, Correggio's capitolo 355 recalls the moment of separation from his lady, laying out (ll. 67-93) a detailed narrative sequence: the speaker takes leave of his beloved; then, having noticed her coldness, he spends the night crying; the following day, upon leaving, he repeatedly falls to the ground; finally, he wanders around the city for long time before being able to find its gate. On this poem, see Gentili 2003, pp. 126-127. On the 'narrativeness' of the elegiac capitolo, see also Vecchi Galli 2003, p. 54.

15 *Libro de natura de amore*, *Libro primo*, ff. 17*v*-18*r*: '[...] raccontando timori, speranze, suspitioni, gelosie, cure, [...] guerre, paci, tregue, partenze, retorni [...]. Cose fora di nostro proposito, per la qual cosa le lasciamo' (throughout this study all quotations from this work are not from the 1525 *editio princeps*, but rather from the first known version of the treatise, probably dating back to 1505-1508, between the author's sojourns in Ferrara and in Mantua: Equicola 1999, p. 229).

16 Tissoni Benvenuti 1976, p. 307.

et vidi un morto all'altro sì vicino
che, senza premer lor, quasi il terreno
a molte miglia non dava il camino;
et da chi alberga tra Garonna e 'l Reno
vidi uscir crudeltà che ne devria
tutto el mondo d'horror rimaner pieno.

(*Rime del canzoniere*, XLV 37-45)

I agree with the most common interpretation, according to which the battle in question is that of Ravenna (11 April 1512).[17] This saw the Estensi allied with the French against the Holy League of Julius II and constituted an important victory for Alfonso I, although both sides suffered significant losses. What enables the modern reader to infer this location is precisely the description of the bloody battlefield and the special emphasis placed on the – historically documented –[18] horrific violence enacted by the French. These aspects are also highlighted by Ariosto in the passages of the *Furioso* where he recalls the same event; in fact, some textual similarities between them and the capitolo may be observed:

Nuoteranno i destrier fin alla pancia
nel sangue uman per tutta la campagna:
ch'a sepelire il popul verrà manco
tedesco, ispano, greco, italo e franco.

(*Fur.*, III 55,5-8 ABC)

morti erano infiniti, e derelitti

(*Fur.*, XII 1,3 AB; XIV C)

quanta n'ingrassa il campo ravegnano

(*Fur.*, XII 5,5 AB; XIV C)

Di qua la Francia, e di là il campo ingrossa
la gente ispana, e la battaglia è grande.
Cader si vede e far la terra rossa
la gente d'arme in amendua le bande.
Piena di sangue uman pare ogni fossa

(*Fur.*, XXXIII 40,1-5 C)[19]

---

17 According to another interpretation, far less likely, the passage refers to the battle of Marignano (Catalano 1930-1931, I, p. 342 footnote 81).

18 See Guicciardini, *Storia d'Italia*, X 12-13.

19 The most extensive reflection on this battle is developed in the proem to the fourteenth canto, from which I have quoted only two lines – see also footnote 26. In all the passages quoted, an echo may be felt of *Inf.*, XXVII 43-44: 'La terra che fé già la lunga prova / e di Franceschi

From a stylistic point of view, in the quoted passage from capitolo XLV, it may also be noted that the contents are predicated on an assertive first person, which gives it a 'chronicle-like' feel. This effect is achieved by Ariosto through the use of verbs of perception: besides the repetitions of 'vidi' (ll. 40, 44, and 47), 'notai' is found at l. 52. Here too parallels may be supplied from the *Furioso*, and especially from those passages where Ariosto-the-narrator declares himself to be a witness or at least a reliable narrator of two historical events: the tragic capture of Ercole Cantelmo ('un Ercol *vidi* e un Alessandro, indutti [...]' *Fur.*, XXXIII 6,3 AB; XXXVI C) and the capture of fifteen Venetian galleys by Ippolito, at the battle of Polesella ('*Nol vide* io già[20] [...] Ma [...] tanto me ne contar, ch'io *ne fui certo*', *Fur.*, XXXVI 3,1-4,4 AB; XL C). Ariosto's use of this type of rhetoric, based on verbs of perception, was in all these cases probably influenced by the *visione allegorica* – a genre whose main models were Dante's *Comedy* and Petrarch's *Triumphi* –[21] but its deployment is completely different between the *Furioso* and the capitolo. While in the former it constitutes the basis for historical reflection, in the latter it serves entirely lyric-elegiac purposes. Indeed, here the speaker, a frustrated lover, is visiting the battlefield as an attempt to remedy his unhappiness, as he is certain that, in such a place, he will encounter greater suffering than his own. The theme is developed along a proto-mannerist strategy, with a hyperbolical use of the Petrarchan pattern of antithesis –[22] an aspect which emerges clearly if the passage in which the speaker reflects on the ineffectuality of this supposed remedy is compared to its Petrarchan source:

Ché s'un contrario all'altro è medicina
non so perché, da l'un pigliando forza,
per l'altro la mia doglia non declina
(*Rime del canzoniere*, XLV 22-24)[23]

sanguinoso mucchio' (Dante is here referring to Forlì, while discussing the political framework of the Romagna). On the genesis of these passages on Ravenna, see Dorigatti 2011, pp. 19-21. In the capitolo Ariosto also resorts to another example of *poesia politica*, that is *Rvf*, XXVIII (cp. the latter's l. 31: 'Chïunque alberga tra Garona e 'l monte' and l. 43 of the capitolo).

20 In the first two versions of the *Furioso*, this concept is further enhanced at the beginning of octave 4: 'Absente ero io [...]' (*Fur.*, XXXVI 4,1 A); 'Lontano ero io [...]' (*Fur.*, XXXVI 4,1 B). According to Catalano 1930-1931, I, p. 317, Ariosto actually witnessed Cantelmo's capture (the scholar bases his statement on a passage from the *epicedio* written by Gabriele Ariosto). On Ariosto's connections to and relationship with these historical events, see also Maldina 2016.

21 Examples of this genre in the Cinquecento are illustrated in Corsaro 1999 (who also considers its echoes in the *Furioso*).

22 On the use of the oxymoron in medieval love poetry, see Gigliucci 1990; for its Renaissance use, see Gigliucci 2004.

23 Cp. *Fur.*, VI 49,1-2 ABC: 'Deh! perché vo le mie piaghe toccando, / senza speranza poi di medicina?'.

Se mai foco per foco non si spense,
né fiume fu già mai secco per pioggia,
ma sempre l'un per l'altro simil poggia,
et spesso l'un contrario l'altro accense,
Amor, tu che' pensier' nostri dispense,
al qual un'alma in duo corpi s'appoggia,
perché fai in lei con disusata foggia
men per molto voler le voglie intense?

(*Rvf*, XLVIII 1-8)

While Petrarch wonders on the laws of nature – by which the addition of similar elements augments their effect and the opposites, too, often become stronger if juxtaposed –, the speaker of the capitolo lays out a strictly medical question. His argument implies a paradoxical identification between love and illness, and, as its counterpart, the identification of distance – and ultimately also of warfare – as a medicine. Ariosto is here foregrounding an antierotic (or, allopathic) strategy which implies his knowledge of a specific Quattrocento genre, that of writings against love. These texts (on which see also the Preamble to Chapter II) articulate a discourse that systematically deploys medical language and is influenced by Ovid's *Remedia amoris*, which was possibly a direct source also for Ariosto. In Ovid, the speaker-preceptor prescribes separation on the assumption that Love especially strikes the idle, in order to 'give the empty mind some business to occupy it';[24] among the activities that can be pursued at a distance from the beloved woman, he recommends warfare, as well as political engagement:

Sunt fora, sunt leges, sunt, quos tuearis, amici:
vade per urbanae splendida castra togae.
Vel tu sanguinei iuvenalia munera Martis
suspice: deliciae iam tibi terga dabunt.
Ecce, fugax Parthus, magni nova causa triumphi,
iam videt in campis Caesaris arma suis:
vince Cupidineas partier Parthasque sagittas,
et refer ad patrios bina tropaea deos.

(*Rem. am.*, ll. 151-158)

---

[24] *Rem. am.*, l. 150: 'Da vacuae menti, quo teneatur, opus'. This concept is also in TEBALDEO, *Rime della vulgata*, 16,1-4: 'Provato ho stare in sdegno i mesi e l'hore, / provato ho far mia vita in monte e in piano, / solcar l'onde del mar, fugir lontano, / per trovar fine al mio sfrenato ardore'.

The speaker of capitolo XLV, however, does not reach his antierotic goal. Indeed, he realises that the pain of the soldiers is incomparably smaller than his agony, because it is soon silenced by death:

> Io notai che 'l mal lor li trahea fuore
> del mal, perché sì grave era che presto
> finìa la vita insieme col dolore;
> il mio mi pon fin su le porte, e questo
> medesmo ir non mi lascia, et torna indrieto
> et fa che mal mio grado in vita resto.
>
> (*Rime del canzoniere*, XLV 52-57)

Eventually, he decides to return to his lady ('Io torno a voi', l. 58): he has failed, therefore, in effecting the cure prescribed by Ovid, who explicitly warned his pupils not to give in to their suffering, or to the desire to end their separation from their beloved.[25]

If we now return to the tercets describing the battlefield, their difference from the purely dramatic tones of the historical passages of the *Furioso*[26] is now fully evident. The capitolo is a clear example of *poesia cortigiana* and was arguably conceived for courtly circulation.[27] Incidentally, the lack of specification regarding the battlefield constitutes a further proof in this sense, as it presupposes a set of shared ideas between the author and his supposed readers – these we may take as belonging to the milieu of Ippolito d'Este, whom Ariosto was serving in 1512. In this light, it may also be supposed that Ariosto actually did visit the battlefield (as Catalano believes),[28] because such use of paradox and the speaker's concern with persuasiveness

---

[25] *Ibid.*, ll. 213-218: 'Tu tantum quamvis firmis retinebere vinclis / i procul, et longas carpere perge vias; / flebis, et occurret desertae nomen amicae, / stabit et in media pes tibi saepe via: / sed quanto minus ire voles, magis ire memento; / perfer, et invitos currere coge pedes'.

[26] As noted by Bigi, in the proem to the fourteenth canto 'il poeta esprime soprattutto la sua grave pietà per le vittime della battaglia e del saccheggio e il suo doloroso sdegno per le violenze commesse dai Francesi' (Ariosto 2012, p. 441).

[27] An example of a similar employment of the theme of opposites is in Correggio, *Rime*, 212,1-8: 'Non fur mai fiamme da le fiamme spente / ma l'una ognor fa più l'altra gagliarda; / pioggia non secca fiume, e non si tarda / per sproni il corso d'un destrer corrente. / Amor, per farmi il mio disio presente, / altro non è che a dir: — Chi è acceso si arda —: / tu mi fai un Tantal che ne l'acqua guarda, / anzi un giaccio propinquo a un foco ardente'. We have no information regarding the circulation of Ariosto's poem; interestingly however, it features, together with XXX and XLIII, in **L3** (Florence, Biblioteca Medicea Laurenziana, Ashburnham 564), a manuscript anthology dated by Segre to the third decade of the Cinquecento. This contains several lyric poems by Ariosto, as well as two of his *Satire* in their earlier version. See Finazzi 2002-2003, pp. 92-93.

[28] Catalano 1930-1931, I, pp. 341-342.

would have been ineffectual if the situation had no basis in reality. If we accept this, the poem may be taken as the elegiac transfiguration of a journey undertaken as part of the author's court duties.

Despite this adherence to the strategies of courtly poetry, some original choices may be noted in Ariosto's approach to the genre of the *dipartita*. First, the increased autobiographical consistency attained through the strategies briefly described above gives the speaker's voice a distinctness that is unusual in the Quattrocento elegy. A parallel case is that of Tebaldeo, to whom Marchand has attributed a pioneering attempt in this direction.[29] Two capitoli, 282 and 285, are worth mentioning, which adopt as a mouthpiece Francesco Gonzaga. See the following passage from the latter:

> Io disegnai, ma i miei disegni vani
> restoro al colorir, e dire io posso
> ch'io vinsi con ducento mantüani;
> pensa da che cordoglio io fui percosso
> quando vidi quei fidi citadini
> quasi tutti giacer su il terren rosso!
> (Tebaldeo, *Rime della vulgata*, 285,127-132)

A second notable matter in Ariosto's case is that his speaker willingly pursues the separation, in such a way that we might even speak of a reversal of the *dipartita*; it may also be observed that while he finds himself on the site of an historical event in which his masters played a central role, he is there not on their orders (as instead regularly happens in this genre). An ironic note may be perceived in this subtle shift: indeed, we may take it as a starting point to note more broadly that also in the *rime* irony is deployed as a fundamental lens through which Ariosto views the situations he describes,[30] something which diverges from the normal manifestations of elegy. Capitolo XLV offers, therefore, a first set of elements to describe Ariosto's strategy of self-fashioning – more specifically as a subject so taken up with love as to read through its lens even the most 'serious' matters. These characteristics are also to be found in the other three capitoli that will be the study of this chapter.

---

29 Marchand 1997, p. 166: 'L'opera tebaldeana ci offre [...] la possibilità di studiare come il racconto dell'io emerga progressivamente dall'elegia per conquistare la sua quasi piena autonomia [...]. Infatti, mentre nella maggior parte dei capitoli il protagonista rappresenta il proprio dolore nel tempo stesso del componimento, alcuni cominciano a dare spazio ad eventi anteriori e posteriori al tempo del racconto [...]'.

30 Among the most recent studies on Ariosto's irony – a well-established critical commonplace regarding the *Furioso* – see Musarra 2013; Sangirardi 2014; Rivoletti 2014; Jossa 2016.

3. A poem addressed to Ippolito d'Este

If in XLV Ariosto was still caught up in the rhetorical modes of the courtly capitolo, in XLIII (*Del bel numero vostro havrete un manco*) a more original elaboration can be detected. The poem was occasioned by an event which took place in October 1514: Ariosto, who was accompanying Cardinal Ippolito to Rome, was forced by a sudden illness to stop at the Furlo Pass.[31] This poem addresses Ippolito himself and is in fact a most interesting testimony to Ariosto's lyric activity at the cardinal's court, allowing us to touch upon the poet's relation to patronage.

In the opening lines, Ariosto apologises to the cardinal for not being able to follow him any further:

> Del bel numero vostro havrete un manco,
> Signor, ché qui rest'io dove Apenino
> d'alta percossa aperto mostra il fianco,
> (*Rime del canzoniere*, XLIII 1-3)
> Tiemme la febre, [...]
> (l. 10)

This opening is an exact calque of the *incipit* of Tibullus, I 3: 'Ibitis Aegaeas sine me, Messalla, per undas, [...] / me tenet ignotis aegrum Phaeacia terris' (ll. 1-3).[32] As a matter of fact, the whole situation outlined by Ariosto mirrors the source, indeed closely following its first half in which Tibullus also tells his lord, Messalla, that an illness has prevented him from following his entourage. Later on, both poets express their fear of dying in a foreign land, far away from the woman they love.[33]

We have, therefore, an outstanding case displaying a coincidence between a real situation and a motif belonging to literary tradition: I will return to this point later. For the moment, it should be observed that the

---

31 This episode is reconstructed in Catalano 1930-1931, I, pp. 374-375.

32 This link was first noted by Floriani 1988*bis*, p. 252.

33 Cp. *Rime del canzoniere*, XLIII 61-67: 'Ché se qui moro, non ho chi mi pianga: / qui sorelle non ho, non ho qui matre / che sopra il morto corpo il capel franga, / né quatro frati miei, che con vesti atre / m'accompagnino al lapide che l'ossa / devria chiuder del figlio allato il patre. / Madonna non è qui [...]' and Tibullus, I 3,5-9: 'abstineas, Mors atra, precor: non hic mihi mater / quae legat in maestos ossa perusta sinus, / non soror, Assyrios cineri quae dedat odores / et fleat effusis ante sepulcra comis, / Delia non usquam [...]'. See also *Rime del canzoniere*, XLIII 52: 'Lasso, chi sa ch'io non sia al fin degli anni?' and Tibullus, I 3,53: 'Quodsi fatales iam nunc explevimus annos'. If the dating to 1514 is correct, Ariosto's beloved must be identified as Alessandra Benucci.

rewriting from Tibullus – an author whose influence is also felt in Ariosto's Latin poetry –[34] is not an end in itself but must be inscribed in Ariosto's overall rhetorical strategy aimed at paying homage to his lord. Through the classical borrowing, he is implicitly praising the figure of the cardinal as a modern Messalla: that is, as a figure of power, but also as a patron of the arts (as Messalla famously promoted the activity of a group of writers – one of whom was Tibullus – who were known as the 'Messalla circle'). Notably, in his choice of representing Ippolito in this way Ariosto only partially follows a strategy of embellishment. Indeed, contemporary historical research on the cardinal has unearthed his profound interest in the arts, music, and the sciences, overall pointing to a cultural background that was certainly superior to that of his brother Alfonso. His passion for literature led him to encourage, along with the composition of the *Furioso*, also the intellectual activity of Equicola and Calcagnini.[35] The statement by the historian Giuseppe Antonelli that Ippolito 'ne' suoi viaggi sempre seco trasportava buon numero di volumi'[36] suggests the intriguing possibility that he might have even read Tibullus during the 1514 journey, and perhaps discussed this reading with Ariosto.

Another homage to the cardinal occurs from l. 13. The speaker, maintaining a tone of bland confidentiality – which significantly diverges from the gloomy funereal register adopted by Tibullus –, jokingly wishes that the fever had come at a more opportune moment and had prevented his setting out in the first place, thus providing him with a 'scusa degna' (l. 23) that may spare him the pain of separation from his beloved lady. Within this statement, he resorts to an equation (highlighted by the *enjambement*) of woman and lord as his 'two lights':

> Ché s'ero per restar privo de l'una
> mia luce, al men non devea l'altra tormi
> la sempre aversa a' miei disir' Fortuna.
> Deh, perché quando honestamente sciormi
> dal debito potea, che qui mi trasse,
> non venne più per tempo in letto a pormi?
>
> (*Rime del canzoniere*, XLIII 13-18)

Equally worthy of note is, in the last part of the poem, the mention of Ferrara, the city in which the speaker hopes to be buried if he dies ('Almen

---

[34] See the notes of the most recent edition (Ariosto 2017).

[35] On the figure of Cardinal Ippolito, see Menegatti 2016; Menegatti 2017, esp. pp. 50-51; Dorigatti 2018.

[36] Quoted in Dorigatti 2018, p. 21.

l'inutil' spoglie habbia Ferrara', l. 91). While paying homage to his lord, Ariosto is here also declaring his ultimate faithfulness to his homeland, following a well-established *topos* of courtly poetry. Further elements may be observed that suggest Ariosto's intention of highlighting here his compliance with the courtly amorous code. At ll. 13-18 (above), he is stressing his own involvement in a pattern of reasoning that was very common within this repertoire, and a constitutive element of the *dipartita*: the ongoing conflict between its two key principles, love and duty, which forces the poet, a servant of both, to make a difficult choice between the two. The ultimate victory of the former is declared in the central section of the text. Here the speaker is tormented by worries caused by Love, who wishes to take revenge on him for setting out against his dictates. An echo of Tibullus is again observable (I 3,21-22: 'Audeat invito ne quis discedere Amore, / aut sciat egressum se prohibente deo'), but what is conspicuously Ariosto's own innovation, one with its roots in his cultural milieu, is the radicalisation of the portrayal of Love as the overpowering ruler of a court – 'tyran', l. 43 –, in open competition with that of Ippolito – 'Signor', l. 2:[37]

> Né per spronare o caricar d'antenna
> si può fuggir, o con cavallo o nave,
> che [Amor] non ne giunga in un spiegar di penna.
> (*Rime del canzoniere*, XLIII 37-39)

> Questo tyran, non men crudel che forte,
> ch'anchor mai perdonar non seppe offesa
> né lascia entrar pietà ne la sua corte,
> perché mille fiate et più contesa
> m'havea la lunga via, che sì m'absenta
> da quella luce in c'ho l'anima accesa,
> de la inobedientia hor mi tormenta [...]
> (*ibid.*, ll. 43-49)

The contrast between love and the claims of duty can also be regarded as a constant centrifugal force of the *Furioso*. Here, too, the outcome is always the victory of love, which takes the form either of an insane over-

[37] The metaphor of Love as a ruler is noted by Mengaldo 1963, p. 328 with a reference to Boiardo: the scholar notes how it stands 'all'incontro della tradizione poetica latina e volgare' but 'ha nel B[oiardo] un'estensione, dettata da una poetica umanistico-cortese, ben più larga che nel Petr[arca]'. For the theme of the 'two lords' in courtly literature, see also Filenio Gallo, *A Safira*, 81,14: 'ch'a due servir non puol un servidore'; Tebaldeo, *Rime della vulgata*, 282,36: 'ché a dui signor' non se sta ben sugetto'.

turning of chivalric values – emblematic is the case of Orlando and Rinaldo, who are seduced away from their obligations towards the Christian army by Angelica's charms – or that of the 'rational' call of marital obligations, as with Ruggiero, who is continually torn between his predestined marriage to Bradamante and his devotion to king Agramante. Significantly, similar lexical choices are observable between the capitolo and a passage whose subject is Ruggiero:

Restomi qui, né, come Amor vorebbe,
posso Madonna satisfar, [...]
(*Rime del canzoniere*, XLIII 7-8)

né per *spronare* o caricar d'antenna
si può fuggir, [...] (*ibid.*, ll. 37-38)
Tal fallo poi di *punition* sì grave
punisce [...] (ll. 40-41)

Tra sé volve Ruggiero e fa discorso,
se *restar* deve, o il suo signor seguire.
Gli pon l'amor de la sua donna un morso
per non lasciarlo in Africa più gire:
lo volta e gira, et a contrario corso
lo *sprona*, e lo minaccia di *punire*,
s'el patto e 'l giuramento non tien saldo,
che fatto avea col paladin Rinaldo.

Non men da l'altra parte sferza e *sprona*
la vigilante e stimulosa cura [...]
(*Fur.*, XXXVI 66 and 67,1-2 AB; XL C)

(emphasis mine)

The speaker of the capitolo, however, cannot even aspire to be regarded as an analogue of Ruggiero. Indeed, his illness prevents him from even choosing between his court obligations and his *servitium amoris*: 'né, come Amor vorebbe, / posso Madonna satisfar, né a voi / l'obligo scior che la mia fe' vi debbe' (ll. 7-9). We therefore encounter here the paradoxical strategy typical of the courtly repertoire of love poetry. Along the same lines, Ariosto also revises another motif drawn from his model, namely, the appearance of the speaker's epitaph at the end of the poem. Indeed, while the tombstone imagined by Tibullus sought to immortalise him only as a comrade of Messalla's (I 3,55-56: 'HIC IACET IMMITI CONSVMPTVS MORTE TIBVLLVS, / MESSALLAM TERRA DVM SEQVITVRQVE MARI'), in the inscription designed by Ariosto he appears as a victim of the sorrow caused by separation from his lady: 'così né anchor chi questo marmo serra / viver lontan da la sua donna puote' (ll. 96-97).

Arguably, the speaker here fashions himself as an 'unwilling' courtier, who sets love above duty. Could such an attitude – even if merely a literary pose – run the risk of alienating favour from his addressee? If one looks at the internal evidence offered by the text, the answer is no. Indeed, the poet assimilated his patron into the logic of the capitolo: the fact that Ippolito himself is a lover binds the two closely and suggests their reciprocal sympathy. One should note in particular how Ariosto-the-speaker invokes his lord's indulgence for his behaviour, counting on the fact that the latter, too, is among those who have felt the sting of love's arrow:

> ma mi fido ch'a voi, che de la fiera
> punta de Amor chiara notitia havete,
> debba la colpa mia parer leggiera.
> Così vi sien tutte le imprese liete,
> com'è ben ver ch'ella talhor v'ha punto,
> né sano forse anchora hoggi ne sete.
> (*Rime del canzoniere*, XLIII 28-33)

In representing Ippolito along these lines, Ariosto certainly met with his lord's approval. Within the system of relationships between those in power and court literati, the lords not only enjoyed appearing as political centres, but also being involved in the fashionable code of love, which constituted the basis of the intellectual exchange between themselves and their entourage and prompted their activity as patrons. Such forms of exchange also encouraged the creation of poems, emblems, mottos, etc. Capitolo 285 by Tebaldeo, for which he used the mouthpiece of Francesco Gonzaga and which has already been mentioned in section 2, is to be taken as a further example stemming from the same cultural milieu. The marquis is obliged to support Venice in its war against France, but all his thoughts are occupied by love, and he deserves forgiveness, he argues, for his lack of military prowess:[38]

> Sendo io al stipendio del Leon condutto,
> ve andai, pensa cum qual ira e travaglia,
> ch'io fui qual pianta svèlta in su il far frutto! [...]
> de altro fastidio fu il combatter mio,
> ché loro [= Camillus and Caesar] ebber la pugna sol cum Galli
> et io cum Galli e cum Amor, che è dio;
> era divisa a dui diversi balli
> la mente mia, e son degno de scusa
> s'io avesse nel pugnar commessi falli.
> (Tebaldeo, *Rime della vulgata*, 285,100-114)

That Cardinal Ippolito, too, was willing to be represented as a lover is confirmed in another capitolo by Ariosto, XXV, which it is worth briefly considering. Here, the lyric voice speaks of a burden that oppresses him

[38] From Tebaldeo's capitolo 282, whose speaker is again Gonzaga, it is also possible to glean the marquis's desire to be represented in poetry as a lover. See the previous footnote, and ll. 16-18: 'ecco, io, per farme in l'arme excelso e magno, / per trar l'afflicta Italia de fatica, / da te, da la qual pendo, me scompagno'.

almost unbearably. In order to describe its strength, he engages in a long series of metaphors and similes which draws on various *topoi* of endurance:

De sì calloso dosso et sì robusto
non ha né dromedario, né elephante
l'odorato indo, o l'ethiope adusto
che possa star, non che mutar le piante,
se radoppiata gli è la soma poi
che l'ha qual può patir, né può più inante.
(*Rime del canzoniere*, XXV 1-6)[39]

In the context of **Vr**, the poem lends itself to be read as the complaint of a lover – albeit one who has almost reached the limit of his endurance of the *servitium amoris* (see Introduction, 4) – but in fact the subject is deployed quite obscurely, in a way that has long defied understanding. It was Bozzetti who eventually grasped the meaning with which it was initially conceived, by linking the opening image of the capitolo – an excessively burdened dromedary – to one of Ippolito's *imprese*, which is known to us thanks to Giovio's description: a kneeling camel accompanied by the Spanish motto 'No suefro mas de lo que puedo'.[40] Arguably, therefore, the capitolo was written at the request of Ippolito, probably when the cardinal, a keen collector of *imprese*, first adopted that of the camel.[41] Incidentally, Ariosto's poetic response to the creation of a device demonstrates that he, too, accepted the well-established vogue of writing works on emblems by means of which court literati tried to 'smooth their way to patronage'.[42]

---

39 See *Purg.*, XXXI 16-19: 'Come balestro frange, quando scocca / da troppa tesa la sua corda e l'arco, [...] / sì scoppia' io sottesso grave carco'.

40 Bozzetti 1985, p. 96 (but Fatini 1934, p. 170 had already advanced a hypothesis in this sense). Indeed, translations and rewritings of this motto recur at various points throughout the capitolo: 'che l'ha qual può patir, né può più inante' (l. 6); 'quando superchia le sue forze il pondo' (l. 15); 'che non si rompa a tirar senza fine' (l. 18); 'ma se de più sol una dramma leve / giunta mi fia, verrei subito a manco' (ll. 29-30), and, in the closing line (l. 43), 'c'ho fatto oltra il poter e a più non basto'. The presence – highlighted by Finazzi 2002-2003, pp. 242-243 – of a variant, in two manuscripts carrying an earlier version of the capitolo, is a further confirmation of this: indeed, in the original version, the last line was 'c'ho fatto oltra il poter e amàs no abasto', where the Spanish hemistich clearly reminds us of the motto. On this poem, see also Chapter III, 4.

41 Giovio 1559, p. 117: 'portò anchora per impresa amorosa un Camelo inginocchiato carico d'una gran soma con un motto, che diceva; NON SVEFRO MAS DE LO QVE PUEDO; volendo dire alla dama sua, non mi date più gravezza di tormenti di quel che posso sopportare'. Giovio does not specify when Ippolito first adopted this *impresa*: it can only be argued that the choice of language was prompted by the fashion for all things Spanish triggered by the arrival of Lucrezia Borgia's court at Ferrara.

42 Schirg 2015, p. 136. Other examples of *imprese* in Ariosto's lyrics are analysed in Chap-

A parallel case may be seen in Equicola's Latin dialogue *De opportunitate* (1507), which illustrates another of Ippolito's devices, whose probable inventor was Leonardo da Vinci:[43] a falcon holding a balancing weight in its beak. It should also be noted that Ariosto's poem is simply a description, not an explanation. As such, this enigmatic quality was itself also a characteristic element in the way the court made use of such devices, as is evident from a letter by Equicola in which he asks Ippolito if he may incorporate some of the cardinal's *imprese* in his writings, specifying that he would not however be so presumptuous as to wish to fully penetrate their meaning.[44] At any rate, what is especially of interest here is that Giovio clearly ascribes the camel *impresa* to an amorous motivation, and this proves that the passion of love belonged to the public self-fashioning of the then young cardinal (Ippolito was born in 1479). This point is confirmed by biographical accounts, which depict him as definitely more devoted to secular life than to religious concerns – an assiduous frequenter of balls and hunting parties, who took a particular interest in expensive purchases, and made no secret of his infatuations.[45] To him, the perfect embodiment of the contemporary courtly code, Equicola apparently gifted the first version of his *Libro de natura de amore*.[46] In this light, it is clear that the lack of dutifulness that Ariosto parades in capitolo XLIII is in fact a pretext to reinforce the closeness between the public image of the courtier and that of his lord.

The degree of sincerity of Ariosto's flattery in this capitolo might perhaps be questioned by the reader. Indeed, the 'myth' of Cardinal Ippolito, fuelled by Ariosto's early biographers and still carrying some authority, is mostly that of an ungrateful lord and patron. It is a myth that stems from Ariosto's own words in satira I, which, one feels, deserve further attention.[47] The satira was famously written after the definitive break between the two men in 1517, when Ariosto, unlike other courtiers belonging to his entourage – such as Ludovico da Bagno and the poet's brother Alessandro, the two addressees of the poem – refused to follow Ippolito to his new

ter III, 4. Also on poetry concerned with devices, in particular that by Serafino Aquilano, see Rossi 1980, pp. 69-74.

43 This was discovered by Schirg 2015. On *De opportunitate*, see also Kolsky 1991, pp. 97-101.

44 The letter is quoted in Kolsky 1991, p. 101.

45 There is documentary record of his infatuation for Angela Borgia (one of Lucrezia's damsels), which would ignite his rivalry with his stepbrother Don Giulio and, as a consequence, trigger the plot of Don Giulio and Don Ferrante (on this event, see Introduction, 5).

46 Equicola 1999, p. 18 and footnote 3.

47 See also *Sat.*, VI 233-234: 'dal giogo / del Cardinal da Este oppresso fui'.

see in Eger (Hungary). After a decidedly uncomplimentary brief opening sketch of courtly life – suggesting that none of Ippolito's other courtiers would ever speak out in defence of Ariosto's decision, so as not to offend the cardinal, ll. 4-9 –, the poet lists the reasons that drove him to his refusal. In a long tirade he voices the disappointment caused by Ippolito's disregard of his poetic activity (he is referring specifically to the *Furioso*, which was written under the cardinal's patronage) and his belief that other court offices, which in fact were degrading and menial, were much more worthy of recompense (a theme he will return to in the sixth satira, re-evoking how 'di poeta cavallar mi feo', l. 238):

> Non vuol che laude sua da me composta
> per opra degna di mercé si pona;
> di mercé degno è l'ir correndo in posta.
>
> (*Sat.*, I 97-99)

> S'io l'ho con laude ne' miei versi messo,
> dice ch'io l'ho fatto a piacere e in ocio;
> più grato fora essergli stato appresso.
>
> (*ibid.*, ll. 106-108)

The apex of the speech comes as the poet stakes his claim to personal freedom (ll. 118-123). In order to enjoy it, he is ready to return all the 'doni' received from his lord (ll. 263-265). The satira and the capitolo may be seen as antithetical in that they capture two extremely different moments in the relationship between Ariosto and Ippolito, but also in that they follow very different classical models. While in the 'elegiac' capitolo the speaker is integrated in the environment of his patron, viewed as a new Messalla, in the satira, which is powerfully influenced by Horace's *Epistulae* and in particular reflects the 'cuncta resigno' of *Epist.* I 7,34, we grasp a representation of the lord as Maecenas just as the poet, who desires his freedom, seeks to cut the cords of his dependence.[48] The anti-courtly impulse that dictates the portrayal in the satira, however, is not absolute, and it is in fact nuanced in its central part. Ariosto explains (ll. 124-135) that his bitterness derives not so much from the cutting of the ties between himself and Ippolito, as from the anger of the cardinal, 'che da l'amor e grazia sua mi esclud[e]' (l. 132), and by his accusations of unfaithfulness. As critics have highlighted, these words suggest that the affection for his former lord still endured – this would

[48] A recent comprehensive analysis on the complex and profound Horatian influences in the *Satire* is CUCCHIARELLI 2019.

be confirmed by Ariosto's choice not to expunge the dedication to Ippolito from either the 1521 or the 1532 versions of the *Furioso*,[49] and, moreover, by his choice to include the capitolo in his provisional canzoniere, at a point in time when the break had already occurred and the first satira had been written. In addition to this passage, I would suggest that a residue of nostalgia for court life may also be felt in the aforementioned ll. 97-99 and ll. 106-108, where Ariosto states his desire to be acknowledged not merely as a poet, but as an author of 'laude', i.e. poetry in celebration of his lord. Celebration was precisely among the aims of the *Furioso*,[50] expressed in its dedication: 'Quel ch'io vi debbo [...] / quanto io posso dar, tutto vi dono' (*Fur.*, I 3,4-8 ABC). This is a passage which shares with capitolo XLIII the emphasis on 'debito', meaning court obligation ('Deh, perché quando honestamente sciormi / dal debito potea', ll. 16-17) and which, according to Masi, may be linked to it for its expression of an 'unadulatory' intention.[51] I also believe that a true sense of gratitude is perceivable in the capitolo, a sentiment which moreover must have lasted even after 1517, although lord and courtier had different conceptions of what was deserving of 'mercé'.[52]

But even if we leave aside their psychological basis, the comparison between capitolo XLIII and satira I also proves fruitful on a stylistic level, as it allows us to identify some relevant elements of continuity and identifying traits between the satirical and the elegiac terza rima. With regard to this, it should be noted that only three years separated the historical occasions that prompted the two works. As he was writing the satira, Ariosto still had in mind the capitolo, and it is tempting to consider the former as a palinode, as it were, of the latter, once the illusion of obtaining any compensation for his poetic homages had lost hold. The fact that Tibullus's poem I 3 was newly echoed in the opening of the satira – cp. ll. 1-3: 'Io desidero intendere da voi [...] / s'in corte è ricordanza più di noi', and, from Tibullus, l. 2: 'o utinam memores ipse cohorsque mei!'[53] – is a clear sign of the link between the two poems in Ariosto's perception.

Among the most relevant differences – leaving aside those mentioned above, and those most obviously ascribable to the respective poetic codes –

---

49 See Russo's commentary in Ariosto 2019, pp. 38-39; pp. 52-54.

50 On the descriptions and praises of Ippolito in the *Furioso*, see Stimato 2009.

51 Masi 2003, p. 83.

52 The conceptual nucleus of service-reward is acknowledged as a fundamental theme of this satira: see again Russo's commentary on this point.

53 Such rewriting was observed, but not discussed, by Floriani 1988*bis*, p. 252. Note however that another possible influence here is from Horace, *Epist.*, I 3,6: 'quid studiosa cohors operum struit? Hoc quoque curo' (see Cucchiarelli 2019, p. 271).

the management of the temporal dimension should be mentioned. While in the *Satire* the speaker is at a certain remove from the events he recalls, the capitolo is entirely played out in the present: the lyric voice here is still in the middle of the situation it describes. This rhetorical solution, despite its difference from that of capitolo XLV, nevertheless achieves a similar effect, that of emotionally involving the reader/listener in the dynamic of the situation recounted. If we turn to examine the analogies, the reader will first note that similar situations (two refusals to Ippolito) are conveyed through the same form: the epistle, whose addressees are Ippolito himself in the capitolo, Alessandro Ariosto and Ludovico da Bagno in the satira. While this is a common formal feature in all the *Satire*, its adoption in capitolo XLIII is a unique case in the *rime*, and this makes the link between the two poems all the more interesting. Another element of affinity may be found, quite unexpectedly, on the level of self-fashioning. It is well known that Ariosto's satirical persona is not only that of an 'imperfect' courtier, but also that of someone who speaks the truth, even though this may have potentially negative consequences.[54] A similar characterisation applies to the speaker of the capitolo, who admits, frankly and against his interests, that he is the only unhappy person in Ippolito's 'joyful retinue' (a phrase in which Fatini and Santoro detect an ironic note):

> Io so ben quanto mal mi si convegna
> dir, Signor mio, che fra sì lieta schiera
> io malcontento sol dietro vi vegna
>
> (*Rime del canzoniere*, XLIII 25-27)

> Ma se in altro biasmarme, almen dar laude
> dovete che, volendo io rimanere,
> lo dissi a viso aperto e non con fraude.
> Dissi molte ragioni, e tutte vere
>
> (*Sat.*, I 19-22)

We shall examine the comparison between the two self-portrayals in greater detail in section 6. By way of conclusion here, I would suggest that a general affinity also exists in the way Ariosto marries biographical concreteness with a closer use of the classical sources. The process by which Ariosto superimposes Horatian influences onto personal events, acknowledged by Piero Floriani as a distinctive trait of the *Satire* ('il punto generativo del codice oraziano [è] la connotazione forte – circostanziata cronisti-

---

54 On this type of characterisation, see at least Marini 2008 and Ugolini 2017.

camente – dell'io recitante [...]'),[55] is very closely paralleled here by his use of Tibullus. In the *Satire*, this process determined a stepping beyond the traditional manner of the moralising capitolo: in XLIII it similarly marks a step forward from the tradition of the *capitolo elegiaco*.

4. A mission to Florence

In capitolo XXX (*Gentil città, che con felici auguri*), the poet speaks from Florence. The fact that he refers to the city being governed by the Medici allows us to infer that the poem was written after September 1512, but it is nonetheless hard to determine exactly which among the numerous journeys Ariosto undertook in that period inspired it. According to Fatini (whose position is generally shared by later scholars) the poem may be referred either to the journey of 30 August-8 September 1516 or to that of February 1519 (the former commissioned by Ippolito, the latter by Alfonso d'Este). However, one should also note that it seems to allude not to a journey commissioned by Ariosto's lords but to one motivated by personal reasons, and we will return to this point below.[56] We shall first examine, however, the most notable stylistic elements of this capitolo.

In the first part, which in fact takes up two thirds of the poem, the speaker praises the beauties of Florence. Ariosto is here following the humanist genre of the *laudatio urbis*, which was extremely popular throughout the Quattrocento.[57] Among the works belonging to this genre written in the second half of the century, one should mention Tebaldeo's *Ad Magnificum Laurentium Medicem* – a Latin poem in hexameters that dates to around 1480, where the praise of Florence acts as a prelude to a celebration of Lorenzo il Magnifico –[58] and Cornazano's *De laudibus urbis Florentiae*, of 1464, a collection of four capitoli in terza rima in praise of Florence, composed to celebrate the city's alliance with Milan.[59] Finally, we should not overlook the proem to Cristoforo Landino's *Comento* on Dante's *Comedy*. Here, Landino articulates a long encomium of Florence (within the context of a defence of Dante against those who accused him of offending his hometown), exalting its political history and the virtues of its people.[60] All these models are to

---

55 Floriani 1988, p. 72.

56 Fatini 1934, pp. 182-184.

57 On this genre, see at least Tateo 1990 and 2002.

58 A description of the poem is in Pasquazi 1966, CIV-CVII; the text is *ibid.*, pp. 58-62.

59 On this poem, see Zancani 2007.

60 See Lentzen 1985. The *Comento* was first printed in 1481.

a certain extent indebted to Leonardo Bruni's pamphlet *Laudatio Florentine Urbis* (1403-1404), by far the most renowned fifteenth-century eulogy of a city – and one which certainly Ariosto selected here as his main model.[61] The points of capitolo XXX that owe a debt to the rhetoric of the *Laudatio* may easily be identified. The opening of the capitolo picks up the *topos modestiae,* which also dominates the first section (pars 1-3) of the pamphlet. The capitolo then touches upon the naturalistic beauties of the city, the fertility of the land, and its breadth,[62] following Bruni also in his praise of the city's cleanliness.[63] Next, the speaker mentions the architectural elements of Florence, which contribute to make this city incomparable to any other.[64] Like Bruni, he insists on the suburban villas and on the *palazzi* lying outside the city centre, as well as on the magnificence of the dwellings of private citizens:

> A veder pien di tante ville i colli
> (*Rime del canzoniere*, XXX 19);
> Se dentro un mur, sotto il medesmo nome
> fusser raccolti i tuoi palazzi sparsi
> (*ibid.*, ll. 22-23)

[...] ita hec extra urbem edificia universos circum montes collesque et planitiem occupant, ut potius e celo delapsa quam manu hominum facta videantur. At quanta horum edificiorum magnificentia est, quantum decus, quantus ornatus! (*Laudatio*, 14-15)

> Chi potrà a pien lodar li tetti regii
> d'i tuoi privati, i portici e le corti
> (*Rime del canzoniere*, XXX 34-35)

Sed redeo ad privatorum domos, que ad delitias, ad amplitudinem, ad honestatem maximeque ad magnificentiam instructe, excogitate, edificate sunt. (*Laudatio*, 11)

---

61 This link was also mentioned by Rinaldi 2000, p. 316. For an overview of the reception and fortune of the *Laudatio*, see Bruni 2000, XXIII-XXVII and its bibliography.

62 *Rime del canzoniere*, XXX 13-15: 'narar quanto si' ameno / et fecondo il tuo pian, che si distende / tra verdi poggi'; *Laudatio*, 5: 'A ceteris autem partibus apricissimi se explicant campi, ad zephiros tamen magis aperti'.

63 *Rime del canzoniere*, XXX 37-39: 'Non ha il verno poter ch'in te mai porti / di sua immondicia, sì ben questi monti / t'han lastricata sin alli angiporti'; *Laudatio*, 8: 'Quid enim mirabilius quam in populosissima urbe nichil usquam limi apparere, imbrem autem quamvis maximum nichil impedire quominus siccis plantis urbem perambules, [...]?'.

64 *Rime del canzoniere*, XXX 24: 'non ti serien da paregiar due Rome'; *Laudatio*, 10: 'Quid est in toto orbe tam splendidum aut tam magnificum quod cum edificiis huius sit comparandum?'.

This is one of the poems that most clearly speaks to Ariosto's humanist interests. At the same time, it reveals the author's penchant for the theme of the 'city', and more specifically Florence, whose urban settings are also alluded to in poems 50 and 56 (these will be analysed in Chapter II, 5 and Chapter III, 2). In this capitolo, however, the eulogy of the city does not constitute the poem's true and ultimate meaning. It is in fact a rhetorical pretext to introduce *e contrario* the elegiac contents, which start at l. 52. All the beauties of Florence, the speaker says, are of no help to his grief, since he has left his lady (she is again referred to – like in XLIII – as 'la mia luce', l. 59). The sudden shift of tone from panegyrical to elegiac undoubtedly catches the reader off-balance, shedding an ironic light on all that came before. This strategy – for which many parallels may be found in Ariosto's lyric technique – is consistent with the witty courtly code. However, I would also suggest that in this structure there may once again be an underlying classical source: Ovid's poem II 16 from the *Amores*. Here the speaker is in Sulmona, and, following an initial description of the beauty of the place – which translates, in this case, into a praise of its anthropised countryside and cultivated land –, he abruptly turns to lamenting his beloved's absence ('At meus ignis abest', l. 11), emphasising the paradoxical unpleasantness of such a *locus amoenus*. We should note that in Ovid, however, the laudatory part is much shorter than the plaintive one.

Though beautiful, therefore, Florence is not the city of love. This point is interesting, because in poems 50 and 56 (which were probably composed years later) the city is recalled as the setting of Ariosto's falling in love with Alessandra Benucci, and also as the place from which Alessandra herself hails – a further reason for it to occupy a privileged place in his heart. More specifically, in canzone 50 Alessandra is portrayed by the poet as a sort of link between Florence and Ferrara – and even as an object of contention between the two cities. Indeed, the fact that she returned to her hometown provokes the lament of the river Po: 'lasciato havendo lamentar indarno / il re de' fiumi, et invidiarvi ad Arno' (ll. 76-77). In the capitolo, on the other hand, the beloved woman is depicted as fully belonging to the environment of Ferrara – which, through the very same mention of the 'king river' Po,[65] is opposed by the speaker to that of Florence:

> Gli tuoi Medici, anchor che sieno tali
> che t'habian salda ogni tua antiqua piaga,
> non han però rimedio alli mei mali.

---

65 This phrase comes from VIRGIL, *Georg.*, I 482: 'fluviorum rex'.

Oltra a quei monti, a ripa l'onda vaga
del re de' fiumi, in bianca et pura stola
cantando ferma il sol la bella maga
che con sua vista può sanarmi sola.
(*Rime del canzoniere*, XXX 70-76)

This clear-cut opposition, and the lack of any allusion to the Florentine origin of his beloved, leads us to suspect that Alessandra may not have been the poem's dedicatee:[66] indeed a dating that precedes Ariosto's falling in love with her (21 June 1513) may even be hypothesised. Because September 1512 must also be taken into account as a *terminus post quem*, we may therefore refer the capitolo to Ariosto's stay in Florence between late December 1512 and mid-February 1513, when he had to collect some money owed to his cousin Rinaldo. If we accept this, the person who prompted the journey ('chi fu cagion ch'io venni', l. 62) may consequently be identified not as one of the Este lords but as Rinaldo.[67] This can be no more than a cautious hypothesis, however, as evidently here autobiographical detail goes hand in hand with a strong formalising drive.

Interestingly, a further memory of Ferrara lies, in the above-quoted passage, in the hint that the woman may be a 'maga'. Though this is perhaps not an intentional rhetorical strategy, nevertheless the use of the figure of the sorceress belies a cultural bias, as it recalls the long-standing Ferrarese predilection for French tales of magic. Intriguingly, moreover, Ariosto employs the same words and rhymes in the *Furioso* to describe the sorceress Melissa,[68] the unrequited lover of the 'cavaliere del nappo', who almost certainly is not simply a homonym of Melissa-the-protector-of-Bradamante, but is actually the same character.[69] The 'maga' of capitolo XXX, therefore, reminds the reader of the Ferrarese sorceress par excellence – who works towards the accomplishment of the union of Bradamante and Ruggiero,

---

66 It is certainly true that Alessandra's relationship with Ariosto was kept secret for a long time; however, the encomium of the city would have offered the perfect opportunity to allude to her at least indirectly, for instance in the context of the praise of Florentine women at ll. 46-48.

67 This stay was troublesome for Ludovico: he was able to collect only part of the credit from Rinaldo's debtor (the merchant Pierfrancesco de' Medici), and not without some difficulty. See CATALANO 1930-1931, I, pp. 396-397.

68 *Fur.*, XXXIX 21,1-4 AB; XLIII C: 'Ella sapea d'incanti e di malie / quel che saper ne possa alcuna maga: / rendea la notte chiara, oscuro il die, / fermava il sol, facea la terra vaga'. As noted by STIMATO 2011, p. 47, in depicting Melissa's magical powers Ariosto drew on *Met.*, VII 690-862, where, in the tale of Cephalus and Procris (arguably the inspiration for the tale of the 'nappo'), these abilities are attributed to Aurora.

69 On this point, see STIMATO 2011 and DELCORNO BRANCA 2019, pp. 18-22.

from which the Este dynasty will originate – and suggests an exchange of ideas between the lyrics and the composition of the *Furioso*.

From the analysis above it is clear that the feeling of homesickness plays a role in this poem, and integrates, as it were, the longing for distant love. This theme does not certainly feel new to readers of Ariosto, whose 'sedentary' nature is tantamount to a critical commonplace. In this regard we may recall satira III, where – above all the other advantages offered by his new condition as courtier of Duke Alfonso – the poet prizes the greater settledness it guarantees, which he evokes through the mention of his home as the 'native nest' where the heart always dwells (an obvious allusion to his beloved Alessandra), even if his physical body is removed from it:

> Chi vuole andare a torno, a torno vada:
> veggia Inghelterra, Ongheria, Francia e Spagna;
> a me piace abitar la mia contrada.
>
> (*Sat.*, III 55-57)

> Il servigio del Duca, da ogni parte
> che ci sia buona, più mi piace in questa:
> che dal nido natio raro si parte.
> Per questo i studi miei poco molesta,
> né mi toglie onde mai tutto partire
> non posso, perché il cor sempre ci resta.
>
> (*ibid.*, ll. 67-72)

Ariosto uses similar arguments also in satira VII, in commenting his refusal to go to Rome as ambassador to Duke Alfonso at the court of Clement VII:

> Da me stesso mi tol chi mi rimove
> da la mia terra, e fuor non ne potrei
> viver contento, ancor che in grembo a Iove.
>
> (*Sat.*, VII 148-150)

> Ma se 'l signor vuol farmi grazia a pieno,
> a sé mi chiami, e mai più non mi mandi
> più là d'Argenta, o più qua del Bondeno.
> Se perché amo sì il nido mi dimandi, [...]
>
> (*ibid.*, 160-163)

Besides appertaining to the 'Horatian' satiric persona as part of its desire for independence,[70] attachment to one's home is a theme that often

---

70 See for instance Horace, *Epist.*, I 14,6-9: 'Me quamvis Lamiae pietas et cura moratur,

featured in lyric poetry and particularly in the *dipartita*: it can be argued that it played a significant role in the case of poems composed for a 'social' use, and destined to circulation among the members of the same milieu.[71] It might be supposed that in this case, too, the mention of the 're dei fiumi' functioned rather as a nod to a courtly readership than as a private outburst. In the absence of evidence that may give us a sense of how widely the text circulated, what may undoubtedly be stated is that it constitutes further proof of Ariosto's dynamic relationship with his numerous and extremely varied models.

5. The journey to the Garfagnana: style and sources

In capitolo XXIX (*Meritamente hora punir mi veggio*), the lyric voice is apparently speaking from the midpoint of a journey that will separate him for some time from his beloved. To add to his pain, a storm has just begun, but he cannot find shelter as his road crosses a wild and mountainous area (ll. 28-30). The widely held view that the poem may refer to one of Ariosto's journeys to the Garfagnana seems persuasive. Indeed, in order to reach that subregion of Tuscany, one had to descend the Apennines through the steep pass of San Pellegrino in Alpe ('ruïnosi balzi', l. 24; 'per lungo trato il monte hor scende hor poggia', l. 30), crossing an area that was, and still is, densely wooded ('folto / bosco', ll. 25-26) and sees the confluence of two waterways, the Serchio and the Turrita ('fiumi', l. 43). Some affinities may be found between this poem and those analysed before, and especially the capitolo addressed to Cardinal Ippolito. Just as in XLIII, Ariosto here explicitly sets up an opposition between the call of duty and personal desire:

Ben poco saggio fui che all'altrui prece,

[...] / tamen istuc mens animusque / fert et amat spatiis obstantia rumpere claustra' (addressed from Rome to the bailiff of his farm). In Horace, the theme is famously inscribed within a general contrast between city and countryside. A possible vernacular precedent for the quoted passages from Ariosto's satira III is Paganelli's *De vita quieta*: see Campeggiani's commentary in Ariosto 2019, p. 105 footnote 17.

71 See, for example, Correggio, *Rime extravaganti*, VII 1-8: 'Dolce mio patrio nido, albergo e vita, / de' mei pianti e suspir fidel ricetto, / ch'io m'avea in vita per sepulcro eletto / come al diserto el povero eremita, / oggi convienmi far da te partita, / né mai più pace in altro loco aspetto. / Addio, delizie mie, dolce studietto! / La nostra compagnia pur è finita'; Sasso, capitolo XVIII, ll. 127-132: 'O patria a me soave, e patria degna, / quanto sia grato a ciascuno il suo nido / l'experientia del partir m'insegna. / Vera è la fama del publico crido: / troppo è dolce el paese ove l'huom nasce / tanto più quanto è più constante e fido'.

a cui devea et potei chiuder l'orecchi,
più ch'al mio desir proprio satisfece.
(*Rime del canzoniere*, XXIX 4-6)

The other conspicuous similarity is that both poems are the fruit of a combination of personal experience and a re-writing of the classics. Indeed, here the situation described is the same as in Propertius, I 17, whose opening line ('Et merito, quoniam potui fugisse puellam!') is also clearly echoed in the *incipit*:

Meritamente hora punir mi veggio
del grave eror che a dipartir mi fece
da la mia donna, et degno son di peggio.
(*Rime del canzoniere*, XXIX 1-3)[72]

In the Latin poem, the speaker has been shipwrecked and reads the event as a revenge Cynthia has taken on him for having abandoned her. Ariosto's lyric voice also feels that he has been punished for wronging the woman ('contra lei più pecchi', l. 7), although he, unlike Propertius, does not explicitly describe her as possessing those almost 'sadistic' traits that characterise Cynthia.

The classical imitation extends to some other devices, such as the sudden interruption of the speaker's flow of thoughts, which causes his attention to shift to the ongoing storm:

Mentre ch'io parlo il turbido austro prende
maggior possanza, et cresce il verno, et sciolto
da ruïnosi balzi il liquor scende;
di sotto il fango, et quinci et quindi il folto
bosco mi tarda, e in tanto l'aspra pioggia,
acuta più che stral, mi fere il volto.
(*Rime del canzoniere*, XXIX 22-27)

The initial phrase of this passage echoes many classical, and especially Ovidian, places. The line 'Dum loquor, increvit latis spatiosior undis' from *Amores*, III 6,85 appears to be the most pertinent, but besides it the follow-

[72] Cp. Tebaldeo, *Rime della vulgata*, 282,49-51: 'e iustamente merto Amore infesto, / che un don mi fe' non mai più conceduto / ch'io lassai per seguir Marte funesto'. As noted by Zampese 2000, p. 470, Ariosto's description of the adverse weather may also have been influenced by Bembo's Latin poem XIV (*Ad Lygdamum*), in turn inspired by Propertius (ll. 13-18: 'At mihi longiquae gentesque urbesque petuntur, / ut toto a domina separer orbe mea: / et modo nimbosas mannis transmittimur alpes, / saxaque vix ipsis exuperanda feris: / nec caeci nemorum tractus suspectaque lustra, / nec tardant nostras flumina adaucta vias').

ing must be mentioned: 'dum loquor hora fugit' (*Amores*, I 11,15); 'Sed iam pompa venit' (*Amores*, III 2,43); 'Dum loquor, et timeo pariter cupioque repelli, / increpuit quantis viribus unda latus!' (*Tristia*, I 4,23-24), and, from Horace, 'Dum loquimur fugerit invida aetas' (*Carm.*, I 11,7).[73] Ariosto may also have recalled Petrarch's rephrasing of them: 'ora mentre che parlo il tempo fugge' (*Rvf*, LVI 3). However, the real-time reference to what he sees around him, producing the effect of pulling the reader into a story, makes him definitely closer to the Latin sources.

In addition to this chronicle-like feel, another notable feature of this capitolo is the special focus on the speaker's interiority. This is achieved through leaps backwards an forwards in time, recollecting first the circumstances of his promise (ll. 4-6 – above – and ll. 16-18) and then envisaging his future life in the Garfagnana (ll. 52-70). Most importantly, the speaker makes a foray into the dimension of impossible desire, as he expresses his wish that the journey may bring the lovers together instead of separating them and also evoking the image of their encounter. The possibility of being reunited at the end of the journey would turn any troublesome route into a *locus amoenus*; conversely, even the most idyllic place would seem unpleasant for him if he did not enjoy in it his lady's presence:

ché se a Madonna io m'appressasi quanto
me ne dilungo, et fusse speme al fine
del rio camin poi respirarle a canto,
et le man' bianche più che fresche brine
baciarle, e insieme questi avidi lumi
pascer de le bellezze alme et divine,
poco il mal tempo et lothi et sassi et fiumi
mi darian noia, et mi parrebbon piani
et più che prati molli erte et cacumi.
Ma quando avien che sì me ne allontani,
l'amene Tempe e del re Alcino li orti
che puon se non parermi horridi et strani?
(*Rime del canzoniere*, XXIX 37-48)

For this point, too, we might suppose the influence of classical models. In poem II 16 from Ovid's *Amores*, already quoted as a possible reference

[73] Some of these are noted also by FLORIANI 1988*bis*, p. 252, which insists on Ariosto's debts to Ovid in expressing 'il richiamo alla simultaneità'. Among the humanist imitations I will mention a poem by Ercole Strozzi, in which the speaker begs the rower of his lady's ship, which is sailing away, to stop: 'Dum loquor, heu diversus abis, rogo navita siste' (STROZZI 1513, I, f. 62*v*, l. 25).

for capitolo XXX in section 4, we find a similar curse of journeys and a comparison between how a place objectively looks like and how it appears to the lover, depending on the presence or absence of his beloved:

tum mihi, si premerem ventosas horridus Alpes,
  dummodo cum domina, molle fuisset iter.
Cum domina Libycas ausim perrumpere Syrtes
  et dare non aequis vela ferenda Notis.
Non quae virgineo portenta sub inguine latrant,
  nec timeam vestros, curva Malea, sinus;
non quae submersis ratibus saturata Charybdis
  fundit et effusas ore receptat aquas.

(*Amores*, II 16,19-26)

At sine te [...]
non ego Paelignos videor celebrare salubres,
[...] sed Scythiam Cilicasque feros viridesque Britannos,
  quaeque Prometheo saxa cruore rubent.

(*ibid.*, ll. 33-40).

The theme of the lover ready to face any metereological adversity in order to reach his beloved's abode is also in the *Ars amatoria*, where it is linked to the concept of *militia amoris*: 'Nec grave te tempus sitiensque Canicula tardet, / nec via per iactas candida facta nives' (*Ars am.*, II 231-232) – among the Ferrarese continuators of this theme are Tito Vespasiano Strozzi and Boiardo, who features it in two sonnets of his *Amorum libri* (I 23 and I 47).[74]

These classical influences mingle, in the capitolo, with elements that recall more closely the contemporary tradition and that may be compared to similar usages in late Quattrocento authors. Among these is the use of a pathetic register:

  Non più tranquille già né più serene
hore attender posso io, m'al fin di queste
pene et travagli, altri travagli et pene

(*Rime del canzoniere*, XXIX 52-54)

  Morto costui, non vissi lieto una hora
né vivrò

(Tebaldeo, *Rime della vulgata*, 285,142-143)

74 See e.g. *Amorum libri tres*, I 47,12-14: 'Or mi par bianca rosa e bianco fiore / la folta neve che dal ciel riversa, / pensando al vivo Sol che io me avicino' (I shall refer the reader to Zanato's commentary to both this poem and I 23). On Strozzi's use of the *topos*, see Tissoni Benvenuti 2003, pp. 95-96.

The last image, an arrow shot from a bow symbolising the wasteful passage of time, echoes the classical – and later Petrarchan – theme of *fuga temporis*, which was also extremely popular in the Quattrocento repertoire. Ariosto however develops this idea further and with deeper psychological insight, lingering on our variable perception of time, which expands and contracts at different speed:

> Et mesi l'hore, e i giorni a parer anni
> comincieranno, et diverrà sì tardo
> che parrà il tempo haver tarpato i vanni:
> che già, aspettando di furar un sguardo
> da la invittà beltà, da l'immortale
> valor, da' bei sembianti onde tutto ardo,
> vedea fuggir più che da corda strale.
>
> (*Rime del canzoniere*, XXIX 64-70)[75]

In this capitolo Ariosto therefore once more proves himself to be at the same time an attentive listener of contemporary poetical trends and a subtle innovator.

The Garfagnana setting inescapably recalls satira IV, and in fact constitutes a link between the two texts. In the satira, as is known, Ariosto offers an account of the difficulties that he faced during his commissionership in that region, telling the reader that one year has elapsed since he took up the position, that is, on 7 February 1522. Most probably, the journey referred to in the capitolo is precisely that of 1522. The chronology proposed by Catalano was entirely different, placing the capitolo in relation to a journey to the Garfagnana that the poet made in February or March 1509, summoned by Rinaldo Ariosto.[76] This position was based on the situation that is described. The speaker says he is travelling to fulfil the earnest request of an unnamed person ('altrui prece', l. 4). While this reflects the events of 1509, it does not reflect – Catalano argues – the events of 1522, when Ariosto himself asked his lord to be given the commissionership on account of his financial difficulties (a point on which I shall be returning later). Catalano's

---

75 Fundamental antecedents for this image in are *Inf.*, VIII 13: 'Corda non pinse mai da sé saetta'; XVII 136: 'si dileguò come da corda cocca'; *Rvf*, CCCLV 3: 'o dì veloci più che vento et strali'; CCCLXVI 89: 'I dì miei più correnti che saetta'. In the courtly repertoire, see Boiardo, *Tarocchi*, II, *Sonetto excusato*, ll. 10-11: 'Che 'l tempo, tanto prezioso e caro, / via manda come corda d'arco un strale'; Correggio, *Rime*, 400,85-88: 'Da la noce sì tosto non si scioglie / spinto da corda uno impennato strale / che 'l veder per prestezza a gli occhi toglie, / como io giongerò al piè de le tue scale'.

76 Catalano 1930-1931, I, pp. 538-539.

hypothesis has not been popular, and critics tend instead to agree with Fatini, who dated the capitolo to 1522 on account of the fact that it seems to describe a permanent move rather than a short trip: see for instance 'Languido il resto de la vita mia / si struggerà di stimulosi affanni, / percosso ognhor di penitentia ria', ll. 61-63.[77]

The 1522 chronology also seems to me to be more convincing and I believe further clues may support it. One is the fact that this poem is only transmitted by the main testimonies:[78] it may be hypothesised that it was written purposely for **Vr** (where, not coincidentally, it is placed right before XXX),[79] in the mid- or late 1520s. Some stylistic and lexical hints, too, suggest this dating. As the following quotation shows, the setting is described with a similar choice of words both in the capitolo and in satira IV; moreover, in both texts the description of the landscape is closely associated with the mention of 'maraviglia' and with the theme of the distant beloved:

> [...] *maraviglia*
> abbi che morto io non sia ormai di rabbia
> vedendomi lontan cento e più miglia,
>   e da *neve, alpe, selve e fiumi* escluso
> da chi tien del mio cor sola la briglia.
>
> (*Sat.*, IV 20-24)

> Pentomi, et col pentir mi *maraviglio*
>
> (*Rime del canzoniere*, XXIX 16)

> ché se a Madonna io m'appressasi [...]
> poco *il mal tempo et lothi et sassi et fiumi*
> mi darian noia
>
> (*ibid.*, XXIX 37; 43-44)

> (emphasis mine)

Some of the lexical choices in the capitolo, moreover, chime with changes made by Ariosto starting from the 1521 *Furioso*. For instance, in describ-

---

77 Fatini 1934, p. 185.

78 Apart from the main testimonies, it is included only in manuscript **P3** (Florence, Biblioteca Nazionale Centrale, Capponi 138 (Palatino 432)): this however is a *descriptus* of the *editio princeps*. See Finazzi 2002-2003, p. 179, who, in turn, follows Chittolina's conclusions.

79 The contiguousness between this capitolo and *Gentil città, che con felici auguri* holds true also in the reconstruction of Volta 2019.

ing Orlando's sleeplessness Ariosto replaces 'selce'[80] with 'sasso', precisely the word used in the capitolo in the same situation:

giù dagli occhi rigando per le gote
sparge un *fiume di lacrime* sul petto:
sospira e geme, e va con spesse ruote
di qua di là tutto cercando il letto;
e più duro ch'un sasso, e più pungente
che se fosse d'urtica, se lo sente.
(*Fur.*, XXI 122,3-8 B; XXIII C)

altre pioggie al coperto, altre *tempeste*
di suspire et de lachryme mi aspetto,
che mi sien più continue et più moleste.
Duro serammi più che sasso il letto
(*Rime del canzoniere*, XXIX 55-58)

(emphasis mine)

The rhyme *fiumi* : *cacumi* (ll. 43-45) is also introduced in the *Furioso* only from the 1521 version onwards (though in the singular form: *fiume* : *cacume*, XXVII 35,2-4 B; XXIX C – there are no other occurrences for 'cacume' in Ariosto's oeuvre). Likewise, the couple 'travagli et pene' (l. 54) is added to the 1521 version as a substitute for the singular form.[81] Finally, in the theme of the journey rendered complicated by adverse weather a similarity may be seen between the capitolo and the description of Bradamante's journey towards Tristan's castle, an episode that is part of the 1532 additions to the *Furioso*.[82] While taken individually these points are not definitive evidence, viewed as part of a more general picture they lend credence to the hypothesis of a relatively late date of composition.

The poem must thus be referred to the most difficult phase of Ariosto's service of Duke Alfonso – when he was given the unwelcome task of bringing order to a border region infested by brigands, whose people were

---

80 *Fur.*, XXI 122,7 A: 'e lo ritrova più duro che selce'.

81 *Fur*, XXXIX 97,4 A: 'che gran travaglio m'havea dato e pena'; *Fur.*, XXXIX 97,4 B; XLIII 101,4 C: 'che gran travagli m'avea dati e pene'. It should at any rate be noted that this phrase is backed by poetic tradition; see e.g. *Inf.*, VII 20: 'nove travaglie e pene'; Tebaldeo, *Rime della vulgata*, 282,27: 'travaglia e pena'.

82 *Fur.*, XXXII 63-74 C; see e.g. 69,1-6: 'La donna, ancor che Rabican ben trotte, / solecitar però non lo sa tanto / per quelle vie tutte fangose e rotte / da la stagion ch'era piovosa alquanto, / che prima arrivi, che la cieca notte / fatt'abbia oscuro il mondo in ogni canto'. On these correspondences see Cabani 2016*bis*, pp. 29-30.

unused to obeying orders. The letters he wrote to the duke in that period reveal his sense of impotence, but also a profound sense of duty, which led him to complete his task with both humanity and moral rigour. This period left a visible trace on the poetry he produced during that period – in particular, in addition to the *Satire*, on the *Cinque canti*.[83] Capitolo XXIX may then be seen as one more piece of this mosaic, a demonstration that Ariosto was also active on the lyric front. Such poetic activity may be seen as contradicting the claims made in satira IV that he received no creative inspiration in the Garfagnana;[84] however, these claims probably appertain to the fictional elements of the *Satire*, which sought to create a specific type of first-person speaker – one besieged by the sense of anguish that such a place, described as truly hellish, communicated to him. As shown by critics, other elements in satira IV may also be ascribed to the universe of self-fashioning rather than to Ariosto's actual biography. An example is his understated self-presentation as a governor unsuited to his role and afraid of undertaking it: this is a different portrayal from that which emerges from his letters, and it is a strategy that obeys to the constraints of the satirical genre.[85] The speaker of capitolo XXIX is also modelled according to the rules of its genre. In the opening lines, he states that he has set off to fulfil 'l'altrui prece': through this point, which, as mentioned before, was used by Catalano to exclude the 1522 dating, Ariosto is actually placing the emphasis on the fact that he is a victim of circumstances. In the satira, conversely, it is Ariosto himself who 'begs' Duke Alfonso to help him financially (his court salary had been suspended due to the financial insolvency of the Estense state), thereby conferring on the lucrative appointment the appearance of a gift (ll. 172-198). This version allows him to reflect on the courtly relationship, and to describe himself as torn between his gratitude and the fact that such a gift constitutes, in Marini's words, 'una vera e propria violenza alla natura intima dell'io ariostesco'.[86]

---

83 The most recent historical account of Ariosto's stay in the Garfagnana is Baja Guarienti 2018. Cabani 2016*bis* tackles the subject from a literary point of view, comparing satira IV to Ariosto's letters. To these should be added Marini's studies on the fourth satira (Marini 2018; see also his commentary to the satira in Ariosto 2019). On the influence of the Garfagnana period on the *Cinque canti*, see Valentina Gritti's notes in Ariosto 2018.

84 See *Sat.*, IV 109-138 (for example, ll. 110-111: 'ti confesso / che qui perduto ho il canto, il gioco, il riso'; ll. 136-138: 'Dove altro albergo era di questo meno / convenïente a i sacri studi, vuoto / d'ogni iocundità, d'ogni orror pieno?'). Although Ariosto's claims specifically refer to the year between 1522-1523, nonetheless he is fashioning the Garfagnana as being at entirely unwelcoming for the arts.

85 See Marini 2018, pp. 12-13.

86 Ariosto 2019, p. 159. See *Sat.*, IV 199-201: 'Obligo gli ho del buon voler, più ch'io / mi contenti del dono, il quale è grande, / ma non molto conforme al mio desio'.

As in the pair constituted by capitolo XLIII and satira I, in this case, too, the different guise of the speakers translates into a different treatment of the temporal dimension. While in the capitolo Ariosto makes us believe he is writing in real time, in the satira he presents us with a stabilised situation, which he analyses through the lens of the experience matured over time. On the other hand, the fact that satira IV in its turn displays some lyric-elegiac influences brings to light a number of similarities with the capitolo. Actually, this is, among the *Satire*, the one where we find most fully articulated the theme of nostalgia, both for Alessandra – the aforementioned ll. 20-24, which betray his sense of desperation at being separated from her, are a case in point – and for his homeland, the only place where he can find that peace so favourable to poetry. This theme is developed, at ll. 115-132, into an emotionally charged recollection of his hometown, Reggio Emilia. As well as this parallel, one may add the description of the landscape, which in both cases makes a prominent use of deictic expression.[87] Finally, these two poems stem from a single organising principle: if in the couple constituted by capitolo XLIII and satira I this was refusal, in this case it is acceptance tinged with regret.

Some closing observations may now be made. Ariosto here resorts to a technique similar to the other poems examined in this chapter, and ideally suited to a courtly destination, though it remains extremely difficult to determine if this text actually circulated at court. This confirms the ambiguous status of the lyrics, whose final destination, whether public or private, is often hard to grasp and judge fully. Finally, the fact that he wrote this poem after the first three satire[88] is also extremely significant, in that it prompts us to challenge the commonly held view according to which the capitoli merely herald the *Satire*,[89] showing how in fact Ariosto was still experimenting with the lyric genre while in the middle of a new project.

---

[87] This was noted by MARINI 2018, pp. 6-7. For instance, see *Sat.*, IV 4-6: '*qui* scesi, dove da diversi fonti / con eterno rumor confondon l'acque / la Tùrrita col Serchio fra duo ponti'; ll. 142-144: '*Questa* è una fossa, ove abito, profonda, / donde non muovo piè senza salire / del silvoso Apennin la fiera sponda' (emphasis mine).

[88] And possibly also after V, which, according to Paoli and Campeggiani, predates the other satire (ARIOSTO 2019, p. 168).

[89] In Bologna's words, 'per Ariosto l'esperienza del capitoli precederebbe immediatamente quella della satira, e [...] fungerebbe quasi da laboratorio formale per la messa a punto della nuova struttura' (BOLOGNA 1998, p. 22).

6. Portrait of the lyric speaker as a lover

Now that each of the four capitoli has been analysed, we should turn our attention to their moralising contents, which appears especially relevant in these poems, consistently with the overall importance of the gnomic theme – a fundamental legacy from the humanist tradition – in Ariosto's oeuvre. In particular, the poet often deploys the 'practical' ethic of *exemplum* – this very word occurs in capitolo XXIX, l. 9, where the speaker wishes 'che nel mio exempio ogni amator si specchi' –, popularised in the culture of Ferrara by Erasmus and by literati such as Alberti, Collenuccio, Calcagnini, all of whom drew on the models of Aesop and of Lucian.[90] To this background one must add the influence of fifteenth-century terza rima writings. Indeed, sententiousness seems to be a typical feature not only of the 'moralistic capitoli' proper, but also of the elegiac ones. An example is the following capitolo by Sasso, where the speaker asks his beloved for *mercede* resorting to arguments that echo popular wisdom:

> Chi ha tempo e 'l ben non usa, in tutto el perde,
> dir se suon un proverbio antico, e vero
> coglier se vol el fior mentre l'è verde
>
> (Sasso, capitolo IV, ll. 1-3)

A demonstration of the influence of these moralising traditions in Ariosto's lyrics is the presence of *exempla* involving animals, a case in point being the beginning of XLV. Here the speaker compares his own situation to that of a wounded bear, whose clumsy attempts to alleviate the pain do nothing but increase his suffering:

> O vera o falsa che la fama suone,
> i' odo dir che l'orso ciò che trova
> quand'è ferito, in la piaga si pone:
> hor un'herba, hor un'altra, et talhor prova
> et stecchi et spini et sassi et acqua et terra,
> che affligon sempre, et nulla mai gli giova.
> Vol pace et egli sol si fa la guerra;
> cerca da sé scacciar l'aspro martire,
> et egli è quel che se lo chiude et serra.
> Ch'io sia simile a lui ben posso dire,

90 On this point should be mentioned at least D'Ascia 1998; Tissoni Benvenuti 2004.

ché, poi che Amor ferimmi, mai non cesso
a nuovi impiastri le mie piaghe aprire
(*Rime del canzoniere*, XLV 1-12)

One is put in mind of the numerous similes and metaphors in the *Furioso* that adopt animal imagery, and whose function is hardly ever strictly ornamental, aiming instead, in Carlo Delcorno's formulation, 'a connotare più o meno esplicitamente una situazione morale, un atteggiamento psicologico'.[91] In the *Satire*, too, frequent gnomic passages involving animals appear, either in the form of the apologue (which may be viewed as a 'narrative expansion' of the *exemplum*)[92] or as briefer rhetorical figures. The latter case is of special interest here.[93] See, for instance, the following tercets of satira III, in which the speaker is illustrating the difference between himself and his fellow courtiers, in their ability to adapt to the duties of courtly life:

Non si adatta una sella o un basto solo
ad ogni dosso; ad un non par che l'abbia,
all'altro stringe e preme e gli dà duolo.
Mal può durar il rosignuolo in gabbia,
più vi sta il gardelino, e più il fanello;
la rondine in un dì vi mor di rabbia.
(*Sat.*, III 34-39)

These terzine share with the opening of the capitolo XLV a popular flavour: in both cases, Ariosto must have recalled the literary tradition of the Quattrocento capitolo, a model which, however, in XLV he seem to wish to keep at a distance, through a technique of rationalisation (not devoid of irony) that he also adopts in the *Furioso* – by evaluating, that is, in the very first line, the possibility that the legend may be false.[94]

Notable, too, is the end of XLIII. The speaker is here envisaging the epitaph he wishes to be carved upon his grave; this inscription deploys three animal images that capture the impossibility of staying away from his beloved:

---

91 Delcorno 1989, p. 319.

92 An examination of the four apologues of the *Satire* is in Villa 2000. On the use of the apologue in humanist Ferrarese texts, see D'Ascia 1998.

93 A recent examination of this subject is Bucchi 2019.

94 See *Fur.*, VIII 52,1 ABC: 'Narran l'antique storie, o vere o false'; VIII 58,1-2 ABC: 'O vera o falsa che fosse la cosa / di Proteo (ch'io non so che me ne dica)'; XLV 105,1 C: 'Marfisa, o 'l vero o 'l falso che dicesse'. As noted by Zatti 1990, p. 190, these asides derive from hypothetical stereotyped formulas that were used by the *canterini*; however, 'Ariosto li estende a usi più generalizzati, che fingono di mettere in questione il suo stesso statuto di narratore onnisciente'.

la causa del mio mal si legga chiara:
  come né pesce a l'aqua, né alla terra
talpe, né al fuoco le piral remote,
così né anchor chi questo marmo serra
  viver lontan da la sua donna puote.
(*Rime del canzoniere*, XLIII, 93-97)

The first two animals mentioned, fishes and moles, are also commonly featured in the moralistic sections of Quattrocento capitoli.[95] Interestingly, the 'piral' instead seems to be extremely rare, and perhaps for this reason this animal was left out by Ariosto in the post-**Vr** version of the poem (in this way, however, he also rendered less understandable the implicit outcome of this set of similes, namely the identification of the woman as air).[96] The *pirali*, or *pyrausta*, was a fictional creature, whose birth and life in fire was first described by classical authors. That Ariosto should prefer it to the more common salamander[97] is perhaps motivated by the influence of an adage by Erasmus, *Pyraustae interitus*. Only in its 1536 version will Erasmus explicitly recommend the adoption of this image to convey the impossibility of living away from one's homeland,[98] but such reading of the myth is intuitive, and it is easy to suppose that Ariosto deployed it with a view to enhancing the importance of the feeling of homesickness in the capitolo (which was pinpointed in section 4).

Besides the *exempla* involving animals, the pervasive use of a lexical repertoire related to the idea of 'error' is a further element that signals the

---

[95] Sasso, capitolo XXXVI, ll. 165-166: 'l'orso sta bene in selva, in acqua el pesce, / el falcon non è bon da porre in gabbia'; Correggio, *Rime*, 35,5-6: 'Che senza alito in aqua viva il pesce / e talpa in terra' (both are also quoted in Finazzi 2002-2003, p. 280).

[96] In the final version, included in **Mn**, **Cp** and **F**, ll. 94-97 are: 'né senza morte talpe da la terra, / né mai pesce da l'acqua si disgiunge / né poté anchor che questo marmo serra / da la sua bella donna viver lunge'.

[97] This animal features in *Rvf*, CCVII 40-41: 'Di mia morte mi pasco, et vivo in fiamme: / stranio cibo, et mirabil salamandra'. Examples of its use in courtly poetry are Tebaldeo, *Rime della vulgata*, 283,1-4: 'cum quel dolor che l'amate aque lassa / pesce iretito e salamandra il foco, / che è tal che in breve la lor vita passa, / cum quel da te mi parto'; Serafino Aquilano, *Sonetti di dubbia attribuzione*, 32,9-10: 'O nova salamandra, o sol fenice, / che nel morir rinasco e vivo in fuoco'.

[98] *Adagia*, 851: '[...] Nec invenuste deflecteretur in eos, qui nusquam vivere possunt nisi in propria patria. Si contingat agere peregre, rebus omnibus offenduntur'. In the version Ariosto could consult, Erasmus had already given some instructions on the metaphorical use of this symbolic image: 'Quod si placet ad hoc referre adagium, convenient et in eos [...] qui celeriter intereunt' (see e.g. Erasmus 1508, f. 98*r*, and Erasmus 1514, f. 134*r*). Interestingly, the 1514 edition of the adages was printed only seven months before Ariosto undertook the journey that occasioned this poem; the printer was Giovanni Mazocco, who was also the editor of the 1516 *Furioso* (on his activity, see Jossa 2019).

importance of the moral theme in these capitoli. The words adopted assume different nuances, from that of transgression to that of sin – though never straying beyond the confines of a lay vision –, and are flanked by others that convey the concept of punishment:

XXIX: 'Meritamente [...] punir' (l. 1); 'grave eror' (l. 2); 'ben poco saggio fui che all'altrui prece [...] / più ch'al mio desir proprio satisfece' (ll. 4-6); 'pecchi' (l. 7); 'pena' (l. 8); 'Pentomi [...] pentir' (l. 16); 'mal consiglio' (l. 18); 'penitentia ria' (l. 63)

XXX: 'da penitentia et da dolor oppresso' (l. 58); 'più a l'altrui che al mio desir m'atenni' (l. 66)

XLIII: 'la colpa mia' (l. 30); 'Tal fallo poi di punition sì grave / punisce' (ll. 40-41); 'perdonar [...] offesa' (l. 44); 'inobedientia' (l. 49)

XLV: 'errore' (l. 63)

As may be expected, this terminology finds several correspondences in the *Satire*, even though its use appears to be completely different in the two genres. Let us look at some examples from the *Satire* first, and to this end the vocabulary related to the concept of madness – which in Ariosto is closely correlated to that of moral error – must also be considered. In the beginning of satira I the speaker calls 'pazzo' whoever breaks the fundamental rule of courtly life by contradicting his lord – the author is obviously alluding to himself, and to his decision not to follow Ippolito to Hungary:

Pazzo chi al suo signor contradir vole,
se ben dicesse c'ha veduto il giorno
pieno di stelle e a mezzanotte il sole.

(*Sat.*, I 10-12)

In satira II, talking of his attempts to obtain the benefice of St Agata, he says that it is highly probable that he may be judged 'folle' for not fully embracing a career in the church:

Questa opinïon mia so ben che folle
diranno molti, che a salir non tenti
la via ch'uom spesso a grandi onori estolle.

(*Sat.*, II 142-144)

Other relevant examples are offered by the fourth satira. The poet imagines the rebuke he might receive by an unnamed friend for complaining about having to stay in Garfagnana, at a great distance from his beloved, and instead praises the wisdom of his addressee Sigismondo Malaguzzi:

liberamente il mio *peccato* accuso
(*Sat.*, IV 27)

– Guata poco cervel! – poi diria seco
– degno uom da chi esser debbia un popul retto,
uom che poco lontan da cinquanta anni
vaneggi nei pensier di giovinetto! –
E direbbe il Vangel di san Giovanni;
che, se ben *erro*, pur non son sì losco
che 'l mio *error* non conosca e ch'io nol danni.
(*ibid.*, ll. 30-36)

Tu forte e *saggio*, che a tua posta muovi
questi affetti da te, [...]
(*ibid.*, ll. 40-41)

perciò non dico né a difender tolgo
che non sia *fallo* il mio; [...]
(*ibid.*, ll. 52-53)

(emphasis mine)

It goes without saying that in all these cases self-accusation is a rhetorical tool in the service of irony and unmasking: 'isola il protagonista in un esclusivo mondo alla rovescia, la cui ammissione equivale in realtà a una condanna degli altri, i veri folli'.[99] Ariosto's protested madness is a *pazzia savia*, an idea borrowed from the satiric genre in its Horatian sense,[100] and that is in fact pursued in the name of values such as personal freedom and love – in satira IV the latter is ironically defined through the metaphor of poison: 'Ma che giova s'io 'l danno e s'io 'l conosco, / se non ci posso riparar, né truovi / rimedio alcun che spenga questo tòsco?' (ll. 37-39). From examples such as the following one may see Ariosto's ironic grasp of his 'errore', a knowledge that goes hand in hand with a heartfelt defence of his personal decisions:

Ma chi fu mai sì saggio o mai sì santo
che di esser senza macchia di pazzia,

99 Berra 2000*bis*, p. 175 – I shall also refer the reader to this study for an analysis of the theme of madness in the *Satire*.

100 See especially *Serm.*, II 3 and II 7. The relevance of these poems for Ariosto is highlighted by Cucchiarelli 2019, pp. 285-286.

o poca o molta, dar si possa vanto?
  Ogniun tenga la sua, questa è la mia:

(*Sat.*, II 148-151)

  S'io ti fossi vicin, forse la mazza
per bastonarmi piglieresti, tosto
che m'udissi allegar che ragion pazza
  non mi lasci da voi viver discosto.

(*Sat.*, VII 178-181)

If, starting from these premises, we return to the capitoli, it should first be noted that 'fallo', a keyword of the fourth satira, is used in capitolo XLIII (see above) with an opposite meaning, denoting the speaker's refusal to follow the call of Love in favour of court duties. The passages from the satira quoted above also openly contrast with the beginning of capitolo XXIX (its 'twin', as they share the Garfagnana setting), in which the lack of wisdom lamented by the speaker consists in the fact that he agreed to leave:

  Meritamente hora punir mi veggio
del *grave eror* che dipartir mi fece
da la mia donna, et degno son di peggio.
  Ben *poco saggio* fui che all'altrui prece,
a cui devea et potei chiuder l'orecchi,
più ch'al mio desir proprio satisfece.

(*Rime del canzoniere*, XXIX 1-6 – emphasis mine)

In short, in the *Satire* 'ragione' backs duty and error/madness means giving in to passions. In the capitoli, on the other hand, the reasonable decision is that which follows the passions, and error is all that leads us away from them.[101] Obviously, this does not mean that Ariosto is here actually being polemical against the sphere of 'duties'. This fashioning is consistent with the elegiac code, in which any external matter must be unconditionally referred to love and subjectivity, and is therefore fully acceptable in the courtly scenario – a similar rhetorical strategy, whose effect is that of voiding the seriousness of the speaker's judgements and declarations, may be observed in Tebaldeo's capitolo 282, where the allegedly wrong deci-

101 In the case of capitolo XLV – where the 'mistake' is the speaker's belief that going to Ravenna might be a remedy (ll. 61-63: 'Havendo dunque de' rimedii il tutto / provato ad uno ad un, fuor che l'absenza / ch'al fin provar m'havea il mio errore indutto') the point I make seems valid especially if we hypothesise that Ariosto actually took the journey as part of his court service.

sion the speaker (Francesco Gonzaga) has made is warfare.[102] In addition however, and most interestingly, it seems to me that here Ariosto is enacting a subtler strategy of self-representation, hinting that the parameters by which the speaker is judging are blurred by his being in the thrall of the irrationality engendered by love. Such characterisation is observable from several textual details, in whose analysis it will of course be necessary to bear in mind the *Furioso*, the epitome of all manifestations of human irrationality, where 'errore' is a leitmotiv of the characters' vicissitudes.

A first interesting passage in this respect is the *exemplum* of the bear which opens capitolo XLV. The bear also appears prominently in the imagery of the *Furioso*. Following the numerous legends that centered on this animal, Ariosto employs it either as a symbol for wrath or for uncontrolled lust,[103] and in any case to denote loss of rationality – examples are the scene of Ruggiero's attempted rape of Angelica, or a number of similes concerning Rodomonte and Orlando.[104] The same meaning can be inferred regarding the use of the bear image in the capitolo, which clearly is used by Ariosto to set the lyric voice under the sign of an almost bestial irrationality, one also implying sexual desire, and which may ultimately lead to the subversion of well-established values. This lyric voice goes as far as to select the tragic scenario of the battlefield of Ravenna as a remedy for unhappy love.

The other three capitoli examined in this chapter also allow us to glimpse the speaker's distorted logic. In XLIII, sickness is preferred by him to health, inasmuch as it makes it possible for him to stay with his beloved:

> Non fu mai sanità che sì giovasse
> a peregrino infermo che tra via,
> da la patria lontan, compagno lasse,
> come giovato a me il contrario havria:
> un languir dolce, che con scusa degna
> m'havesse havuto di tener balia.
>
> (*Rime del canzoniere*, XLIII 19-24)

---

102 See Tebaldeo, *Rime della vulgata*, 282,52-57: 'Prender mai non dovea lancia né scuto, / se non per te, quando me fussi tolta: / perisco, ahimé, per dare ad altri aiuto! / Ma fallando se impara! Una altra volta / aprirò meglio gli occhi; hora che il piede / ho inviato al camin, non vo' dar volta'.

103 Notably, these two meanings also conflate in Dante's *Così nel mio parlar*; see Dante, *Rime*, 46,66-71: 'S'io avessi le belle trecce prese, / che fatte son per me scudiscio e ferza, / pigliandole anzi terza, / con esse passerei vespero e squille: / e non sarei pietoso né cortese, / anzi farei com'orso quando scherza' (an analysis of the meaning associated with the bear image in this poem is in Martinez 1993).

104 The relevant passages are analysed by Delcorno 1989, pp. 319-322.

In XXIX he regards the undertaking of his duties as a foolish decision ('come io potessi *uscir sì di me stesso* / ch'io mi appigliasse a questo *mal consiglio*', ll. 17-18).[105] His condition of insanity is here suggested by his envisaging of future sleepless nights ('Duro serammi più che sasso il letto', l. 58). This finds a parallel in the three episodes of love irrationality of the *Furioso*, those of Orlando, Bradamante and Rodomonte, all of which feature references to a bed, hinting at the idea of unsatisfied desire.[106] Additionally, the rhyme *tempeste* : *moleste* (ll. 55-57; see above) possibly echoes the fifth canto of the *Inferno*, which deals with the punishment of carnal lust (*tempesta* : *molesta*, ll. 29-33).[107] Finally, in capitolo XXX the speaker even goes as far as cursing himself, together with the person who commissioned his journey to Florence and with his travelling companion:

[...] ch'odio talor me stesso.
   L'ira, il furor, la rabbia mi conduce
a biastemar chi fu cagion ch'io venni
et chi a venir mi fu compagno et duce;
   et me che senza me di me sostenni
lasciar, ohimè, la meglior parte, il core,
et più a l'altrui che al mio desir m'atenni.

(*Rime del canzoniere*, XXX 60-66)

Besides noting the triple repetition of 'me' at l. 64, which suggests a condition of restlessness, attention must be called to the lexical cluster *ira-furor-rabbia*. The use of these words (which can, in this context, be taken as synonyms) in the *Furioso* is analysed in depth by Raffaella Anconetani, who highlights the pathological nuances they carry and their accumulation in the episode of Orlando's frenzy:[108] '[...] in lui non restò dramma / che

---

105 The speaker's supposed foolishness is symbolised by his inability to close his ears to the request received ('a cui devea et potei chiuder l'orecchi', XXIX 5). Conversely, in the *Furioso* the action of closing one's ear is attributed to Cardinal Ippolito as an expression of his wisdom. See *Fur.*, XVI 2,3-4 AB; XVIII C: 'o riserbargli almen, fin che presente / sua causa dica, l'altra orecchia chiusa', and the commentary to this passage in Fórnari, *Spositione*, I, p. 373: 'solevano i scultori le statue de' giustissimi principi così alle volte formare, che una mano tenevano a una orecchia supposta, a dinotare che si riserbavano, per più diritta sentenza darne, d'ascoltare anco la contraria parte'.

106 This is suggested by Weaver 2003, pp. 127-128. Ariosto also probably remembered Dante's simile in *Purg.*, VI 149-151: 'vedrai te somigliante a quella inferma / che non può trovar posa in su le piume, / ma con dar volta suo dolore scherma'.

107 The same rhyme occurs in *Amorum libri tres*, I 47; according to Zanato this is tantamount to a 'confessione diretta della condizione di *peccator carnale*' of Boiardo (Boiardo 2012, p. 293).

108 Anconetani 2009, pp. 22-30 (I refer the reader to this study for a more detailed examination of the vocabulary of madness in Ariosto's poem). It should nevertheless be noted that

non fosse odio, rabbia, ira e furore' (*Fur.*, XXI 129,6-7 B; XXIII C).[109] A similar lexical sequence is displayed by Ariosto in Bradamante's jealous rage ('di gelosia, d'ira e di rabbia piena [...] / ritornò furibonda alla sua stanza', *Fur.*, XXX 31,6-8 A; XXX 35 B; XXXII 35 C),[110] as well as in an exordium in which the narrator reflects on the consequences of irrationality:

> Quando vincer da l'impeto e da *l'ira*
> si lascia la ragion, né si difende,
> e che 'l cieco *furor* sì inanzi tira
> o mano o lingua, che gli amici offende;
> se ben dipoi si piange e si sospira,
> non è per questo che l'error s'emende.
> [...]
> Ma simile son fatto ad uno infermo,
> che dopo molta pazienza e molta,
> quando contra il dolor non ha più schermo,
> cede alla *rabbia* e a bestemmiar si volta.
> (*Fur.*, XXVIII 1-2 AB;[111] XXX C – emphasis mine)

This proem allows us to gather further samples. Ariosto-the-narrator is here comparing himself to a sick person, also with an explicit reference to Orlando, as an excuse for his unfairness to the female sex ('Voi scusarete, che per frenesia, / vinto da l'aspra passion, vaneggio [...] / Non men son fuor di me, che fosse Orlando', 3,3-4 and 4,1). The verb 'bestemmiare' should especially be noted: it constitutes one further link with capitolo XXX, where it also appears at l. 62. In the conceptual universe of the *Furioso*, blasphemy, too, appertains to the sphere of folly. Ariosto mostly associ-

in the *Furioso* 'l'impiego dei termini presi in esame, spesso accostati in serie dittologiche in contesti di guerra e d'amore è [...] molto esteso' (*ibid.*, p. 28). The scholar also explores the values of these words in classical culture and also recalls *Rvf*, CCXXXII, which takes up Seneca's definition of *ira* while listing a series of historical figures which were overcome by it (ll. 12-14: 'Ira è breve furore, et chi nol frena, / è furor lungo, che 'l suo possessore / spesso a vergogna, et talor mena a morte').

109 The version in A is: 'non rimase dramma / di lui ch'ira non fusse, odio e furore' (*Fur.*, XXI 129,6-7 A).

110 Note that the word 'rabbia' was added to the Orlando episode from the 1521 *Furioso*, and 'ira' was added only to the 1532 version of the Bradamante episode: Ariosto progressively 'reinforced the pathological and linguistic similarities between the two episodes' (WEAVER 2003, p. 130).

111 In AB, octave 1 reads slighty differently. I will quote from A, ll. 1-6: 'Deh, come invan si piange e si suspira / drieto all'error, e non gli vale emenda, / se avien ch'el sdegno e l'impeto de l'ira / a cacciar d'alto la ragione ascenda, / quando con forza irreparabil tira / o lingua o man, sì che li amici offenda'.

ates it with Rodomonte: 'che 'l re di Sarza, pien d'ira e di sdegno, / grida e bestemmia, e non può star più a segno' (*Fur.*, XII 108,7-8 AB; XIV C); 'egli bestemmia Dio' (*Fur.*, XII 117,8 AB; XIV C); 'bestemmia il ciel con spaventoso grido' (*Fur.*, XIII 5,8 AB; XV C); 'e bestemmiò l'eterna Ierarchia' (*Fur.*, XXI 33,6 AB; XXIII C); 'e lo bestemmia sempre e maledice' (*Fur.*, XXI 33,6 AB; XXIII 38,4 C); 'Bestemmiò il cielo e gli elementi' (*Fur.*, XXIV 80,1 AB; XXVI 83 C). Rodomonte blasphemes even as he dies, which is interesting because this detail is not featured in the Virgilian source of the passage ('bestemmiando fuggì l'alma sdegnosa', *Fur.*, XL 112,7 A; 111 B; XLVI 140 C). The fact that Ariosto chooses to associate blasphemy precisely with Rodomonte, rather than with the Saracens in general – as was customary in chivalric literature –,[112] means that he intended it less as a topical signal for unbelief, than as a symbol of the the pathological irrationality that is specific to Rodomonte's personality (what Mario Santoro has called 'defezione della ragione').[113] In this light, the fact that Ariosto-the-narrator should also refer the act of blaspheming to himself, in the proem to the thirtieth canto, is extremely significant. Through this device he is establishing a parallel between himself and Rodomonte – indeed the existence of a privileged link between the narrator and this character (they share a certain mutability in their judgment of events and situations) had early on been noted by Durling.[114] As a matter of fact, although so far I have quoted the *Furioso* mainly in order to find narrative parallels for the themes that characterise Ariosto's lyric and satirical self-fashioning, it is nevertheless important to take it into account also in questions relating to self-reflexivity.[115] After all, the narrator often refers to his own experience and especially to his condition of lovesickness, which causes him and his characters to mirror each other, as common sharers in the universal irrationality that is the distinguishing mark of human existence. A significant passage in this respect is the proem to the twenty-fourth canto, where, after stating – commenting upon Orlando's story – that 'non è in somma amor, se non insania' (1,3), he considers his own situation:

> Ben mi si potria dir: – Frate, tu vai
> l'altrui mostrando, e non vedi il tuo fallo. –

---

112 In the *Furioso*, the Saracens are generally defined as 'folli', accepting the moral connotation that the adjective carried in Christian ethics (Anconetani 2009, p. 46).

113 Santoro 1989, pp. 263-274.

114 Durling 1965, pp. 169-173.

115 A certain continuity between the narrator of the *Furioso* and the speaker of the *Satire* in terms of moral self-fashioning has also been noted by Bruscagli 2003.

Io vi rispondo che comprendo assai,
or che di mente ho lucido intervallo;
et ho gran cura (e spero farlo ormai)
di riposarmi e d'uscir fuor di ballo:
ma tosto far, come vorrei, nol posso,
che 'l male è penetrato infin all'osso.

(*Fur.*, XXII 3 AB; XXIV C)

Also worth considering is the famous complaint about the loss of his own wits – coming once again close on the heels of the vicissitudes of Orlando – in the proem of the thirty-fifth canto:

Chi salirà per me, madonna, in cielo
a riportarne il mio perduto ingegno?
che, poi ch'uscì da' bei vostri occhi il telo
che 'l cor mi fisse, ognior perdendo vegno.
Né di tanta iattura mi querelo,
pur che non cresca, ma stia a questo segno;
ch'io dubito, se più si va sciemando,
di venir tal, qual ho descritto Orlando.

(*Fur.*, XXXII 1 AB; XXXV C)

Because the narrator's madness is punctuated by intervals of lucidity,[116] during which he is able to recognise his disease, a similarity may be noted between him and the speaker of the *Satire*, who is also able to observe his weakness from an 'external' standpoint and in fact adopts it as a conscious life choice. It is perhaps no coincidence that in the proem to canto XXIV an echo from Horace's *Sermones* (a work that exerted great influence on the *Satire*) may be noted.[117] Moreover, in the proem to canto XXXV, the narrator declares that he wishes to seek for his lost wits among the beauties of his beloved: 'Ne' bei vostri occhi e nel sereno viso, / nel sen d'avorio e alabastrini poggi / se ne va errando; et io con queste labbia / lo corrò' (*Fur.*, XXXII 2,5-8 AB; XXXV C). As observed by Ferroni, this decision to im-

116 The phrase 'lucido intervallo' is indebted to a passage of St Jerome, according to which Lucretius composed his *De rerum natura* 'per intervalla insaniae' (see Saccone 1974, p. 245).

117 Compare ll. 1-2 in its third octave and *Serm.*, I 3,19-20: 'Nunc aliquis dicat mihi: Quid tu? / nullane habes vitia?' (mediated through *Rvf*, XCIX 12-14: 'Ben si può dire a me: Frate, tu vai / mostrando altrui la via, dove sovente / fosti smarrito, et or se' più che mai'). On this aspect in the self-fashioning of Ariosto-the-narrator, see Durling 1965, p. 168: 'He is mad, but he knows it, and he is not as mad as Orlando'; Ascoli 1987, p. 333: 'By splitting himself into a madman and the detached critic who views that madness, Ariosto simultaneously moves outside of himself and recovers himself'.

merse himself in the passion of love is essentially tantamount to a repudiation of the idea of recovery, and an acceptance of madness as a necessary element – the 'ragion pazza' of the *Satire*.[118] Within this framework, as we have seen, the speaker of the capitoli speaks from a perspective that is exclusively 'internal' to the love malady, of which he remains unconscious, and this fact triggers the mechanism of paradoxicality that underlies the poems. However, this crucial difference is inscribed within the wider continuum that is Ariosto's interest in this theme. Interestingly, the exordium of the thirty-fifth canto has been the basis for Federica Pich's interpretation of the narrator in the *Furioso* as the protagonist of a vicissitude which 'focuses on his continuous struggle to save his wits from amorous folly' and which is, therefore, 'to a great extent lyric in inspiration and expression'.[119] Whether or not one accepts the more general argument within which this observation is placed (according to Pich, the narrator must not be seen as the author's projection but as a character proper of the poem), nevertheless I believe that the emphasis placed on the osmosis between Ariosto's different poetic personas is correct, and indeed confirmed by our examination of these poems.

From the observations made so far, it can be argued that both the satirical and the lyric code are generated by an imbalance between the 'letter' and its meaning. The lyric persona defines as 'errore' all that stands in the way of love, but this is an unreliable speaker; the satirical persona labels as error passions and self-interest, its actual aim however being an apology of these 'faults'. In other words, I believe that in the capitoli it is possible to detect the influence (to the extent to which this is possible within the lyric code) of the logic of the *spoudaiogeloion*, the principle which sets the rules for Alberti's and Erasmus's concepts of folly and which appears to have been deeply assimilated by Ariosto in both the *Satire* and the *Furioso*. This entailed the description of things through an estranged or reversed perspective and explored the dialectical intertwining between reason and folly.[120]

---

118 Ferroni 1975, p. 87. Another comparison between the speaker's folly and Orlando's is in the proem to canto IX (see 2,1-4: 'Ma l'escuso io pur troppo, e mi rallegro / nel mio difetto aver compagno tale; / ch'anch'io sono al mio ben languido et egro, / sano e gagliardo a seguitare il male').

119 Pich 2015, p. 338 and p. 337 respectively.

120 On the points of contact between these authors and Ariosto in terms of their conception of madness, I will refer the reader at least to Ferroni 1975, Ossola 1976 and (for a comparison between Erasmus and Ariosto) Scianatico 2014, pp. 1-40. The serio-comic mode has been famously theorised by Bakhtin 1984, pp. 106-132; see also Zatti 1990, pp. 129-132 for Ariosto's relation to it.

On the strictly pathological nuance attributed to the concept of irrational mistake it is worth dwelling further. As has partly been shown, the medical theme is foregrounded to various extents by all these poems. Capitolo XXX develops a word pun on the 'Medici' family who cannot be helpful against the author's disease (see section 4). The theme of infirmity also underlies the whole text of XLIII, in which the real illness of the poet ('Tiemme la febre', l. 10) is juxtaposed to the illness induced by love, among whose victims are himself and Cardinal Ippolito ('né sano forse anchora hoggi ne sete', l. 33). Emphasis is placed on this motif here through the comparison of his own state to that of a sick pilgrim (ll. 19-21; see above). In capitolo XLV, the role of this theme is prominent, as has already been noted in section 2: the way it is laid out resembles that of sonnet XXXVIII (*Madonna, io mi pensai che 'l stare absente*), a poem that probably dates to Ariosto's stay in the Garfagnana. Here the speaker is allowed only to make brief visits to his beloved; these, however, are ineffectual in relieving his pain, and actually contribute to enhance it. The underlying concept is that a medicine, if wrongly administered, can easily become a deadly poison:

> Giovava il rivedervi, se sì breve
> non era, ma per la partita dura
> mi fu un venen, non che un rimedio leve.
> Così suol trar l'infermo in sepoltura
> interrotto compenso: o non si deve
> incominciare, o non lasciar la cura.
>
> (*Rime del canzoniere*, XXXVIII 9-14)

In this sonnet, the pain is caused by the condition of absence, for which its opposite – reconnection – is supposed to act as a remedy. Conversely, in capitolo XLV the speaker's pain derives from the proximity of the beloved, and the situation of absence consequently takes on the role of the proposed cure:

> Io volsi al fin provar se la partita,
> s'il star da le repulse et sdegni absente
> potessi risanar la mia ferita,
> quando provato havea ch'era possente
> trarmi ad irreparabile ruina
> a voi senza mercé l'esser presente.
> Ché s'un contrario all'altro è medicina
> non so perché, da l'un pigliando forza,
> per l'altro la mia doglia non declina:
> piglia forza da l'uno et non s'ammorza

per l'altro già; né già si minuisce,
anzi più per l'absenza si rinforza.

(*Rime del canzoniere*, XLV 16-27)

According to the theory of humoralism, which was popular in medieval and Renaissance medical handbooks as a legacy of Hippocrates's and Galen's theories, disease is the result of a state of imbalance between the four humours which fill the human body: in order to re-establish the correct balance, a treatment by opposite should be pursued (*contraria contrariis*).[121] The poems we have been looking at seem to translate into metaphor precisely this medical concept. More in general, Ariosto is arguably following the traditional definition of the lover as affected by *melancholia*, an excessive amount of black bile –[122] a malady that is explicitly mentioned in satira VII, where the speaker supposes that his interlocutor will think he is suffering from it on account his refusal to accept the position of ambassador at Rome:

Proponendo tu questo, s'io ricuso
l'andata, ben dirai che triste umore
abbia il discorso razional confuso.

(*Sat.*, VII 142-144)

The presence of these themes in Ariosto is easy to understand if we take into account the cultural background against which he moves. Ferrara at the time was, thanks to figures such as Niccolò Leoniceno or Giovanni Manardi,[123] at the forefront of the development of medical philosophy, in a way that enabled writers and court physicians to mingle and exchange ideas. In addition, it should be considered that the discourse on malady, which had always been suited to poetical use, had penetrated the Quattrocento amorous culture as part of worldview that was open to absorb the most varied components – a noteworthy example of this eclecticism being

---

121 Hippocrates, *Nature of Man*, IX: '[...] the treatment carried out should be that opposed to the cause of the disease'. On the theory of humoralism, Klibansky – Panofsky – Saxl 1964 remains a fundamental reference.

122 Literature on melancholy is extemely vast; in addition to referring the reader again to Klibansky – Panofsky – Saxl 1964, I will mention Gigliucci 2009 and its bibliography. On this concept in the Renaissance, it will also be useful to consult the contributions gathered in Rotondi Secchi Tarugi 1999.

123 Both are mentioned in the third *Furioso*: 'Veggo il Mainardo, veggo il Leoniceno, / il Pannizzato, e Celio e il Teocreno' (*Fur.*, XLVI 14,7-8 C). On medical knowledge in Renaissance courtly culture, I shall refer the reader to the contributions in Crisciani – Zuccolin 2011.

Equicola's *Libro de natura de amore*, where, in a discussion on the nature of love that also touches on lovesickness, examples drawn from poetry sit next to medical sources proper.[124] In medical treatises, lovesickness is defined as *amor hereos*, a concept which entertains a complex and variable relationship with that of melancholy,[125] and presupposes an alteration of the imaginative processes, causing the mind to obsessively focus on a fixed idea. It is described in these terms by Michele Savonarola, a court physician in Ferrara in the first half of the fifteenth century, in his most successful *Practica maior*.[126] As an example of the poetic application of this concept,[127] see the following tercet by Correggio:

> e mi facesti qual languido infermo,
> che vede quel che a sua salute è amaro,
> pur l'occhio col pensier lì sempre ha fermo.
>
> (Correggio, *Rime*, 212,12-14)

The episodes of love insanity in the *Furioso*, and especially that of Orlando, have also been connected by scholars to the concept of 'clinical' lovesickness, and suggest that Ariosto was familiar with specific medical issues.[128] I shall add to this framework that the feeling of homesickness, implicity foregrounded in capitoli XXX and XLIII, was also viewed as a pathology within in this milieu. Michele Savonarola codifies it as such in his illustration of the phenomenon of *ilischi*, when he specifies that this word – despite being often adopted as a generic synonym of *amor hereos* – originally defined a pathological form of desire for one's homeland (Savonarola's actually represents one of the earliest descriptions of nostalgia in clinical terms).[129] Even if a direct intertextual link is not established, it is

---

124 See esp. *Libro de natura de amore, Libro secondo*, f. 102 (Equicola 1999, pp. 330-331).

125 An exhaustive bibliography on the *amor hereos* is provided by Cracolici 2011, p. 40, footnote 31. I shall mention at least Ciavolella 1976 and Agamben 1977.

126 On Savonarola, see again Crisciani – Zuccolin 2011.

127 A previous poetic formulation of *amor hereos* is in *Rvf*, CLXXVI 7-8: 'ch'i' l'ò negli occhi, et veder seco parme / donne et donzelle, et sono abeti et faggi'.

128 On this point, besides the works cited in the previous footnotes, see also Beer 1987, pp. 83-108; Rinaldi 1988. It is worth remembering that Ariosto mocks the medical milieu in the controversial prose speech *Herbolato* (composed after 1530) whose speaking subject is a quack who wishes to advertise an allegedly miraculous medicine. On this work, see Looney 2013, Liboni 2018 and their bibliographies.

129 Savonarola 1486, f. 63*v*: 'Tales quidem secundum plurimum sunt cupientes dominas quas inordinato amore diligent. Dicitur secundum plurimum, quia etiam aliqui non dominas cupiunt, sed reverti ad patriam, quam summe et summe amant. Unde aliqui primam dispositionem nominaverunt hereos, secundam vero, quae est amor repatriandi, ilischi appelaverunt.

extremely probable that Ariosto felt the influence of this set of beliefs and moved within this cultural framework.

In these poems, it often happens that the concept of love medicine merges with that of love magic. 'Sorceresses' often feature in these lyrics. This point was noted by Rinaldi, who claimed the poet's indebtness to a variety of classical models that include the figures of Medea from Ovid's *Metamorphoses* and of Erichto from Lucan's *Pharsalia*.[130] To the classical line of influence may be added that of courtly literature, in which this motif enjoyed great popularity. Among the treatises should be mentioned Calcagnini's *Amatoriae magiae compendium*, which was dedicated to Niccolò da Correggio and listed several examples of amorous magic from classical literature.[131] As for the lyric genre, two recurring situations, both inherited from the Latin elegy (one recalls Tibullus, I 1 and Propertius, I 1), should be noted: the speaker resorts to the aid of sorceresses in order either to make his beloved reciprocate his love, or, conversely, to rid himself of it. The numerous possible examples include the following sonnet by Boiardo:

> Ma in che me affido, lasso! Che arte maga
> soglia da amore? E non sciolse Medea
> con l'erbe scythe e' canti di Thesaglia!
> Lei non pòte saldar l'ardente piaga
> che avea nel cor, con quanto ella sapea,
> ché contro amor non è forza che vaglia.
>
> (*Amorum libri tres*, II 37,9-14)

Ariosto follows this tradition in capitolo XLV, where the speaker considers appealing to 'maghe [...] di Tessaglia' (l. 67), who however are too far away, to fall out of love. A different elaboration of the sorceress theme is in XXX and XLIII: here, it is the beloved woman herself that is fashioned as such.[132] In XXX, as mentioned at section 4, Ariosto adopts a phrasing similar to that used for Melissa, and endows her beloved with abilities typical of the classical sorceress: those of stopping the sun in its course and of

Ego vero feci ilischi terminum communem'. For the concept of nostalgia in ancient medical literature, see Roscher 1993.

130 Rinaldi 2000, pp. 317-321.

131 This can be read in Calcagnini 1544, pp. 497-503.

132 To mention but one among the possible parallels, in sonnet VIII of Cornazano 1502, the poet says that the woman's faculties combine those of legendary creatures and herbs, i.e. she can kill with her gaze and she is both the cause and the cure of 'fatal heating'. He concludes (ll. 10-14): 'Che gli è il suo sguardo la mia sepultura, / et di duo bianche man l'una m'impiaga, / l'altra insensibilmente m'unge e cura: / tale è la incantatrice e la mia magha'.

healing with her gaze ('cantando ferma il sol la bella maga / che con sua vista può sanarmi sola', ll. 75-76).[133] The lady's gaze is again represented as having healing powers for the speaker (in the moment in which he imagines his death) in XLIII:

> Che s'ella anchor l'exanimata faccia
> mira, a quel punto ho quasi certa fede
> ch'esser non possa che più il corpo giaccia.
> (*Rime del canzoniere*, XLIII 73-75)

This motif is closely intertwined with the very typical metaphor of the lady as Sun,[134] in the context of a mythological comparison: if Prometheus was able to give life to clay, by heating it with a flame he stole from Phoebus' chariot,[135] then he himself, too, may be resurrected thanks to the 'rays' coming out from the woman (ll. 76-81). In addition to noting that the Prometheus myth was apparently enjoying popularity in Ferrara at the turn of the century – again thanks to Calcagnini, who dedicated to Correggio a pamphlet summarising its several versions –,[136] it may be argued that in this capitolo the beloved woman is represented both as a natural phenomenon and as one who controls natural phenomena.

Madness and magic, therefore, are themes that not only intertwine in Ariosto[137] but link together these poems. If considered alongside the moral vocabulary employed, the picture that emerges – although arguably maintaining its receptiveness to the courtly literature of the time – confirms certain inclinations on the part of the poet, while some of the decisions he makes here may be seen as forming a continuum with what in the *Satire* and in the *Furioso* become fully-fledged organising principles.

---

133 Also in sonnet XVII Ariosto endows his beloved with powers of natural magic: see Chapter II, 5. Note that Equicola, too, in reviewing the *topoi* applied by modern love poets to their beloved ladies, includes among them the 'più che humane actioni, parole che 'l sole fermano et il mare fanno tranquillo' (*Libro de natura de amore*, *Libro primo*, f. 18*r*, in Equicola 1999, p. 229).

134 This is consistent with the definition of her and Cardinal Ippolito as his 'two lights' in this poem (see section 3).

135 Ariosto is probably following Boccaccio, *Genealogie deorum gentilium*, IV 44.

136 On this pamphlet, which was not published in the comprehensive edition of Calcagnini's works (1544), and whose *terminus ante quem* is 1508 (the year of Correggio's death), see Sandrolini 2004. Prometheus also features in a sonnet by Ariosto, on which see Chapter II, 5.

137 Ferroni 1975, p. 84: 'La magia è nel *Furioso* una delle matrici fondamentali della pazzia: [...] attraverso di essa passa quella creazione di immagini fittizie ed illusorie che costringono gli uomini a perdere coscienza di sé'.

7. Conclusion

It may be useful to recall, by way of conclusion to this discussion, some observations made by Floriani in his analysis of the birth and early development of Italian sixteenth-century satire. This process, the scholar believes, was influenced by the Latin literature of the Augustan age: an influence that is especially exerted on the quality of the speaker, who does not limit himself to generic moral precepts but presents himself in a way that echoes actual biographical features. This ambition to engage directly with the literature of the age of Augustus is motivated, Floriani argues, with the similarity in the social position of poets, who, enjoying a privileged status in the context of a centralised state, felt the urge to protect their intellectual autonomy:

> Un carattere proprio dello *speaker* [...] della poesia latina, da Catullo all'età imperiale, è il forte tasso di *realismo*. Intendo con questa pregiudicatissima parola indicare [...] il fatto che *io* è una realtà testuale che si pone come corrispondente perfetto della realtà biografica del poeta [...]. Lo *speaker* latino è un cittadino di Roma [...] è titolare di una competenza letteraria e insieme di un *ethos*, che gli permette di celebrare i valori pubblici di Roma, ma anche di distinguersi, di esprimere la sua puntuale *recusatio*, quando è in gioco la sua sostanziale autonomia. [...] Proprio su questo punto, io dico, fa leva la cultura volgare primo-cinquecentesca per organizzare un rinnovato sistema letterario, alternativo a quello in vigore nella poesia cortigiana tardo-quattrocentesca. [...] è ben possibile proiettare sul presente e sul volgare lo schema dello *speaker* antico. Perché, innanzitutto, quella *figura* complessiva trova una corrispondenza larga e significativa nella situazione presente.[138]

It was Ariosto who initiated this process, thus injecting new life, as is acknowledged by Floriani and later also by Godioli, into the fifteenth-century capitolo, whose speaker had thus far expressed his stance 'in termini astratti e vaghi'.[139] The points that have been debated in this chapter make it possible, I believe, to further enrich this framework. I have shown that the elegiac capitolo is also handled by Ariosto in a way that reacts to tradition, in some cases converging with the *Satire* themselves in terms of the tools adopted for such an innovation. The 'classical' and the 'autobiographical' components, which in these poems on the theme of distance achieve a harmonious fusion, return, in different doses, as it were, and in a varied manner, in the rest of Ariosto's lyric work, and will therefore also play an important role in the following chapters of this book.

---

138 Floriani 1988, p. 14.

139 Godioli 2010, p. 120.

Chapter II

ARIOSTO, THE LYRIC LOVER

Preamble

In the poems analysed in the previous chapter, the speaker was entirely moulded by love, a state before which any duty took second place. It is now time to delve deeper into the subject, in order to understand more about the type of love relationship Ariosto envisages in his *rime*. Once again, this is a theme that has often been considered in relation to the *Furioso,* although it is essentially – constitutionally, one may say – lyric, and indeed the fundamental contribution of this genre, especially of the lyric poetry of Petrarchan descent and of the love elegy, to Ariosto's chivalric-epic poem has been observed by many scholars.[1]

Throughout the *rime*, the theme is attributed a particular complexity: the reader is shown all the possible degrees and nuances of the experience of love and, as a consequence, is presented with a highly multifaceted speaking subject. This is certainly due to the status of the corpus itself as a 'layered' compilation of poems, but it is also a result of both Ariosto's personal inclination (this is also evident in the *Furioso*, where his propensity to maintain the ambivalence of the emotion of love emerges fully) and of the influences he received.

Ariosto's interest in investigating 'love cases' emerges already from two capitoli that very probably belong to his youthful output,[2] and which he kept on in **Vr**. XLIV (*Piaccia a cui piace, et chi lodar vuol lodi*) and XLVI (*Chi pensa quanto il bel disio d'amore*) share the same structure, and their contents

---

[1] I will mention in particular Cabani 1990; Matarrese 2005; Praloran 2005. Pich 2015 provides a radical interpretation of the entire *Furioso* by arguing that its narrative is embedded in a story, that of the Narrator, whose nature is essentially lyric (see Chapter I, 6). Other studies will be cited where relevant.

[2] See Cabani 2016, p. 121, who in turn takes up a hypothesis formulated by Bigi and Fatini.

mirror one another: both are organised as a series of counterarguments on the part of the speaker to the objections against his choice of life, in XLIV for, and in XLVI against love.[3]

> Piaccia a cui piace, et chi lodar vuol lodi,
> et chiami vita libera et sicura
> trovarsi fuor de gli amorosi nodi,
> ch'io per me stimo chiuso in sepultura
> ogni spirto che alberghi in petto, dove
> non stilli Amor la sua vivace cura.
>
> (*Rime del canzoniere*, XLIV 1-6)

> Chi pensa quanto il bel disio d'amore
> un spirto pelegrin tenga sublime,
> non voria non haverne acceso il core;
> se pensa poi che quel tanto n'opprime
> che l'util proprio e il vero ben s'oblia,
> piange in van del suo ardor le cagion prime.
>
> (*Rime del canzoniere*, XLVI 1-6)

The specularity between the two texts, and their development as lists of arguments in support of opposite theses (set out in the form of an adversarial debate), may be seen as following the genre of the *tenzone*. It also recalls the dialogue form, and in particular the *Asolani*, a fundamental reference point for early sixteenth-century writers, which offers a systematisation of the various possible positions that may be taken on the subject of love.[4] The first book of Bembo's treatise, which articulates Perottino's arguments against love, and the second book, dominated by Gismondo's celebration of it, mirror each other closely in the layout and organisation of their contents:[5] they are, therefore, linked in a manner that is very similar to that of Ariosto's capitoli. If we focus on XLVI, furthermore, another genre – which in turn exerted its influence over Bembo – also comes to

---

3 Comboni 2000, p. 298 speaks of a 'disposizione chiastica che lega saldamente i due testi in questione'. Note that in **Vr** the presence of XLV (for which see Chapter I) between the two poems probably aims at anticipating the speaker's renunciation of love in XLVI. It should also be observed that the quoted passage from XLIV echoes *Amorum libri tres*, I 1,12-14: 'Ma certo chi nel fior de' soi primi anni / sanza caldo de amore il tempo passa, / se in vista è vivo, vivo è sanza core' (this has been noted by Zampese 2000, p. 477).

4 On the dialogic form in the *Asolani*, see Berra 1996, pp. 45-46 (which provides a rich bibliography); Bolzoni 2010. On Cinquecento love dialogues, see at least Tateo 1990*bis*; Quondam 1995; Masi 1996; Favaro 2012.

5 See Berra 1996, pp. 193-194.

mind: the *dialogo antierotico*, already mentioned in Chapter I. This was especially popular during the Quattrocento (one of its first examples being Alberti's *Deifira*) and other examples may be instanced toward the close of the century, such as Pietro Edo's *Antierotica, sive de amoris generibus* (1492) or Battista Fregoso's *Anteros* (1496). Its interlocutors are typically an 'elegiac' lover, in the thrall of *aegritudo amoris*, and a friend who tries, and often succeeds, to make him fall out of love by means of rational arguments, which are accorded the status of a medical cure (thus explaining the frequent borrowings from Ovid's *Remedia amoris* or from actual medical theories).[6]

The antierotic genre seems moreover to have exerted its influence on a capitolo *extravagante*, XXIII in Fatini's edition, which also pivots on a rigid rhetorical structure, as a tercet in which the speaker re-evokes the pain and suffering he has endured on account of his beloved is followed by another in which he spurs himself on to place indignation where once there reigned desperation:

> Non è più tempo ormai sperar ch'io pieghi
> un'alma altiera, un'indurata spoglia,
> con lunga servitù, con lunghi prieghi;
> ma ben tempo è sperar ch'un sdegno scioglia
> il laccio in che mi prese, e, preso, a lei
> mi diede Amor con mia perpetua doglia.
> (*Rime*, capitolo XXIII ed. Fatini, ll. 1-6)

Another capitolo by Ariosto, also not included in the 'canzoniere', *Sì come a primavera è dato il verno* (XXV ed. Fatini), develops an analytical description of Jealousy, the natural companion of Love. The list of the opposite effects these passions exert on the human soul is framed by an anaphoric pattern:

> Lui [= Amor] con speranza mostra lieta faccia,
> lei [= Gelosia] con desperazion trista ti affronta,
> lui cerca di piacer, lei che dispiaccia.
> Lui quel ch'agrada sol intende e conta,
> lei rapresenta sempre offesa e scorno,
> lui sempre al ben, lei sempre al mal fu pronta.
> (*Rime*, capitolo XXV ed. Fatini, ll. 7-12)

While the technique of the personification of sentiments was well-established since Late Antiquity, the specific focus on Jealousy saw a num-

[6] On this genre see CRACOLICI 2001; DILEMMI 2000*bis*, pp. 236-243. On the figure of Anteros, see also below, section 2.

ber of antecedents in the Quattrocento tradition, among which should be mentioned its description in Lorenzo il Magnifico's *Selve*,[7] and in a capitolo by Gaspare Visconti (who probably took inspiration from Lorenzo himself).[8] Furthermore, two capitoli from Boiardo's *Tarocchi* describing Love and Jealousy deserve particular note, as they resemble Ariosto's poem in its use of the anaphora:

> Amore, un che cum te cerchi bon stato,
> sollicito, animoso e prompto sia,
> ché nel fin a chi dura el pregio è dato.
> Amor, dubio non è che gelosia
> in qualche parte ognor non te acompagni:
> ma poca è bona, e troppa cosa è ria.
>
> (*Tarocchi*, 2, ll. 1-6)

> Gelosia un vero amor non po' smarrire,
> ché si uno amante va cum pura fede,
> Amor il premia al fin del suo servire.
> Gelosia è dura cosa, ove esser vede
> commodo al concorrente dello amore:
> ché al spesso supplicar segue merzede.
>
> (*ibid.*, 4, ll. 1-6)

It may be said that Ariosto's analytic take on the subject of love, despite being influenced by earlier authors, is also the result of what may be termed his own personal poetics. Jealousy, for instance, seems to be a subject particularly dear to him. This is proved by its prominence in the *Furioso*, where, besides permeating many of the characters' vicissitudes, it is on two occasions represented as a personification,[9] and is given a lengthy description in the proem to canto XXXI, through an analysis of feelings

---

[7] LORENZO DE' MEDICI, *Selva seconda*, oct. 39-49; see in particular 46: 'D'ombre vane e pensier tristi si pasce: / rode un cor sempre l'infelice bocca; / e come è consumato, allor rinasce: / o miser quel a cui tal sorte tocca! / Nelle sue prime cune e nelle fasce, / nel petto tristo invidia, odio trabocca. / Fugge sempre ove il mio bel Sole arriva, / né si parte però la morte viva'.

[8] See VISCONTI, *I canzonieri*, XLVI (capitolo 4); this poem, written in a female voice, presents a description of the effects on the speaker of the personified Jealousy (see, for instance, ll. 73-79: 'Vidi una smorta et increspata vechia / ch'avea cento ochi e ognun lacrime versa, / longa e deforme l'una e l'altra orechia; / la vesta era del pianto suo conspersa, / de incerto stame e de colore incerto, / in un bizzarro cogitar summersa'; ll. 94-96: 'Ella inalzando la sua faccia austera / incominciò: – Germana son d'Amore, / e d'ogni suo subiecto consigliera').

[9] 'Gelosia' is part of the cortege of Discordia in *Fur.*, XVI 28-33 AB; XVIII C; it reappears as 'un strano mostro in feminil figura', fighting against Rinaldo, in *Fur.*, XXXVIII 43-54 A; XXXVIII 46-57 B; XLII 46-57 C.

that closely echoes that of capitoli XLIV and XLVI.[10] Moreover, it should not escape attention that the rigid rhetorical schemes of the three capitoli seen above look odd even by the standards of courtly poets, where similar patterns are normally restricted to a limited portion of the text: perhaps a sign that Ariosto, in his youthful verses, was searching for a 'formal' equivalent to express the articulations of the emotion of love.

This propensity is all the more evident in his mature lyric poems, where it is backed by a more skillful technique. As anticipated in the Introduction, when it came to arranging the poems for **Vr**, Ariosto apparently tried to create a narrative, but in fact, and despite the presence of thematic connections, the overall unfolding of the 'story' of **Vr**'s poetic speaker is anything but straightforward. This has been described by Bozzetti as a transition from an initial state of restlessness caused by conflicting sentiments, 'nel loro rampollare l'uno dall'altro e nel loro mutevole avvicendarsi e sopraffarsi', through a phase of satisfaction in love, to a new 'tumultuoso scontrarsi di certezze e dubbi, sospetti e proteste e riconferme' that eventually gives way to a wiser perspective.[11] Following the new ordering of the central capitoli proposed by Volta 2019, this specific logical sequence may be reconsidered. In any case, what we see is an ever-changing psychological dynamic involving desire, emotions, and reason, whose interplay Ariosto chooses to display from the very first poem of the collection:

O messaggi del cor, sospiri ardenti,
o lacrime che 'l giorno io celo a pena,
o prieghi sparsi in non feconda arena,
o del mio ingiusto mal giusti lamenti,
o sempre in un voler pensieri intenti,
o desir' che ragion mai non rafrena,
o speranze che Amor drieto si mena,
quando a gran' salti et quando a passi lenti;
serà che cessi o che s'allenti mai
vostro lungo travaglio e il mio martire,
o pur fia l'uno et l'altro insieme eterno?

10 The textual similarities between the capitoli and the proem have been noted by Cabani 2016, pp. 121-122. Here I will only quote the first octave of the latter, namely *Fur.*, XXIX 1 AB XXXI C: 'Che dolce più, che più giocondo stato / saria di quel d'un amoroso core? / che viver più felice e più beato, / che ritrovarsi in servitù d'Amore? / se non fosse l'uom sempre stimulato / da quel sospetto rio, da quel timore, / da quel martìr, da quella frenesia, / da quella rabbia detta gelosia'. The description runs for several stanzas, as the narrator compares the states of mind of those who do and those who do not feel jealousy (it is here especially that the textual contacts with the two capitoli occur, to the point that the hypothesis of an actual borrowing may be advanced).

11 Bozzetti 1985, pp. 92-93.

Che fia non so; ma ben chiaro discerno
che mio poco consiglio et troppo ardire
soli posso incolpar ch'io viva in guai.

(*Rime del canzoniere*, I)

Both the *progressione del senso* of **Vr** and its *punto α* – to use the parametres laid out by Comboni – Zanato 2017 – comply to some extent with the Quattrocento canzonieri. In these, too, as the two scholars observe, the 'plot' is not always clear-cut. For instance, in some canzonieri only the beginning shows a clear narrative progression, while others adopt a sort of 'circular structure' and end up repeating very similar situations.[12] As for Ariosto's *punto α*, scholars have often pointed out that this sonnet (an exercise in the imitation of *Rvf*, CLXI, for which several parallels may be found among Ariosto's contemporaries)[13] is unsuited to the proemial position. Indeed, they write, the fact that Ariosto refrains from any repentance and starts off *in medias res* (with the lyric subject still experiencing to the full the alternating vicissitudes of love) sets his sonnet apart from the standard incipitarian poems of Renaissance canzonieri, which customarily follow *Rvf*, I and, accordingly, display a discrepancy between the past – when love was experienced – and the present, which rejects this experience defining it as an 'errore'.[14] These scholars, however, examined only a number of examples as a touchstone for Ariosto, and if the scope of the investigation is extended to the whole of the Quattrocento repertoire, the anomaly will appear less marked. Indeed, from Comboni and Zanato's comprehensive comparison of the fifteenth-century *punti α* it emerges that less than one-fifth features the word 'errore', and a mere eighth of them clearly places

---

[12] Comboni – Zanato 2017, XXVIII-XXIX; see also Introduction, 3.

[13] A number of these (which include examples by Giusto de' Conti, Tebaldeo, and Sannazaro) are listed by Dilemmi 2000, p. 485. I will call attention especially to Sannazaro, *Sonetti et canzoni*, LXXXI, ll. 1-4: 'Interditte speranze e van desio, / pensier fallaci, ingorde e cieche voglie, / lacrime triste, e voi, sospiri e doglie, / date ormai pace al lasso viver mio'. The ultimate model is *Rvf*, CLXI, ll. 1-8: 'O passi sparsi, o pensier' vaghi et pronti, / o tenace memoria, o fero ardore, / o possente desire, o debil core, / oi occhi miei, occhi non già, ma fonti! / O fronde, honor de le famose fronti, / o sola insegna al gemino valore! / O faticosa vita, o dolce errore, / che mi fate ir cercando piagge et monti!'. Other borrowings from Petrarch in Ariosto's poem are listed in Bozzetti – Vela 2000, p. 225. Also worth mentioning as another important poetic exposition of the *status amantis* is Bembo, *Le rime*, 6, ll. 1-8: 'Moderati desiri, immenso ardore, / speme, voce, color cangiati spesso, / veder, ove si miri, un volto impresso, / et viver pur del cibo onde si more, / mostrar a duo begli occhi aperto il core, / far de le voglie altrui legge a se stesso, / con la lingua et lo stil lunge et da presso / gir procacciando a la sua donna honore'.

[14] Cabani 2016, pp. 100-101; Dilemmi 2000, pp. 480-483.

the experience of love in the past. Moreover, little attention is paid to Petrarch's *vergogna*, to his *mutatio animi* and to his being a *fabula vulgi*. These are signs that these poets 'non considerano, se non blandamente, l'amore una colpa di cui vergognarsi [...] dunque in esso perseverano, senza una sincera volontà di cambiamento'.[15] In this light we may say, at least judging from the beginning of **Vr**, that Bozzetti was right in ascribing to Ariosto an 'affermazione di fedeltà'[16] towards the poets writing in the Po valley in the previous generation.

The 'simultaneity' we note in sonnet I – in other words, the fact that the poetic subject is speaking at the time of the (psychological) events it describes – in fact applies to most of Ariosto's love lyrics. This confirms a characteristic of the *rime* that had already emerged in the previous chapter, namely, their connection to the present: not in the sense that Ariosto's poetry is, strictly speaking, 'occasional' (that is, meaningful only in relation to its circumstances of writing), but rather in the sense that he privileges the investigation of ongoing feelings and situations over the dimension of recollection.

My analysis, in what follows of this chapter, of the nuances Ariosto attributes to the love relationship will not be based on the order of **Vr**, this being a problematic, and to some extent artificial order. Rather, it will identify a number of relevant aspects that are found throughout Ariosto's lyric output, including some of his uncollected poems. I will, nevertheless, be providing references to the poems' arrangement in **Vr** in a limited number of cases, where this serves to illuminate additional meanings. Another point that I will not be primarily focusing on is the matter of whether the poems were actually inspired by Ariosto's relationship with a woman, and in what cases that woman should be identified as Alessandra Benucci. As mentioned in the Introduction, it is difficult to provide a satisfactory answer to this question. Actually, many poems included in **Vr** are entirely justifiable as based on literary tradition, without the need to infer the presence of a real woman behind them. Of course, it is still possible that Ariosto did have Alessandra in mind, and that he chose to endow her with a stylised representation in order to conceal her identity, at a stage in which their relationship could not be publicised. But although in general I will not be tackling this problem, the supposed dedication to Alessandra of the few poems exclusively included in **F** and/or **Mn** is a case in which I will make an exception, as these lyrics display unique (and unifying) stylistic choices,

---

15 Comboni – Zanato 2017, XIX-XX.

16 See Introduction, 3.

which acquire an even greater significance if one posits that they are inspired by Alessandra. Additionally, this endorses Finazzi's assumption (see Introduction, 1) that it was not **Vr**, but rather Ariosto's later attempt at a canzoniere that was dedicated to his life companion.

1. Love encounters: a classical theme

At a thematic level, a striking characteristic of Ariosto's lyric poems is the presence, in some of them, of references to encounters between lovers. In this respect the poet is following not so the celebration of Eros pursued in the 'popular' genres, such as the *poesia comico-realistica* or Carnival poetry, but rather a tradition stemming from Latin love elegy. To exhaustively retrace its history is beyond the scope of this book. I shall just note that the theme of the amorous meeting is passed down from the Middle Ages (the encounter between Troiolo and Criseida in Boccaccio's *Filostrato* comes to mind)[17] to the Quattrocento, a century whose lyric repertoire is, as Bartolomeo 2012 shows, most often permeated by a sensual vein. It was down to each individual poet to choose whether to simply allude to the erotic situations (see, for instance, the case of Boiardo),[18] or to render them explicit, sometimes under the influence of a classical source: the latter is the case of Cosmico's canzone CCCVII, where the poet shamelessly asks his beloved to open the door to him at night, while her husband is sleeping (in this theme he is following a poem by Tibullus).[19]

The theme is foregrounded by Ariosto most explicitly in capitoli XXI and XXII, which are first-person accounts of, respectively, a fortunate and an unsuccessful night of love, and are among the poems by Ariosto which traditionally received most critical praise. The fortune of capitolo XXI, *O più che 'l giorno a me lucida et chiara*, is proved by its rich tradition (it features in thirty-five testimonies).[20] It was written either just before the beginning

---

17 Boccaccio, *Filostrato*, III 31-32: 'Lungo sarebbe a raccontar la festa, / ed impossibile a dire il diletto / che 'nsieme preser pervenuti in questa; / ei si spogliaro ed entraron nel letto, / dove la donna nell'ultima vesta / rimasa già, con piacevole detto / gli disse: – Spogliomi io? Le nuove spose / son la notte primiera vergognose. // A cui Troiolo disse: – Anima mia, / io te ne priego, sì ch'io t'abbi in braccio / ignuda sì come il mio cor disia. – / Ed ella allora: – Ve' ch'io me ne spaccio. – / E la camiscia sua gittata via, / nelle sue braccia si ricolse avaccio; / e strignendo l'un l'altro con fervore, / d'amor sentiron l'ultimo valore'.

18 According to Zanato 2014, p. 21, 'l'Eros di Boiardo non è mai esplicito, non si spinge a espressioni o situazioni sessualmente evidenti, come spesso accade negli elegiaci latini'.

19 The poem is quoted in Bartolomeo 2012, pp. 58-59; see also *ibid.*, p. 55.

20 Finazzi 2002-2003, p. 229.

of the sixteenth century or in its very early years, and immediately earned notoriety (indeed, an imitation of this poem was printed in the edition of Liburnio's *Selvette* as early as 1513).[21] In it, the speaker expresses his gratitude for all those things that permitted his encounter to take place: the night, the stars which refrained from shining too much, the people in the city overcome by sleep, the door that opened silently (all elements suggesting the clandestine nature of the rendezvous, 'furti d'amor', l. 4, recognisable as the the elegiac *furtivus amor*). Finally, he goes on to recall the intercourse itself and the items within the room that witnessed it, including the bed (ll. 31-33) and the lamp ('lucerna', l. 37) which lighted the scene, thus increasing the overall pleasure of the lovers:

> per te fu duplicato il mio contento,
> né veramente si pò dir perfetto
> uno amoroso gaudio a lume spento.
>
> (*Rime del canzoniere*, XXI 40-42)

In the last part of the capitolo, the speaker laments the approaching of Dawn, who forces him to leave. In fact he accuses Aurora of being envious as she cannot enjoy the same pleasure with her old husband Tithonus:

> Perché lassasti, ohimé, così per tempo
> invida Aurora il tuo Titone antico
> et del partir m'accelerasti il tempo?
> Ti potessi io, come ti son nimico,
> nocer così! Se 'l tuo vecchio t'annoia,
> ché non ti cerchi un più giovene amico?
>
> (*Rime del canzoniere*, XXI 58-63)

As already pointed out by scholars, in this poem a rich layering of models is detectable. Indeed, its ultimate source, an elegy of Propertius (II 15), had been the subject of a particular revival on the part of humanists, the most relevant works in this sense being Piccolomini's *Historia duobus amantibus*, and two poems in elegiac couplets respectively by Tito Vespasiano Strozzi (*Amica potitus, gloriatur*) and by his son Ercole (*Amica tandem potitus exsultat*).[22] The two latter also feature the final accusation (or appeal, in

---

21 See Berra 2000, pp. 180-181. Another proof of its success is its employment in the love treatise *Gradenico* by Ludovico Zuccolo, in support of the author's arguments against Platonic love (Favaro 2010, p. 128). Also Stampa, *Rime*, CIV, and Barignano, *Rime*, CXXXVII, were probably influenced specifically by Ariosto rather than by the generic *topos* of the *beata notte*.

22 They can be read in Piccolomini 2001, p. 100; Strozzi 1513, I, ff. 74*v*-76*r* and II, ff. 7*r*-8*v*. It should be observed that the first line of Propertius's poem is quoted by Equicola in an

Ercole's case) to Aurora, which may be traced back to Ovid, *Amores*, I 13 (ll. 27-44). To these Latin examples, many Italian elaborations of the theme of the *beata notte* may be added.[23] Their authors chose the form of the sonnet, so the fact that Ariosto should instead have opted for the capitolo may reveal his attempt to move closer to the Latin sources. An indication of Ariosto's skill in *imitatio* is the fact that this very capitolo was translated into Latin elegiac distichs, as testified by a little-known manuscript brought to scholarly attention by Finazzi. The translation is anonymous and might have been authored by Calcagnini.[24]

Far less popular in terms of literary reception has been capitolo XXII, *O ne' miei danni più che 'l giorno chiara*, which illustrates an opposite situation, i.e. the hindrance to an amorous encounter caused by an excess of moonlight and a surfeit of stars. This poem deserves to be reconsidered afresh, at the very least on account of its relationships with XXI,[25] whose structure it mirrors so closely that it uses the same rhyme-words in the same position in the two opening lines and resorts to the same rhetorical patterns. Indeed, in both 'notte' is described by three adjectives, and the third line expresses the overturning of an expectation:

O più che 'l giorno a me lucida et chiara,
dolce, gioconda, aventurosa notte,
quanto men ti sperai, tanto più cara!

(*Rime del canzoniere*, XXI 1-3)

O ne' miei danni più che 'l giorno chiara,
crudel, maligna et scelerata notte,
ch'io sperai dolce et hor trovo sì amara!

(*Rime del canzoniere*, XXII 1-3)

Another indication of the close relationship between the two capitoli is the presence, in both, of a vehemently indignant appeal to a god. In XXI, as

---

overview of classical examples of erotic success (*Libro de natura de amore*, *Libro primo*, f. 13*v*; see Equicola 1999, p. 223).

23 Examples are provided in Malinverni 2000, pp. 503-513: they include Lorenzo de' Medici (*Canzoniere*, CVII), Visconti (*I canzonieri*, LVI-LVII (217-218)), Tebaldeo (*Rime della vulgata*, 189). See also Comboni 2000, pp. 306-307, and Bartolomeo 2012, pp. 55-56 (on the theme in Quattrocento authors) and p. 59 (it provides the text of Cosmico, *Rime*, CLXVI, which also belongs to this tradition). Salza 1914, pp. 71-80 is the first attempt of analysis of the sources of Ariosto's capitolo.

24 Finazzi 2002-2003, p. 89 and p. 230.

25 Also according to Bozzetti 1985, p. 94, the two poems show 'connessioni [...] collaboranti allo svolgimento dello stesso tema'.

has been shown, this is Aurora, while in XXII it is the too luminous Luna, whose pity the speaker begs, reminding her of her own pleasure when visiting her beloved Endymion.[26] Like the passage that refers to Aurora this, too, is inspired by Ovid's *Amores*, I 13 (where 'Luna' is mentioned at l. 42).

This network of mutual references suggests that the two capitoli should be evaluated as a single lyric experience, or even as an actual diptych.[27] Such a configuration is sometimes found in courtly elegiac poems, the most typical case being the exchanges of epistles in terza rima between lovers, after the model of Ovid's *Heroides*.[28] I believe that one of these 'sets' of poems in particular may be recalled as a parallel case, or even a source for Ariosto: that is, Serafino Aquilano's two capitoli *Della luna* and *Dell'aurora* (which, together with a third, *Del somno*, constitute a triptych inspired by the elegiac genre, including *Amores*, I 13).[29] There, too we may find a list of appeals and curses, to the Moon and to Dawn respectively.[30] But unlike that of Aquilano, Ariosto's approach to the subject is definitely a narrative one: he is able to suggest temporality and create a sense of tension as he approaches, or tries to approach, the object of his desire. Most importantly, he suggests the context where the events take place – the city, with its myriad prying eyes:

---

26 *Rime del canzoniere*, XXII 10-12: 'Rimembriti il piacer ch'alhora havesti / d'abbraciar il tuo amante, et altro tanto / conosci che mi turbi et mi molesti'. This myth also features in *Fur.*, XVI 185,1-4 AB; XVIII C: 'La Luna a quel pregar la nube aperse / (o fosse caso o pur la tanta fede), / bella come fu allor ch'ella s'offerse, / e nuda in braccio a Endimion si diede'.

27 Other textual connections between the two poems are noted by Comboni 2000, p. 296 footnote. It should be specified that these connections should not include the fact that they appear in consecutive order in **Vr**, as such ordering is the outcome of Finazzi's reconstructive hypothesis, which cannot be entirely proved, on account of the philological problems that concern this section of the manuscript (see below).

28 This genre is analysed in Longhi 1989.

29 These are capitoli 5, 6 and 7 of Serafino Aquilano 1967.

30 I will provide some textual similarities between the two sets of poems: 'Ingrata al Sol, per cui *vai tanto altera*' (*Della luna*, l. 21) and 'Tu che *di sì gran luce altiera vai*' (*Rime del canzoniere*, XXII 7); 'di Vener bella e soi *amorosi furti*' (*Della luna*, l. 27) and 'Stelle a' *furti d'amor* soccorrer dotte' (*Rime del canzoniere*, XXI 4); 'Ma a che più dir di te la lingua mïa? / Ché io vedo ogn'hora più tua luce abonda' (*Della luna*, ll. 60-61) and 'Ma priego et parlo a chi non ode; e il giorno / s'appressa intanto' (*Rime del canzoniere*, XXII 43-44); 'Ben mi bastava Amor per *inimico* / senza le insidie tue; ma credo el fai / per non voler al mondo un solo *amico*' (*Dell'aurora*, ll. 13-15) and 'Ti potessi io, come ti son *nimico*, / nocer così! Se 'l tuo vecchio t'annoia, / ché non ti cerchi un più giovene *amico*?' (*Rime del canzoniere*, XXI 61-63); 'Ma teco, ohimè! più Cephalo non giace, / ché cercaresti rallentare el corso, / qual tanto amasti con passion tenace' (*Dell'aurora*, ll. 70-72) and 'quando al tuo pastorel nuda scendesti, / Luna, io non so s'havevi tanti rai' (*Rime del canzoniere*, XXII 8-9). Aquilano's capitolo *Della luna* was analysed, in an overview on the anti-lunar theme (for the rest especially considering late sixteenth- and early seventeenth-century poems) in Gigliucci 2001, which also makes references to Ariosto's capitolo XXII.

Ma priego et parlo a chi non ode; e il giorno
s'appressa intanto,[31] et senza frutto, ahi lasso,
hor mi lievo, hor m'accosto, hor fuggio, hor torno.
Tutto nel manto ascoso, a capo basso,
vo per intrar; poi veggio apresso o sento
chi può vedermi et m'allontano et passo.
Che deb'io far? Che posso io far tra cento
occhi, fra tanti usci et finestre aperte?
(*Rime del canzoniere*, XXII 43-50)

It should also be noted that in XXI and XXII Ariosto makes a point of exploring different possible values of the theme of light/darkness. In capitolo XXI, the night obscures the stars and is therefore seen as an ally of the poet ('minuisti il lume', l. 5). This darkness creates a rhetorical contrast with the metaphorical 'clarity of night'[32] at l. 1. Conversely, in capitolo XXII the night is filled with light and becomes, therefore, the target of the poet's curse:

Sperai ch'uscir da le cimerie grotte
tenebrosa devessi et veggio c'hai
quante lampade ha il ciel teco condotte.
(*Rime del canzoniere*, XXII 4-6)

Ariosto refers to the moon and the stars through the metaphorical word 'lampade', normally used for an artificial source of light,[33] thus reminding the reader of the 'lucerna' which lights up the room in XXI. Through this mirroring, and through the opposition between different values of light, he is contrasting a public context with the intimacy of the site where love takes place: 'o camera che poi così m'affidi!' (*Rime del canzoniere*, XXI 18).

There are two other poems by Ariosto, sonnets XVIII and XIX – both probably composed at the time of the compilation of **Vr** –, which develop the theme of the room as the place where the satisfaction of love is made possible and all the tensions that torment the poetic subject come to an end. What makes them remarkable is that this clearly non-Petrarchan

---

31 For this syntagm, see Ovid, *Amores*, I 11,15: 'dum loquor hora fugit' (also echoed by Ariosto in *Rime del canzoniere*, XXIX 22-23: see Chapter I, 5).

32 On the oxymoronic juxtaposition of light and darkness in Italian lyric poetry up to the Renaissance, see the list compiled by Gigliucci 2004, pp. 251-254. This paradoxical theme is sometimes mingled by poets with the *topos* of the lady as the Sun. See, for example, Tebaldeo, *Rime della vulgata*, 301,1-4: 'Ove è il bel sol che cum sua luce chiara / te facea giorno a meza nocte oscura, / nuda fenestra, che già tanto dura / me fusti a torto, e sì sdegnosa e avara?'

33 This meaning is already in *Par.*, XVII 5: 'santa lampa'.

theme is here worked into a poetic situation that is respectful of Petrarchan conventions in terms of language, style, and imagery. We shall start by looking at the following:

> O sicuro, secreto et fidel porto,
> dove fuor di gran pelago due stelle,
> le più chiare del cielo et le più belle,
> dopo una lunga et cieca via m'han scorto;
> hora io perdono al vento e al mare il torto,
> che m'hanno con gravissime procelle
> fatto sin qui, poiché, se non per quelle,
> io non potea fruir tanto conforto.
> O caro albergo, o cameretta cara
> ch'in queste dolci tenebre mi servi
> a goder d'ogni sol notte più chiara:
> scorda hora i torti e i sdegni acri et protervi,
> ché tal mercé, cor mio, ti si prepara
> che appagarà quanto hai servito et servi.
>
> (*Rime del canzoniere*, XVIII)

This sonnet, too, tackles the light/darkness contrast, by resorting to the traditional Petrarchan metaphor of the woman's eyes as guiding lights and, conversely, of the poet himself as blind unless he is in their presence. This motif is intertwined with another leading image of the *Fragmenta*, namely, the safe harbour, an archetypal symbol (with an age-long tradition)[34] of man's final state of inner peace. Ariosto's reference to the 'cameretta' suggests that the specific Petrarchan poem he is drawing from is *Rvf*, CCXXXIV, *O cameretta che già fosti un porto* – where the diminutive indicates the poet's little room, which (like his 'letticciuol', l. 5) is no longer able to give him rest.[35] Only at l. 9 does Ariosto's equation between harbour and room become clear, thus releasing the tension created by this delayed explanation: it should be noted that the feeling of expectation Ariosto is able to elicit in the reader corresponds to the state of mind of the speaker himself ('ti si prepara', l. 13).

In this poem, however, the Petrarchan metaphor is completely refashioned: the room is here a place of delight, which, after the 'procelle' (sym-

---

[34] On the nautical metaphor in poetry a fundamental reference is Curtius 2013, pp. 128-130. This, however, mainly examines the image in its metaliterary value (that of Dante's 'navicella del mio ingegno', also employed by Ariosto himself in the final canto of the *Furioso*).

[35] The room as a place where secret tears are shed had of course a long tradition: see at least *Vita nuova*, XII, XIV, XXIII.

bolising the long hesitation on the part of the woman), is finally ready to welcome the two lovers.[36] At this point, Ariosto introduces what we may regard as a textual connection with capitolo XXI, namely, the oxymoronic mentions of sweet darkness and bright night (ll. 10-11). As also noted by Cabani, who regards this sonnet as actually a parody of the Petrarchan code,[37] the theme of the room also appears when Ruggiero waits for Alcina 'in una adorna e fresca cameretta' (*Fur.*, VII 22,7 ABC). Here, the hero's anxiety as he waits is remarkably depicted over several octaves, and the arrival of Alcina is accompanied by the metaphors of 'ridenti stelle' (27,2) and of navigation ('Or sino agli occhi ben nuota nel golfo / delle delizie e de le cose belle', 27,5-6). Moreover, Ariosto subtly communicates the privacy afforded by the place: 'Queste cose là dentro eran secrete, / o se pur non secrete, almen taciute' (30,1-2).

Also the ultimate meaning of sonnet XIX is most probably a variation on the theme of the 'little room':

> Aventuroso carcere soave,
> dove né per furor né per dispetto,
> ma per amor et per pietà distretto
> la bella et dolce mia nemica m'have,
> li altri prigioni al volger de la chiave
> s'attristano, io m'allegro, ché diletto
> et non martir, vita et non morte aspetto;
> né giudice sever né legge grave,
> ma benigne accoglienze, ma complessi
> licentiosi, ma parole sciolte
> da ogni fren, ma risi, vezzi et giuochi;
> ma dolci baci dolcemente impressi
> ben mille et mille et mille et mille volte,
> et se potran contarsi ancho fien pochi.
>
> (*Rime del canzoniere*, XIX)

This poem exemplifies many innovative aspects of Ariosto's lyric poetry, and will therefore be discussed again later. What I wish to focus on now is that the paradoxical image of the delightful prison may hint at the room itself. This meaning is supported by the poem's context in **Vr**. Indeed, it is placed immediately after XVIII, but it is also linked to it by a common feeling of tension and expectation ('aspetto', l. 7). Furthermore, a similar

---

36 Among the previous employments of a 'cameretta' as a setting for erotic encounters, I will only recall that in *Decameron*, IX 6.

37 Cabani 2016, p. 114.

rhetorical development underlies the two poems: the two quatrains, composed by words and syntagms clearly recalling the *Fragmenta*, and therefore inducing in the reader the impression of a straightforwardly Petrarchan poem, are followed by the unfolding of the actual theme in the tercets.[38] Moreover, at l. 9 of both we find a semantic upending of a word used in the tradition of *poesia aulica*, namely 'cameretta' in XVIII and 'accoglienze'[39] in XIX, the latter being employed to signify the amorous embraces. Note that in XIX a real stylistic shift occurs, as the tercets (as well as the last line of the quatrains) lose all connections with Petrarch and turn instead to recognisable classical models, i.e. Catullus and Propertius.[40]

Two more elements enhance the sensual feel of this sonnet. One is the characterisation of the woman as endowed with 'pietà' (l. 3): it is implied that her previous coldness (cp. 'sdegni acri et protervi', XVIII 12) in the end turns to sympathy, and what may easily be seen as sexual availability in response to the poet's endurance. The other is the description of the enjoyment of love in first tercet, which feels similar to a passage of capitolo XXI where the word 'complessi' is also found:

> O complessi iterati, che con tanti
> nodi cingeste i fianchi, il petto, il collo
> che non ne fan più l'edere o li acanti!
> Bocca ove ambrosia libo, né satollo
> mai me ritorno; o dolce lingua, o humore
> per cui l'arso mio cor bagno et rimmollo.
>
> (*Rime del canzoniere*, XXI 19-24)[41]

All these points suggest a spatial continuity between the events taking place in the two sonnets and in capitolo XXI, and show Ariosto's concern with the poetic exploration of the private space, displaying what may be called a 'realistic' taste.

---

38 On this point, see RONCACCIA 2012, p. 154 (the article is a close reading of sonnet XIX).

39 See CINO, canzone CXXIII, l. 15: 'oimè, dolce accoglienza'; *Purg.*, VII 1: 'Poscia che l'accoglienze oneste e liete'; *Rvf*, CCCXLIII 9: 'O che dolci accoglienze, et caste, et pie'.

40 CATULLUS, V 2: 'rumoresque senum severiorum' (and *Rime del canzoniere*, XIX 8); ll. 7-9: 'da mi basia mille, deinde centum / dein mille altera, dein secunda centum, / deinde usque altera mille, deinde centum' (and ll. 12-13 of Ariosto's poem); PROPERTIUS, II 15,50: 'omnia si dederis oscula pauca dabis' (and l. 14 of Ariosto's poem).

41 The theme of the successful achievement of erotic goals is also developed by Ariosto in the Latin poem XVII (*De Megilla*), which lingers on the obstacles that have ultimately been overcome ('Lux, qua plena meis amplaque gaudia / commuto lacrimis, quaque laboribus / munus grande reporto!', ll. 37-39) and mentions 'lusus, illecebras, delitias, iocos, / risus, quicquid et almo est / regno dulce Cupidinum' (ll. 26-28).

Anyone looking at the pages that, in **Vr**, feature the two capitoli and the two sonnets we have considered, would notice at ff. 11*v*-12*v*, between XIX and the beginning of XXI, the last part (ll. 22-46) of another capitolo, *Forza è ch'al fine scopra et che si veggia*, whose subject is the need for the speaker to keep silent on the true cause of his extreme happiness. Further portions of this poem are scattered in later pages of the manuscript. This disorder must be ascribed to a mistake of the copyist, who was transcribing from wrongly ordered quires: the same mistake also caused the displacement of part of the text of XXII. Whether these poems were actually related to each other in the antigraph is, therefore, difficult to say. The reconstructive hypothesis put forward by Bozzetti sees *Forza è ch'al fine* as number thirty, and *O ne' miei danni più che 'l giorno chiara* as number twenty-four: consequently, he excluded both poems from the kernel – sonnets XVIII e XIX and the capitolo on the 'beata notte' – that formed, according to his interpretation, an important narrative linkage (that is the 'realisation' of the love relationship). On the other hand, Finazzi's placing of *Forza è ch'al fine* at number twenty – I therefore also refer to it as XX – and *O ne' miei danni* at number XXII, identifies a different narrative sequence, and, most importantly, assimilates XX into the kernel of poems that form the narrative link. She does not, however, furnish a literary, but only a philological explanation for this ordering.[42] According to Volta, the narrative link must be entirely dismantled: *O ne' miei danni* must be pushed forward to number thirty, and the two sonnets, XVIII and XIX, are followed by other capitoli, before one comes to *Forza è ch'al fine* (at number twenty-five) and *O più che 'l giorno a me lucida et chiara* (twenty-six).

What it is interesting to point out here is that in both Finazzi's and Volta's hypotheses, *Forza è ch'al fine* is contiguous to the capitolo on the 'notte d'amore'. I shall add that, although this poem was probably not written for the canzoniere,[43] Ariosto's decision to place *Forza* just before XXI makes a lot of sense not only from a philological point of view, but also on the level of meaning. As I mentioned before, here the poet needs, in order to keep envy at bay, to conceal his joy – of a clearly amorous nature –, which, nevertheless, manifests itself powerfully through real physical symptoms:

> Forza è ch'al fine scopra et che si veggia
> il gaudio mio dianzi a gran pena ascoso,
> anchor ch'io sappia che tacer si deggia,

---

[42] A table of the contents of **Vr**, page by page, is found in Finazzi 2002-2003, p. 130. A table with the provisional reconstruction of its antigraph is *ibid.*, 131; the problem is discussed *ibid.*, 133-136.

[43] Indeed, it has also come down to us in a slightly different version (*ibid.*, pp. 226-227).

et quanto dirlo altrui sia periglioso:
perché sempre chi ascolta è più proclive
ad invidiar che ad esserne gioioso.

(*Rime del canzoniere*, XX 1-6)

This articulation of the theme of silence has several antecedents in the courtly repertoire, among which capitolo XXII of Correggio's *Rime extravaganti* (*Vive in me più che mai quel gran disio*) stands out.[44] Here, too, the poet is unwilling to reveal the cause of his happiness, to avoid the 'ardente invidia maculata e accesa' (l. 9) of Fortuna. Compared to Correggio, Ariosto focuses in more detail on the physical manifestation of joy:

Tentano altro camin, poi ch'io li exclusi
da quel che per la bocca, da chi viene
dal petto, par che per più trito s'usi.
Di passar quindi homai tolta ogni spene,
se ne vengon per gli occhi et per la fronte,
dove raro, o non mai, guardia si tiene

(*Rime del canzoniere*, XX 28-33)

In the end, the speaker allows these outward signs to finally manifest themselves, but still strives to hide the origin of his happiness:

Sappil chi 'l vuol saper, ch'io son sì pieno,
sì colmo di leticia et di contento
che non lo cape a una gran parte il seno.
Ma la cagion del gran piacer ch'io sento
non vuo' che soni voce o snodi lingua;
et faccia Dio, se mai di ciò mi pento,
che l'una svelta sia, l'altra s'extingua.

(*Rime del canzoniere*, XX 40-46)

Rinaldi, who mentions this poem in his overview of the occurrences of the theme of silence in Ariosto's lyrics, ascribes it to the vernacular tradition of the *segni d'amore* which 'out' the speaker as a lover, exposing him to the 'manifesto accorger de le genti' (*Rvf*, XXXV 6). He also notes, however, that Ariosto's use of this tradition is quite personal, since in the most common version of this motif the lover is unrequited: he concludes that

44 This link had been noted by Comboni 2000, p. 304; Rinaldi 2000, p. 335. It should also be noted that the opening syntagm of Ariosto's capitolo, 'Forza è', is recurrent in court poetry and correspondences may be found, among others, in Tebaldeo, Serafino and Correggio (Finazzi 2002-2003, p. 227).

the true highlight of the capitolo is rather the 'forte sottolineatura morale' conferred by the motif of silence, traditionally associated with wisdom.[45] The emphasis Rinaldi places on this point is important and marks one relevant aspect of Ariosto's humanist background (which I shall be examining in greater detail in Chapter III, 4). Among the texts where the theme features, and which may have been a source for Ariosto, I shall mention in particular one of Erasmus's *Adagia* (*In sinu gaudere*). Here Erasmus resorts to several examples drawn from the classics in order to underline the concept of the 'silent joy'. In this context he specifically refers to the bosom as the place where the emotion of love is enclosed – cp. *Rime del canzoniere*, XX 42: 'che non lo cape a una gran parte il seno' –, a sealed receptacle from whence no sign of the lover's joy transpires:

> In sinu gaudere est tacitam apud se voluptatem sentire neque quod vulgo faciunt foras proferre gaudii notas. Tibullus: 'Qui sapit, in tacito gaudeat ille sinu'. Propertius item: 'In tacito cohibe gaudia clausa sinu'. Idem: 'Alter in alterius mutua flere sinu'. De amantibus dictum, qui secretas animi curas invicem effundunt, quas aliis caelant tamen. [...] Perinde dictum est in sinu, quasi dicas: in pectore tuo, non in labiis aut fronte, quibus partibus vulgus consuevit prodere quid in animi penetralibus occultat. (*Adagia*, 213)

This aside, however, I would suggest that the point of the poem is precisely the 'unsaid': the reason for the joy, which the poet challenges his readers to guess. The probability that the cause of this happiness may be erotic success turns into certainty following a survey of other possible sources, and especially two consecutive sonnets by Boiardo, *Amorum libri tres*, I 52 and I 53. In the former, Boiardo limits himself to general claims of the 'alegreza del mio stato' (l. 3), without specifying its cause. It is only in the latter that, reprising the theme and also introducing the motif of the 'segni d'amore',

> La smisurata et incredibil voglia,
> che dentro fu renchiusa nel mio core,
> non potendo capervi, esce de fore,
> e mostra altrui cantando la mia zoglia.
>
> (*Amorum libri tres*, I 53,1-4)

also praises his own 'Felice bracia' (l. 9), thus revealing the erotic nature of his 'ben passato' (l. 14). In turn, this poem is influenced by the ballata re-

---

[45] Rinaldi 2000, pp. 332-335.

cited by Panfilo that concludes the eighth day of Boccaccio's *Decameron*.[46] Note that its l. 7 is exactly replicated at l. 3 of Boiardo's poem:

> L'abondante allegrezza ch'è nel core,
> dell'alta gioia e cara
> nella qual m'hai recato,
> non potendo capervi esce di fore,
> e nella faccia chiara
> mostra 'l mio lieto stato; [...]
>
> (*Decameron*, VIII 4-9)

Panfilo, too, needs to conceal his joy. In the last stanza he alludes to the involvement of 'braccia' (l. 22), although his audience fails to decipher this confused passage: 'quantunque varii varie cose andassero imaginando, niun per ciò alla verità del fatto pervenne'. Through this ballata, which was certainly known by Ariosto (as well as by Boiardo and Correggio), it is possible to read XX as being ultimately a poem on sensual love. This bears out Finazzi's and Volta's hypotheses regarding its close association with capitolo XXI, where the meeting has just taken place and the poet, no longer able to keep silent, finally gives vent to his happiness.

2. *Fides* and constancy

After assessing the significance of the theme of sensual love in Ariosto's lyrics, we must now widen the perspective and investigate how the psychological aspects of the love relationship are treated. Predictably, the Latin love elegy plays a crucial role in shaping the amorous situations, some of which may be regarded as truly genre-defining: the poet/lover experiences the driving force of desire, frustration at the woman's sudden coldness, fear of her infidelity, sorrow for her absence (this last emotion has been examined in Chapter I). We will shortly see, however, that Ariosto's interpretation of these *topoi* is quite free, as is his refashioning of the 'slavery of love' (*servitium amoris*), the typical attitude of the elegiac lover – and of his forerunners or pioneers, such as Catullus – which is characterised by an inversion of the relationship between power and gender that places the woman in psychological control of the affair.[47]

---

[46] On this point, see Tissoni Benvenuti 2003, pp. 92-93; Zanato 2014, p. 37. A classical antecedent for this theme is Ovid, *Amores* II 12,1-2: 'Ite triumphales circum mea tempora laurus! / Vicimus: in nostro est, ecce, Corinna sinu'.

[47] The studies on this subject are very numerous; I will only recall Fulkerson 2013 (on

In this context, a concept that seems to be endowed with a particularly key role within the world of the *rime* is the classical notion of faith, or *fides*. This must be understood as a mutual ethical bond between the two lovers, by which both equally ought to abide. The principle of fidelity may qualify as fully Ariostean as it also regulates several plots of the *Furioso*, where it applies not only to love situations, but more in general to social relationships, playing a fundamental role in the chivalric system of values. It must be seen, as Ascoli puts it, as a 'normative bond for all interpersonal and institutional relationships, from the erotic to the diplomatic, and one that sealed a connection between the inner person and the society and state of which he [...] is a part'.[48] Cabani and Favaro more than any other scholar have pointed out the relevance of *fides* also in Ariosto's lyric poems.[49] Nevertheless, it is worthwhile to further investigate the matter and examine in greater detail the poems in which it features.

Ariosto's interest in this theme probably developed in his youthful years. This is demonstrated by an uncollected capitolo, XX ed. Fatini (*Quel fervente desio, quel vero ardore*), where a vast repertory of tropes specifically connected with fidelity are explored and indeed form what may well be described as an allegorical system. More specifically, the image of the fortress is made to signify the constancy of the lover, which rules over his own soul ('ché una fondata rocca, alta e sicura, / mi guarda il regno mio, detta costanzia', ll. 7-8). The faculties aiding it and those challenging it are depicted by means of the components of the fortress itself (for instance, perseverance as the stones, endurance as its impenetrable walls)[50] and the concept of siege respectively. In the end, constancy is said to overcome all possible enemies, 'ché una rocca di fé mai non si atterra' (l. 40). Not only does such military imagery bear the mark of the elegiac concept of *militia amoris* – particularly known through its Ovidian formulation[51] and

---

the *servitium amoris*), Miller 2007 and bibliography (on the relationship between Catullus and the Roman elegists) and their bibliographies.

48 Ascoli 1997, p. 12. The concept of ethical faith in the *Furioso* is also tackled by Ascoli 1987, pp. 284-286 and *passim* (here the scholar argues for the inextricable intertwining of this concept, in Ariosto's poem, with questions of religious faith); Saccone 1968; Zatti 1990, pp. 99-105; Ascoli 2003; Bucchi 2016, pp. 274-277.

49 Cabani 2016, pp. 131-135; Favaro 2010 and 2011, pp. 103-104.

50 I will quote some tercets in full: 'Li fondamenti, ove si posa e stanzia, / son di stabilità viva fermezza; / la calce e pietre è sol perseveranzia; / l'inespugnabil mur viva fortezza; / le sue difese, scudi e bastïone, / son fé che ogni timore fugge e sprezza' (ll. 10-15); 'Castellano è un amor fermo e provato, / che scorge il tutto; li sergenti èn poi / solliciti pensier, ciascun fidato' (ll. 19-21).

51 Ovid, *Amores*, I 9 is the poem which most thoroughly develops the metaphor of the lover as a soldier (ll. 1-2: 'Militat omnis amans, et habet sua castra Cupido; / Attice, crede mihi,

deployed by Ariosto himself in one of his Latin epigrams.[52] It could also be understood as belonging to the tradition of the *rocca interiore*, especially popular in medieval literature and the subject of a monograph by Ilaria Gallinaro (GALLINARO 1999). The scholar singles out two possible versions of the theme, which had begun to take on a clear-cut physiognomy since the time of Petrarch. One is the *arx rationis*, deriving from ancient philosophers (Plato, Cicero, and Seneca), which associates the image to the self's firmness in the pursuit of virtue. The other is the *arx cordis*, which originated in late Latin literature and which presents different variations of the theme, all of which, however, underscore the irrational subservience of the poet to Love.[53] Although the *arx cordis* had become more popular in love poetry,[54] it cannot escape notice that Ariosto's use of the metaphor in this capitolo seems rather to reconnect to the *arx rationis*. The fortress should indeed be understood as the rationality of the poet, and reason and foresight are the supreme faculties presiding over the hope of success:

> Regge speranza il mastro torrïone
> sotto due guardie; una, fedel, chiamata
> prudenzia, e l'altra, svegliata, ragione.
>
> (*Rime*, capitolo XX ed. Fatini, ll. 16-18)

while the enemies are the worries that may arise in a relationship, caused both by the male lover himself ('gelosia, timor', l. 32) and by the lady, the latter being the traditional iniquities of the elegiac woman ('odio, disdegno, / disprezzo, crudeltà, lunga dimora', ll. 32-33).

We find another 'rocca di fè' in the *Furioso*, in a passage that has rightly been associated with this poem. Odorico, trying to justify himself to his friend Zerbino for having attempted to rape the latter's beloved Isabella, compares his own 'fede' – in this case the word must be taken not as amo-

---

militat omnis amans'), but the concept of *militia amoris* is overall very relevant to the Latin elegy; the subject is explored by DRINKWATER 2013.

52 *Carmina*, XLII (*In Venerem armata Lacedaemone*). In this poem, in turn inspired by a number of epigrams from the Palatine Anthology, the goddess Venus is presented as equipped with the weapons of Mars and in the process of fighting a mortal (ll. 1-2: 'Arma Venus, Martis sunt haec; quid inutile pondus, / mortali bellum si meditare, subis?').

53 GALLINARO 1999, pp. 103-104; Ariosto's capitolo is also analysed *ibid.* at pp. 210-213.

54 In one of the most popular medieval versions of the theme (featured, among others, in Dante's *Fiore*), the fortress is the beloved woman herself, who has to be conquered by the male lover: this often assumes a sexual connotation. Ariosto follows this version in his description of Ricciardetto's 'amorous assault' (l. 2) of Fiordispina in *Fur.*, XXIII 66,6-8 A; XXIII 68 B; XXV 68 C: 'Io senza scale in su la ròcca salto / e lo stendardo piantovi di botto, / e la nimica mia mi caccio sotto'.

rous faithfulness, but as loyalty towards a friend – to a fortress he was not able to defend against a too powerful enemy (the temptation constituted by Isabella).[55] Although this passage and the capitolo clearly share a common inspiration, and although in both the fortress symbolises fidelity (in the one case maintained, in the other broken), the different value attributed to 'fede' leads to a subtle shift between the two in terms of the construction of the image. In the passage from the *Furioso*, Love is the enemy of Reason ('Prudenzia', in this case), the guardian of the fortress of fidelity. Similarities are therefore evident with *Rvf*, II, where the 'poggio faticoso et alto', that is the seat of rationality, is the place where the speaker hopes to seek refuge from the assault of Love – vainly, as it turns out, because he was unprepared for such an attack.[56] In capitolo XX ed. Fatini, on the other hand, Love is not the enemy, but the lord of the castle ('Castellano è un amor fermo e provato', l. 19): he, Constancy and Reason fight on the same side, attemping to stave off the attacks of the irrational part of the soul.

The grounding of constancy in reason, rather than in passion and desire alone, is a trait which often appears in Ariosto's lyric output.[57] That it belongs to the Renaissance mindset is confirmed by looking at a similar articulation of the same metaphor in Castiglione's *Cortegiano*: 'Però quanto qualche grazioso aspetto di bella donna lor s'appresenta [...] deve in questo principio provedere di presto rimedio, e risvegliar la ragione e di quella armar la ròcca del cor suo'.[58] The dialogue also highlights the relationship between fidelity and the rational faculty, articulating it through the lens of Neoplatonism and prescribing it as one of the fundamental ethical virtues of the courtier (*Cortegiano* I.XVII: 'integrità di fede [...] animo invitto').[59]

The opposite scenario, that of a blind fidelity in love induced by irrational passion, is far less explored in the *rime*. Some exceptions will be an-

---

55 *Fur.*, XXII 31-32 AB; XXIV C. I will quote from 32,3-8: 'Mia fé guardar dovea non altrimente / ch'una fortezza d'ogn'intorno chiusa: / così, con quanto senno e quanta mente / da la somma Prudenzia m'era infusa, / io mi sforzai guardarla; ma al fin vinto / da intolerando assalto, ne fui spinto'. The similarity with the capitolo in the use of the image has been noted by Bigi in his commentary (Ariosto 2012, p. 801) and by Favaro 2011, pp. 103-104.

56 *Rvf*, II 9-14: 'Però, turbata nel primiero assalto, / non ebbe tanto né vigor né spazio / che potesse al bisogno prender l'arme, / overo al poggio faticoso et alto / ritrarmi accortamente da lo strazio / del quale oggi vorrebbe, et non pò, aitarme'. On this poem, and in general on the *arx rationis* in Petrarch's oeuvre, see Rigo 2014; Zacchetti 2018.

57 This point had already been noted (also with a specific reference to capitolo XX ed. Fatini) by Favaro 2010, pp. 124-125, and connected by him to contemporary love treatises, where the question on the possible coexistence of love and reason is often raised.

58 *Cortegiano*, IV.LXII (I am quoting from the third version of the work).

59 A discussion on this point is found in Gallinaro 1999, pp. 205-208.

alysed in the next section; here I would like to make a note on capitolo XXIV ed. Fatini (*Vo navigando un mar d'aspri martìri*), as it presents a similar construction to that of the capitolo we have just examined. Here, too, we encounter a single image developed at length – one which is antipodal to the *arx rationis* –, the image of navigation in a turbulent sea ('Vo navigando un mar d'aspri martìri / in fragil barca, perigliosa e grave', ll. 1-2) towards the woman-harbour ('voi sète il porto del mio navicare, / voi calamita sète e la mia stella', ll. 10-11 – a theme similar, incidentally, to that adopted in the above-discussed sonnet XVIII). Military imagery is also present here, but its aim is to represent the speaker as a 'loser' against the woman, who has conquered his heart ('e diedi a voi di me la potestate', l. 24). In other words, the poem foregrounds the dispossession of rational control, with a clear allusion to the *arx cordis* in the last line ('tenendo voi la ròcca del mio cuore', l. 28), which constitutes an inversion of the concept of XX ed. Fatini. These elements suggest that the two capitoli may have been conceived together as part of a diptych such as that constituted by capitoli XXI and XXII.

Following these attempts, the theme of constancy is newly explored, possibly at a considerable distance of time, by Ariosto in capitolo XXIV, which, unlike those just seen, is included in the main tradition. This time the subject is entrusted to a female poetic persona, who claims her absolute faithfulness to her beloved:[60]

> Qual son, qual sempre fui, tal esser voglio,
> alto o basso fortuna che mi rote,
> o siami Amor benigno, o mi usi orgoglio.
> Io son di vera fede imobil cote
> che 'l vento indarno, indarno il flusso alterno
> del pelago d'amor sempre percote;
> né già mai per bonaccia, né per verno,
> di là dove il distin mi fermò prima,
> luoco mutai, né mutarò in eterno.
>
> (*Rime del canzoniere*, XXIV 1-9)

This capitolo shares strong textual similarities with an episode introduced only in the 1532 version of the *Furioso*: the monologue (XLIV, 61-66 C) spoken by Bradamante so that it may be transmitted to Ruggiero, in order to dissolve the latter's doubts on her fidelity induced by the notice

---

60 In **Vr** this poem is placed immediately after *O lieta piaggia, o solitaria valle* (for which see below), as if it were an 'answer' to the complaints of the male speaker in the preceding poem. It is moreover followed by *De sì calloso dosso et sì robusto* (mentioned in Chapter I, 3) which is a further reply by the lover. Such a sequence is valid also according to the reconstruction of Volta 2019.

of her imminent (unwilling) marriage to Leone.[61] As a matter of fact, the theme of *fides* appears especially important in the 'Leone *giunta*', to which this passage belongs.[62] It is no coincidence that scholars have pointed out how Bradamante becomes an 'elegiac woman' at this stage of her story: indeed, in this claim of fidelity Ariosto was following a tradition which ultimately originated in Ovid's *Heroides*.[63] In addition, several vernacular examples, in turn inspired by Ovid (and by *Rvf*, CXLV 13-14: 'sarò qual fui, vivrò com'io son visso, / continüando il mio sospir trilustre'), could be produced as antecedents, or parallel cases, to Ariosto's use of the theme.[64]

As has been noted by Pich, Ariosto's choice of a female speaker in the capitolo is a rather innovative feature. Indeed, in the poetic tradition this kind of pattern was most often attributed to the male lover: that it should then pass on to the female warrior Bradamante only further accentuates her androginousness.[65] Here however, rather than on this aspect, I would like to focus once more on Ariosto's use of metaphors. A rich net of images is woven into the theme of constancy, either by the choice of hard materials as vehicle[66] – see above, 'imobil cote', i.e. the rock amid the waves – or by resorting to the language of warfare, as the following excerpt shows:

A voi di me tutto il dominio ho dato;
so ben che de la mia non fu mai fede
meglior giurata in alcun nuovo stato. [...]

---

61 This textual relationship is generally acknowledged by commentaries; see, furthermore, Pich 2008; Cabani 2016, pp. 122-127. Scholars agree that the capitolo preceded (and served as poetic material for) the episode of the *Furioso*. Note that there exists another version of this capitolo, witnessed by **Mn**, that identifies the poetic speaker as Bradamante (the first line is, in this version: 'Ruggier, quel sempre fui, tal esser voglio'); it is uncertain whether the author of this different version is Ariosto himself (see Finazzi 2002-2003, pp. 239-240).

62 This point is explored by Ascoli 2003, who also provides as an appendix a list of the words related to the concept of fidelity which are found in the *giunta*.

63 On this point, see Ferretti 2008; Pich 2008.

64 See *Amorum libri tres*, I 57,1-2: 'Io sono e sarò sempre quel ch'io fui, / e se altro esser volesse, io non potrei'; Tebaldeo, *Rime della vulgata*, 28,1: 'Io son quel che io fui sempre et esser voglio'. These were already noted by Comboni 2000, p. 307.

65 Pich 2008, pp. 262-264. But see also an excerpt of Visconti, *I canzonieri*, XLVI (cap. 4), where the female speaker displays a similar metaphor to claim having been absolutely faithful: 'Io salda e ferma qual immobile torre / che non se move per soffiar de' venti, / ma la lor forza qual vil cosa abborre, / spreggiava i pianti e 'lor sospiri ardenti' (ll. 25-28).

66 In this point of the text (ll. 34-49), the speaker also resumes a metaphorical imagery related to the art of sculpture, as she declares that no artist could ever succeed in modifying the image of the beloved one, firmly imprinted with the hardest material in her heart. This reconnects to another line of tradition, that of the picture of the beloved portrayed inside the lover's heart. On this *topos*, see Pich 2010, *passim*; Bolzoni 2010, pp. 317-322. Moreover, some Quattrocento examples that make specific reference to sculpture are listed by Zanato in Boiardo 2012, pp. 326-327.

Quel ch'io v'ho dato ancho difesso tegno,
per questo voi né d'assoldar persona,
né de riparo havete a far disegno.
Nessuno, o che m'assalti, o che mi pona
insidie, mai mi trovarà sprovista,
o mai d'havermi vinta havrà corona.

(*Rime del canzoniere*, XXIV 16-27)[67]

Among the possible parallels for this metaphoric exposition of female perseverance, a passage of the *Cortegiano* should be pointed out. While praising woman's chastity, in contrast to the misogynist arguments of Gasparo Pallavicino and of Frigio, Cesare Gonzaga states 'che molte se ne trovano invittissime, che ai continui stimuli d'amore sono adamantine e salde nella loro infinita constanzia più che i scogli all'onde del mare' (*Cortegiano*, III.L). Despite the different context – a discussion on the subject of chastity rather than of fidelity –, the metaphor is analogous, and is interesting that this passage should be present in all versions of the dialogue, including the *Lettera al Frisia in difesa delle donne* (ca. 1508), which probably constitutes its first plan.[68]

If we now return to the passage quoted from XXIV, it should be noted that it brings together the *arx cordis* and the *arx rationis*. The speaker yields power on herself to the beloved-conqueror and offers her vassalage to him (ll. 16-18) – thus translating into military language the theme of 'loss of oneself' expressed through the nautical metaphor in capitolo XXIV ed. Fatini – but at the same time she is ready and willing to pursue a defence strategy against assaults from outside through her strong will, exactly like the speaker of the capitolo XX ed. Fatini. I think this intertwining of two opposite conceptions is significant: indeed, it does justice to the psychological complexity of the lover and offers a multifaceted picture of fidelity, as

---

67 A very similar metaphorical repertoire also occurs, in the *Furioso*, in the second-degree story of Filandro, Argeo and Gabrina (XIX AB; XXI C), this time one already present in the 1516 version, which is also underpinned by the concept of *fides*: the similarity was noted by Ascoli 2003, pp. 115-116. It is impossible to state whether the capitolo pre-dated (and influenced) this elaboration of the theme.

68 See Ghinassi 1967 (the *Lettera* can be read in its Appendix). This is not the place to discuss Ariosto's knowledge of the *Cortegiano*. The elaboration of the dialogue, as is well known, took about twenty years, starting from ca. 1508: see, besides Ghinassi, Floriani 1976; Quondam 2000; Motta 2003. As claimed by Cabani 2016, pp. 142-143, Ariosto probably read it only after 1516: consequently, only the second and third versions of the *Furioso* could have been influenced by it. In this light, any resemblance between Ariosto's lyrics and the *Cortegiano* either suggests a post-1516 composition of the former or (more cautiously) is to be ascribed to a common cultural framework.

characterised by a coexistence of reason and self-abandonment, which will emerge more clearly from the poems that will be analysed next.

As a matter of fact, with the exception of the capitoli just presented, Ariosto's constant elaboration on the theme of fidelity seems rather to suggest its possible contradictions than to celebrate its power uncritically. Throughout the *Furioso*, the demonstrations of 'fede' (like any other chivalric tenet) elicit ambiguous responses on the part of the narrator. As showed by Ascoli, the characters that commit themselves to an unconditional application of that precept often end up doing more harm than good. The most exemplary case is that of Zerbino who, from the moment he pledges his word to protect the hag Gabrina, will be defending the epitome of all evils and treacheries.[69] Through the story of Zerbino, Ariosto calls into question not the importance of fidelity in itself, but its absoluteness, which does not stand up to the test of the real world. We would be hard put to find the same ethical complexity in the *rime*, also on account of the fact that they lack a proper narrative development. Nonetheless, as we shall shortly see, Ariosto's lyric treatment of fidelity departs to some extent from the traditional views, and is rather characterised by irony and by a more participatory approach on the part of the male speaker.

This may be easily seen if one compares the poems that exemplify this matter (i.e. those where an actual interaction between the two lovers is outlined) with those by the classical poet who provided him with the most important inspiration for this theme, namely, Catullus. In the latter we find the same pervasiveness not only of *fides* itself, but also of its concretisation as a *foedus* which binds both partners equally: something very different from the spiritualised, one-sided love that will prevail in the vernacular tradition. As we know, Catullus's relationship with Lesbia was characterised by her repeated breaches of this bond, which caused him pain but also prompted his proud claims of integrity despite all her ingratitude:

> Siqua recordanti benefacta priora voluptas
> est homini, cum se cogitat esse pium,
> nec sanctam violasse fidem, nec foedere in ullo
> divum ad fallendos numine abusum homines,
> multa parata manent in longa aetate, Catulle,
> ex hoc ingrato gaudia amore tibi. (Catullus, LXXVI 1-6)

[69] On the story of Zerbino (which is narrated at *Fur.*, XIX AB; XXI C, and also embeds the tale of Filandro mentioned at footnote 67), see Ascoli 1997 and 2003, pp. 106-109.

nulla fides ullo fuit umquam foedere tanta
    quanta in amore tuo ex parte reperta meast.

(*ibid.*, 87,3-4)

On its first occurrence in **Vr**, in sonnet IX (*Madonna sète bella et bella tanto*), fidelity is exalted by the speaker above all values in a manner that ostensibly recalls Catullus ('che più mirabil molto è la mia fede', l. 14). In this case, however, what is esteemed inferior is no moral value, but rather, physical beauty. Indeed, the abrupt introduction of 'fede' in the last line sounds very much like an *aprosdoketon* (not devoid of irony) in an enumeration of female beauties.[70]

The word 'fede' is then returned to in the first line of the poem which immediately follows,[71] ballata X, where the comparison between his fidelity and the beauty of the woman is further illustrated:

    Se voi così mirasse alla mia fede
com'io miro a vostr'occhi e a vostre chiome,
exceder l'altre la vedreste, come
vostra bellezza ogni bellezza excede.
    Et come io veggio ben che l'una è degna
per cui né lunga servitù né dura
noiosa mai debbia parermi o grave,
così vedreste voi che vostra cura
dev'esser che quest'altra si ritegna
sotto più leve giogo et più soave,
et con maggior speranza che non have
d'esser premiata; et se non hora a pieno
come devriase, al meno
con un dolce principio di mercede.

(*Rime del canzoniere*, X)

The ballata is organised around a rhetorical construct expressing parallelism, which is replicated throughout ('così [...] come', etc.), so as to reflect the equality which should characterise the *foedus* in the poet's hopes. The articulation of the poem as a logical argument addressed to the woman (which would run as follows: just as much as he is ready to undergo the *servitium amoris*, reckoning her beauty as being worth the bondage, so she should reckon his own faithfulness as deserving some reward) feels

70 On this poem, see also Chapter III, 1. A similar concept is in TEBALDEO, *Rime della vulgata*, 40,10-11: 'in me è gran fede, se in te è gran beltate, / non ebbi io da le stelle minor dono'.

71 The role of this keyword as an internal connector between the two poems has been noted by BOZZETTI 1985, p. 94; BOZZETTI – VELA 2000, p. 235.

unfamiliar for the reader of Catullus, who instead infuses the theme with the highest possible bitterness, hardly ever succeeding in processing this resentment by rational means. Furthermore, in Ariosto's case the poet is even ready to wait for the fulfilment of the duty she owes to him, of whose sexual nature he is entirely aware ('come devriase', l. 13).

The same attitude of rational persuasion underlies sonnet XXXV:

> Perché simil' le siano et de li artigli
> et del capo et del petto et de le piume,
> se l'acutezza anchor non v'è del lume,
> riconoscer non vuol l'aquila i figli:
> una sol parte che non le somigli
> fa che esser l'altre sue non si presume.
> Magnanima natura, alto costume,
> degno onde exempio un saggio amante pigli,
> ché la sua donna sua creder che sia
> non dee, s'a' suoi piacer', s'a' desir' suoi,
> s'a tutte voglie sue non l'ha conforme!
> Non siate, dunque, in un da me diforme,
> perché mi si confaccia il più di voi:
> ché o nulla, o voi convien tutta esser mia.
>
> (*Rime del canzoniere*, XXXV)

In the two quatrains the speaker lays out an *exemplum* ('exempio', l. 8) for the benefit of all lovers, beginning with himself: he exploits the famous legend according to which the eagle, once her eaglets are born, only acknowledges them as her own if they share her same ability, that of fixing their eyes on the sun.[72] In moralistic and religious literature, this legendary gift had led to interpreting the eagle as a symbol of contemplation.[73] It was also often put to poetic use, insofar as it allowed the comparison between the lady and the Sun, by fixing which the speaker is led to the contemplation of God. An example is *Rvf*, CCCXXV 59: 'Tien' pur li occhi come aquila in quel sole'. Among courtly poets, the case of Serafino Aquilano is worth noting, because he also features the theme of the refusal of the eaglets in his sonnet I. Indeed, his comparison of himself to the eagle (a comparison also backed by the onomastic pun: aquila-Aquilano) is motivated precisely by his discarding all thoughts that do not regard his beloved, who constitutes his

---

[72] One of the most famous formulations of the story, much inspirational to medieval bestiaries, is that by Isidore of Seville, *Etymologiae*, XII 7,10-11.

[73] I will only mention the simile comparing Beatrice to an eagle (who transmits her peculiar quality to Dante himself) in *Par.*, I 46-48: 'quando Beatrice in sul sinistro fianco / vidi rivolta e riguardar nel sole: / aguglia sì non li s'affisse unquanco'.

only contemplative aim.[74] The use of this motif in Ariosto is entirely different. He also engages in a comparison with the eagle, but his beloved is not associated with the sun (any possible celebratory intention is thus severed from the theme) but with the eaglet: she thereby risks rejection unless she fully and exclusively conforms to his desires. According to Turchi's 1567 commentary, the sonnet illustrated an *impresa* which Ariosto had adopted, seeing that his beloved's attitude did not satisfy him entirely.[75] Be that as it may, the message we are left with is the lover's (self-)recommendation of wisdom ('saggio amante', l. 8) when pondering the behaviour of his woman and conducting himself accordingly. While the eagle *exemplum* is traditionally an illustration of wisdom, I would suggest that in this case it also promotes equality between lovers ('simil', l. 1; 'somigli', l. 5) against the narcissistic propensity of the lady, who seemingly aspires to the manipulative position typical of the object of desire in the Latin love elegists. Indeed, the poet is ready to relinquish the relationship ('nulla', l. 14) if he himself is not satisfied.[76] This drastic idea is also foregrounded by Ariosto in his Latin poem VII, addressed to Bembo, where an explicit reference to the woman's promiscuity is found: 'Parte carere omni malo, quam admittere quemquam / in partem; cupiat Iuppiter, ipse negem' (ll. 17-18).

The reader will find a similar concept in sonnet 51 (*Aventurosa man, beato ingegno*), where the speaker, in seeing his woman entirely absorbed in meticulously copying the pattern of a dress, wishes – again in the tercets, in which he addresses the dress itself – that she would rather imitate his own attitude of constancy:

> Felice voi, felice forse anche io,
> se mostrarle o con gesti o con parole
> voi potesse altro exempio che ella toglia:
> quanto meglio di voi, ch'imitar vuole,
> serà se la fede imita, se 'l mio
> constante amor, se la mia giusta voglia.
>
> (*Rime del canzoniere*, 51,9-14)

---

74 Serafino Aquilano, *Sonetti*, I: 'L'aquila che col sguardo affisa el sole / tutti i soi figli ancor prova a la spera, / e qual fissar non può, sdegnata e fiera / morto lo tra' del nido e non lo vole. / Simile spesso far mia mente suole / de' soi penser poi che son nati a schiera; / che qual non mira a la mia donna altiera / presto l'occide e mai non si ne duole. / Questo è quel sol ch'ogn'altra vista abaglia, / che se 'l vedesse ognun come el vidi io / dirria ch'al mio nisiun stato se aguaglia; / perché la mente e ciascun penser mio / spesso convien per lei tanto alto saglia / che conoscer mi fa che cosa è Dio'.

75 Ariosto 1730, II, p. 362.

76 Favaro 2010, p. 126 also observes that in the last tercet 'non traspare alcuna subalternità dell'amante: anzi, si può affermare che è lui a voler dettare risolutamente le regole'.

Note that in both XXXV and 51 this take on the theme of *somiglianza* sets Ariosto dramatically apart from the lyric vernacular tradition, in which the beloved, a divine creature, cannot be 'similar' to anybody, and it is rather the lover who makes an effort to be more like her, in order to elevate his soul.[77]

A similar moral outlook is expressed by the speaking subject also in sonnet XXXIX (*Se con speranza di mercé perduti*), where his *servitium amoris* is identified with the writing of grieving poetry, in keeping with an equivalence well-established in the elegiac genre. Having so far failed to move his woman to pity through his verse, he gives up, hoping to save himself from the fate of the legendary Greek inventor Perillus:

> Se voi Phalare sète, io mi v'excuso,
> che non voglio esser quel che per udire
> dolce doler fu nel suo toro chiuso.
>
> (*Rime del canzoniere*, XXXIX 12-14)

According to the classical legend, Perillus presented Phalaris, the tyrant of Agrigento, with a newly created torture device, a bronze bull into whose side the condemned would be pushed and beneath which a fire would be kindled. This was further provided with an acoustic apparatus designed to convert screams into the actual lowing of a bull. The tyrant, disgusted by this cruel invention, ordered Perillus himself to test it first. This legend, which features in Dante[78] and in the humanist tradition (it is the subject of one of Erasmus's *Adagia*, number 986), was also popular in late-Quattrocento poetry, where Perillus became the perfect embodiment of the poet himself, who sings because of the pain caused by the sadistic will of a tyrannical woman.[79] The speaker of Ariosto's poem, however, detaches himself from this stereotype in that he chooses *not* to sing. The focus on his falling

[77] Examples of this entirely different value of the concept of *somiglianza* are *Rvf*, CLX 4: 'che sol se stessa, et nulla altra, simiglia'; CCCXLII 5-6: 'Ma chi né prima simil né seconda / ebbe al suo tempo'; CCCLX 127-128: 'di lei ch'alto vestigio / li 'mpresse al core, et fecel suo simìle'.

[78] *Inf.*, XXVII 7-12: 'Come 'l bue cicilian che mugghiò prima / col pianto di colui, e ciò fu dritto, / che l'avea temperato con sua lima, / mugghiava con la voce de l'afflitto, / sì che, con tutto che fosse di rame, / pur el pareva dal dolor trafitto'.

[79] See, for instance, Tebaldeo, *Rime estravaganti*, 443,1-8: 'Come del bue sicilïano usciva / un flebil grido de chi dentro vi era, / che non human lamento, ma una vera / voce parea d'un thoro a chi l'udiva, / così il dolente carme che deriva / da me, che in te Amor chiuse aciòch'io pèra, / esce de la tua bocca in tal manera / che mortal harmonia non par, ma diva'; Correggio, *Rime*, 78,1-4: 'Sì dolce è il lamentar, sì dolce è il pianto / ch'e dolci amanti in dolce foco fanno, / che 'l buò che fu di Faleri tiranno / non diè nel foco mai concento tanto'.

silent ('Dunque è meglio il tacer, Donna, che 'l dire', l. 9) may remind us of another 'metapoetic' poem, sonnet XI, where he also decides to abandon his poetic efforts ('ove tacendo io moro', l. 14 – see next section). The difference is that in the latter the speaker is moved by no personal interest and his renunciation is caused by his awareness of his inability to properly celebrate his beloved (a common *topos*), while in XXXIX the singing ceases because it does not elicit from the woman the desired response.

As a final example of the importance in Ariosto of the speaker's role in dictating the rules of the relationship, sonnet XXXIII (*Deh, voless'io quel che voler devrei!*) should be mentioned. After voicing, in the quatrains and in the first tercet, his lament for not being able to restrain his love, the speaker suddenly turns to his beloved, and seems to actually threaten to interrupt the *servitium amoris* which has been long and greatly taxing: 'Ben vi vuo' ricordar ch'ogni cavallo / non corre sempre per spronar, et vegio, / per punger troppo, alcun farsi restio' (ll. 12-14). To indicate that his patience is wearing thin he ironically resorts to an equine metaphor which, as noted by Cabani, inescapably reminds the reader of the episode of the *Furioso* involving the hermit's attempted rape of Angelica, where the 'destrier' has a clear sexual connotation (*Fur.*, VIII 49 ABC).[80] Incidentally, this poem is a perfect example of Ariosto's adoption of a typical pattern of courtly sonnets, in which the last tercet is occupied by a witty and unexpected conclusion (see Introduction, 3).

While the situation of unrequited love – where the poet reprimands his beloved for not rewarding his fidelity – often features in Ariosto's lyrics, another typically elegiac *topos*, namely, the open accusation of betrayal, is very rare. As is well known, the woman's sexual promiscuity dominates the vicissitudes of the speaking subject in Catullus, Tibullus, and Propertius, as well as in the early modern reworking of the Latin elegy. It also features, for instance, in the second book of Boiardo's *Amorum libri tres*. The marginalisation of this theme by Ariosto is another fact that contributes to reducing the elegiac manifestations of *pathos*, and conversely enhances the importance, in his vision, of the idea of equality between the two partners. It is therefore worth dwelling on the only poems featuring clear references to treachery, capitoli XXIII and XXXI.

The former (*O lieta piaggia, o solitaria valle*) has come down to us in two different authorial versions – which, in Fatini's edition, have two distinct numbers, XII and XII*bis*. The earlier one, which is forty-nine lines long (XII*bis*), is found in thirteen miscellanies; the other is a reworking of

---

[80] Cabani 2016, pp. 112-113; see also Favaro 2010, p. 126.

the former in view of the compilation of **Vr**, Ariosto's main intervention being the addition of fifty-nine lines. Both versions are in keeping with the long-established tradition of the lover who vents his sorrow in solitude amid a *locus amoenus* – a strand deriving from Propertius, I 18, through the fundamental mediation of *Rvf*, XXXV and CXLVIII. From this tradition Ariosto also borrows the *topos* of the lovers' names cut into a tree bark, which he also uses in the love idyll of Angelica and Medoro.[81]

The 'short' version may more easily be inscribed within the tradition of court literature. In fact, it could be linked to a youthful capitolo by Bembo, 192 (*Fiume, che del mio pianto habondi et cresci*), which is of similar length and displays similar thematic and lexical choices.[82] Only in this version, and particularly in its final lines, is the cause of the poet's sufferings (i.e. the woman's betrayal) revealed:

> Quella che sì lodar m'odiste, a cui
> tanto creder solea, m'ha rotto fede:
> per lei sola arsi et alsi, ma non fui
> solo, come al servir, alla mercede.
>
> (*Rime*, capitolo XII*bis* ed. Fatini, ll. 46-49)

Ariosto deleted this passage when he added the new portion of text, and as a result, in the longer version of the capitolo any overt mention of betrayal disappears. In its place, the poet introduces a description of the progressive change of attitude of his beloved, who, after a period of happiness, has inexplicably turned cold towards him. In this context, the

---

81 *Rime del canzoniere*, XXIII 31-33: 'Io son quel che solea, dovunque o dritto / arbor vedeva, o tuffo alcun men duro, / de la mia dea lasciarvi il nome scritto'; *Fur.*, XVII 36 AB; XIX C: 'Fra piacer tanti, ovunque un arbor dritto / vedesse ombrare o fonte o rivo puro, / v'avea spillo o coltel subito fitto; / così, se v'era alcun sasso men duro: / et era fuori in mille luoghi scritto, / e così in casa in altritanti il muro, / Angelica e Medoro, in varii modi / legati insieme di diversi nodi'. The classical source is PROPERTIUS, I 18,21-22: 'ah quotiens vestras resonant mea verba sub umbras, / scribitur et teneris Cynthia corticibus!'. On the basis of this model (but also of VIRGIL, *Buc.*, V 13-15: 'Immo haec, in viridi nuper quae cortice fagis / carmina descripsi [...] / experiar'), bucolic literature often features the *inscriptio corticis*, i.e. the bark of the tree as the place where the lover carves the name of his beloved, or messages addressed to her. On this theme, see DANZI 2017, pp. 132-139 and 2018, pp. 206-209. Another passage of Ariosto's poem that may be linked to Propertius's is at ll. 28-30: 'Ma stommi in dubio che l'acerbe et molte / pene amorose sì m'habbiano afflitto / che le prime sembianze mi sien tolte' (cp. PROPERTIUS, I 18,17-18: 'an quia parva damus mutato signa colore, / et non ulla meo clamat in ore fides?').

82 This similarity has been noted by TISSONI BENVENUTI 1976, p. 307. Both poems start with an invocation to the various elements of nature. Moreover, we may compare the following syntagms: 'gelate e lucid'onde' (BEMBO, *Le rime*, 192,2) and 'gelid'onde' (ARIOSTO, capitolo XII*bis* ed. Fatini, l. 9). Both also feature the rhyme *fronde*: *onde*.

vocabulary of *fides* and *foedus* is resumed, and the final phrase of the last line of ballata X, 'principio di mercede' (see above) is used again:

> Quella, ohimè, quella, quella, ohimè, da cui
> con tant'alto principio di marcede
> tra i più beati al ciel levato fui,
> che di fervente amor, di pura fede,
> di strettissimo nodo, da non sciorse
> se non per morte già speme mi diede,
> hor non m'ama, né prezza, et odia forse
> et sdegno et duol credo che 'l cor le punga
> che ad essermi cortese unqua si torse.
>
> (*Rime del canzoniere*, XXIII 46-54)

Arguably, Ariosto expanded the capitolo so that it could be linked to other poems of **Vr**, in order to establish what may be seen as a narrative sequence. Significantly, the memory of past nights of passion is expressed in a language that recalls the capitolo on the happy night of love ('Non pur al süavissimo abbracciarse / de l'amorose lotte, e a i dolci furti[83] / le dolce notte a ritornar son scarse', ll. 64-66). But the reworking for the final version brings about further effects. The reader is now presented with a new nuance of suffering, deriving not from unilateral love but rather from the woman's falling *out* of love ('L'esserne privo causa maggior lutti, / poi ch'io n'ho fatto il saggio, che non fora / s'havuti ognhor n'havesse i denti asciutti', ll. 97-99).[84] Most importantly, the elimination of the reference to treachery shifts the focus away from the woman and onto the speaker himself, specifically, on his reaction and his attitude. This is evident in the last part of the final version, where he no longer addresses the elements of nature, but the woman herself, engaging in a long rebuke that has the effect of emphasising by contrast his own moral righteousness. What is even more interesting, he suggests that he controls her reputation: one word from him and she will be irreparably dishonoured.

> Ogni lingua di voi serà mordace,
> se s'ode mai ch'un sì benigno giogo
> rotto habbia, o sciolto il vostro amor fugace.
>
> (*Rime del canzoniere*, XXIII 82-84)

---

[83] For the expression 'dolci furti', related to the concept of *furtivus amor*, see also *Fur.*, XXXII 74,1-2 C: 'un bene acceso amante / ch'ai dolci furti per entrar si trova'.

[84] This too, is a *topos*. See for instance *Asolani*, I.xxiii, where Perottino highlights the ephemerality of the amorous 'allegrezze', concluding that 'tanto ci appare la miseria più grave, quanto la felicità ci è paruta maggiore'.

Although he chooses to remain 'secreto' (l. 104), we still gather that it is the speaker, and not the woman, who has the upper hand. As a matter of fact, Ariosto refuses to adopt the tones of the *disperata*, very much used in the Quattrocento elegiac capitoli (which featured exaggerated curses on the woman, often culminating with the threat of suicide),[85] and in general seems to reduce the *pathos* of the capitolo in its revision for **Vr**, in order to align it with his ideal pursuit of moral equality in the love relationship.

An even more accomplished elaboration on the theme of infidelity is in capitolo XXXI (*Ben è dura et crudel, se non si piega*), which may have been written for the canzoniere.[86] Here, too, the male lover is rebuking his woman – with whom he used to be happy ('Hor chi di noi / eran più d'amor giunti? / Et chi fidarsi / puote mai più ch'io mi facea di voi?', ll. 70-72) – for no longer reciprocating his faithfulness.[87] He next tries to understand the possible reasons for this behaviour: either she has simply changed her mind, ll. 19-27, or she was untruthful even as she first made her promise, ll. 28-36. While the former scenario is already reproachable, the latter is a deception or even a betrayal, and as such is condemned as the opposite of faithfulness, ll. 32-33. At this point he launches into a moralistic tirade on the absolute value of faithfulness:

> La fede mai esser non dee corrotta,
> o data a un solo o data che odan cento,
> data in palese o data in una grotta.
> Per la vil plebe è fatto il giuramento,
> ma tra li spirti più ellevati sono
> le simplici promesse un sacramento.
>
> (*Rime del canzoniere*, XXXI 43-48)

As some critics have already noted, this portion of text appears in an almost identical form in the proem to *Fur.*, XXI,[88] thus confirming the ex-

[85] Some examples of *disperata* are listed by Tissoni Benvenuti 1976, p. 306 (the scholar also underscores the absence of *disperate* in Ariosto's output, *ibid.*, p. 307). See also, with a special reference to Tebaldeo, Marchand 1997. On the characteristics and the tradition of this genre between Italy and France, see Scarlatta 2017 (who argues for its substantial difference, also in the contemporary perception of the times, from other genres such as the elegy).

[86] Finazzi 2002-2003, p. 259.

[87] Here, too, Ariosto employs a metaphor already seen in XXIV, that of the rock, to which he thought he could compare her firmness: 'le speranze mie sparsi ne l'onde / credendomi fondarle in stabil scoglio', ll. 23-24.

[88] *Fur.*, XIX 2 AB; XXI C: 'La fede unqua non debbe esser corrotta, / o data a un solo, o data insieme a mille; / e così in una selva, in una grotta, / lontan da le cittadi e a le ville, / come dinanzi a tribunali, in frotta / di testimon, di scritti e di postille, / senza giurare o segno

change of influences between Ariosto's lyrics and narrative, and the prominent role of *fides* in both. Indeed ingratitude in love is a common thread that regularly reappears in the tapestry of the *Furioso*, where it is part of the poem's more general interest in the theme of 'unrewarded effort'.[89] In the capitolo as well as in the proem, the speaker insists on the force of faithfulness beyond any legal endorsement (in other words, on the superiority of the promise over the oath) and on its sacredness. This feature, probably borrowed from Catullus – 'sanctae foedus amicitiae', CIX 6 –, leads him to predict the gods' vengeance over thc unfaithful woman:

> Et non sa anchor di quanto mal radice
> questo gli sia, se ben non va col fallo
> la pena alhor alhor vendicatrice;
> ma lo segue ella con poco intervallo,
> et ogni cor, che qui par sì coperto,
> trasparente è là su più che cristallo.
>
> (*Rime del canzoniere*, XXXI 10-15)

Along these lines, he also implicitly resorts to an ordering of the gravity of sins which follows Dante's *Inferno*, in order to justify his evaluation of her sin as the most grievous: 'più si perdona a l'homicidio e al furto / ch'al pergiurarsi e a l'inganar chi crede' (ll. 35-36); 'Et chi serà che con più biasmo s'oda / notar di quel ch'a gli congiunti suoi / o di sangue o d'amor cerchi usar froda? / Tanto più a chi si fida' (ll. 67-70).

In this framework, however, it is the speaker's psychological attitude that makes this poem, too, outstanding. In his opinion, the most compelling reason for his lady to keep faith does not seem to be the sacredness of the promise, but rather, his own merit: 'quel che, oltra l'havermi / promesso voi, mi si devea per merto' (ll. 17-18). The love relationship is thus clearly likened to a relation of exchange. Within this framework any imbalance must be dealt with and remedied by the guilty party, if it wishes to avoid the terrible punishment of divine justice:

---

altro più espresso, / basti una volta che s'abbia promesso'. It is impossible to exactly determine what was written before. Finazzi supposes that the first formulation of the tirade was in the first *Furioso* (Finazzi 2002-2003, p. 259). The link between the capitolo and the octave is noted by Bigi in his commentary (Ariosto 2012, p. 706) – the scholar also compares the stanza with *Inn.*, I, XXVIII 28,5-8: 'egli è chiaro e palese / che tra gentile e generosa gente / solo a parole se observa la fede; / senza giurare l'uno all'altro crede'.

[89] See Durling 1965, p. 167; Zatti 1990, pp. 126-171; Residori 2018 (who considers this theme in the framework of a wider Renaissance debate). Also the motto PRO BONO MALVM appended to the end of the poem has been explained by several critics in the light of the concept of ingratitude: see Santoro 1989, pp. 317-320; Masi 2002.

S'a voi per mia cagione o macchiar l'unge
o vedessi un crin mosso, ohimè, che doglia!
Solo il pensarvi me da me disgiunge.
Voi de periglio et me di pena toglia
un pentir presto, un satisfarmi intiero;
che sia il debito vostro, et quel ch'io voglia,
ch'a sapere habbia altri che voi non chero.
(*Rime del canzoniere*, XXXI 79-85)

The reader may be reminded of Boccaccio's novella of Nastagio degli Onesti, the eighth of the fifth day of the *Decameron*: the young lady beloved by Nastagio finally accepts to reciprocate him when she witnesses the awful torment inflicted on women who die without regretting their coldness. But most of all, we feel the echo of the story of Lidia in the *Furioso*, whose debt to the story of Nastagio is commonly accepted. Lidia, whom Astolfo encounters in the underworld, gives him an account of her vicissitudes and explains that the reason why she – and many others like her – are in hell is her ingratitude (*Fur.*, XXXI 11-44 AB; XXXIV C). The infernal setting, also reminescent of Dante, reconnects to the threats voiced by the speaker in capitolo XXXI; but the most evident unifying trait is the use of a vocabulary that expresses the idea of exchange.[90]

Actually, other poems by Ariosto also reveal his concept of love as a mutual bond, described in terms of an actual contract between the two parties and ultimately regulated by the gods. A noteworthy formulation of it is in capitolo XLII. Here the speaker is ready to waive his 'love credit' if this helps his beloved's recovery back, thereby implicitly recognising in her illness the divine punishment also envisioned in XXXI ('Così quanto di lei creditor sono / del mio lëal server di cotanti anni, / dipenno tutto et volentier le dono', ll. 28-30). Actually, in the capitolo that immediately follows it in **Vr**, XLIII (that addressed to Ippolito; see Chapter I) the speaker takes on the role of the debtor: indeed, he is bound to his lord and to his woman by a double debt, having left both ('Restomi qui, né, come Amor vorebbe, / posso Madonna satisfar, né a voi / l'obligo scior che la mia fe' vi debbe', ll. 7-9). However in most of the poems, as has been shown throughout this section, it is the vocabulary related to the deserved reward (*mercede*) that resonates most clearly, with a marked sexual allusion: the concrete val-

90 Both points are also noted, with regard to the Lidia episode, by Zatti 1990, pp. 138-139 (the scholar interprets Lidia as a reversal of the figure of Francesca in the *Inferno*). Residori 2018, pp. 171-172 also proposes a comparison between this episode (which he extensively analyses) and the capitolo.

ue of this lexicon, which is also noticeable in several places of the *Furioso*, has led Cabani to speak of a 'logica "commerciale"'.[91] As a further example of this topic, sonnet XXXIV (*Occhi miei belli, mentre ch'i' vi miro*) should be mentioned. Here the poet describes the 'dolcezza ineffabil', l. 2, which he feels when he sees his lady, a joy far higher than that afforded by merely thinking of her – which incidentally underscores the concreteness of this love, although here we do not find specifically sexual innuendos.[92] He next claims that she ought not prevent him from such contemplation as it does not entail any loss for her, and lays out this issue in terms that evoke financial exchange: 'nulla a voi perde, et a me tanto acquista' (l. 14).

But, to return to XXXI, what especially matters is that the envisioning of a magnified divine punishment, and the request for satisfaction as a way to avoid this punishment, are infused with irony and archness: again, an attitude at the furthest remove from that, say, of Catullus, who was always on the verge of collapsing into desperation when faced with Lesbia's infidelity. This feeling, which emerges from the last lines, retrospectively casts an ambiguous light on all the preceding tirade. Suddenly, the reader feels that it is nothing more than a persuasive argument directed at the woman in order to achieve his goal, and that the poet himself is the first not to believe his own claim about the absoluteness of this value. It is not accidental, in this light, that the context of the *Furioso* where these lines are replicated is that in which Zerbino's absolute coherence with his ideals is proved – an episode not devoid of interpretative ambiguity, as mentioned before.

Commenting on the tragic or paradoxical outcome of the plots of the *Furioso* involving an unconditional observation of *fides* (as is the story of Zerbino), both Ascoli and Zatti have noted the relativistic attitude of Ariosto-the-narrator towards this concept,[93] pointing out how it tallies with Machiavelli's perspective, in which the ability to respond to external factors is regarded as the prince's fundamental virtue. We may now conclude that a similar attitude can be attributed to the poetic persona of several of Ariosto's lyrics. Furthermore, I would suggest that this was already evident in some early poems. These include two capitoli mentioned at the beginning

---

91 Cabani 2016, p. 136 (and see in general pp. 132-136).

92 On this point see Favaro 2010, p. 129.

93 See, in particular Zatti 1990, pp. 98-102. The scholar points out juxtapositions between cases such as those of Zerbino and Filandro and that of the 'unscrupulous' Mandricardo, who, after becoming attracted to Rodomonte's beloved Doralice and deciding to steal her from him, offers Marfisa to Rodomonte as compensation, 'se quando una ne perde, una n'acquista' (*Fur.*, XXIV 67,8 AB; XXVI 70 C), with a pragmatism that apparently remains uncondemned by the narrator.

of this chapter, XLVI (which is structured as a weighing up on the part of the poet of the pros and cons of love), and XXIII ed. Fatini. In the latter, incidentally, in addition to the 'customary' language of accounting, we also find him hinting at a theme that became very dear to him, i.e. the soaring height achieved by amorous thought:

> Non è più tempo stare in quel pensiero
> ch'alto mi leva sì che abbrucia l'ale,
> ma poi torna cadendo al luoco vero;
> ma ben tempo è pensar quanto sia 'l male,
> quanto il bene, e stimar l'utile e 'l danno,
> render alla fatica il premio uguale.
>
> (*Rime*, capitolo XXIII ed. Fatini, ll. 19-24)

Of course, the development of such an idea of relationship is made possible within a wider framework of thought, which considers and reflects on the issue of reciprocity. Here, too, a strong connection can be established with the *Furioso*, where it is exploited in all its narrative possibilities and elevated to the level of a structural principle, its types ranging from the betrothal and/or marital bond (Ruggiero and Bradamante, Brandimarte and Fiordiligi), to the 'irregular' relationship (Isabella and Zerbino). The proem of the second canto aptly epitomises the difficulty of achieving it: 'Ingiustissimo Amor, perché sì raro / corrispondenti fai nostri desiri?' (*Fur.*, II 1,1-2 ABC). The motif of reciprocity is extraordinarily complex, and it would be hard to summarise all the shapes it takes in Renaissance culture. In line with this book's attention towards the courtly milieu, I would like to call attention to the mythological figure of Anteros, which often features in this cultural context.

Anteros, the son of Venus and Mars according to Cicero, takes on very different identifying traits in his various embodiments in humanist texts, at times being the destroyer of love (under whose 'sign' the above-mentioned *letteratura antierotica* should be placed), at others the god of celestial love, as opposed to Eros, the symbol of vulgar love. The latter is the Neoplatonic interpretation, which inspired an iconography that was especially popular at the courts of Milan and Mantua, particularly keen on these subjects (key figures in this respect were Paride Ceresara and Antonio Fileremo Fregoso).[94] One further strand which is of interest here sees Anteros as the

---

94 The apparitions of Anteros in early Renaissance literature have been investigated by Dilemmi 2000*bis* (pp. 221-243) and Comboni 2000*bis*; see also Lucioli 2010 (the article focuses on a specific case, namely a poem by Sigismondo Paolucci Filogenio constituting a continuation of the *Furioso*). These three studies also provide exhaustive bibliography on this mytho-

god of mutual love, taking the Greek prefix 'anti-' as an expression of reciprocity rather than contrast and supporting this position with several classical examples. Among the works that espouse this position are Equicola's *Libro de natura de amore*[95] and a learned essay by Calcagnini, entitled *Anteros sive de mutuo amore*. This was dedicated to the diplomat Antonio Costabili and inspired the design for the fresco decoration of the Stanza del Tesoro in his own Palazzo Costabili in Ferrara. Indeed, the eighteen lunettes of the room – executed by Benvenuto Tisi 'Il Garofalo' by 1512 – illustrate the eighteen poetic couplets which conclude the essay.[96] It should be noted that Ariosto, too, was well acquainted with Antonio, as they shared the role of vice-chancellor of Milan, and a meeting between the two took place in the Stanza del Tesoro in 1520.[97]

In his essay – which is in his customary erudite style – Calcagnini claims that he wishes to re-establish the correct opinion of Anteros, mistakenly believed by many to be the god of lovelessness: instead, he should be interpreted as the 'grown-up' counterpart of Cupid, who heals the damages caused by the latter, ensuring reciprocation and avenging unrequited lovers.[98] The same concept also emerges from two other works by Calcagnini, namely, a Latin poem (*De Anterota*) and an apologue, in both of which this god is featured.[99] Ariosto may have had this figure in mind when threatening the intervention of generic deities in capitolo XXXI – just as he was thinking of Cupid, in his traditional representation as a capricious blind boy, in the poem immediately following it in **Vr**, sonnet XXXII (*Mal*

---

logical figure and on individual instances of its literary employment. I will only mention two seminal studies: PANOFSKY 1939, pp. 95-128, and MERRILL 1944.

95 *Libro de natura de amore, Libro quarto*, f. 192*r* (EQUICOLA 1999, p. 438): 'La opinione di quelli che credeno Antheros volere denotare "opposito et non conrespondente amore" noi la reputamo totalmente falsa, et lo significato suo essere "mutuo, equale et reciproco amore" dicemo, ché, benché *anti* "contra" denote, denota anchora "equale" [...]'.

96 See PATTANARO 2007, p. 78 and footnote 10; WATTEL 2018. The essay can be read in CALCAGNINI 1544, pp. 436-442.

97 WATTEL 2018, p. 34.

98 CALCAGNINI 1554, p. 438: 'Huic itaque naturae consortio, mutuaeque animorum coniunctioni, veterum superstitio Anterota praefecit: eumque existimavit mutuis vinculis per quasdam vicissitudines ac reciprocationes animos et rerum genios illigare: hominesque parum in amore gratos ulcisci'.

99 I have no information on the chronology of either work. The poem reads: 'Hic unus colitur, sed unus ille / implet munia numinum duorum, / et potest geminus vocari, et unus, / et quod vix licet aestimari, in illo / bis unum duo non facit, sed unum, / haec vis scilicet Anterotis illa est, / haec vis mutua mutui est amoris, / haec binas animas coire cogit: / atque una geminum calere pectus' (PIGNA 1553, I, p. 179). The apologue is quoted below, footnote 168. Calcagnini mentions Anteros also in another poem, addressed to Lilio Gregorio Giraldi (*ibid.*, p. 184, ll. 7-8: 'Quem si dixeris Anterota, dices / recte per superos, et eleganter').

si compensa, ahi lasso, un breve sguardo). Here, the speaker, in the course of a conventional complaint about his unrequited love – in which we again find the idea of parity: 'non fu pare il dardo', l. 5 –, blames the winged god for having hit him alone and not the lady, who would have been a far more desirable prey for him:

> Pensai che ad ambi havesse teso Amore,
> et voi devesse a un laccio coglier meco;
> ma me sol prese e lasciò andar voi sciolta.
> Già non vid'egli molto a quella volta
> che, s'havea voi, la preda era maggiore,
> et ben mostrò ch'era fanciulo et cieco.
> (*Rime del canzoniere*, XXXII 9-14)

Even setting aside the figure of Anteros, it should be noted that mutual love is the subject of a long-standing discussion in some Cinquecento love treatises, which debate how the lover should succeed in achieving reciprocity, and if such reciprocity is deserved by him at all. Favaro, who deals with this topic in his study on the Renaissance amorous treatise, explores a wide range of possible answers provided by various authors and justified by them through literary examples (in this context Petrarch and also Ariosto are often quoted).[100] A remarkably elaborate case is constituted by the precepts for unrequited lovers included in the *Ragionamento d'Amore* by Verino, which nevertheless adopts a different perspective from that of Ariosto and is rather in line with traditional Petrarchan poetry: Verino's advice starts with the assumption that the lover is in an inferior position, and that all he can do is to celebrate the woman or elicit her compassion.

In addition to the works examined by Favaro, another text should be taken into consideration in this context, namely, Castiglione's *Cortegiano*. In its third book, while fashioning the ideal *donna di palazzo*, the interlocutors also discuss the reciprocation of love. Giuliano de' Medici, who is leading the discussion, believes it possible that the lady may return the courtier's love on account of their affinity: this is in line with his overall conception of her as the ideal female equivalent of the courtier himself. Giuliano's argument, however, is developed on an 'abstract' level, in keeping with the Neoplatonic view, and disregards any reference to physical love (a gaze or a smile of hers being enough reward),[101] which is only acceptable in the

100 Favaro 2010, pp. 167-172.

101 *Cortegiano*, III.LVII: 'Colui adunque che sarà da tal donna amato, ragionevolmente devrà contentarsi d'ogni minima demostrazione, ed apprezzar più da lei un sol sguardo con

case of marriage. On this point Giuliano is answered by Bernardo Accolti, who, taking a rather different perspective on the subject – one ostensibly inspired by the courtly-elegiac genre – claims that the lover should always have his due reward for his fidelity, something that in his experience does not happen often since beauty tends to be paired with cruelty.[102] Accolti's disguise as a frustrated elegiac lover is dismantled by Emilia Pia, who insinuates that he, who is in fact a well-known ladies' man, is pretending to be the opposite 'per nasconder le grazie, i contenti e i piaceri da voi conseguiti in amore, ed assicurar quelle donne che v'amano e che vi si son date in preda, che non le publichiate'.[103]

Emilia's argument clearly hints at sensual (and transgressive) love. This is somewhat difficult to integrate in the economy of the dialogue, predictably so, because of the diffused prevalence in it of the Neoplatonic perspective, which is certainly not limited to Bembo's final intervention, but a structural element of the dialogue as a whole. Strictly speaking, however, such prevalence is visible only in the final formulation of the *Cortegiano*. If we consider its previous versions, what prevails is still a vision of love as a social and 'earthly' phenomenon, elegiac-Ovidian, as it were (and analogous to that professed by Gismondo in Bembo's *Asolani*), while the theme of spiritual love is far less developed.[104] In particular, it may be noted that in the second version the person called to speak about love is Accolti himself: the audience appears to marry his point of view and display hostility towards the Neoplatonic theses expressed quite tentatively only by Bembo and the Duchess.[105]

It is clear that in the poems seen so far (and most clearly in capitolo XXXI) Ariosto's views on love are closer to the courtly-elegiac perspective. A further confirmation of this is offered by the theme of secrecy. The point is

---

affetto d'amore, che l'essere in tutto signor d'ogni altra; ed io a così fatta donna non saprei aggiunger cosa alcuna, se non che ella fosse amata da così eccellente cortegiano come hanno formato questi signori, e che essa ancor amasse lui'.

102 *Ibid.*, III.LX: 'Ben è conveniente [...] insegnar alle donne lo amare, perché rare volte ho io veduto alcuna che far lo sappia; ché quasi sempre tutte accompagnano la lor bellezza con la crudeltà ed ingratitudine verso quelli che più fidelmente le serveno e che per nobiltà, gentilezza e virtù meritariano premio de' loro amori'.

103 *Ibid.*, III.LXII.

104 Its importance progressively increases among the different versions of the dialogue (consequently, the importance of Bembo as a character also increases). On this issue see Ghinassi 1967, pp. 159-160; Floriani 1976, p. 179.

105 Floriani 1976, pp. 179-182. See in particular sections 101-104 of that version, featuring a playful banter between Accolti and Emilia Pia, which partly survives in the final version. The second *Cortegiano* can be read in Ghinassi's edition (Castiglione 1968).

discussed by the interlocutors of the *Cortegiano*, in a way that provokes the irritation of Bembo.[106] Sonnet 419 from Tebaldeo's *Rime estravaganti* should also be mentioned. Here the speaker, in order to bend his beloved (who worries about her own reputation) to his will, promises that 'se me soccorri, il saperem sol nui', reassuring her that 'Di cosa occulta non po' biasmo uscire' (ll. 11 and 12). In Ariosto, the promise of secrecy is brought up in the last line of XXXI, and the theme is also present in the whole text of capitolo XX (the one describing the *segni d'amore*) and also in capitolo XXIII, where the theme of calumny is introduced, although only as an option rejected by the speaker. These concepts apply to some extent also to the poems that adopt a female point of view: we will return to this point in Chapter III.

3. Another path of the love discourse: the 'courtly-Petrarchan' celebration of woman

If it is the code of the love elegy – in its various Latin and Italian expressions – that offers Ariosto most of the ideas for his elaboration on the theme of love, in other texts he proves receptive to a more spiritualised vision, which derives from a mingling of literary memories ranging from Petrarch (undoubtedly the most influential)[107] to the Stilnovo and the Neoplatonic thought. Although ostensibly the two strands ('earthly' and 'celestial' love) are incompatible, courtly authors managed to find compromise solutions, even within a single work. Clear examples are the *Asolani* and the aforementioned passages of the *Cortegiano*.

I will now analyse the poems by Ariosto that bear the mark of this undercurrent, which for convenience I will denominate 'courtly-Petrarchan'. The principle on which these texts are elaborated is the celebration of the

---

106 In the second version of the dialogue, Bembo interrupts the discussion on love secrecy 'come chi non regga più a sentir parlare di un amore che abbisogna di precetti e accorgimenti e che s'apprende, ovidianamente, come una qualsiasi 'arte'' (Ghinassi 1967, p. 168). He is not taken seriously by Gaspare Pallavicino, who turns to Camillo Paleotto and prays him to continue on the theme (*ibid.*, p. 172). The theme of *segretezza* is already present in the first edition of the dialogue (*ibid.* p. 167).

107 It should be specified that, despite the fact that numerous situations inherited from the Latin love elegy (such as those briefly described in the preceding section) are clearly non-Petrarchan, it would be somewhat limiting to take Petrarch's Italian works as a model entirely 'alternative' to that of the elegiac code – since, as is known, he himself felt the influence of the Latin poets (it will be sufficient here to mention Tonelli 1998 and 2003). It is instead more correct to say that often it is the *Fragmenta* themselves that constitute the link with some motifs already present in that code. See for example the 'solo et pensoso' *topos*, which ultimately originates from Propertius.

lady. The beloved woman is here characterised as an idealised figure, unattainable by the speaker, who is overwhelmed by the contrasting feelings caused by the sight and the thought of her (expressed through frequent antitheses and oxymorons). This fact suggests that in these texts the canonical balance of power typical of lyric poetry is re-established, with the poet being subjected to his beloved, as in the following ballata:

Oh, se quanto è l'ardore
tanto, Madonna, in me fusse l'ardire,
forse il mal c'ho nel core   osarei dire.
A voi devrei contarlo,
ma per timore,   ohimè, d'un sdegno resto,
che faccia, s'io ne parlo,
crescergli il duol sì che l'uccida presto.
Pure io vi vuo' dir questo:
che da voi tutto nasce il suo martire,
et s'el ne more   il fate voi morire.

(*Rime del canzoniere*, V)

Although it is on the whole methodologically incorrect to look for single specific sources for the poems by Ariosto we are now examining (their inspiration should rather be sought in a poetic *koiné*), an exception may be made for the young Bembo, already a leading figure in the Italian vernacular style in the early sixteenth century (see Introduction). For example, a link can be established between a canzone belonging to the uncollected poems, *Dopo mio lungo amor, mia lunga fede* (III ed. Fatini) and Bembo's canzone 79 (*Gioia m'abonda al cor tanta et sí pura*), probably written for Maria Savorgnan in 1500-1501.[108] This link is suggested by the identical metre adopted by the canzoni (both are composed of only three stanzas with the rhyme scheme ABB.AAC/cDD; envoy: YyZZ)[109] and by the similarity between their themes, i.e. the choice of love in spite of the lady's indifference. The connection is further enhanced by the identity of some lexical choices:

---

108 See Donnini's notes in Bembo 2008, I, p. 180.

109 Note that the same rhyme scheme, although without the envoy, is adopted by Trissino in his canzone LXXII (*Deserte piagge e boschi ombrosi et hermi*), which is however in theme and tone not as close to the other two. It seems likely, as argued by Gorni 1993, p. 51, that of the three poets it was Bembo who inaugurated this metre and inspired Ariosto and Trissino. Indeed, the innovation is in line with Bembo's experimentation on Petrarchan patterns in those years, during which (as claimed by Dionisotti 1974, pp. 109-110) his major efforts were directed to the form of the canzone. As to Ariosto, we saw in Introduction, 3 how he found the canzone uncongenial.

'*Né* mi *pento* d'amar, né pentir posso' (canzone III ed. Fatini, l. 19) – '*Né* fia per tutto ciò che quella voglia [...] / rallenti il nodo suo' (Bembo, *Le rime*, 79,19-22); '*di lui mai non mi pento*' (*ibid.*, l. 26)

'quantunque vada la mia carne in *polve*' (canzone III ed. Fatini, l. 20) – '[...] poca *polve* et ombra' (Bembo, *Le rime*, 79,12)[110]

(emphasis mine)

Another interesting case is sonnet 58*, a poem that was excluded from Ariosto's selections – it is featured in the *editio princeps*, but not in the manuscripts constituting the main tradition –, perhaps on account of its rather involved style. Here a metaphor is developed of the woman as the Sun. This enables the poet to term 'blessed' ('Felice', 'beato') anything that benefits from her contact, from the land where she was born to the people for whom she constitutes a source of life:

Felice stella, sotto ch'il sol nacque,
chi di sì ardente fiamma il cor m'accese;
felice chiostro ove i bei raggi prese
il primo nido in che nascendo giacque.
Felice quell'humor che pria li piacque,
il petto onde l'humor dolce discese:
felice fè la terra in che 'l piè stese,
beò con gli occhi il fuoco, l'aere e l'acque.
Felice patria, che per lui superba
con l'India e con il ciel di par contende,
più felice che 'l parto che lo serba.
Ma beato chi vita da quel prende,
ove 'l bel lume morte disacerba,
ch'un molto giova e l'altro poco offende.

(*Rime del canzoniere*, 58*)

In this case also, a link with Bembo may be established. His canzone 26 (*Felice stella il mio viver segnava*), probably written for Maria Savorgnan,[111] has an identical beginning which consists, in turn, in the reversal of *Rvf*, CLXXIV 1: 'Fera stella [...]'. Moreover, the two poems display the same joyful and ecstatic conception of love, depicting the poet's falling in love and also sharing the metaphorical repertoire of light.[112]

---

110 See *Rvf*, CCXCIV 12: 'Veramente siam noi polvere et ombra'.

111 See Bembo 2008, I, pp. 67-69.

112 See Bembo, *Le rime*, 26,8: 'preso al primo apparir del vostro lume'; l. 11: 'si mise, vago, a gir di raggio in raggio'.

The solar metaphor was almost a commonplace in Petrarchism,[113] insofar as it enabled the speaker to digress on the 'divine' nature of the lady and to engender other metaphors: the poet burnt by passion, his awe in looking at her or, conversely, the impossibility of fixing his gaze on her (see the variations mentioned above on the myth of the eagle). If we examine the courtly repertoire, some examples may be found comparable to Ariosto, with the metaphor being developed throughout the entire length of the poems. For instance, in the following sonnet by Boiardo the sunset reminds the poet of 'his other' Sun, who has departed from him. This poem, however, is dominated by a grieving mood:

> Colui che il giorno porta è già ne l'onde,
> on forsi oltre a Moroco splende ancora,
> e fammi sovenir sempre quest'ora
> dell'altro Sol che Crudeltà me asconde.
>
> (*Amorum libri tres*, III 17,1-4)[114]

Most importantly, however, I believe that Ariosto's use of the solar theme may here be taken as evidence of a poetic exchange with Ercole Strozzi.[115] The first tercet of the sonnet, in particular, displays the same motif – the competition between the lady's homeland and the Orient, where the real sun rises – as the first tercet of Strozzi's sonnet *Euro gentil, che gli aurei crespi nodi*:

> Potrai ben dir, se torni al tuo soggiorno,
> né restar brami con mille altri preso,
> come 'l nostro levante al tuo fa scorno.
>
> (Strozzi, *Sonetti*, I 9-11)

Sonnet 58* may therefore be regarded as another of Ariosto's juvenilia and a testimony of his adhesion to an intellectual milieu which, under Bembo's influence, was elaborating in the very first years of the Cinquecento on specific lyrical ideas, and especially on the concept of love as a source of paradisiac 'beatitudine' (see e.g. Bembo, *Le rime*, 79,8-9: 'su nel ciel non è spirto sì beato / con ch'io cangiassi il mio felice stato').

---

113 I shall only note one of the longest references to this metaphor in Petrarch's canzoniere, namely *Rvf*, CCXIX 9-14: 'Così mi sveglio a salutar l'aurora / e 'l sol ch'è seco, et più l'altro ond'io fui / ne' primi anni abagliato, et son anchora. / I' gli ò veduti alcun giorno ambedui / levarsi inseme, e 'n un punto e 'n un'hora / quel far le stelle, et questo sparir lui'.

114 Other occurrences of the solar theme in the *Amorum libri* are listed by Zanato in Boiardo 2012, p. 747.

115 I also develop this thesis in Guassardo 2018, pp. 352-353.

The woman-Sun metaphor also underpins Ariosto's sonnet II, which is a poetic elaboration on the myth of Icarus:

Del mio pensier, che così veggio audace,
timor freddo come angue il cor m'assale:
di lino et cera egli s'ha fatto l'ale,
disposte a liquefarsi ad ogni face.
Et quelle, del desir fatto seguace,
spiega per l'aria, et temerario sale;
et duolmi ch'a ragion poco ne cale,
che devria ostarli, et sel comporta et tace.
Per gran vaghezza d'un celeste lume
temo non poggi sì ch'arrivi in loco
dove s'incenda et torni senza piume.
Seranno, ohimè, le mie lacrime poco
per soccorrergli poi, quando né fiume
né tutto il mar potrà smorzar quel foco.

(*Rime del canzoniere*, II)

According to this classical story,[116] Icarus, son of the craftsman Daedalus, was imprisoned by King Minos together with his father in the Labyrinth of Crete; he tried to escape with wings made of wax and feathers, but flew too close to the sun and fell into the sea. This theme easily lent itself to metaphoric elaborations in love poetry: if the woman is identified with the sun, Icarus's flight represents the doomed attempt of the poet to obtain her favours.[117] Here in particular, Icarus (not mentioned by name, but clearly alluded to through the reference to crafted wings at l. 3) personifies the poet's Thought, which attempts to follow Desire up through the air[118] to approach the Woman-Sun ('celeste lume'). The poet-speaker witnesses the event, deploring the passivity of Reason, who is supposed to take action, and fearing that Thought may get too close and be incinerated. The myth symbolises the ontological discrepancy between the 'divine' lady and the poet, whose approach to his object of desire cannot but be equated with an act of hubris ('audace', l. 1; 'temerario', l. 6).

---

116 This is mostly familiar from *Met.*, VIII 183-235 and *Ars amatoria*, II 15-98; but it is featured also in Virgil, Horace, Seneca. Its most influential classical versions are illustrated by Prandi 2004, pp. 103-109.

117 See, in Ariosto's poetry, also capitolo XXIII ed. Fatini, ll. 19-21 (already quoted at section 2).

118 For the topic association wings-desire, see *Purg.*, IV 28-29: 'con l'ale snelle e con le piume / del gran disio'; *Amorum libri tres*, I 15,3-4: 'Chi darà piume al mio intelletto et ale / sì che volando segua el gran desio?' (other similar cases are considered by Zanato in his commentary to this poem).

Ariosto could certainly be inspired by the numerous occurrences of the Icarus myth in the *Fragmenta*.[119] At the same time, his choice is also consistent with a Renaissance fashion. Indeed, the Icarus story, often paired with the similar story of Phaethon, appears frequently in treatises on love such as the *Libro de natura de amore* and the *Asolani* (in Perottino's pessimistic review of the experience of love),[120] as well as in early sixteenth-century poetry.[121] In these cases, Icarus's fall symbolises the lover, ruinously drawn to his woman despite the awareness of her superiority, only to end up burnt by passion. In particular, sonnet II can be linked to Tebaldeo's sonnet 347 (*De gran periglio son le grandi imprese*). In it the speaker explicitly compares his own 'troppo ardir' to that of Icarus and Phaethon, weaving into this theme that of the endless tears (as in the last tercet of Ariosto's poem).[122] Eventually he is drawn to the sententious conclusion that 'chi del suo grado esce / convien che alfin in pianto si consume', ll. 13-14. Another possible match is sonnet 600, also by Tebaldeo (*Ove ne vai, cor mio cieco? Misura*). Here the poet warns his 'blind heart', l. 1, about the dangers of such a flight, and again resorts to the *exempla* of Icarus and Phaethon ('Dovria Phetonte pur farte paura / et Icar, che 'l volare intese male', ll. 5-6).

The idea exemplified in both the story of Icarus and that of Phaethon, the dangers of daring too much (and the impossibility of controlling desire), appears also in canzone VI (*Quante fiate io miro*).[123] The speaker is

---

119 The closest Petrarchan reference is *Rvf*, CCXXX (*I' piansi, or canto, ché 'l celeste lume*), which includes an allusion to Icarus at l. 8: 'ma scampar non potienmi ale né piume'. From this poem Ariosto may also have drawn the syntagm 'celeste lume' and the final comparison between his tears and a river (cp. *Rvf*, CCXXX 5: 'onde e' suol trar di lagrime tal fiume'). See also *Rvf*, CXCIV 12-14: 'I' chiedrei a scampar, non arme, anzi ali; / ma perir mi dà 'l ciel per questa luce, / ché da lunge mi struggo e da presso ardo', as well as the whole text of *Rvf*, CCCVII (*I' pensava assai destro esser su l'ale*), for which see also below.

120 *Libro de natura de amore, Libro primo*, f. 12*v* (Equicola 1999, p. 222): 'ma volendo più alto che le forze non supportano volare, Icari et miserabili Phaetonti ci retrovamo; nel che nostra imprudentia, non amor si deve accusare'; *Asolani* I.xxv: 'o ali che bene in alto ci levate perché, strutta dal sole la vostra cera, noi con gli homeri nudi rimanendo, quasi novelli Icari, cadiamo nel mare'.

121 On the myth of Icarus in Italian and French sixteenth-century lyric poetry, see Prandi 2004.

122 See its ll. 5-11: 'E a me del troppo ardir che 'l cor mio prese / non men doglioso fin nato si vede: / ché, se a l'antica auctorità si crede, / il fulmine un, l'altro il sol caldo offese, / me la fiamma de Amor che assai più incresce. / E se l'un cade in mar, l'altro nel fiume, / dentro a una acqua cadi io che ognhor più cresce'. The link between this sonnet and Ariosto's has already been established by Prandi 2004, pp. 113-114. Fedi 1990 also identifies in Ariosto's poem a 'disposizione lirica che ancora rinvia alla tecnica ed alle proposte concettuali dell'officina di un Tebaldeo' (p. 100).

123 This is featured, alongside a miscellaneous manuscript, in **Vr**, **Mn**, **Pc**, **Cp**, but not in **F**: Ariosto probably excluded it from the most mature stage of his lyric project.

aware of the audacity of Desire and of the 'forbidden journey' of Hope in its pursuit:

> non posso far ch'un passo
> voglia andar la speranza
> dietro al desire audace.
> La misera si giace
> et odia et maledice l'arroganza
> di lui, che la via tiene
> molto più là che non se gli conviene.
>
> (*Rime del canzoniere*, VI 33-39)

This awareness culminates in the fear of some punishment ('però ch'ancor m'aspetto / de la mia audacia pena', ll. 17-18). Although both metaphorical terms – Icarus and Sun – have disappeared, yet the subject is very similar to sonnet II, as both poems centre on the theme of flight. Likewise, the poetic discourse is similar: in both, the envisioning of an uncertain punishment shapes the tense of the poem as a 'present moment', making it very different from Tebaldeo's sonnets, whose atemporality is determined by their moralistic messages.

The connection between sonnet II and canzone VI is even stronger if one looks at the earlier version of the former, which at l. 1 reads 'sperar' (to be compared with 'speranza' at VI 34) in place of 'pensier'. Incidentally, this fact shows that, in the sonnet, Hope was originally the ground for Icarus's metaphor, and indeed Hope and Desire are treated as closely related terms also elsewhere in the *rime*: 'et sì in alto poggiar dietro al desire / che non osa seguire / la speme' (IV 6-8 – see below); 'Deh, Madonna, l'andar fussi interdetto / dove non va la speme ai disir' miei!' (XXXIII 3-4). The substitution of 'pensier' was probably prompted by the principle of *variatio*, but it also gives more complexity, and a hint of paradoxicality, to the theme, suggesting that even the rational faculty of thinking loses its role, and aspires to a reconnection with the sensual self.

Indeed, it is very important to note that the Icarus myth, besides suggesting the lover's inferiority, is employed in these poems in its archetypal value as a symbol of amorous irrationality. Not coincidentally, we find it in the following passage from Bradamante's lament:

> Ma di che debbo lamentarmi, ahi lassa,
> fuor che del mio desire irrazionale?
> ch'alto mi leva e sì ne l'aria passa,
> ch'arriva in parte ove s'abbrucia l'ale;
> poi non potendo sostener, mi lassa
> dal ciel cader: né qui finisce il male;

che le rimette, e di nuovo arde: ond'io
non ho mai fine al precipizio mio.
(*Fur.*, XXX 17 A; XXXII 21 B; XXXII 21 C)

Sonnet II features, as we have seen, the theme of the annihilation of Reason (ll. 7-8); this is interesting to note, in that it constitutes a slight divergence from the medieval tradition of the conflict within the soul (*psychomachia*), where Reason is usually one of the fighters rather than a passive witness. A famous example of this are Dante's lussuriosi 'che la ragion sommettono al talento' (*Inf.*, V 39), but of course the fundamental reference here is Petrarch, whose canzoniere pivots precisely on the soul's inner conflict, and on the tensions between its different parts. In this regard it will be enough to quote *Rvf*, CI 12, 'La voglia e la ragion combattuto ànno', where the fight between desire and reason 'è anche il sotterraneo contrasto dei *Fragmenta* tra Vita attiva (Lia) e Vita contemplativa (Rachele)', as Rosanna Bettarini writes in her commentary.[124] More recent examples are Bembo's sonnet 55 – in which Desire, together with false Thoughts and Hope, engages in a battle against Reason,[125]

Con la ragion nel suo bel vero involta
l'ardito mio voler combatte spesso
di speme armato, et muovono con esso
falsi pensieri a larga schiera et folta.
(Bembo, *Le rime*, 55,1-4 – emphasis mine)

and, again from Bembo, sonnet 96 (*Amor, mia voglia e 'l vostro altero sguardo*), included in the first version – the *redazione queriniana* – of the *Asolani*, which also centers on the conflict between Reason and Desire:

Al foco de' vostr'occhi, qual ésca, ardo,
a cui l'ingordo mio voler mi mena,
et se ragion alcun tempo l'affrena,
Amor poi 'l fa più leve et più gagliardo.
(Bembo, *Le rime*, 96,5-8)

The irrationality of the lover, and the motifs connected with this topic (including its pathological excesses), is something we have already exam-

---

124 PETRARCH 2005, p. 472. For further information I refer the reader to the commentaries to *Rvf*, CXL, CXLVII, and CCXI.

125 The deceptiveness of Hope also features in BEMBO, *Le rime*, 57,1-4: 'Speme, che gli occhi nostri veli et fasci, / sfreni et sferzi le voglie e l'ardimento, / cote d'amor, di cure et di tormento / ministra, che quetar mai non ne lasci'.

ined in Chapter I, where this condition was an effect of the speaker's distance from his beloved. It is worthwhile to return to this subject, because as we have now seen this is not the only condition that Ariosto imagines to be available to the lover. Reason is also taken as a component of his psychology: this is demonstrated by the poems analysed in the previous section, where reason appears as a fundamental principle (although the term itself does not appear), which effectively directs the speaker's behaviour towards the woman, with the final aim of achieving reciprocity and equality. In the 'Icarian' lyrics, on the other hand, the scenario is different, and, not only is reason lost, but if it were present it would lead the speaker to the opposite behaviour, i.e. self-restraint and respect for the woman's superiority.[126]

It is clear that these two concepts are inspired by different interpretations of the female figure, one influenced by the love elegy, the other not. But it should be noted that in both cases the concept of reason is given a mundane meaning. It is, therefore, free from any Neoplatonic connotation, according to which it should rather be an instrument for the contemplation of God, as opposed to all types of earthly love, which are only driven by senses.[127] In Ariosto's poetry, only one poem among those that feature an 'Icarian flight' – which, incidentally, are very close to each other in **Vr** and constitute a sort of nucleus, placed at the very opening of the canzoniere – may be related to a Neoplatonic framework, namely madrigal IV:

Quando vostra beltà, vostro valore,
Donna, et con gl'occhi et col pensier contemplo,
mi volgo intorno et non vi trovo exemplo.
Sento ch'allhor mirabilmente Amore
mi leva a volo et me di me fa uscire,
et sì in alto poggiar dietro al desire
che non osa seguire
la speme, ché le par che quella sia
per lei troppo erta et troppo lunga via.

(*Rime del canzoniere*, IV)

---

126 Ariosto's dialogic capitolo *Amor che voi* also tackles the same theme: see Introduction, 5.

127 This connotation of Reason is featured in two famous passages inspired by Neoplatonism, i.e. the intervention of the hermit in the third book of the *Asolani* (on the hermit's doctrine, which in fact combines Neoplatonic and Aristotelian principles, see Berra 1996, pp. 240-255), and that of Pietro Bembo in the fourth book of the *Cortegiano*. Both speak in favour of old age as being the most suitable for love, just because, 'quando il fervor naturale comincia ad intepidirsi, s'accendono della bellezza e verso quella volgono il desiderio guidato da razional elezione' (*Cortegiano*, IV.LIII); 'Ché miglior parte della vita nostra è per certo quella [...] in cui la parte di noi migliore, che è l'animo, dal servaggio de gli appetiti liberata, regge la men buona temperatamente, che è il corpo, et la ragione guida il senso' (*Asolani*, III.xvi).

Here, what rises up is the poet's soul itself, prompted by the contemplative act: 'di me fa di me uscire' resembles the mystical *excessus mentis*.[128] And indeed, Hope, which belongs to the sensual self, this time remains earthbound. Ariosto is following an idea ultimately derived from Plato's *Phaedrus* (249d ff.), according to which the lover's contemplation of beauty triggers the heavenly ascent of his soul, towards its union with God.[129] This theme is filtered by Ariosto through the clear mediation of Petrarch[130] and constitutes the connecting element between this poem and the one that precedes it in **Vr**, sonnet III (*Quando muovo le luci a mirar voi*). The latter also portrays a situation of contemplation. Its object, however, in this case is not the lady herself, but rather the idea of her ('la forma che nel cor m'impresse Amore', l. 2), which, prompting an alternation of feelings that is once again clearly of Petrarchan origin,[131] would appear to be on the point of guiding the soul – a philosophically connoted term – towards ascent: 'Di che l'anima avampa, poi che degna / a tanta impresa par che Amor la chiami', ll. 9-10.

The theme of rapturous ascent to the skies through amorous contemplation had already been developed in poetry in the Ferrarese context, with notable examples in Boiardo.[132] This milieu certainly influenced Ariosto, but his friendship with Bembo must have especially contributed to his interest in Neoplatonism (see Introduction, 4). As a matter of fact, in his 1564 notes to the *rime,* Francesco Sansovino states that, in using the word 'contemplo' (or *contempio*) in madrigal IV, Ariosto was imitating a sonnet by Bembo.[133] Sansovino may be referring to *Le rime*, 145 (*Caro et sovran de*

128 Both in **F** and in one miscellaneous manuscript, l. 5 reads '[...] e senza di me uscire'; according to Finazzi 2002-2003, p. 208, this is the earliest reading, substituted for **Vr** and then resumed (it is unclear whether intentionally or by chance) much later.

129 On the Neoplatonic exegesis of the myth of Icarus, see Prandi 2004, p. 111; pp. 126-127, footnote 30. The theme of the flight with a similar meaning is, understandably, well established also in spiritual poetry (at least since *Par.*, XV 54: 'ch'a l'alto volo ti vestì le piume'). See, for instance, Bembo, *Le rime*, 177,13-14: 'da levarse / et rivolar a te vesta le piume'; Colonna, *Rime*, S1 93,12-14: 'sì che dei propri affetti ogni alma schiva / voli con l'ali del verace amore / a la beata Tua celeste riva'.

130 See *Rvf*, XVII 13: 'l'anima esce del cor per seguir voi'; XXIII 147: 'I' seguì' tanto avanti il mio desire'; CCXXXIV 11: 'che, seguendol, talor levommi a volo'. These links were noted by Bozzetti (Bozzetti – Vela 2000, p. 228).

131 See again Bozzetti – Vela 2000, p. 227.

132 See *Amorum libri tres*, I 13,1-4: 'Ride nel mio pensier la bella luce / che intorno a li ochi di costei sintilla, / e lèvame legier come favilla / e nel salir del ciel se me fa duce', and l. 11: 'Così, rapto nel ciel fuor di me stesso'; see also I 15.

133 Ariosto 1730, II, p. 363: 'Contempio, a imitazion del Bembo in un luogo de' suoi Sonetti'.

l'età nostra honore), in which Bembo praises Vittoria Colonna's virtues. This shares four rhyme-words (*exempio* : *contempio*; *amore* : *valore*) with Ariosto's madrigal. Furthermore, in both poems a distinction is made between a 'physical' and a 'non-physical' kind of sight: 'et con gli occhi et col pensier contemplo' (*Rime del canzoniere*, IV, l. 2); 'scorgo et contempio' (*Le rime*, 145,7). Bembo's sonnet, however, was certainly composed between 1530 and 1531,[134] while Ariosto's poem is attested in **Vr**, which is commonly dated *before* the first edition of Bembo's lyrics (1530).[135] It is therefore safer to suppose that the two poems may be independent: both may ultimately draw on the coupling of the 'two sights' which appears in Petrarch ('vedere e contemplare', *Tr. Mor.*, I 110), as well as in other texts inspired by Neoplatonism.[136] Alternatively, we may suppose that Sansovino was referring to *Le rime*, 41 (*L'alta Cagion che da principio diede*), a sonnet probably composed by Bembo for Lucrezia Borgia in 1503: though less close to Ariosto's madrigal in terms of word choices, this is definitely more similar to it in its theme. Here, the poet says he only enjoys happiness when he looks at his beloved, to whom he always turns 'come helitropio al sole' (l. 14): the beatitude he feels is similar to that caused by the contemplation of God ('et come è sol beato / a cui per gratia il contemplarla è dato', ll. 6-7).

Although it features in poems such as III and IV, however, this version of the 'flight' image remains at the margins in Ariosto's *rime*.[137] He instead favoured a version which, besides complying with his own vision (that was not primarily interested in the transcendent), also afforded him more scope for psychological exploration. We may see this if we return to sonnet II, where the speaking voice seemingly witnesses the event from an external standpoint. In other words, the misbehaviour of the components of the self is paradoxically analysed by the entity that can only exist if those components act in unison – and who is here, therefore, both *agens* and a detached *auctor*. This fashioning of the lyric voice is close to that in the aforementioned sonnet 600 by Tebaldeo (where the speaker addresses his

---

134 See Donnini's notes in Bembo 2008, I, p. 345.

135 An earlier version of it is also known (Finazzi 2002-2003, p. 208).

136 See, for example, *Asolani*, III.xx: 'Ma vie maggior diletto ti sarà [...] se tu da questi cieli che si veggono a quelli che non si veggono passerai, et le vere cose che ivi sono contempierai'. Ariosto also adopts similar pairings in the *Furioso*. See *Fur.*, VI 69,5-6 ABC: 'che a l'uom, guardando e contemplando intorno / bisognerebbe aver occhio divino'; XXI 34,7 AB; XXIII C: 'Lo mira, lo contempla, e dice spesso'. The verb 'contemplare' indicates non-physical sight also in *Fur.*, XXI 6,7-8 AB; XXIII C: 'ma sempre, o vegli o dorma, con la mente / contemplando Ruggier come presente'.

137 The lack of 'trasfigurazioni platonizzanti' in Ariosto's lyrics has been noted by Bigi 1953, p. 39; Fedi 1990, p. 91.

own heart). At the same time, it is also very Ariostean, in that it recalls the characteristics of the narrator of the *Furioso* – who is at once the victim of love-induced madness and he who is able to see it rationally and foresee its likely course (*Fur.*, XXXII 1,5-8 AB; XXXV C: 'Né di tanta iattura mi querelo, / pur che non cresca, ma stia a questo segno; / ch'io dubito, se più si va scemando, / di venir tal, qual ho descritto Orlando').

4. The flight of the poet: cases of metapoetry

As briefly mentioned above, during the Renaissance the literary elaborations of the story of Icarus often associated it with that of Phaethon.[138] The possible symbolic meanings of the two stories go beyond the field of love casuistry, a point that deserves some attention.

The myth of Phaethon should first be briefly outlined. Phaethon, the son of Apollo, dared to drive his father's chariot and lost control of it, only to be struck down by Jupiter's lightning and fall into the river Po.[139] As it offered the possibility of connecting the city of Ferrara to mythological events, this story was a favourite at the Este court, and features prominently in Ferrarese literature at least from the first half of the fifteenth century.[140] Ariosto's lyrics also contain one explicit mention of Phaethon, in sonnet XVII, which will be analysed later. Most importantly, Ariosto also includes it in his genealogical review of the Estensi in *Fur.*, III 34 ABC, where he defines Ferrara as 'la bella terra che siede sul fiume, / dove chiamò con lacrimoso plettro / Febo il figliuol ch'avea mal retto il lume' (ll. 2-4). Taking these lines of the *Furioso* as a starting point, Looney has sug-

---

138 See, for instance, Tebaldeo, *Rime della vulgata*, 34,9-11: 'Icar non son, che con le finte piume / cerchi volar [...] / né quel che ardendo ruinò nel fiume'; Correggio, *Rime*, 377,5: 'Ma se Icar perse le incerate penne', l. 36: 'e Fetonte el mostrò, che cadde in l'acque'. The two stories are associated already in *Inf.*, XVII 106-111: 'Maggior paura non credo che fosse / quando Fetonte abbandonò li freni, / per che 'l ciel, come pare ancor, si cosse; / né quando Icaro misero le reni / sentì spennar per la scaldata cera, / gridando il padre a lui: "Mala via tieni!"'.

139 The most familiar version of the story is in Ovid's *Metamorphoses* (I 750-II 339). For its metaphoric use, see Horace, *Carm.*, IV 11,25-26: 'Terret ambustus Phaethon avaras / spes'.

140 Some examples earlier than Ariosto (and including capitolo I ed. Fatini, a poem whose attribution to Ariosto is now in question – see Introduction, 5) are recalled in Looney 2005, pp. 2-4. The myth also features in *Fur.*, XXIX 69,6-8 A; XXIX 70 B; XXXI 70 C: 'e gran rimbombo al ciel ne riede, / simile a quel ch'uscì del nostro fiume, / quando ci cadde il mal rettor del lume'. I shall also note its presence in *Sat.*, III 109-111: 'Una stagion fu già, che sì il terreno / arse, che 'l Sol di nuovo a Faetonte / de' suoi corsier parea aver dato il freno' (here the myth serves to illustrate a drought: Phaethon had driven the chariot of the Sun too close to the earth, provoking fires and aridity).

gested that another factor should be considered as playing a part in the endurance of this myth, namely, that it could be interpreted politically as an image of the weaknesses of the duchy and of 'the Este family's difficulty in maintaining its precarious position in the shifting political realities of early modernity'.[141]

But if one considers the Icarus and Phaethon stories jointly, another aspect comes to light, which may be termed metapoetic in that it reflects on the role of literature, illustrating the limits inherent in creation and the risks connected to artistic ambition. From classical literature onwards, the Icarus/Phaethon figure is evoked self-referentially by writers who experienced (or felt they were about to experience) failure in their attempts: to push poetry to ultimate perfection, to grasp the metaphysical through human language, to achieve eternal fame.[142] As anticipated above, Petrarch also explored this theme in several poems. The most significant are *Rvf*, CCCVII-CCCIX,[143] where he confronts the limits of his own 'ingegno', symbolised by wings ('I' pensava assai destro essere su l'ale', *Rvf*, CCCVII 1) and reminds himself that divine grace is needed in order to accomplish the endeavour ('A cader va chi troppo sale, / né si fa ben per huom quel che 'l ciel nega', *ibid.*, ll. 7-8). Here Icarus/Phaethon does not feature openly, but his presence is subtly worked into the text of the poems through allusions.

Returning to Ariosto, a metapoetic value may also be ascribed to the mention of Phaethon at *Fur.*, III 34, which is incorporated in the poem, according to Looney, 'through a careful network of associations that illuminate, among other things, the potential danger of poetic inspiration'.[144] And indeed, the context of the octave is overall rich in allusions to poetic activity. First of all, this meaning is associated with the theme of flight at the opening of the canto: the narrator, just as he is about to illustrate the deeds of the Estensi, asks himself 'chi l'ale al verso presterà che vole / tan-

---

141 Looney 2005, pp. 1-2. According to Ascoli 1987, p. 341, 'The poet ironically situates the Este family at the site of the fall of the Sun's son, Phaeton, and he later makes Alfonso and Ippolito into (Phaeton-like?) imitators of the sun'.

142 There are many scholarly works, usually concerned with individual authors or works, which explore the metapoetic meaning of these myths. Prandi 2004, Degl'Innocenti Pierini 2012 and Giusti 2013 are overviews on the subject othat cover a wide period of time, from classical antiquity to Italian (French and Italian, in Prandi's case) literature. See also Velli 1983 (on Sannazaro). Among the poets belonging to courtly milieus, an example of an explicit mention of Icarus as a metaphor for the poet is in Tebaldeo, *Rime della vulgata*, 286,1-3: 'Sacre, legiadre, honeste, immortal' dive, / senza il favor de cui smarito resta / come Icaro qualunque in versi scrive'.

143 On this point, see at least Giusti 2013, pp. 101-102.

144 Looney 2005, p. 4.

to ch'arrivi all'alto mio concetto?' (*Fur.*, III 1,3-4 ABC).[145] Shortly after, he invokes Apollo, in a passage clearly inspired by Neoplatonism, where we also find references to *furor poeticus* (octaves 1-3).[146] Furthermore, together with Phaethon, in the mention of Ferrara at octave 34 Ariosto refers to his lover Cycnus ('e Cigno si vestì di bianche piume', l. 6). According to Ovid, Cycnus mourned Phaethon until he was changed by the gods into a swan, thus becoming another archetypal figure of the poet.[147]

The 'flight' and the 'swan' also occur together, at a very short distance, in the lunar sequence – another episode where the discussion on poetry takes on a primary importance. Here the reference to the flight is part of the self-reflexive utterances of the narrator, when, just as he is about to interrupt this story plot and resume that of Bradamante, declares that he cannot remain suspended in the sky: 'Resti con lo scrittor de l'evangelo / Astolfo ormai, ch'io voglio far un salto, / quanto sia in terra a venir fin dal cielo; / ch'io non posso più star su l'ali in alto' (*Fur.*, XXXII 31,1-4 AB; XXXV C).[148] The swans instead are seen by Astolfo among the inhabitants of the lunar valley and constitute the pretext for St John to voice his well-known reflection on writing (*Fur.*, XXXII 14-30 AB; XXXV C). Specifically, what Astolfo sees are two swans, which safely carry in their beaks a number of nameplates picked out of the river Lethe towards the temple of Immortality. Their ability to hold the nameplates despite their weight clearly differentiates these birds from the surrounding ravens and vultures – whose strength is insufficient to this task, and who eventually drop them back into the water. As St John explains, the weaker birds correspond to Earth's adulators and sycophants, who are often rewarded more than the true poets (the swans): here Ariosto introduces the theme of court

---

[145] The passage is probably directly indebted to that from Boiardo quoted at footnote 118. For the possible influence on it of a passage in Deuteronomy, see CASADEI 1993, p. 80. ASCOLI 1987, p. 340 links the passage to *Asolani*, III.viii, 64-65: 'chi mi darà tante ali, / ch'io segua lei [...]?'.

[146] See at least ASCOLI 1987, pp. 339-342; PICH 2015, p. 337.

[147] *Met.*, II 370-380. The stories of Phaethon and of Cycnus occur together in Petrarch's so-called *canzone delle metamorfosi*. See *Rvf*, XXIII 50-60: 'Né meno anchor m'agghiaccia / l'esser coverto poi di bianche piume / allor che folminato et morto giacque / il mio sperar che tropp'alto montava: / ché perch'io non sapea dove né quando / me 'l ritrovasse, solo lagrimando / là 've tolto mi fu, dì et nocte andava, / ricercando dallato, et dentro a l'acque; / et già mai poi la mia lingua non tacque / mentre poteo del suo cader maligno: / ond'io presi col suon color d'un cigno'.

[148] ASCOLI 1987 interpretes these lines as (p. 305) 'presumably an allusion to Icarus' abuse of Daedalus' art or to Bellerophon's fall from the horse of soaring imagination' and locates them within the overall self-representation of the narrator as mad: 'There is thus a clear suggestion that the lunar perspective is provisional even for the poet and that he is bound to find himself back at ground level, narrating the doings of characters whose blindness and folly he shares' (*ibid.*).

patronage through a dispassionate polemic – which has already been mentioned in Introduction, 5 – against the ignorance and avarice of rulers, who should not neglect the poets if they wish to be immortalised.[149]

In the *rime*, Cycnus is featured, again with an implicit metapoetic value, in the last tercet of sonnet XI:

> Com'esser può che degnamente io lodi
> vostre bellezze angeliche et divine,
> se mi par che a dir sol del biondo crine
> volga la lingua inettamente et snodi?
> Quelli alti stili et quelli dolci modi
> non basterian che già greche et latine
> scole ensegnaro, a dire il mezzo e il fine
> d'ogni lor loda a gli aurei crespi nodi;
> e 'l mirar quanto sian lucide et quanto
> lunghe et ugual' le ricche fila d'oro
> materia potria dar d'eterno canto.
> Deh, morso havess'io, come Ascreo, l'aloro!
> Di queste, se non d'altro, direi tanto
> che morrei cigno, ove tacendo io moro.
>
> (*Rime del canzoniere*, XI)

The poem's subject is the inadequacy of poetry to praise his lady's beauty, and it takes her blonde hair as an example of this. Notably, the poetic

[149] I will just quote *Fur.*, XXXII 23-24 AB; XXXV C: 'Son, come i cigni, anco i poeti rari, / poeti che non sian del nome indegni; / sì perché il ciel degli uomini preclari / non pate mai che troppa copia regni, / sì per gran colpa dei signori avari / che lascian mendicare i sacri ingegni; / che le virtù premendo, et esaltando / i vizii, caccian le buone arti in bando. // Credi che Dio questi ignoranti ha privi / de lo 'ntelletto, e loro offusca i lumi; / che de la poesia gli ha fatto schivi, / acciò che morte il tutto ne consumi. / Oltre che del sepolcro uscirian vivi, / ancor ch'avesser tutti i rei costumi, / pur che sapesson farsi amica Cirra, / più grato odore avrian che nardo o mirra'. This passage acts as a prelude to Ariosto's reflection on literature, whose main function – as he satirically suggests – is to tell lies: for an interpretation of this passage, see Introduction, 5. The symbolism of the (white) swan as opposed to the (black) raven, conveying the difference between sincere courtiers and adulators in a context where the lord's discernment is called into question, is in *Sat.*, IV 106: 'e stima il corbo cigno e il cigno corbo' (referred to the dispotic 'Laurino', probably Lorenzo de' Medici, Duke of Urbino). For this passage Ariosto was probably inspired by Erasmus, *Adagia*, 2297 (*Tunc canent cygni, cum tacebunt graculi*). For other occurrences of the crow as a generic symbol of slander in the lyrics (this time with no metapoetic connotation), see Chapter III, 4. As for the swan, it is a symbol for the 'poet' also in *Fur.*, XXXVII 13,1-4 C (where it is referred to Ercole, son of Alfonso I, who dabbled in poetry): 'C'è 'l duca de' Carnuti Ercol, figliuolo / del duca mio, che spiega l'ali come / canoro cigno, e va cantando a volo, / e fino al cielo udir fa il vostro nome'. Finally, I shall note than the swan-crow juxtaposition also occurs in the earlier version of the capitolo on the happy night of love, where the beloved's naked body is said to be so white that 'apo sé fa parer corvi / i bianchi cigni' (Finazzi 2002-2003, p. 229).

discourse becomes richer, more complex and even more technically skilful as the theme of ineffability is reaffirmed. Indeed, throughout the second quatrain and the first tercet the use of the *enjambement* increases and the poet proposes a *variatio* of fixed canonical expressions and adjectives to describe blonde hair: 'aurei crespi nodi', 'ricche fila d'oro', 'lunghe', 'ugual'. The poem actually centres on the issue of the expressive possibilities of poetry and of language itself. At the very moment in which the poet-speaker talks about his limits, he is also trying to overcome them by attempting to raise his style to the highest possible degree of refinement. Not coincidentally, the figure he fails to imitate is Hesiod ('Ascreo'), whose poetry Boccaccio had classified as lofty.[150] In particular, Ariosto refers to the legend according to which Hesiod acquired limitless communicative abilities after eating the laurel leaves that the Muses gave him in his dream. Without that special gift, the speaker says, the poetic act will always be hampered by limits, which are inherent not only in the vernacular,[151] but also in every Greek or Latin poetic form (the two antithetic styles mentioned, 'alti stili' and 'dolci modi', are probably the epic and the lyric). Finally, he refrains from any further utterance ('tacendo'), and in the last image of the poem alludes to himself as a failed Cycnus. The fundamental classical reference here is Horace, *Carm.*, II 20, where the poet imagines metamorphosising, as he dies, into a swan that will embark on a journey around the world (an image that serves to express his desire for posthumous glory).[152] Ariosto is therefore establishing a negative comparison with both Hesiod and Horace. At the same time, the metaphor of the swan also allows him to allusively pay homage to his homeland (Cycnus died while singing in the river Po, the same place where Phaethon had fallen).

Such a display of the metapoetic theme is therefore infused with a classical taste and is intended to compete with the classics themselves. Significantly, the Hesiod legend is also evoked by Ariosto in satira VI, which is addressed to Bembo, once again within the framework of a discussion on humanist knowledge, being among the myths he wishes his son Virginio to learn.[153] To know the chronology of this sonnet would be, in this case,

---

150 Boccaccio, *Amorosa visione*, IV 72: 'Essiodo almo'.

151 Bozzetti talks of an 'umanistica riflessione sulla inadeguatezza del volgare' (Bozzetti – Vela 2000, p. 236).

152 Horace, *Carm.*, II 20,9-12: 'iam iam residunt cruribus asperae / pelles et album mutor in alitem / superne nascunturque leves / per digitos umerosque plumae'.

153 *Sat.*, VI 137-138: 'e quel che da le morse fronde / par che poeta in Ascra divenisse'. To this point I shall add another, more veiled, allusion to the myth in the fourth satira, where the Muses are described as the 'dee che guardano la pianta / de le cui frondi io fui già così giotto'

especially useful, as it would allow us to understand the exact circumstances of its writing and its possible recipients. Nevertheless, there are some hints that suggest a connection between it and Ercole Strozzi's vernacular poetry. The complexity and elegance of its style, and the use of classical mythology, are in fact consistent with the poetic manner of the seven extant sonnets by Strozzi (whose style is clearly influenced by his mastery of Latin). Moreover, the rhyme between 'snodi' and the syntagm 'aurei crespi nodi' occurs identically in *Euro gentil, che gli aurei crespi nodi,*[154] which may also have played a role in the composition of Ariosto's 58* (see above, section 3). While 'aurei crespi nodi' is shared by Strozzi, its rephrasing in the next tercet as 'fila d'oro' is definitely Ariostean, as it occurs in the opening lines of other two poems by Ariosto. We do not know their chronology, but one of them, sonnet VII (*La rete fu di queste fila d'oro*) most probably belongs to an early poetic phase and even shares other textual connections with Strozzi.[155] Thus it seems that Ariosto may have wanted to engage in a dialogue on the exploration of the possibilities of poetry and on the ways of achieving *variatio* and stylistic elevation with a friend who, at the time (namely, in the months preceding his death in 1508), was concerned with moulding the vernacular so as to achieve in it the same proficiency he had in Latin.[156]

In this context, I would like to suggest that the allusion to Cycnus may also bear out this poetic intellectual and poetic relationship. To understand this point, we should recall the most famous appearance of Ercole Strozzi in literature: that is, his inclusion among the speakers of Bembo's *Prose della volgar lingua*. As a matter of fact, the aim of those who take part in the dialogue is precisely to instruct Ercole in the vulgar tongue and convert him to its use. In the opening of the second book (II.III), Giuliano de' Medici recounts a dream he had: while resting along the bank of the Arno, he

(ll. 14-15). As noted by Marini in his commentary to this passage (Ariosto 2019, p. 138), 'l'io satirico [...] proietta [...] il suo profilo su quello di un sommo poeta della classicità, Esiodo'. Marini also mentions the classical and Late Antique occurrences of the Hesiod legend, on which Ariosto may have drawn.

154 Strozzi, *Sonetti*, I 1-4: 'Euro gentil, che gli aurei crespi nodi / hor quinci hor quindi pel bel volto giri, / guarda non, mentre desioso spiri, / l'ale intrichi nel cor, né mai le snodi'. This sonnet had long been assigned to Castiglione; Strozzi's authorship was finally ascertained by Vagni 2011 in his overview on Strozzi's vernacular poetry.

155 For this point see Guassardo 2018, p. 354. This is one of the poems by Ariosto with the richest tradition (Finazzi 2002-2003, p. 212). The other occurrence of the phrase is in *Rime del canzoniere*, 54,1 ('Qual volta io penso a quelle fila d'oro'). This poem, however, was probably written later: see the next section on this point.

156 On this point see Introduction, 4.

saw a flock of swans paying homage to one swan. This was Ercole, 'del Po figliuolo', who had moved first to the Tiber, then to the Arno: the dream clearly alludes to the shift from Latin to the vernacular that Giuliano wishes Ercole to make. Could it be that the metaphorical name of 'cigno' in Ariosto's sonnet XI, in addition to subverting the Horatian concept (which is undoubtedly alluded to, given the reference to metamorphosis at the point of death), hides a homage to his friend's poetic talent, which the speaker admits he cannot equate? Another possible hypothesis is to connect the 'swan' of the sonnet to that in Bembo's canzone *Se 'l pensier che m'ingombra*: this was included by the poet in the second book of the *Asolani*, where it is recited by Gismondo. The poem foregrounds precisely how the 'canto' falls short of the amorous thought it would like to express. If this could be manifested fully in his verse, the speaker says,

> io che fra gli altri sono
> quasi augello di selva oscuro humile,
> andrei, cigno gentile,
> poggiando per lo ciel, canoro et bianco
>
> (Bembo, *Le rime*, 81,10-13)

Whether we choose to link Ariosto's poem to Strozzi, or to the youthful Bembo (whose poetry had formed both men),[157] and whether or not we accept that a direct referent may be found for his 'swan', it remains a testimony to a specific poetic season.

As a final observation on sonnet XI, it should be noted that, as it includes Ariosto's statement of his poetic intention, it may be compared to sonnet XIII (*Altri lodan il viso, altri le chiome*), which will be analysed in greater depth in Chapter III, 3. What matters here is that in XIII the poet's objective, i.e. to leave aside the celebration of the lady's outward appearance in favour of her intellectual qualities, is articulated through classical quotations. See the opening *priamel*, reminiscent of Horace and Propertius ('Altri lodan il viso, altri le chiome [...] Me [...]', ll. 1-5),[158] and its closing lines, in which the speaker regrets not being able to create with his art a 'viva / statua che dureria più d'una etade' (ll. 13-14), once again with a quotation from Horace[159] and a veiled reference to another myth, that of Pygmal-

---

157 A new research by Amelia Juri on the theme of the 'swan' in humanist and sixteenth-century poetry, and on the way Bembo's adoption of it influenced his contemporaries, is forthcoming.

158 Horace, *Carm.*, I 7,1: 'Laudabunt alii [...]'; Propertius, II 3,9: 'nec me tam facies, quamvis sit candida, cepit'. These echoes are also noted by Floriani 1988*bis*, pp. 256-257.

159 Horace, *Carm.*, III 30,1: 'Exegi moumentum aere perennius'.

ion. Despite the self-awareness of his insufficiency thereby conveyed, the poet's attitude towards his own activity is far more confident in this sonnet than in the one mentioned before. Indeed, he is opposing his own ambitious, classicising style to the majority of love poets who can do nothing but repeat the *topoi* imposed by the trite convention of Petrarchism, such as the 'canonical' celebration of beauty. Precisely because of the similarity in the speaker's attitude, XIII in turn may be linked with the already quoted sonnet XIX (*Aventuroso carcere soave*; see section 1), to which, in addition to the meanings we have enumerated, a subtle metaliterary meaning may be attributed. Indeed, this sonnet is also grounded in a juxtaposition, between 'li altri prigion' (l. 5) and the speaker himself. The former we may take to be Petrarch's more pedestrian imitators, from whom he consciously stands apart because of his different views on love. Such views lead him to deploy a classicising poetical language, to the extent that the poem closes with an evident loan from Catullus.

5. Between realism and myth

The poems we have just examined offer us the opportunity to embark on another overview, the object of which is to scan the employment of classical myths in Ariosto's lyrics, and especially in those poems on whose stylistic maturity scholars generally agree. The presence of myths in itself cannot certainly be regarded as Ariosto's prerogative, and is rather a constant of humanism (even in its courtly declension). This is not the place for an exhaustive description of the poetic deployments of myth, but it should be pointed out that these range from the most broadly conventional to the extremely personal, as with Boiardo. With specific reference to the latter's use of mythology, Mengaldo noted that 'non risente solamente di un atteggiamento culto di quattrocentista, ma certo anche dell'intenzione di creare attorno alla propria vicenda amorosa un alone di antiche e nobili leggende che contribuiscano a sollevarla su un piano di esemplarità'.[160] Ariosto is also able to achieve original results in this sense: the main aspect to note is his superimposition of myth – which is accompanied by a highly refined poetic register – onto situations that are drawn, or at least appear to be drawn, from reality.

A remarkable example is sonnet XVII, which is beyond doubt one of the most celebrated among Ariosto's poems, and one of those with the

160 Mengaldo 1963, pp. 265-266.

richest tradition (in addition to the main testimonies, it appears in eleven manuscripts).[161] On a stormy day, the poet suddenly witnesses the epiphany of his beloved on the shore of the turbulent river Po. Her presence determines a change in the weather, as the winds and the waters are immediately calmed:

> Chiuso era il sol da un tenebroso velo
> che si stendea fin all'extreme sponde
> de l'orizonte, et murmurar le fronde
> s'udiano, et tuoni andar scorrendo il cielo.
> Di pioggia in dubbio, o tempestoso gelo,
> stav'io per ire oltra le torbide onde
> del fiume altier che 'l gran sepolcro asconde
> del figlio audace del signor di Delo;
> quando apparir su l'altra ripa il lume
> de' bei vostr'occhi vidi, e udi' parole
> che Leandro potean farmi quel giorno.
> Et tutto a un tempo i nuvoli d'intorno
> si dileguaro, et si scoperse il Sole;
> tacquero i venti et tranquillossi il fiume.
>
> (*Rime del canzoniere*, XVII)[162]

This is the only poem by Ariosto where the landscape features prominently. The accurate description of nature – which occupies the first quatrain, part of the second, and the last tercet – serves as a sort of frame that encloses the development of the event. At the same time, the dimension of myth is projected onto the event itself. Indeed the speaker, when he sees his beloved's eyes and hears her words, would appear to be ready to replicate the story of Leander. According to Ovid,[163] Leander swam across the Hellespont every night to meet his beloved Hero, a priestess of Aphrodite, who would light a lamp (whose equivalent in the sonnet are the lady's eyes: 'lume', l. 9) to help him see his way. It was during a storm that Leander

---

161 FINAZZI 2002-2003, p. 222.

162 We find very similar textual material in an octave of the *Furioso* (which already appeared in the 1516 version) where the beginning of a storm is described – it is impossible, however, to determine which of the two elaborations of the theme came first: 'Stendon le nubi un tenebroso velo / che né sole apparir lascia né stella. / Di sotto il mar, di sopra mugge il cielo, / il vento d'ogn'intorno, e la procella / che di pioggia oscurissima e di gelo / i naviganti miseri flagella: / e la notte più sempre si diffonde / sopra l'irate e formidabil onde' (*Fur.*, XVI 142 A; XVIII BC). According to Bozzetti (BOZZETTI – VELA 2000, p. 242), this description is indebted to STATIUS, *Theb.*, V 364-367: 'inde horror aquis, et raptus ab omni / sole dies miscet tenebras, quis protinus unda / concolor; obnixi lacerant cava nubila venti / diripiuntque fretum [...]'.

163 *Her.*, XVIII (*Leander Heroni*).

drowned, in a situation therefore similar to that described in this sonnet. Indeed, evil omen seems to wind its way through the poem. To this sense of foreboding contribute not only the metereological elements, but also the identification of the Po as Phaethon's sepulchre ('figlio audace del signor di Delo'): he, too, was died in water, and his hubristic boldness would appear implicitly to be projected onto that of the protagonist. The sonnet actually has a happy ending: nature favours the speaker, and what the gods in the myth had made unachievable, is here possible. Yet it remains ultimately unclear whether the speaker crosses the river. The sonnet has no development: the mythological projections, therefore, belong solely to the speaker's imagination and are not lived out in the events that constitute the 'reality' of the poem. It is precisely this element that has led Cabani to detect an ironic note (which I also feel is present), in what she describes as a 'divertito e quasi paradossale ingigantimento di un evento di per se stesso inconsistente'.[164]

According to Rinaldi, the woman is here depicted as a good sorceress, capable of controlling Nature's elements through words as well as of casting a love spell on the poet.[165] This reading is certainly tenable: indeed her 'parole' seem to be the trigger for the speaker's action and, at the same time, for the clearing up of the weather. Such a portrayal is also consistent with other representations of sorceresses across Ariosto's oeuvre (see Chapter I, 6), and is probably indebted, as again argued by Rinaldi, to that of Medea in Ovid's *Metamorphoses*.[166] But in addition to this, I should note that a further classical reference is at play in this situation which has hitherto escaped critics, the last tercet being modelled on the following passage of the proem of Lucretius's *De rerum natura* (which also contains a reference to the crossing of a river):

> te, dea, *te fugiunt venti, te nubila caeli*
> adventumque tuum, tibi suavis daedala tellus
> summittit flores, *tibi rident aequora ponti*. [...]
> Inde ferae pecudes persultant pabula laeta
> *et rapidos tranant amnis*: ita capta lepore
> te sequitur cupide quo quamque inducere pergis.
> (Lucretius, *De rerum natura*, I 6-16 – emphasis mine)

The passage is part of the famous hymn to Venus, the goddess of pleasure and desire who rules over the cosmos: it describes the awakening of

164 Cabani 2016, p. 117.

165 Rinaldi 2000, pp. 315-316.

166 *Ibid.*, p. 317.

spring, when her power is at its height. These specific lines had also been significant for Boiardo, who, in *Amorum libri tres*, I 6, represented his beloved Antonia as a modern Venus: 'Al suo dolce guardare, al dolce riso / l'erba vien verde e colorito il fiore / e il mar se aqueta e il ciel se raserena' (ll. 12-14).[167] Ariosto's beloved, therefore, is embodied by both Hero *and* Venus. The ultimate meaning of the poem is related to mutual, and also sensual, love, and it is perhaps no coincidence that in **Vr** this sonnet should precede the two sonnets on the 'room' (see above, section 1). It should be noted that in one of his apologues Celio Calcagnini explicitly links the Hero and Leander story to the figure of Anteros, the god of reciprocated love (and the subject of his essay mentioned at section 2). Although the chronology of the apologue cannot be established, it is nonetheless worth mentioning it in relation to this poem, as both may be regarded as evidence of a 'hot topic'.[168] Another quotation of the story to a similar end is in the *Asolani*, where it is used by Gismondo to prove the sweetness of love.[169]

Incidentally, it is interesting to compare this poem with Bembo's sonnet *Fiume, onde armato il mio buon vicin bebbe* (*Le rime*, 117), which shares a similar theme.[170] Bembo stages an analogous situation: the woman is caught in a shower of rain while sailing on the river Brenta; the sky soon repents its mischief, and clears up. Bembo, too, accomplishes the description of nature through the lens of myth, but the classical hints end up appearing as little more than ornamental[171] and do not contribute to the overall meaning of the poem.

---

[167] For Lucretius's influence on Boiardo, see Zanato 2014, pp. 26-28. See also Boiardo 2012, pp. 89-92. This passage by Boiardo has been considered to be a possible source for Ariosto also by Bianchi (Ariosto 1992, p. 233).

[168] Calcagnini 1544, p. 638: 'Post Leandri et Herus infortunium ferunt Sestiacos lucernam illam nocturnae natationis testem Anteroti consecrasse, addito titulo: "Anteroti sacrum. Qui se felicem in amore probaverit, hanc succendito. At qui eam succenderit, ad hanc diem inventus est nemo"' (punctuation mine).

[169] *Asolani*, II.xxv: 'Le narrate dolcezze de gli amanti, o donne, essere vi possono segno et dimostramento delle non narrate [...] non è hoggimai da maravigliarsi di Leandro, se egli, per vedere la sua donna pure un poco, largo et periglioso pelago spesse volte a nuoto passava'. As noted by Berra 1996, p. 197, 'la infelice giovane di Sesto' (i.e. Hero) also features in the first book of the *Asolani* (I.xvii), as an example of love suicide which serves Perottino to argue against love.

[170] Bembo's sonnet was written close to 1530 (Bembo 2008, I, p. 288) and is therefore, very probably, more recent than Ariosto's (at least, it is more recent than the octave from the *Furioso* with which it shares textual material: see footnote 162). Turchi's statement that Ariosto wrote the poem 'ad imitazione di quello del Bembo' (Ariosto 1730, II, p. 364) is therefore incorrect; it should rather be supposed that Bembo imitated Ariosto.

[171] The Brenta is identified through the memory of the battle of 302 B.C., narrated by Livy, which saw the victory of the Paduans against the Spartan king Cleonymus ('quando del

But to return to Ariosto, a similarity with his use of ancient legends in sonnet XVII may be noted in capitolo XLII (*O qual tu sia nel cielo, a chi concesso*). The speaker is worried about his beloved's illness and prays to God for her recovery. This is an extremely popular theme in the *poesia occasionale*, where the preference was however to decline it in the form of the sonnet.[172] In this light Ariosto's choice of the capitolo in fact bespeaks his classicising intention, and indeed, although he invokes the 'Padre eterno' (l. 40), the poem is infused with classical reminiscences. In particular, it recalls a poem by Propertius, II 28, where the speaker also appeals to the gods to save Cynthia from a serious illness, and tries to guess at the reasons why they should punish her so harshly. But while there emerges from Propertius's poem a recognition of Cynthia's guilt (at the very least for not having revered the gods enough),[173] Ariosto openly claims his woman's innocence, except on the count of not having reciprocated his love for so long:

> Innocente è Madonna, se non d'una
> colpa forse: che l'avida mia voglia
> sempre ha lasciata oltre il dover digiuna.
>
> (*Rime del canzoniere*, XLII 22-24)

In the last part of the capitolo, l. 34 ff., the speaker asks God to transfer onto him the punishment inflicted on the woman. Here he resorts to examples of self-sacrifice drawn from the Roman history, showing an erudite poetic attitude that may be ultimately inspired by his Latin model (also Propertius's poem features some myths, although in a different context) but especially draws on Petrarch's *Triumphus Famae*.[174] Rather than to these *exempla*, however, I would like to call attention to the myth that concludes the poem – the story of Admetus:

---

gorgo e de la destra riva / fugò lo stuol di Sparta', ll. 2-3); at the end of the sonnet, the waters are embodied by Thetis ('rendendo a Theti chiaro et puro il giorno', l. 14). CABANI 2016, pp. 117-118 footnote, notes that the two poems 'mostrano due atteggiamenti opposti nell'uso del repertorio classico oltre che due concezioni assai diverse del far poesia', also on account of the different treatment of the poetic 'I' (in Bembo simply a spectator; in Ariosto the protagonist – albeit of a narrative situation without any actual development).

172 To mention but a few examples, TRISSINO, *Rime*, 32 (ll. 9-11: 'Ma tu, Re de le stelle, eterno padre, / non consentir ch'a torto altrui ne prive / del maggior nostro bene, e del più caro'); TEBALDEO, *Rime della vulgata*, 25; CORREGGIO, *Rime*, 249.

173 PROPERTIUS, II 28,5-6: 'sed non tam ardoris culpast neque crimina caeli / quam totiens sanctos non habuisse deos'.

174 More specifically, he mentions the stories of Curtius and of the two Decii, father and son, following *Tr. Fam.*, I 67-72. This debt is acknowledged by Segre's commentary (ARIOSTO 1954, p. 206).

Odiosa fu la tua contraria sorte,
ingratissimo Admeto, che, agli casti
prieghi inclinando, la fedel consorte
morir per te nel più bel fior lasciasti.
(*Rime del canzoniere*, XLII 52-55)

According to Valerius Maximus, Admetus, the king of Pherae, learnt that he would recover from his illness only if his wife Alcestis agreed to die in his place, upon which Alcestis accepted to undergo this fate. This myth serves Ariosto as an 'anti-exemplum', since letting Alcestis die was proof of ingratitude (to his mind, the worst sin possible in a love relationship). Ariosto juxtaposes it, in the lines preceding this quotation, to the positive case of Tiberius Sempronius Gracchus who, again in Valerius's recount,[175] had no hesitation in giving his own life in order to spare that of his wife. In this case too, the use of myths is not merely decorative, but aims to better describe a specific amorous situation, that of reciprocated love in marriage or in a marriage-like relationship.

Ariosto's tendency to express through myth a situation of reciprocity reaches its highest degree of originality in a number of sonnets belonging only to **F**/**Mn** and not included in **Vr**. Whatever the reason for this – Ariosto may have written them later, or he may not have wanted them to circulate until late in his life because of the private nature of the feelings they describe –, the female protagonist here does not seem to be a stereotypical lady, as in most of Ariosto's lyrics, but rather a concrete person, whom we may identify as Alessandra Benucci. Her relationship with the poet was not made public for a long time: she and Ariosto eventually got married between 1526 and 1530, in great secret (possibly on account of her fear of losing custody of her children and the management of the legacy of her late husband Tito Strozzi).[176] These poems constitute the most significant integrations of Ariosto's 'last canzoniere', making the supposition likely that in this final form it was to be dedicated to Alessandra. To these should be added canzone 50, the poem where the figure of Alessandra is most successfully portrayed, which will be extensively analysed in Chapter III.

Four of these lyrics, sonnets 52, 53, 54, and 55 – which appear in consecutive positions in manuscripts **F1** and **F2** – allow us to reconnect to the theme of illness. They can be regarded as a mini cycle, as they were probably prompted by the same occasion, that is, by a period of illness suffered

[175] Valerius Maximus, *Factorum et dictorum memorabilium libri IX*, IV.V 6 (see *ibid.*, p. 207).

[176] See Catalano 1930-1931, I, pp. 610-618.

by Alessandra, which made it necessary for her to cut her hair (the theme is tackled also in the more conventional ballata 57, *Se mai cortese fusti*). At first sight, Ariosto may appear here to be writing strictly 'occasional' poems, and to be superficially indulging in the description of female hair (we shall return to this point in Chapter III, 2). What he is actually doing is playing variations on this everyday event so as to refine it into myth.

A common pattern among these sonnets should be pointed out. This is the effort made, in the last lines of each, to link the event to a classical legend: an attempt which (at least in 53 and 55) may be classified as aetiological. In the tercets of sonnet 53 (*Son questi i nodi d'or, questi i capelli*), Ariosto first reproaches the incompetent doctor ('Phisico indotto', l. 9) for not being able to find a cure more respectful of Alessandra's beauty. He then concludes that it must have been Apollo, the god of medicine, to wish for this, in order to eliminate a dangerous rival of his own hair ('Ma così forse ha il tuo Phebo voluto / acciò la chioma sua, levata questa, / si possa inanzi a tutte l'altre porre', ll. 12-14). In sonnet 54 (*Qual volta io penso a quelle fila d'oro*) the poet once again thunders against the doctor, and seeks revenge on his 'empie mani et stolte' (l. 8). Thereafter he turns his barrage of accusations onto Cupid, who should have taken action, as Bacchus did against Lycurgus:

> Ch'elle [= the doctor's hands] non sieno, Amor, da te punite
> ti torna a biasmo: Bacco al re de' thraci
> fe' costar cara ogni sua tronca vite;
> e tu, maggior di lui, da queste audaci
> le tue cose più belle et più gradite
> levar ti vedi, e tel comporti e taci.
>
> (*Rime del canzoniere*, 54,9-14)

The idea around which the poem revolves is that of mutilation. Because Lycurgus cut down Bacchus's sacred vines, the god punished him by driving him insane and compelling him to chop off one of his feet:[177] a similar punishment should be inflicted by Cupid on the doctor's hands, which are responsible for an equally serious 'cut'. All this suggests that Alessandra's hair, too, is dear to the gods, and particularly to the god of love. Interestingly, the attitude of passive acceptance attributed to Cupid, at l. 14, is identical to that of 'ragion', that is guilty of not taking action to prevent Thought's flight, in sonnet II ('et sel comporta et tace' – see section 3).[178]

Sonnet 52 is perhaps the most skilfully crafted among the four and as such is worth quoting in full:

---

177 The version of the legend is narrated by Pseudo-Hyginus, *Fabulae*, 132.

178 This in turn is indebted to *Rvf*, CL 8: '– Questo ch'è a noi, s'ella sel vede, et tace?'.

Qual avorio di Gange, o qual di Paro
candido marmo, o qual hebano oscuro,
qual fin argento, qual oro sì puro,
qual lucid'ambra, o qual cristal sì chiaro,
qual scultor, qual artefice sì raro
faranno un vaso alle chiome che furo
de la mia donna, ove riposte, il duro
separarsi da lei lor non sia amaro?
Ché ripensando all'alta fronte, a quelle
vermiglie guancie, alli occhi, alle divine
rosate labra, e all'altre parti belle,
non potrian, se ben fosson come il crine
de Beronice assunto fra le stelle,
riconsolarsi et porre al duol mai fine.

(*Rime del canzoniere*, 52)

The hair itself, argues Ariosto, must be in despair at being separated from such a beautiful creature, and not even its being held in the most precious jar will ease the pain of separation. At the end the poet alludes to the possibility that the hair may be placed in the sky by some god, although this does not sufficiently console the tresses themselves. Ariosto creates a link to the story of the Lock of Berenice, the subject of one of Callimachus's *Aetia*, a Latin version of which was authored by Catullus (poem LXVI). In Catullus's account, the Egyptian queen vowed to cut off a lock of her hair and dedicate it to Aphrodite if her husband safely returned from a military campaign. In the epilogue, the lock was transformed by the goddess into a constellation. In Ariosto's poem, not only is the classical legend explicitly mentioned at ll. 12-13, but the author's overall empathy with the hair's perspective is fully consistent with that of the sources: both Callimachus's and Catullus's poems speak through the voice of the lock, which on several occasions articulates its unwillingness at being parted from Berenice's head.[179]

The choice of this myth establishes a link between this poem and the above-mentioned sonnet 54, in which it is also implied that the beloved's hair is dear to the gods of love. Furthermore, however, Ariosto is able to hint that the poem's underlying event is part of a situation of mutual love. Indeed, it is precisely the theme of fidelity that underpins the story of Berenice. Moreover, at the end of Catullus's poem the speaker encourages young brides not to give themselves to their husbands unless they have

---

179 Catullus, LXVI 39-40: 'invita, o regina, tuo de vertice cessi, / invita: adiuro teque tuumque caput'; ll. 75-76: 'non his tam laetor rebus, quam me afore semper, / afore me a dominae vertice discrucior'.

first treated their hair with ointments from ritual onyx jars:[180] the fact that Ariosto also includes a 'vaso' in 52, within a context of generalised mythological preciosity, may be further evidence of his memory of Catullus (although he employs the motif to a different end). If we accept this, we should see this borrowing as also containing a hint at the 'marital' nature of the relationship between himself and Alessandra, whether or not it was written after the wedding itself had been celebrated.

Finally, we should note the witty poetic expedient of starting sonnet 52 with a proliferation of nouns describing precious materials. This tricks readers into thinking that they are looking at yet another variation of the *descriptio puellae*, which usually deploys such terms with a metaphorical value: see *Rvf*, CCCXXV 16-17, which compares Laura's body to a luxurious building ('Muri eran d'alabastro, e 'l tetto d'oro, / d'avorio uscio, et fenestre di zaffiro') and see Ariosto's own sonnet 51, *Aventurosa man, beato ingegno* (mentioned at section 2). The latter also belongs to the new additions for **F** and is contiguous to 52: here the beloved's beauties are 'avorio et perle et un tesoro' (l. 6), and are described as being even more desirable than a kingdom girded by the Ganges, the same river mentioned at 52,1. In 52, however, the reader is not actually presented with metaphors, but rather with a 'concrete' object:[181] only late in the second quatrain does this become clear. This expedient also enhances the parallelism between the actual description of the attributes of the woman, in the first tercet, and the hypothetical 'substitute' for the woman herself, that is, the jar.

Sonnet 55 (*Giorno a me sol più che la notte oscuro*) is also constructed similarly to those mentioned above. The poet cannot stop crying for his beloved's illness, whose effects are accurately described ('d'acerbo et duro / mal è premuta et ogni membro ha stanco, / tanto gli arde la febre il petto e il fianco', ll. 5-7). The context of the poem is a festive journey during which all other people rejoice: 'stan gli altri in festa, in gioia', l. 3.[182] At this point, Ariosto calls upon the myth of Prometheus ('mercé di Prometeo malvaggio et

---

180 *Ibid.*, ll. 80-83: 'non prius unanimis corpora coniugibus / tradite nudantes reiecta veste papillas / quam iucunda mihi munera libet onyx, / vester onyx, casto colitis quae iura cubili'.

181 In this acception as a concrete object – and not as a metaphorical receptacle of virtue or vices – the vase sometimes appears in late-Quattrocento occasional poetry, and particularly so in Correggio. See, from his *Rime*, numbers 50, 82, and 248, in the latter of which the vase contains an unguent. Here however the function of the vase is not the same as in Ariosto's sonnet: it is, rather, an object that acts as an intermediary between the poet and his beloved, following a stylistic motif typical of courtly Petrarchism (on objects 'allied' with the lover in Serafino Aquilano, see Rossi 1980, pp. 36-44).

182 As a matter of fact, the second line, 'più del solito agli altri puro et bianco [giorno]', probably alludes to a precise event: the day in question may be Easter, or Candlemas.

duro', l. 8) to justify the woman's illness: enraged at Prometheus's theft of fire as a gift for mankind, Zeus punished the latter by sending down into the world Pandora, whose jar contained all the evils[183] ('poi fece segno con la destra mano / ai mali che scendessero a 'sto loco', ll. 13-14). For Segre, Prometheus was introduced in this poem only as a symbolic representation of fire: therefore, he argues, Alessandra's illness can be read as the effect of a burn, which would have caused the cutting of her hair.[184] Be this as it may, it should be noted that Ariosto is able to establish a chain of correspondences among the characters involved through the use of the identical rhyme: Prometheus is 'duro' just as 'duro' is Alessandra's illness; each of the woman's limbs is 'stanco', but the poet himself is also 'stanco' (l. 3). The latter link certainly enhances the feeling of empathy between the two lovers.

Such feeling also emerges from sonnet 56 (*Qui fu dove il bel crin già con sì stretti*). This is closely related to canzone 50, which describes the circumstances in which Ariosto fell in love with Alessandra, during the Florentine feast of St John the Baptist in 1513.[185] In this sonnet, the poet remembers that day, addressing (l. 4) the architecture of the city:

> Qui fu dove il bel crin già con sì stretti
> nodi ligommi, et dove il mal che poi
> m'uccise incominciò; sapestel voi,
> marmoree loggie, alti et superbi tetti,
> quel dì che donne et cavallieri elletti
> haveste, quai non hebbe Peleo a' suoi
> conviti, alhor che, scelto in mille eroi,
> fu alli himenei che Giove havea suspetti.
> Ben vi sovien che de qui andai captivo,
> traffisso il cor; ma non sapete forse
> come io morissi et poi tornassi in vita,
> et che Madonna, tosto che s'accorse
> esser l'anima in lei da me fuggita,
> la sua mi diede, et ch'hor con questa vivo.
>
> (*Rime del canzoniere*, 56)

Such articulation is rather unusual, as in the lyric tradition it was the elements of nature, not those of architecture, that were chosen by poets

183 Hesiod, *Work and Days*, ll. 44-105; Horace, *Carm.*, I 3,27-33. Ariosto alludes to this myth also in *Sat.*, VII 43-45: 'Non vuo' più che colei che fu del vaso / de l'incauto Epimeteo a fuggir lenta / mi tiri come un bufalo pel naso' (he is referring to Hope, the last to leave Pandora's jar).

184 Ariosto 1954, pp. 145-146.

185 See Chapter III, 2.

as their confidants. In other words, we are witnessing a refashioning of the 'solo et pensoso' *topos*, whose effect is now to project the poet's experience not onto a conventional chronotope, but onto a real place (this makes this poem very different, for instance, from those on the love encounter that were discussed at section 1). What is described seems to be something that actually happened. It is also clearly an experience that takes place within the city,[186] whose setting and elegance acquire here a positive value, moving away from the myth of the idyllic simplicity of the rural landscape. Such an explicit contrast between the town and the country is deployed, to mention but two examples from Ariosto's times, in the following poems by Serafino Aquilano and Bembo:

Palazzi, loggie, palchi, anfiteatri,
cibi, pompe, gemme, argento e fama,
luxurie, invidie ora non n'è sorte.
Poveri eletti fur li antiqui patri,
ma le ricchezze che ognun tanto brama
ci toglion pace, e dànno guerra e morte.
(Serafino Aquilano, *Rime*, 116,9-14)

Triphon, che 'n vece di ministri et servi,
di loggie et marmi, et d'oro intesto et d'ostro,
amate intorno elci frondose, et chiostro
di lieti colli, herbe et ruscei vedervi
(Bembo, *Le rime*, 140,1-4)

In Ariosto's poem, the speaker is apparently visiting Florence sometime after the 'fatal day' and recounts what has changed since then. The news is, significantly, that his one-sided love has turned into a reciprocated one, as illustrated through the image that appears in the final tercet of the mutual exchange between the two souls (a motif popularised by two youthful canzoni by Bembo).[187] As I anticipated, in this case also the ultimate meaning of the poem, the happiness of the love relationship with Alessandra, is both filtered through and enhanced by the use of myth: in the second quat-

[186] We may compare the architectural references to those featuring in the description of Florence in capitolo XXX (on which see Chapter I, 4). See ll. 34-36: 'Chi potrà a pien lodar li tetti regii / d'i tuoi privati, i portici et le corti / di magistrati et le corti e li seggi?'; l. 40: 'Piazze, mercati, vie marmoree, ponti'.

[187] Bembo, *Le rime*, 26 and 27; the latter is probably a reworking of the former so that it could be included in the *Asolani*. See 27,20-21: 'così cangiaro albergo, e da quell'hora / meco 'l cor vostro e 'l mio con voi dimora'. In turn, Bembo drew this theme from Giovanni Aurelio Augurello; see Donnini's commentary (Bembo 2008, I, p. 68) for details.

rain, he compares the luxury of the feast in which he took part (for which see Chapter III, 2) to the marriage banquet of Peleus and Thetis. Ariosto was probably thinking of Catullus's version of the myth in poem LXIV. While Catullus also lingers on the splendour of the occasion,[188] what is especially relevant in Ariosto is that the use of this classical episode leads the reader to establish a connection between it and the poet's own situation. The marriage between a goddess and a mortal could indeed be an effective metaphor to describe a happy love relationship in lyric terms (it implied, for example, the traditional recognition of the woman's superiority) and the possibility should not be ruled out that Ariosto wrote this poem when he eventually married Alessandra.

6. The conclusion of **Vr**

By way of conclusion of this overview of the love theme in Ariosto's lyrics, I shall look at the last poem of **Vr**, sonnet XLVIII (*Come creder debbo io che tu in ciel oda*):

Come creder debbo io che tu in ciel oda,
Signor benigno, i miei non caldi prieghi,
se, gridando la lingua che mi sleghi,
tu vedi quanto il cor ne'·llacci goda?
Tu che 'l vero conosci, me ne snoda
e non mirar ch'ogni mio senso il nieghi;
ma prima il fa' che, di me carco, pieghi
Charon il legno alla dannata proda.
Escusi l'error mio, Signor eterno,
l'usanza ria, che par che sì mi copra
gli occhi che 'l ben dal mal poco discerno.
L'haver pietà d'un cor pentito ancho opra
è di mortal; sol trarlo da l'inferno
malgrado suo pòi tu, Signor, di sopra.

(*Rime del canzoniere*, XLVIII)

It is probable that this sonnet was written with a view to including it in **Vr**. As noted by Gorni, 'poco discerno' at l. 11 seems to engage in a dialogue with 'chiaro discerno' of sonnet I, l. 12 (both rhyme with 'eterno'), thus

188 Catullus, LXIV 43-46: 'Ipsius at sedes, quacumque opulenta recessit / regia, fulgenti splendent auro atque argento. / Candet ebur soliis, collucent pocula mensae, / tota domus gaudet regali splendida gaza'.

sealing that connection between *punto ω* and *punto α* that often occurs in the canzonieri.[189] The possibility that it was conceived as a final poem is made even more convincing by the textual conversation observable with the final ballata of Bembo's canzoniere (which was already in **VM**$_5$), *Signor, quella pietà che ti constrinse* (*Le rime*, 138): a point which I briefly examined in Introduction, 3. These affinities, however, are limited to the intertextual level,[190] and extend neither to the tone of the speech nor to the way the repentance is described. In Bembo's ballata, the speaker prays for God's forgiveness for his amorous mistake. In this context he also tries to attenuate his fault first by drawing attention (ll. 4-10) to the power of worldly temptations, then (ll. 11-18) by underscoring that the fault is indeed necessary for the goodness of God to manifest itself, and finally (ll. 19-24), by expressing his hope that God, who showed his great mercy by forgiving mankind for Christ's death, may extend this mercy even to the poet himself.[191] Indeed, the general tone of such an argument prompted Dionisotti to see in Bembo's ballata 'una certa facilità spirituale e quasi un modo di contrattare famigliarmente e speditamente con Dio la propria salvezza'.[192] On the other hand, the speaker's abandonment to divine grace is nowhere to be found in Ariosto's lyrics, and although this is the only poem by him to tackle spiritual subjects, expressed as was customary within the boundaries of the Petrarchan poetic convention,[193] and despite the presence of the word 'errore', regularly employed by Petrarch's followers to condemn the past experience of love, it definitely does not qualify as an actual religious poem. The speaker appeals to God so that he may be freed from the 'lacci', but what emerges is rather the opposite, namely, what is in fact his unwillingness to relinquish this love (and be spared from hell). Indeed, his prayer is defined as 'cold' (l. 2), and is refused by his sensual self (l. 6). The syntagm expressing the contrast between God's will and his own, 'malgrado suo' (l. 14), reverses the meaning it is given by Petrarch: in the latter's lyrics it rather indicated an inner con-

---

189 GORNI 1989, p. 39.

190 The textual affinities between the two poems have been pointed out *ibid.*, and in DI-LEMMI 2000, p. 484. The invocation 'Signor benigno' (l. 2) in Ariosto corresponds to 'Signor' and 'Signore' at ll. 1 and 11 of Bembo's poem respectively. Ariosto's l. 4 may be likened to Bembo's ll. 4-8: 'Vedi, Padre cortese, / l'alto visco mondan com'è tenace, / et le reti, che tese / ne son da l'aversario empio et fallace, / quanto hanno intorno a sé di quel che piace'; Ariosto's l. 5 to Bembo's ll. 18-19: 'Tu, Padre, ne mandasti / in questo mar, et tu ne scorgi a porto; Ariosto's l. 6 to Bembo's ll. 11-12: 'Non si nega, Signore, / che 'l peccar nostro senza fin non sia'. Finally, Bembo's poem also features the keywords 'errore', 'copra', and 'pietà'.

191 See BEMBO 2008, I, p. 333.

192 BEMBO 1960, p. 649.

193 The echoes from Petrarch have been noted by FEDI 1990, pp. 92-93 footnotes.

flict, between the poet's soul, which tended towards God, and his body 'che *mal suo grado* "consente" ai legami con la terra'.[194]

This is not the proper place to discuss Ariosto's religious views.[195] It is clear, however, that his lyric poetry has to be inscribed within an entirely human, down-to-earth perspective. Interestingly, Ariosto is here implicitly separating the domain of poetry from that of prayer. The former alone is associated by him with the truthful expression of sentiments, while prayer, entrusted to the 'lingua', is nothing but an exterior ritual which, precisely on account of its shallowness, may not even reach God (ll. 1-2).

This peculiar fashioning of the spiritual theme invites comparison with the Quattrocento repertoire analysed in Comboni – Zanato 2017. First of all, we shall note that, while most fifteenth-century canzonieri conclude with a spiritual poem, others choose different themes.[196] But even if one leaves aside the *punti ω*, we shall observe that the *testi di pentimento religioso* (one of the parameters adopted by the two scholars to describe the canzoniere) are entirely missing from some authors, e.g. Liburnio or Cosmico.

The almost complete absence of repentance of love from Ariosto's lyrics[197] may therefore be seen as being in line with the late-Quattrocento trend, which sonnet XLVIII also follows in some of its lexical choices.[198] By that time, however, Ariosto most probably also took as his reference point the 'mature' (Bembian) type of Petrarchism. In this context, the peculiar use he makes of Petrarch's language and conventions may have been a personal response to the latter's orthodoxy, as if he wished to propose an alternative formula (note that he also includes a reminiscence of Dante's *Inferno* at l. 8). This is not an isolated instance. A similar challenge to the Petrarchan tradition occurs, as I have previously observed, in sonnet XIX

---

194 See *ibid.*, pp. 92-94 (the quotation is here at p. 93); Dilemmi 2000, p. 484.

195 A new inquiry into this subject by Stefano Jossa is forthcoming. See also Fragnito 1992.

196 Comboni – Zanato 2017, XXIII-XXIV.

197 Sonnet 60* (*Lasso, i miei giorni lieti e le tranquille*), attested only in the *editio princeps*, may be regarded as an exception: in it, the speaker longs for his past freedom, before he fell in love. In this case, too, the speaker's feeling, however, is not that of religious penitence, and the tercets are rather informed by a generic moralism: 'O folle cupidigia, o mai al merto / pregiata libertà, senza di cui / l'oro, e la vita ha ogni suo pregio incerto: / come beato e miser fate altrui! / E l'un de l'altro è morte e caso certo; / hor, ché piangendo penso a quel ch'io fui?' (ll. 9-14).

198 The opening syntagm of the poem may be compared with Tebaldeo, *Rime della vulgata*, 185,1: 'Come creder debbo io che quella fede' (the syntax of this sonnet is similar: its l. 3 also opens with 'se', and its l. 5 also opens with 'Tu') and Serafino Aquilano, *Strambotti*, 328,1: 'Come creder poss'io che ardi sì forte'; for the final line of the first tercet, see Tebaldeo, *Rime della vulgata*, 35,14: 'che discernere il ben non scia dal male' (the affinities with Tebaldeo are noted by Comboni 2000, pp. 307-308).

(*Aventuroso carcere soave* – see section 1). Here it is especially perceptible in the juxtaposition of Petrarchan and classical (i.e. Catullian and Propertian) textual echoes, but also in the use of the typically Petrarchan syntagm 'bella et dolce mia nemica' (l. 4), which is here used ironically as the beloved is in fact very willing to return the poet's love.[199]

We may further explore this point by looking at the theme of love enslavement, which links XIX and XLVIII. The metaphors of the prison and of the 'lacci' belong to the same image cluster of 'tying'. While this metaphor is in fact typical of the western tradition,[200] apparently Ariosto attached special importance to it and – crucially – attributes a positive value to the image, associating it with happiness and enjoyment:[201]

> Io son ferito, io son prigion per loro [= her hair],
> la piaga in mezo 'l core aspra et mortale;
> la prigion forte: et pur in tanto male
> et chi ferimmi et chi mi prese adoro.
>
> (*Rime del canzoniere*, VII 5-8)

> Deh, dite come avene
> che d'ogni libertà m'havete privo
> et menato captivo.
> Né più mi dolgo ch'altri si dorria
> sciolto da lunga servitute et ria.
> Mi dolgo ben che de' soavi ceppi
> l'inefabil dolcezza,
> e quanto è meglio esser di voi prigione
> che d'altri re, non più per tempo seppi.
>
> (*Rime del canzoniere*, 50,139-147)

These and other instances of the *topos* in Ariosto's lyrics have been analysed by Georges Güntert: the scholar concludes that this output lacks all 'ansia inesausta dell'assoluto'[202] and instead celebrates Ariosto's adhesion

---

199 'Dolce nemica' features in *Rvf*, XXIII 69; LXXIII 29; CXXV 45; CLXXIX 2; CCII 13; CCLIV 2. In the *Furioso*, the two occurrences of the word 'nemica' in the Petrarchan amorous meaning are also ironic. See *Fur.*, XXIII 66,8 A; XXIII 68,8 B; XXV 68,8 C: 'e la nimica mia mi caccio sotto' (this belongs to the description of a sexual encounter between Ricciardetto and Fiordispina), or the narrator's excuses at XXVIII 3,5-6 AB; XXX C: 'Date la colpa alla nimica mia, / che mi fa star, ch'io non potrei star peggio'.

200 The tradition of this theme is recalled by Gigliucci 2000, p. 298.

201 This concept may be traced back to the poetry of the trobadours. On this point see Santagata's commentary in Petrarch 2004, pp. 441-442.

202 Güntert 1971, p. 37.

to all aspects of earthly life. The same point has also been explored by RONCACCIA 2012, who contrasts sonnet XIX with Bembo's sonnet 123 (*Tanto è ch'assenzo et fele et rodo et suggo*), which, unlike the aforementioned ballata, is datable to the poet's maturity. Bembo takes up the Petrarchan psychological intonation,[203] describing the speaker's repeated attempts to wriggle out of the 'net' in which he was caught. This point is emphasised by the use of the rhymewords *fuggo* : *rifuggo* (ll. 5-7: 'Et se del carcer tuo pur talhor fuggo / per fuggir da la morte, et tanto ardisco, / tosto ne piango et a pregion rifuggo').

While the difference from Bembo is evident, a conspectus of Quattrocento literature also reveals some similarities with Ariosto's treatment of the theme of enslavement. Boiardo's *Amorum libri tres*, III 3 (ll. 9-11: 'Io non posso fugir, né fugir voglio, / ché tanto libertà prezar non degio / quanto il bel laccio d'or che il cor me anoda'), or I 20 are cases in point:

> Né più lieto di noglia esce e di stento,
> sciolto da' laci, il misero captivo,
> quanto io, di poter privo
> e posto in forza altrui, lieto me sento.
> Quel vago cerchio d'or che me tien vivo
> et hami l'alma e il core intorno avento,
> me fa tanto contento,
> che de alegreza sù nel cielo arivo.
>
> (*Amorum libri tres*, I 20,4-11)[204]

I will also mention Correggio's sonnet 123, where the speaker explicitly refuses to call his amorous slavery an 'errore' and foregrounds instead the sweetness of such condition:

> Ma pur se il danno col piacer misuro,
> non posso dir che abbia commesso errore,
> puoi che in sì dolce carcer non si mòre
> e il custode non è feroce o duro:
> anzi sì dolci son le sue catene
> che se per qualche meritar le scioglie,
> restano i sciolti in libertà con pene.
>
> (Correggio, *Rime*, 123,5-11)

---

203 I will only quote *Rvf*, LXXXIX: 'Fuggendo la pregione ove Amor m'ebbe / molt'anni a far di me quel ch'a lui parve, / donne mie, lungo fôra a ricontarve / quanto la nova libertà m'increbbe. [...] / Onde più volte sospirando indietro / dissi: Oimè, il giogo et le catene e i ceppi / eran più dolci che l'andare sciolto. / Misero me, che tardo il mio mal seppi; / et con quanta faticha oggi mi spetro / de l'errore, ov'io stesso m'era involto!'.

204 ZAMPESE 2000, pp. 468-469 provides three further examples, also from Boiardo.

It should also be noted that this line of tradition was continued later in the Cinquecento. This emerges from the survey carried out by Gigliucci of the various type of Renaissance oxymorons, where several occurrences for the theme of the *amata prigionia* are found, in works by such authors as Colonna, Della Casa, Stampa, and Tarsia.[205]

Returning now to sonnet XLVIII, it should be observed finally that what is at work here is a process similar to that which was noticed in sonnet II, the poem featuring the 'Icarus-like' flight. In both works the lyric voice acts as a detached observer, powerless before the fragmentation of his *animo*, which has succumbed to its irrational component (in XLVIII, the 'cor', l. 4, agrees with the sensual self, 'ogni mio senso', l. 6). This affinity creates a short-circuit between the opening and the end of **Vr**, further confirming that no real development takes place within the soul of the poet-speaker: his condition of enslaved lover cannot but be recorded in the form of individual snapshots of the present time, escaping nearly all possibilities of recollection or careful reflection.

We may now see one of the potential reasons for the 'failure' of **Vr**: it is constituted by autonomous moments, which, although often developed and endowed with internal complexity, are only in a handful of cases truly interconnected by their physical juxtaposition. The predisposition shown by Ariosto-the-lyric poet for depicting individual moments meant that the assembly of these pieces did not lead to an actual internal development. It is this crucial drawback that lies at the core of the radical difference between his canzoniere and the highly accomplished orchestration of the theme of love in the *Furioso*.[206]

7. Final note: Ariosto's 'Catullian' lyric poetry

As this analysis has demonstrated, Ariosto shows no predilection for the *Venere celeste* and appears rather to be inspired by a mundane concept of love, which is given an apt poetic form through recourse to the classics as well as to court poetry.

To conclude, I would like to highlight (and concisely evaluate) the relevance for Ariosto's *rime* of a particular poet, that is, Catullus – an au-

---

205 Gigliucci 2004, pp. 144-154.

206 This is also the position of Cabani 2016 (see p. 121: 'Ciò che nelle rime rimane irrelato e semplicemente contrapposto, all'interno del poema si traduce in un discorso dialetticamente assai più articolato').

thor whose presence can also be felt in the *Furioso*[207] and in Ariosto's Latin lyrics.[208]

It is possible to identify a 'Catullian thread' which weaves its way through the *rime*. While in sonnet XIX the purpose of the Catullian intertextuality is to enhance the sensual undertones of the poem, elsewhere its role is to offer a more generalised support to Ariosto's idea of reciprocated love.

It is significant that some borrowings from the *Liber* seem to appear in the poems inspired by Alessandra, where they contribute to enhance the idea of marital love that subtly emerges in them. But it is even more interesting that Catullus's influence should also apply to poems probably *not* featuring Alessandra, namely, those that explore the concept of *foedus* (see above, section 3), where Catullus seems indeed to be a constant presence, albeit one not openly acknowledged through quotation. Furthermore, I would like to call attention to the 'narrative plot' of **Vr**: close to the outset, the possibility of the woman's reciprocation is announced through a Catullian rewriting, in sonnet XIV (*Quel capriol che, con invidia et sdegno*). The poet is speaking about a deer, a pet belonging to his beloved who, saddened by its death, has granted it 'honesto sepolcro' (l. 8). Having discovered that she is capable of pity, the poet is now certain of his own future reward, 'ché, quando s'incomincia a scior la neve, / che appresso il fin sia il verno è chiara fede' (ll. 13-14). The sonnet is a blatant rewriting of two poems by Catullus (II and III) that were extremely influential throughout the Renaissance,[209] with Lesbia's sparrow changed into the 'capriolo'. It should be

---

207 Catullus was one of Ariosto's favourite authors according to his son Virginio (see Introduction, footnote 50). Pigna also noted the Catullian influence on Ariosto's Latin poems (Pigna 1554, p. 73). The passages of the *Furioso* textually indebted to Catullus have been noted by commentators. I will mention the comparison between young maidens and roses voiced by Sacripante (*Fur.*, I 42 ABC and Catullus, LXII 39-47), or Dardinello's death, for which Ariosto borrows the words employed by Catullus to describe the fading of his love for Lesbia (*Fur.*, XVI 153 AB; XVIII C, and Catullus, XI 21-24 – this simile, however, is also present in Virgil and Ovid: see Ariosto 2012, p. 622).

208 Among Ariosto's *Carmina*, IX (*Ad Albertum Pium*) takes inspiration for its structure from Catullus's poem IX; XX (*De catella puellae*) is inspired by Catullus's II and III (on Lesbia's sparrow), and by XII; XXI (*[In Lenam]*) can be compared to Catullus's XLII; XXII is tame compared with Catullus's VIII; the last lines of XXXII (*[De Glycere et Lycori]*) adopt the rhetorical structure of Catullus's LXXXV; finally, the epithalamium on Alfonso d'Este's marriage to Lucrezia Borgia (LIII) is modelled after Catullus's LXII. Ariosto would have been able to consult the 1502 edition of Catullus's poems, published in Venice by Manutius (this edition also included Tibullus's and Propertius's poems). In addition to these precise calques, various scattered echoes must also be taken into account. These are examined in the comments by Segre and Looney-Possanza (Ariosto 1954 and Ariosto 2017 respectively). On the sources of Ariosto's Latin poems see also Severi 2018. For an overview of Catullus's humanist reception, see Gaisser 1993 and 2007.

209 See Gaisser 2007, p. 444. An example of Italian rewriting of these poems by Catullus is Tebaldeo, *Rime della vulgata*, 23.

pointed out that these two poems by Catullus were also imitated in Latin by Ariosto in poem XX (*De catella puellae*), this time on his beloved's dog.[210]

Thus, it appears that, despite the undeniable importance of Horace, Propertius and Ovid, Catullus is a prominent poetic touchstone for Ariosto's elaboration of the love theme, and provides him with the means to conflate the elegiac situation of *furtivus amor* with one closer to the marital status, characterised by equality between the two lovers. Prompted by these literary memories, Ariosto ultimately achieves a balance that even allows scope for irony – something that crucially links the elegiac lover of these poems to the narrator of the *Furioso*.

210 Rossi 1980, p. 43 emphasises the great fortune enjoyed by the theme of the little dog in poetry from the second half of the fifteenth century onwards.

Chapter III

THE PORTRAYAL OF WOMEN

Preamble

In the preceding chapter, my discussion of Ariosto's treatment of the love relationship necessarily touched upon the fashioning of the beloved woman in the *rime*. I have tried to show the originality of the poet's elaboration of this theme, especially in those cases in which a balanced relationship between the two lovers is hinted at. Intriguingly, in certain cases, in the way this relationship is depicted on page one sees how the traditional *topoi* make way for an intimate dimension which seems to spring from some more private autobiographical source.

It is now time to set aside the theme of the relationship in order to examine more in depth the female portraits he paints. To speak of the female figure in Ariosto means, it would appear, to return to a subject which has received an inordinate amount of scholarly attention: indeed, critics have long tried – not without encountering some difficulties – to extrapolate the author's position with regard to the *querelle des femmes*.[1] The debate, however, is far from having run its full course. Indeed, another declension of the female theme, the stereotypical representation of beauty, has received less attention, leaving us uncertain as to Ariosto's relationship to the tradition of the *descriptio puellae*. Studies on this subject (which nevertheless remain critically valuable) have rarely focused exhaustively on Ariosto, and the preferred line of investigation has been to examine the wider range of the *topos* and to position Ariosto within this range. Moreover, where Ariosto *has* been considered, the focus has been exclusively on the *Furioso,* and his other works have been overlooked.

---

[1] On female characters and / or on the *questione femminile* in the *Furioso*, see at least Durling 1965, pp. 150-163; Tomalin 1976; Peirone 1988; Shemek 1989; Finucci 1992; Mac Carthy 2007; Stoppino 2012; Weaver 2016.

The focus in this chapter will therefore be the *descriptio puellae* in his lyric output. I will first, however, give a brief overview of the salient features of the *topos*, for which Giovanni Pozzi's studies (later developed by Amedeo Quondam) are still relevant.[2] In his close analysis of the detailing of the portrayals of women in terms of words, syntax, and the ordering of concepts, Pozzi had identified two possible options for the Renaissance catalogue of beauties: the *canone breve*, established by Petrarch, which selects only a few physical attributes of the poet's beloved (her hair, eyes, eyebrows, lips, cheeks, and occasionally her neck),[3] and the *canone lungo*, fully developed by Boccaccio (in his *Comedia delle ninfe fiorentine*, *Filocolo* and *Teseida*), in which the description includes several more elements (the chin, feet, and breast as well as some detail of clothes). Both types, according to Pozzi, can be detected in the *Furioso*: the portraits of Alcina (*Fur.*, VII 11-16 ABC) and of Olimpia (*Fur.*, XI 64-72 C) are examples of *canone lungo*; that of Angelica (*Fur.*, IX 83-84 AB; X 95-96 C) follows the *canone breve*. Pozzi's analysis of the structure of the canon shows that it adopts fixed metaphors for each physical feature, recalling tactile or visual sensations (e.g. roses in place of lips; gold for hair) and highlights the symmetrical distribution of such metaphorical attributes, a fact that leads to the presence of regular schemes. This – intrinsically 'visual' – pattern seems (again in Pozzi's view) an attempt to reproduce, through the tools of rhetoric, the traits of painting, in a textual situation where the various elements of the description have no visual potential, the canon being by its very nature highly formalised and non-referential.[4] Indeed, the history of the catalogue has often been interpreted in the perspective of *ut pictura poesis*, i.e. as an effort to mirror the process of portraiture, by aiming at visual effects through non-pictorial devices.[5]

The characterisations put forward by Pozzi's rhetorical-semiological method, however, run the risk of being excessively rigid, and this has prompted María de las Nieves Muñiz Muñiz to adopt a fresh approach to the question of the *descriptio puellae* in her recent monograph (Muñiz Muñiz 2018). Here, rather than the structure of the canon (which is, as

---

2 Pozzi 1974, 1979 and 1993; Quondam 1991.

3 On the Petrarchan canon, see also Fedi 2007, pp. 65-74.

4 Pozzi 1979, pp. 7-22. On the idealised nature of the *canone*, see also Quondam 1991, pp. 291-328.

5 Among the numerous studies that reconstruct the history of the concept of *ut pictura poesis*, from its theoretical formulations in classical antiquity to the Cinquecento, see Quondam 1991, pp. 83-95 and p. 310; Jossa 2008, as well as the bibliography in these books (among the pioneering studies on this concept I will only mention Lee 1940 and Praz 1970).

she demonstrates, typologically much more various than has hitherto been supposed), what is foregrounded is the minute analysis of its components. By re-examining the various branches of the *topos* over the centuries, the aim is to demonstrate the continuity of certain aesthetic ideals – from the classics, through medieval Latin and Franco-Provençal literature, down to medieval and Renaissance Italian literature. Muñiz Muñiz shows, in other words, that the ideal female physiognomy, as well as the use of certain metaphorical attributes, can be traced much further back than the early Renaissance, although the role played in the stabilisation of these attributes by Petrarch and Boccaccio remains unquestioned.

Despite his apparent faithfulness to the canon, Ariosto in fact turns out to be a subtle and often bold innovator. Moreover, as will be seen, it would be an artificial constriction to limit the *topos* of the *descriptio puellae* exclusively to its aesthetic components, while it extends to observations on the psychology and behaviour of the woman described. Significantly, these aspects are also subject to stylisation: there is, in other words, an 'inner canon', which has not so far enjoyed the same critical recognition as the physical canon. This inner canon is not entirely absent from the earlier Italian poetic tradition – one need only think of Cino, who, in his canzone CXXIII (*Oimè lasso, quelle trezze bionde*), after listing some of his lady's aesthetic characteristics, continues with the memory of his beloved's 'caro diporto e bel contegno', of her 'dolce accoglienza' and her 'accorto intelletto' (ll. 14-16). It is, however, in the Cinquecento that this canon acquires complexity, also thanks to a new interest in the female world. This interest – which writers cultivated both as theory and as poetical practice – is central to Ariosto's poetry, and will be the subject of the second part of this chapter.

1. Experiments on the canon

While it is impossible to show exactly how Ariosto's development of the theme evolved through time, we do however have one poem (which belongs to the *rime extravaganti*) that takes it as its subject, which dates back to the early years of the Cinquecento. This is sonnet XXXIII ed. Fatini (*Se senza fin son le cagion ch'io v'ami*). As mentioned in Introduction, 4, this was composed by Ariosto as a personal contribution to a *tenzone*, datable to ca. 1504, between the members of a Venetian society called the 'Compagnia degli Amici': the theme of the poetical exchange was precisely the *descriptio puellae*. As Gnocchi argued, the *tenzone* probably originated as a response to a diptych of sonnets by Bembo – *Crin d'oro crespo et d'ambra ter-*

sa et pura and *Moderati desiri, immenso ardore* – composed with Lucrezia Borgia in mind,[6] and consisted in a triptych of sonnets by Niccolò Tiepolo and one sonnet by Vincenzo Querini, in addition to Ariosto's poem.[7] The link between these sonnets may be evinced from the presence in all of them of the same line, which is repeated in almost identical manner, although it is placed at the very end of the poems of the *amici* (see e.g. 'senza fin le cagion perch'io sempre ami', l. 14 of Tiepolo's third sonnet),[8] while it is used as an opening line by Ariosto, whose poem should be quoted in full:

> Se senza fin son le cagion ch'io v'ami,
> e sempre di voi pensi e in voi sospiri,
> come volete, oimè! ch'io mi ritiri,
> e senza fin d'esser con voi non brami?
> Son la fronte, le ciglia e quei legami
> del mio cor, aurei crini, e quei zaffiri
> de' bei vostri occhi, e lor soavi giri,
> donna, per trarmi a voi tutti ésca ed ami.
> Son di coralli, perle, avorio e latte,
> di che fur labra, denti, seno e gola,
> alle forme degli angeli ritratte;
> son del gir, de lo star, d'ogni parola,
> d'ogni sguardo soave, insomma, fatte
> le reti, onde a intricarsi il mio cor vola.
> (*Rime*, sonnet XXXIII ed. Fatini)

The sonnet provides a detailed account of the lady's beautiful features as prescribed by the *canone breve*, most of which are associated with their typical attributes: milk with the throat (because of its whiteness); ivory with the breast (whiteness + hardness), pearls with the teeth (whiteness + hardness + lucidity) coral with lips (redness), sapphires and gold respectively with the eyes and hair. In spite of the unquestionable conventionaliy of this description, the stylistic concern with a balancing of *variatio* and symmetry should be noted. Ariosto creates a scheme in which the first two items ('fronte' and

---

[6] See Gnocchi 1999, pp. 282-293. The poems are Bembo, *Le rime*, 5 and 6. I will quote, from the former, ll. 1-8: 'Crin d'oro crespo et d'ambra tersa et pura / ch'a l'aura in su la neve ondeggi et vole, / occhi soavi et più chiari che 'l sole / da far giorno seren la notte oscura, / riso ch'acqueta ogni aspra pena et dura, / rubini et perle, ond'escono parole / sì dolci ch'altro ben l'alma non vòle, / man d'avorio, che i cor' distringe e fura'.

[7] These sonnets have recently been re-examined by Vagni 2019, pp. 214-217. The scholar has also attempted to establish the exact succession of the poems (first Querini, then Tiepolo, then Ariosto).

[8] The poem can be read *ibid.*, p. 216.

'ciglia'), which are not paired with metaphors, are followed by two items ('crini' and 'occhi'), which are preceded by metaphorical attributes, and by a sequence of four metaphorical words each of which refers to one of the items in the following line ('labra', 'denti', 'seno' and 'gola'). Moreover, at the end of the second quatrain and of the second tercet the overall effect of the items mentioned is metaphorised by an image expressing the idea of allurement ('ésca ed ami'; 'reti'),[9] thus creating a macro-structure into which the others fit.[10] If we move on to examine the contents of the poem, we notice that it insinuates a subtle variation from the other sonnets of the *tenzone*. While these, as well as Bembo's *Crin d'oro crespo*, are entirely taken up with praise of the (physical and, in Tiepolo's case, moral) attributes of the woman, Ariosto's sonnet begins with a description of the speaker's feelings, which are expressed directly to the dedicatee. The classic situation of lyric poetry is hinted at, with a female figure 'rejecting' or pushing away the male speaker, who strongly desires her presence ('esser con voi'). The list of the attributes, moreover, is no end in itself but aims to illustrate the allure they exert over the speaker (this is clear from ll. 13-14). The absoluteness of the portrait of the woman is thus dispelled and it is made more psychological:[11] although this is not an isolated case in contemporary poetry, attention should nevertheless be called to it as the earliest manifestation of a trend that would also become important in later poems by Ariosto, and would in fact come to be seen as one of their typical features.

The first truly original element in Ariosto's use of the canon regards the description of female nudes. Here, the capitolo on the happy night of love (*O più che al giorno a me lucida et chiara*), which was also written early in the Cinquecento (see Chapter II, 1) once again comes into play. In the following excerpt the narrating voice indulges in contemplating the naked beauties of his beloved:

> Quanto più giova in sì suave effetto
> pascer la vista hor de gli occhi divini,
> hor de la fronte, hor de l'eburneo petto;

---

9 On the idea of 'tying' in Ariosto's lyrics, see Chapter II, 5.

10 This pattern may be seen as diverging from a late-Quattrocento tendency noted by Pozzi 1979, pp. 8-11, in which the catalogue of beauties was solely achieved through the strategy of accumulation, often without any enhanced connection between items and metaphorical words. This trend should, however, be verified by a thorough sounding of the Quattrocento repertoire.

11 It could be hypothesised that Ariosto wished to bring together the subjects of the two sonnets of Bembo's diptych. Indeed *Crin d'oro crespo* foregrounds the female description, while *Moderati desiri* focuses on the lover's psychological troubles.

mirar le ciglia et l'aurei crespi crini,
mirar le rose in su le labra sparse,
porvi la bocca et non temer de' spini;
mirar le membra, a cui non può uguargliarse
altro candore e giudicar mirando
che le gratie del ciel non vi fur scarse,
et quando a un senso satisfar, et quando
all'altro, sì che ne fruiscan tutti,
et pur un sol non ne lasiare in bando.

(*Rime del canzoniere*, XXI 43-54)

Rather than to the texts derived from Propertius's poem, which normally simply recount the enjoyment of the sexual act,[12] this catalogue of the various parts of the woman's body may be linked to a poem from Ovid's *Amores*. Indeed, the two poems present a similar use of anaphoric exclamations as well as a striking resemblance in the scene they describe (Ovid, who is about to have sex with Corinna, unveils her and contemplates her beauty):

Deripui tunicam – nec multum rara nocebat;
pugnabat tunica sed tamen illa tegi.
Quae cum ita pugnaret, tamquam quae vincere nollet,
victa est non aegre proditione sua.
Ut stetit ante oculos posito velamine nostros,
in toto nusquam corpore menda fuit.
Quos umeros, quales vidi tetigique lacertos!
forma papillarum quam fuit apta premi!
quam castigato planus sub pectore venter!
quantum et quale latus! quam iuvenale femur!
Singula quid referam? nil non laudabile vidi
et nudam pressi corpus ad usque meum.

(*Amores*, I 5,13-24)

The eventual outcome of this poetic situation, as reworked by Ariosto, is a particular version of the Petrarchan *canone breve*, developed following, albeit quite freely, the traditional top to bottom rule and introducing metaphorical attributes ('eburneo petto'; 'rose'; 'aurei crespi crini').[13]

---

12 An exception is Piccolomini, *Historia duobus amantibus*, p. 100: 'et nunc os, nunc genas, nunc oculos commendabat, elevataque nonnunquam lodice, secreta, que non viderat antea, contemplabatur [...] quid his membris formosius, quid candidius? [...] o pectus decorum, o papile premende, vosne tango?'. Descriptive elements that may have furnished Ariosto with inspiration may also be found in *Ad Stellam* by Giovanni Pontano.

13 An earlier version of this capitolo exists, where l. 46 is: 'et le ciglia mirar d'ebano e i crini' (Finazzi 2002-2003, pp. 228-230). Finazzi, evidently referring the attribute 'd'ebano' to

The combination of Petrarchan language with a situation dominated by eroticism has already been pointed out in Chapter II, 1 as relevant to both this and other poems by Ariosto. Also, it has been anticipated that it testifies to some extent to the poet's continuity with the Quattrocento tradition. In analysing a sample of authors from that period, Beatrice Bartolomeo observes that their versions of the canon also occasionally includes 'gli elementi più sensuali della fisicità femminile', thereby setting up an ambiguous relationship with the Petrarchan model.[14] The validity of these considerations may easily be extended to the first years of the Cinquecento, especially within the courtly milieu. A sonnet by Tebaldeo, *Dui vivi soli, or fino, hebeno raro* (*Rime estravaganti*, 325) constitutes an interesting case. This mentions 'dui pomi, quai non so se altro horto rende, / che cela un velo ingiurïoso e avaro' (ll. 3-4): an allusion that seems to neatly fall within the typology outlined by Bartolomeo. This framework is complicated, however, by the fact that this sonnet, which is datable between 1502 and 1508, was probably intended by Tebaldeo (as Albonico has suggested) as an imitation of Bembo's *Crin d'oro crespo et d'ambra tersa e pura*: a decidedly singular homage since, in placing the accent on sensuality, Tebaldeo strikingly diverges from Bembo. To this end he takes up a hint from a poem by Tito Vespasiano Strozzi (*Laudat Anthiam a forma et moribus*), which Bembo himself had used, albeit in a form that was 'cleansed' precisely of this sensuality.[15] As Vagni, who has pondered the dynamics of this imitation, has

both 'ciglia' and 'crini', believes that this version of the poem was dedicated to a woman with brown hair and that this detail was changed by Ariosto to make the capitolo fit the 'canzoniere'. However, as brown hair is too uncommon a feature for a canonical description, one finds it easier to link 'd'ebano' only with 'ciglia', and suppose that the hair was blonde already in this early version. Indeed, the brownness of eyebrows was common in the canon of beauty since the Middle Ages (since women used to dye only their hair blonde: on this point see Renier 1885, pp. 41-42, and Torraca 1888, pp. 339-342; on hair colouring, see Fedi 2007, *passim*; Motta 2018, pp. 96-99). This attribute also appears in two of the poems involved in the *tenzone* on female beauty: Tebaldeo writes 'Dui vivi soli, or fino, hebeno raro' (cited in this section); Tiepolo 'ciglia d'hebeno tranquille' (l. 2 of *Crespe chiome d'or fin, serena fronte*, cited in Vagni 2019, p. 215) – and I shall further mention *Libro de natura de amore, Libro primo*, f. 18*r* (Equicola 1999, p. 229): '[poets describe] de oro li crini, de hebeno le ciglia'. There are, of course, some cases of brown-haired women in literature preceding Ariosto, but they are exceptions. Among them could be mentioned the description of Eleuterillide in *Hypnerotomachia Poliphili* (Fedi 2007, pp. 43-44) and Correggio, *Rime*, 376,31-32: 'le chiome su il bel fronte, in ch'io mi annodo, / d'ebano loro, e quel de avolio e lacte'– regarding the latter, Fenzi 2006, pp. 153-154 suggests that the author may have wished to conceal the true addressee of the poem, Lucrezia Borgia, who was actually blonde. On brown hair in Renaissance literature, see also Motta 2018, pp. 95-96. On hair in the context of the *descriptio puellae*, see also Macinante 2011.

14 Bartolomeo 2012, p. 43.

15 Albonico 2017, pp. 93-95. Strozzi's poem can be read in Strozzi 1513, II, ff. 5*v*-6*r*.

observed, Tebaldeo's sonnet should be read as an actual 'Ferrarese reply' to Bembo's Neoplatonic concept of woman and of love.[16] In turn, again according to Vagni, it would have prompted some response, i.e. precisely the *tenzone* mentioned at the beginning of this section, which probably originated from the desire of the 'Compagnia degli Amici' to express their agreement with Bembo's idea of love against Tebaldeo.

If I have briefly turned away from my main argument it has been to better clarify how vital and debated the theme of the *descriptio puellae* was among the early sixteenth-century poets of Northern Italy. Within this debate may also be placed the nude in Ariosto's capitolo. His treatment of the subject should be seen as diverging not only from the 'Bembian' line, but also from the fifteenth-century line continued by Tebaldeo. Indeed, the latter tends to allude – rather than explicitly refer to – any bodily part that may be eroticised: an equivalent to Ariosto's 'mirar le membra' (l. 49)[17] may hardly be found in this repertoire, though I should qualify this statement by adding that Quattrocento poetry has yet to be systematically examined. At any rate, it appears that Ariosto goes beyond the most common contemporary elaborations on this theme, including those in Latin by the two Strozzis, and fully embraces the classical model.

The descriptions of Angelica and, especially, of Olimpia, in the *Furioso*, are also as a matter of fact nudes. These descriptions occur when the two princesses, imprisoned at different points of the story on the island of Ebuda, are tied to a rock so that they may be devoured by the sea monster that haunts the island. That a fully developed Petrarchan canon (far more elaborate here than in the capitolo) should be applied to a naked body is an outstanding achievement, and one which most scholars have attempted to interpret through the lens of *ut pictura poesis*, that is, as a case of *ekphrasis* of figurative themes involving nudes. According to these readings, this imitation presupposes two conditions: first, that Ariosto was referencing actual works of art, especially classical sculpture and the revival of its tradition in Ferrara,[18] and secondly, that it was his *intention* to mirror the traditional pictorial process of giving nudes a narrative/mythological pretext – what Pozzi describes as '[rivestire] di un pretesto narrativo gl'indugi voyeuristici sul corpo delle sue eroine'.[19] Such interpretations, which overall point

---

16 Vagni 2019, p. 213.

17 I shall note that this phrasing may be indebted to *Purg.*, XIX 10-12: 'Io la mirava: e come 'l sol conforta / le fredde membra che la notte aggrava, / così lo sguardo mio [...]'.

18 Among the most relevant studies on this aspect, I will mention Savarese 1984, pp. 53-70; Ceserani 1985; Gnudi 1975; Conte 2004; Farinella 2016.

19 Pozzi 1979, p. 26. The example he offers is Titian's 'Dresden Venus'.

(correctly) to a classicising conception on Ariosto's part, were undoubtedly prompted by the numerous figurative metaphors and similes he adopts. For instance, Phidias (*Fur.*, XI 69,4 C) and Zeuxis (*Fur.*, XI 71,2 C) are called upon to express the perfection of Olimpia's body, and the author even goes as far as to reverse the traditional logical priority of Nature over art – *ars simia naturae* – in his description of Angelica: 'Creduto avria che fosse statua finta / o d'alabastro o d'altri marmi illustri / Ruggiero, o su lo scoglio così avinta / per artificio di scultori industri' (*Fur.*, IX 84,1-4 AB; X 96 C).[20]

But in fact, Ariosto's challenge here addresses not just the visual arts, but also the lyric tradition itself.[21] Arguably, he reworks the literary canon, with the aim of upping the dose of sensuality, indeed of eroticism, of the description:

> *Un velo non ha pure*, in che richiuda
> i bianchi gigli e le vermiglie rose,
> (*Fur.*, IX 83,5-6 AB; X 95,5-6 C)

> ma discendendo giù da le mammelle,
> *le parti che solea coprir la stola*,
> fur di tanta escellenzia [...]
> (*Fur.*, XI 67,5-7 C)

> I rilevati fianchi e le belle anche,
> e netto più che specchio il ventre piano,
> pareano fatti, e quelle coscie bianche,
> da Fidia a torno, o da più dotta mano.
> *Di quelle parti debbovi dir anche*
> *che pur celare ella bramava invano?*
> (*Fur.*, XI 69,1-6 C – emphasis mine)

The insistence on the absence of veils ironically contrasts with the *topos* of the gown that hardly conceals the limbs, but still allows the observer's imagination to roam its delights – a motif which we have just seen in Tebaldeo's sonnet and which originated in Ovid,[22] and which later features significantly in Boccaccio as well as in Quattrocento authors.[23] As a conse-

20 Farinella 2016, pp. 41-42.

21 As is also hypothesised, especially with regard to Angelica, by Padoan 1978, pp. 356-359.

22 See the descriptions of Daphne in *Met.*, I 502: 'siqua latent, meliora putat' and of Cidippe in *Her.*, XX 61-62: 'cetera si possem laudare, beatior essem, / nec dubito, totum quin sibi par sit opus'.

23 Boccaccio, *Comedia delle ninfe fiorentine*, IX 26-28; *Filocolo*, III, XI 5-7; *Teseida*, XII 63. See Maffia Scariati 2008, pp. 472-473. Examples of the Quattrocento employment of the theme

quence, new parts of the body, namely hips, haunches, belly and thighs, are introduced into Olimpia's portrait, and associated with new metaphorical attributes (a mirror for the belly, while the others are likened to sculpted limbs). It is highly significant, too, that the narrator juxtaposes, albeit implicitly, this type of beauty to the traditional 'dressed' or 'half-dressed' canonical beauty, and states its superior effectiveness in triggering love and passion (that of Oberto, in this case – and it is also said that if only Bireno could have seen Olimpia without veils, he would never have abandoned her).[24] Interestingly, this approach to description is applied not only to the poem's fictional characters, but also to the woman the narrator loves. In comparing himself to Orlando, based on the fact that he, too, has lost his wit, he states his intention of searching for it among the woman's beauties, where most certainly 'se ne va errando'. Her nudity is alluded to through a reference to the whiteness of her breast:

> Ne' bei vostri occhi, e nel sereno viso,
> nel sen d'avorio, e alabastrini poggi
> se ne va errando; et io con queste labbia
> lo corrò, se vi par ch'io lo riabbia.
>
> (*Fur.*, XXXII 2,5-8 AB; XXXV C)

This is one of the passages on which Pich bases her reading of the narrator as the protagonist of an amorous story of a strictly lyric nature,[25] an interpretation also confirmed, I believe, by the female portrayals that appear in the poem, which (as we have just seen) engage in a close relationship with the lyric genre. Incidentally, precisely regarding this point, I would suggest that in Olimpia's description Ariosto might still feel – well after writing capitolo XXI (the episode was added only to the 1532 version of the *Furioso*) – the echoes of Ovid's poem I 5 from the *Amores*. The similarity regards the newly introduced body parts: 'netto più che specchio il ventre piano' corresponds to 'planus sub pectore venter', whereas the succession of 'quantum et quale latus' and 'quam iuvenale femur' reminds us of 'I rilevati fianchi e le belle anche'. Innovation therefore proceeds in parallel to a return to the classics.

---

of the female 'hidden parts' are provided in Bartolomeo 2012, pp. 44-45. See, e.g., Giusto de' Conti, *Rime estravaganti*, XIII 10-11: 'dolce parte secrete, di che spesso / dolcemente Amor meco ne ragiona'; Correggio, *Rime*, 179,12-13: 'la gola e il pecto e quelle che nascose, / per non dar morte a tanti, usa a tenerle'.

24 *Fur.*, XI 72,1-4 C: 'Io non credo che mai Bireno, nudo / vedesse quel bel corpo; ch'io son certo / che stato non saria mai così crudo, / che l'avesse lasciata in quel deserto'.

25 Pich's reading has been touched upon in Chapter I, section 6.

In his descriptions, Ariosto allows the reader to perceive the differences that distinguish them from the regular canon. This has been noted by Muñiz Muñiz, who reads the female portrayals of the *Furioso* both as a progressive approach to the concept of *ut pictura poesis*, and as an ambiguous and unsettling dissolution of the ideal of beauty:[26] the most glaring example of this, which ought here to be briefly re-examined, is the scene of the epiphany of Alcina. Following Boccaccio's example, the woman is dressed, and the typical allusion to hardly concealed parts of the body also appears ('Ben si può giudicar che corrisponde / a quel ch'appar di fuor quel che s'asconde', *Fur.*, VII 14,7-8 BC).[27] However, Ariosto once again establishes a comparison with the visual arts ('Di persona era tanto ben formata, / quanto me' finger san pittori industri', 11,1-2 ABC) that allows him to play on the ambiguity between the real and the fictitious. As a matter of fact, the emphasis on the perfection of Alcina's physical appearance, which is so accurately described as to make the reader assume that it is natural ('gli angelici sembianti nati in cielo', *Fur.*, VII 15,7 ABC), contrasts with what will be later revealed as her true essence. In VII 72-73 all her beauties will turn out to be an enchantment, which, lifted, allows the sorceress's true ugliness to shine through: this, in turn, is described in a sort of anti-canonical counterpoint to the earlier description.[28] Once again, a difference is perceived between a type of description that is somehow expected, and its (equally unexpected) subversion. We may therefore agree with Muñiz Muñiz's 'manieristic' reading; nevertheless, I believe that it has to be integrated by also factoring in the role played by irony.

In the *rime*, too, we find at least one clear example of irony applied to the canon. This is in sonnet IX, where the speaker appears at first to

---

26 Muñiz Muñiz 2018, pp. 90-91.

27 In A the distich is: 'non che di fuor perhò, il giudicio manchi / ch'in mezo è stretta, e rilevata a fianchi'.

28 *Fur.*, VII 72-73 ABC: '[...] donna sì laida, che la terra tutta / né la più vecchia avea né la più brutta. // Pallido, crespo e macilente avea / Alcina il viso, il crin raro e canuto, / sua statura a sei palmi non giungea: / ogni dente di bocca era caduto; / che più d'Ecuba e più de la Cumea, / ed avea più d'ogn'altra mai vivuto. / Ma sì l'arti usa al nostro tempo ignote, / che bella e giovanetta parer puote' (on this passage, see Bolzoni 2010, pp. 189-193). A key precedent for the subversion of canonical categories in the description of the lady is *Purg.*, XIX 7-9: 'mi venne in sogno una femmina balba, / ne li occhi guercia, e sovra i piè distorta, / con le man monche, e di colore scialba'. I shall note that we find a brief 'anti-canon' in the lyrics, too: more precisely in capitolo XXXI, the poem where the speaker accuses his beloved of having broken the *foedus* (see Chapter II, 2). Here, he envisions the loss of all beauties as a divine punishment for her and for those women who behave like her: 'Se da le guancie poi cadon le rose, / fuggon le gratie; se riman la fronte / crespa et le luci oscure et lacrimose, / se l'auree chiome et con tal studio conte / mutan color, se si fan brevi et rare, / di vostri danni è vostra colpa fonte' (ll. 55-60).

be straightforwardly following the *canone lungo*, listing the lady's neck, her breast, arms and hand, as well as alluding to the concealed parts of her body ('quanto se ne crede', l. 11). However, in the last tercet the whole catalogue is unexpectedly dismantled, as the poet's own faithfulness is proclaimed superior to all those beauties:[29]

> Madonna sète bella et bella tanto
> ch'io non veggio di voi cosa più bella:
> miri la fronte o l'una et l'altra stella
> che mi scorgon la via col lume santo,
> miri la bocca a cui sola do vanto,
> che dolce ha il riso e dolce ha la favella;
> et l'aureo crine onde Amor fece quella
> rete che mi fu tesa d'ogni canto;
> o di terso alabastro il collo e il seno,
> o braccia, o mano, e quanto finalmente
> di voi si mira, et quanto se ne crede.
> Tutto è mirabil certo, non di meno
> non starò ch'io non dica arditamente
> che più mirabil molto è la mia fede.
>
> (*Rime del canzoniere*, IX)

The trigger for the irony is the adjective *mirabile*: formerly a keyword of the *dolce stil novo*, in which it always signified the divine essence of the lady,[30] the word now loses that exclusivity of reference and is associated instead to the poet's faithfulness. Why is this faithfulness so 'remarkable'? The implied idea is that the woman, albeit beautiful, does not deserve to be loved (probably on account of her coldness towards the speaker). The poet processes his feelings from the outside and recognises their strangeness, without however yet being able to fully detach himself from them: a mechanism, this, with its admixture of lucidity on the one hand and difficulty in behaving rationally on the other, that we have already seen in the poems examined in Chapter II. In this case, the sudden shift in the sonnet's centre of gravity – from the beloved to the poet, from idealised beauty

[29] According to Jossa 2016, p. 190, Ariosto's irony is a 'strumento dissacratorio e insinuante [...] un atteggiamento diffuso che mette sempre in discussione ciò che è scontato e propone continuamente l'imprevedibile'. Cabani 2016, pp. 114-116 argues in favour of an ironic reading specifically of this poem. On this sonnet in the context of Ariosto's concept of *fides*, see Chapter II, 2.

[30] Ariosto uses 'mirabilmente', referring to the *excessus mentis* prompted by contemplation, in *Rime del canzoniere*, IV 4-5: 'Sento ch'allhor mirabilmente Amore / mi leva a volo [...]' (see Chapter II, 3).

to the psychological relationship proper – combined with the semantic modification of *mirabile* produce an effect of concreteness. While the core of this process could already be detected in sonnet XXXIII ed. Fatini (see above), it is here turned into a witty desecration of the *descriptio puellae*.[31]

Here too, moreover, the revisiting of the *topos* is filtered through the classics. It is probable that the sonnet was influenced by the description of Daphne in Ovid's *Metamorphoses*, as may be inferred from the disposition of the elements, from the anaphor of verbs of perception ('miri') and from the emphasis on the eyes, compared to stars, and the lips:

> [...] videt igne micantes
> sideribus similes oculos, videt oscula, quae non
> est vidisse satis; laudat digitosque manusque
> bracchiaque et nudos media plus parte lacertos:
> si qua latent, meliora putat
>
> (*Met.*, I 498-502)[32]

This is a further confirmation that, although it is entirely legitimate to interpret Ariosto's canon through the concept of *ut pictura poesis*, at the same time its roots in an age-long literary tradition should be recognised.

2. The 'dressed beauty' and her social context

The irony applied by Ariosto to the catalogue of beauties and his elaboration of a provocative 'canon of nudities' belong to the same process of de-absolutisation of the *topos*, which has the effect of leading the female figure back to an earthly dimension. This attitude also induces him to focus on another aspect: the social context in which the woman's charms exert their power. This happens in canzone 50 (*Non so s'io potrò ben chiudere in rima*), which recalls the circumstances of his first falling in love with Alessandra Benucci (and is in fact the only document we have that regards that momentous occasion).[33] The event is described as having taken place on 24 June 1513 in Florence, during the celebrations for St John the Baptist. The reader is not told how much time has elapsed since then; as a matter of

[31] Also according to Favaro 2010, p. 126, the poet's aim here is 'smorzare i toni sulla bellezza muliebre, sottraendola alla sublimazione petrarchista'.

[32] See also *Amores*, III 2,35-36: 'Suspicor ex istis et cetera posse placere, / qui bene sub tenui condita veste latent'.

[33] See Fatini 1934, p. 137 and pp. 196-202.

fact, the dating of the poem is unknown. We only know that the canzone is not featured in **Vr** and that it belongs to the poems newly added in the later phases of selection, together with the poems that have been analysed in Chapter II, 5.[34]

The situation described in canzone 50 is inescapably reminiscent of *Rvf*, XXIII, the celebrated canzone where Petrarch recalls his first meeting with Laura, which is also precisely echoed in many places.[35] What results from such a comparison is that Ariosto, unlike Petrarch, endeavours to place the fact in its context, a context that is even assigned partial responsibility for the event. The speaker is already acquainted with his future beloved when he sees her on the 'fateful day'. His is not a case of love at first sight: rather, it is described as a confused feeling, at first unrecognised by the poet himself because of the difficulties involved in its practical realisation (ll. 23-33 – the allusion is perhaps to Alessandra's husband, Tito di Lionardo Strozzi, who was still alive at that time), and finally breaking out when he becomes fully aware of Alessandra's charm.[36] Such charm is in turn a combination of her own personal qualities and the atmosphere in which the meeting takes place: a different context, Ariosto seems to say, would not have prompted his desire to the same extent. The object of love is thus deprived of the absoluteness of her powers, the very thing that had invariably qualified her as 'divine' in the lyric tradition.

It is for this reason that the first stanzas of the canzone contain such an accurate illustration of the feast of St John the Baptist – which in 1513 must have been even more elaborate than usual, as it also honoured Giovanni de' Medici, who had been recently elected Pope Leo X:

> Ne la tosca città che questo giorno
> più riverente honora,
> la fama havea a spettacoli solenni
> fatto raccor, non che i vicini in torno,
> ma li lontani anchora;
> anchor io, vago di mirar, vi venni. [...]
>
> [...] da preghi vinta et liberali inviti
> di vostra gente, con honesta et cara

34 Moreover, in addition to these testimonies, the canzone is also transmitted in **Vb**, which is the only autograph we have of Ariosto's lyrics (see Introduction, footnote 1).

35 See Bianchi's commentary in Ariosto 1992, pp. 203-209.

36 See *Rime del canzoniere*, 50,29-33: 'Ma selve, monti et fiumi / sempre dipinsi inanzi al mio desire, / per levarli l'ardire / d'entrar in via dove, per guida porse, / io vedea la speranza star in forse'.

compagnia, a far più liete
le feste, a far più splendidi i conviti
con li doni infiniti
in ch'ad ogn'altra il ciel v'ha posta inanzi,
venuta erate dianzi, [...]

Porte, finestre, vie, templi, theatri
vidi pieni de donne
a giuochi, a pompe, a sacrificii intente,
et mature et acerbe, et figlie et matri
ornate in varie gonne;
altre star a conviti, altre agilmente
danzare; et finalmente
non vidi, né senti' ch'altri vedesse,
chi di beltà potesse,
d'honestà, cortesia, d'alti sembianti
voi pareggiar, non che passarvi inanti.
(*Rime del canzoniere*, 50,56-61; 69-75; 78-88)

This description is probably reminiscent of a poem from Tito Vespasiano Strozzi's *Eroticon libri*, where the speaker recalls his falling in love during the feast of St George in Ferrara ('Candida lux aderat Maiis vicina Calendis, / quam festam veteres instituistis avi. / Quam pia solemni celebrat Ferraria cultu, / aurea cum admissis praemia ponit equis').[37] In addition, it reminds us of some passages from the *Furioso*, such as that describing the joust of Damascus: 'Adorna era ogni porta, ogni finestra / di finissimi drappi e di tapeti, / ma più di belle e ben ornate donne / di ricche gemme e di superbe gonne. // Vedeasi celebrar dentr'alle porte, / in molti lochi, solazzevol balli' (*Fur.*, XV 20,5-8 – 21,1-2 AB; XVII C). Also, the festive occasion that draws gentlemen and ladies from far and wide is a situation that often features in chivalric poems, being typically associated with tournaments (see *Fur.*, XI 6,3-4 AB; XIII C: 'Trasse la fama ne le terre nostre / cavallieri a giostrar di più paesi').

The same atmosphere is evoked in sonnet 56 (*Qui fu dove il bel crin già con sì stretti*), which has already been quoted in the overview on Ariosto's use of myths in Chapter II, 5. As observed there, in this poem, too, the speaker recalls the occasion on which he fell in love and mentions some architectural elements of Florence (with a phrasing that in turn reminds us

[37] *Quod die solemni Divi Georgii amare Anthiam coepit*, ll. 1-4 (quoted from Strozzi 1513, II, f. 2*v*). This link has also been noted by Zampese 2000, p. 464.

of capitolo XXX, the poem featuring the *laudatio urbis*). The city, he says, on that day gathered 'donne et cavallieri eletti', l. 5: Ariosto here is clearly echoing the famous opening words of the *Furioso*, 'Le donne, i cavallier'.[38] As a matter of fact, the insistence on the details of the festivity in these poems may have been a consequence of the ongoing exchange between the poems and the *Furioso*. The epiphany provoked by the vision of Alessandra in the canzone recalls, even more markedly than the *topos* of the 'woman seen among other women' from the *Vita nuova*,[39] the first appearance of Alcina in the *Furioso*:

> Non tanto il bel palazzo era escellente,
> perché vincesse ogn'altro di ricchezza,
> quanto ch'avea la più piacevol gente
> che fosse al mondo e di più gentilezza.
> Poco era l'un da l'altro differente
> e di fiorita etade e di bellezza:
> sola di tutti Alcina era più bella,
> sì come è bello il sol più d'ogni stella.
>
> (*Fur.*, VII 10 ABC)

> [...] spesso in conviti, e sempre stanno in feste,
> in giostre, in lotte, in scene, in bagno, in danza
> (*Fur.*, VII 31,5-6 ABC)

The common ground is the context of splendour and refinement within which social interactions are enacted and made possible. This is, of course, of the world of the court. As a matter of fact, the aforementioned excerpts may be compared to a passage from Ariosto's 1506 eclogue, in which one of the interlocutors, Tirsi, recalls the scene of the marriage between Alfonso d'Este and Lucrezia Borgia (who appear under the guise of the shepherds 'Alfenio' and 'Licoria'). The latter is seen 'in mezo onesta schiera / di bellissime donne, anzi pur dive' (ll. 245-246). As in canzone 50, the statement about the protagonist's outstanding beauty is introduced by an *excursus* that describes a gathering of ladies, mentioning their different dresses and the ways in which they are grouped:

---

38 Because this sonnet does not feature in **Vr**, I am assuming that the occurrence of the *Furioso* – in A the reading is 'Di donne e cavallier') is earlier. The phrase derives from *Purg.*, XIV 109: 'le donne e' cavalier, li affanni e li agi'; it also appears in *Rvf*, CCCLX 111: 'ch'a donne et cavalier' piacea il suo dire'. On this opening, see Zampese 2018*bis*.

39 See *Vita nuova*, XIV: 'avenne che questa gentilissima venne in parte ove molte donne gentili erano adunate [...] levai li occhi, e mirando le donne, vidi tra loro la gentilissima Beatrice'. Later occurrences of the theme are listed in de' Medici 1992, p. 84.

Io vidi tutte l'altre, e vidi questa,
or sole ad una ad una, e quando in coro,
e quando in una e quando in altra vesta.
Quale è il peltro all'argento, il rame all'oro,
qual campestre papavero alla rosa,
qual scialbo salce al sempre verde alloro,
tale era ogn'altra alla novella sposa;
gli occhi di tutti in lei stavano intenti,
per mirarla obliando ogn'altra cosa.
(*Rime*, eclogue I ed. Fatini, ll. 250-258)

The relationship these examples entertain with the preceding tradition is characterised both by continuity and innovation. The description of female beauty against the background of courtly entertainments often features in late-Quattrocento poetry, a typical situation being that which featured the 'dancing lady' (cp., in Ariosto's canzone, 'altre agilmente / danzare', ll. 83-84). Correggio's sonnet 391, whose protagonist is also, most probably, Lucrezia Borgia,[40] is a good example of this:

Se parla, uscir di lei se ode un concento
che l'aër d'armonia dolce aura rende;
se respirando dà el fiato e 'l reprende,
de odor se empie quel loco in un momento;
se in mezo ornate donne e in balli o festa
non prima el delicato piede move,
che ognun lei mira, e vincta ogni altra resta.
E da i belli occhi suoi tal grazia piove
che se ben nega a un che a danzar l'ha chiesta,
col suo sguardo el sdegno puoi da quel rimove.
(Correggio, *Rime*, 391,5-14)

Although Niccolò is inspired by Propertius, II 1 (a description of the attitudes in which the poet observes Cynthia: walking, playing the lyre, sleeping),[41] he eschews the self-celebratory lyric voice of this model, in which the poet uses description as an opportunity to proclaim his own poetic glory, and insists rather on describing the surrounding environment and the way in which Lucrezia interacts with it: her voice impresses the air;

[40] See Fenzi 2006, p. 157 and footnote.

[41] Propertius, II 1,9-12: 'sive lyrae carmen digitis percussit eburnis, / miramur, facilis ut premat arte manus; / seu compescentis somnum declinat ocellos, / invenio causas mille poeta novas'.

her breath fills it with a sweet scent; her movement in dance inspires awe in those who watch; her eyes bestow grace on her admirers. His portrayal is, therefore, closer to those of Ariosto. However, this sonnet still pays tribute to the medieval representation of the lady as a divine creature (also on account of the socially superior status of its dedicatee), and echoes Dante and the *dolce stil novo*,[42] this time with a proper use of the verb 'mirare'. An idealised conception of the court lady, in other words, still prevails in it.

Something similar happens in the lyric poetry by Boiardo, from whose canzoniere I will single out only two examples, both of which capture Antonia, the young maiden beloved by the poet, in the act of dancing on a social occasion (in the former, she is accompanied by two friends):

> Qual nei prati de Idalo on de Cythero,
> se Amor de festegiar più voglia avea,
> le due sorelle agiunte a Pasithea
> cantando di sé cerchio intorno féro,
> tal se fece oggi e più legiadro e altero
> essendo in compagnia de la mia dea
> e de l'altre doe belle, onde tenea
> la cima di sua forza e il summo impero.
>
> (*Amorum libri tres*, I 30,1-8)

> Ben se è ricolto in questa lieta danza
> ciò che può far Natura, il Cielo e Amore;
> ben se dimostra a' nostri ochi di fuore
> ciò che dentro dal petto avean speranza.
> Ma quella dolce angelica sembianza
> che sempre fu scolpita nel mio core
> è pur la stella in cielo, in prato il fiore,
> che non che l'altre ma sé stessa avanza.
> Il suave tacere, il stare altero,
> lo accorto ragionar, il dolce guardo,
> il perregrin dansar ligiadro e novo
> m'hano sì forte acceso nel pensiero,
> che sin ne le medole avampo et ardo,
> né altrove pace che in quel viso trovo.
>
> (*ibid.*, I 54)

---

[42] For the phrase 'dolce aura' see, besides the obvious references from the *Fragmenta*, *Purg.*, XXVIII 7 ('un'aura dolce'); further on in the same canto (ll. 52-54) a simile on a dancing woman is also present. MENGALDO 1963, pp. 306-316 notes the persistence of the vocabulary of the *stil novo* in Northern late fifteenth-century lyric poetry (he especially analyses Boiardo's case) and argues that it was prompted by the influence of chivalric literature.

As in Correggio, in Boiardo the portrayal of the 'socialite' also obeys the criterion of the idealising transfiguration. In I 30 this happens through the superimposition of myth, as a simile is established between Antonia and Pasithea, one of the three Graces. In I 54, too, despite the 'realistic' reference to the choreography the young lady is following, which is described as new (l. 11),[43] and despite the presence of a sensual vein which originates precisely from the maiden's moves, the portrayal is ideal: Antonia is endowed with an 'angelica sembianza' (a phrase for which Zanato supplies parallels in Petrarch and Cavalcanti).[44] Most importantly, the poet himself, subscribing to a Platonic *topos*, declares that the image of his beloved engraved in his heart – which he imagines to live in all the elements of nature, the skies and the meadows – is more beautiful yet than the woman herself (ll. 5-8).[45] Significantly, the site of the meeting, i.e. the court of Reggio Emilia, also appears similarly transfigured through this ideal, two sonnets earlier: 'alor questa aula de angelico canto / sembrava e de adorneza un paradiso' (*Amorum libri tres*, I 52,7-8).

Against this pattern, as we have seen, Ariosto develops his descriptions in entirely 'human' terms. A related fact is his peculiar treatment of certain specific details of the female portrait. Let us return to canzone 50: the description of the feast of St John is followed by a comprehensive portrayal of Alessandra. This proceeds from top to bottom and the parts described correspond to the *canone lungo*, with frequent borrowings of Petrarchan words and syntagms. However, one striking feature may be noted, and indeed has been noted by Lina Bolzoni: among the woman's beauties, her 'bel volto' (l. 89), her 'biondo et spesso crine' (l. 91) and the 'avorio bianco' (l. 96) of her shoulders receive only the briefest of mentions.[46] Instead, what is given importance is her fine outfit, as well as details of her hairstyle and clothing – in other words, all that contributes to a social characterisation of her beauty.

Stanza 9 and part of stanza 11 develop the representation of the woman's coiffure. It consists of a thin net that gathers the hair (parted in the middle) on the nape, and then flows down the neck and reaches as low as the shoulders;[47] it is embellished by a laurel-shaped diadem decorated with gemstones:

---

43 This is probably a *bassadanza*, as hypothesised by Zanato (Boiardo 2012, p. 325).

44 *Ibid.*, p. 326.

45 On the theme of the image of the beloved woman portrayed or engraved in the lover's heart, see Chapter II, footnote 66.

46 See Bolzoni 2010, pp. 184-185.

47 In fact, what descends at ll. 96-97 may be either the net or the shadow that it casts.

Trovò gran preggio anchor, dopo il bel volto,
l'artifitio discreto
ch'in aurei nodi il biondo et spesso crine
in rara et sotil rete havea raccolto;
soave ombra dirieto
rendea al collo et inanzi alle confine
de le guancie divine,
et discendea fin all'avorio bianco
del destro homero et manco.

(*Rime del canzoniere*, 50,89-97)

non senza [mistero] anchor fu quel gemmato alloro
tra la serena fronte e il calle assunto
che de le ricche chiome
in parti ugual va dividendo l'oro.

(*ibid.*, ll. 113-116)

This is not the only instance of the special attention Ariosto pays to hair. In the *Furioso*, when Dalinda describes how she masqueraded as princess Ginevra, she highlights the '[...] rete pur d'or, tutta adombrata / di bei fiocchi vermigli al capo intorno' (*Fur.*, V 47,3-4 ABC). The theme is frequently found throughout the lyrics: the mini cycle of poems that was occasioned by the cutting of Alessandra's hair – *Rime del canzoniere*, 52, 53, 54, 55, and 57 (for which see Chapter II, 5) may be usefully recalled here. It was in fact not uncommon, especially in Quattrocento lyric poetry, for authors to dedicate poems to the celebration of a single part of the body.[48] In such cases, however, the object of the praise occupies the entire poem, and it is rather unusual to intermingle elements of the canon with a 'realistic' occasion,[49] although occasionality itself is a typical feature of courtly poetry of that period. This is something which also helps distinguish, by contrast, Ariosto's case: as I already showed in the last chapter, the poet introduces reality in a context built up through Petrarchan *topoi* and classical

48 This is also noted by Bartolomeo 2012, pp. 49-53, who, in the context of her analysis of sensual themes in fifteenth-century lyric poetry, focuses on four canzoni by Cosmico which celebrate solely (under the influence of Pontano) the beloved's bosom. To these we may add countless instances from other authors: to mention but a few, Giusto de' Conti's canzoniere famously dedicates poems to his lady's hand or eyes, highlighting the psychological effects that their sight causes in the speaker (see Pantani's notes in Comboni – Zanato 2017, pp. 232; 236-237); Sasso wrote two sonnets (LXII-LXIII) on his lady's hand. Another relevant example is the *Amorosa opra* (a *prosimetro*) by Muzzarelli, within which a cycle of lyrics is dedicated to each physical trait of the woman, hair included (see Dilemmi 2000*bis*, pp. 285-286).

49 On the idealised nature of the *canone*, see Pozzi 1979, p. 22; Quondam 1991, pp. 291-328.

mythology, producing an effect of good-tempered irony. See, for example, the details used to describe Alessandra's various hairstyles before her hair was cut:

> Son questi i nodi d'or, questi i capelli
> c'hor in treccia, hor in nastro et hor raccolti
> fra perle et gemme in mille modi, hor sciolti
> et sparsi all'aura sempre eran sì belli?
>
> (*Rime del canzoniere*, 53,1-4)

The gathered hair may seem an unrenounceable element of the canon, appearing in both Petrarch and Boccaccio.[50] As Muñiz Muñiz observes, it is principally the latter who develops this theme, by introducing garlands of flowers as the privileged beauty accessory of the *ninfe fiorentine*:[51] Boccaccio's aim, however, is not to guarantee verisimilitude, but rather to harmonise the female figure with the surrounding *locus amoenus* (and even in later poetry, the theme of the gathered hair follows this type of stylisation). Conversely, regarding sonnet 53 it should first be noted that, in lamenting the event that has taken place, the speaker adopts the deictic 'questi', suggesting that perhaps the shorn locks are lying before him; in so doing Ariosto both evokes and refashions the Petrarchan model (*Rvf*, CCCLIX 56: 'Son questi i capei biondi, et l'aureo nodo'), which used the same deictic but in the context of a dream, in which Laura had appeared to Petrarch.[52] Secondly, a uniquely minute descriptive attention may be noted. Indeed, the styles of coiffure mentioned in the excerpts quoted above correspond quite closely to those that may still be seen in portraits of noblewomen painted in Northern Italian courts in the early Cinquecento, which probably, as Uberto Motta observes,[53] carried a symbolic meaning, linked to the values of nobility and chastity.

In the literary panorama, one particularly relevant text in this context is Gian Giorgio Trissino's dialogue *I ritratti* (which, although only published in

---

[50] The canon normalised by Petrarch actually includes two hairstyles: gathered hair and loose locks, the latter being the most frequent one (the 'capei d'oro a l'aura sparsi' of *Rvf*, XC 1). For this point, see Motta 2018, pp. 85-90.

[51] Muñiz Muñiz 2018, pp. 65-67; see also Maffia Scariati 2008, p. 476-477.

[52] Note that at ll. 3-4 Ariosto also echoes the blatantly traditional syntagm from *Rvf*, XC 1 (see footnote 50).

[53] Motta 2018, p. 89: 'l'elaborazione di acconciature particolarmente complesse [...] assunse una duplice e polisemica connotazione: quale segno di convenienza e decoro per le donne sposate, nonché prova della loro ricchezza, e come documento di tendenziale autogoverno del potenziale erotico ai capelli tradizionalmente connesso'. The scholar also provides figurative references.

1524, had already been finished ten years earlier).[54] Its contents should first be briefly recalled. In it, Vincenzo Macro tells his interlocutor Pietro Bembo about a beautiful unknown lady he has just seen: from his description of her, Bembo eventually understands that she is Isabella d'Este, and draws on Macro's account for his own speech in her praise. This dialogue shows that an attempt was being made to enrich the canon. Indeed, the description is developed in three distinct steps: at the beginning, Macro recalls the lady's physical features, following the *canone lungo*; then (in response to Bembo's plea) the details of her outfit; finally, Bembo's speech insists on Isabella's intellectual qualities. What is offered is therefore a more complete and individualised female portrait,[55] and, importantly, in addition to pure beauty, the dialogue emphasises other elements that were rapidly gaining importance in that cultural context: the ability to distinguish oneself in society through behaviour and through intellect. To this I shall be returning later.

What is most immediately relevant here is the second section of this literary portrait, which concerns Isabella's outfit and also lingers on her hair. It is well known that Isabella was particularly fond of experimenting with hairstyles (*fogie da testa*) and is even credited with having invented some herself: such as the one worn at her brother Alfonso's wedding with Lucrezia Borgia in 1502, or the particular kind of turban named *capigliara*.[56] In Trissino's text, her chosen style reminds us of that of Alessandra in Ariosto's canzone:

> Ella, disse Macro, aveva i capegli in capo diffusi, in guisa, che sopra i candidi, e dilicati umeri ricadeano; e questi tutti erano raccolti da una rete di seta di color tanè, con maestrevole artificio lavorata, i groppi de la quale mi pareano essere di finissimo oro; e fra mezo le maglie di questa rete, le quali erano alquanto larghette, vi si vedeano scintillare i capegli [...]. Ne la sommità poi de la fronte, dove questi in due parti si divideno, vi aveva un bellissimo, e fiammeggiante Rubino, dal quale una lucidissima e grossa perla pendeva [...].[57]

---

54 On this work (whose model is Lucian's *Eikones*), see Beer 1990 and Pich 2010, pp. 228-230.

55 As observed by Pich 2010, from Trissino's perspective 'Ciò che permette di distinguere bellezze altrimenti tutte uguali è l'*habitus*, un complesso insieme di elementi che comprende i dati visibili più individualizzati: composto di aspetto e di atteggiamenti, è un luogo di connotazione sociale e morale e di caratterizzazione temperamentale' (p. 229).

56 See Bonoldi 2002-2003, pp. 59-69.

57 Trissino 1729, pp. 272-273. The elaboration of the former section, dedicated to Isabella's physical features, is quite different: here the canon is developed along entirely ideal lines. Macro offers a contemporary version of the myth of Zeuxis: just as Zeuxis had composed the portrait of Helena by using the features of the five fairest women of Croton, he can describe Isabella's beauty only by assembling the physical traits of five renowned Italian beauties of his

However, unlike Isabella's, Alessandra's hairstyle – though elegant and precious – is not elaborate in a showy way. Ariosto presents it exactly as it must have been, suited to the social status of its owner. Moderation, moreover, is counted as a positive quality, and is in fact the highlight of Alessandra's portrait: the expression 'artifitio discreto', which means both 'accurately chosen' and 'not showy' (l. 90 of canzone 50, probably in direct reference to Horace, *Carm.*, I 5,5: 'simplex munditiis') should be duly noted as it suggests at the same time the elaborateness of her look and her ability in concealing the effort behind it. Thus, Alessandra perfectly conforms to the aesthetic ideal of moderation of the Renaissance, which Castiglione in his *Cortegiano* labels as 'sprezzatura'.[58]

Ariosto's description of his beloved's hair is followed by that of her gown, which she herself has embroidered (with 'aco dotta', l. 109). Again, Alessandra's sewing skills are probably drawn from reality as they also feature in sonnet 51, where the woman is caught in the act of reproducing on her dress the pattern she saw embroidered on another:

> Aventurosa man, beato ingegno,
> beata seta, beatissimo oro,
> ben nato lino, inclito bel lavoro
> da chi vuol la mia dea prender dissegno [...]
> (*Rime del canzoniere*, 51,1-4)[59]

It also occurs in a simile from the *Furioso*, introduced by the narrator to describe Zerbino's blood, which gently oozes from his armor:

> Così talora un bel purpureo nastro
> ho veduto partir tela d'argento

time (*ibid.*, pp. 271-272). Shortly after, in order to make his verbal portrait more complete (he uses the word 'colorire'), Macro resorts not to a realistic description but rather to the Petrarchan metaphorical attributes: 'il quale primieramente colorirà le chiome [...] facendole di oro fino [...] et il volto farà di calda neve [...]' (*ibid.*, p. 272). One further *descriptio* of Isabella along these ideal lines is foregrounded by Trissino in his canzone LIX; see ll. 34-45: 'Orω mai nωn si tolse / d'alcuna vena a le sue kiome εquale, / nε credω mai che cωsì nerω fusse / guajacω che da l'India si cωndusse, / nuovω rimεdiω a l'insanabil piaghe, / cωme le bεlle cilja; ε sì lucεnti / nωn sωnω in Ciεl seren due stelle ardεnti, / cωme sωn di cωstεi le luci vaghe; / nε gilji o neve han biancω sì perfεttω, / cωm'ella ha 'l viſω ε 'l pεttω, / in cui qualche rωsseza vi si poſa, / che pare in latte una vermilja roſa (I shall refer the reader to Francesco Davoli's commentary to this canzone in Davoli 2017-2018, pp. 207-224).

58 *Cortegiano*, I.XXVI-XXVIII.

59 On this poem, see also Chapter II, 2. Cp. Tebaldeo, *Rime della vulgata*, 43,5-8: 'e ordì con le sue man' sì bel lavoro, / che Pallade tra nui più non se stima: / onde, se pria de lei io facea stima / per sua belleza, hor per virtù l'honoro'.

da quella bianca man più ch'alabastro,
da cui partire il cor spesso mi sento.
(*Fur.*, XXII 66,1-4 AB; XXIV C)[60]

The canzone also offers some further details on the gown. It is, for example, made of black silk:

Non fu senza sue lode il puro e schietto
serico habito nero,
che, come il sol luce minor confonde,
fece ivi ogn'altro rimaner negletto.
(*Rime del canzoniere*, 50,100-103)[61]

Also, it is entirely covered with embroidery featuring an *impresa* of two intertwined grapevines. Nothing is said about the colour of the threads used for the embroidery: grapevines may suggest green, though a darker colour (black on black perhaps) is more likely, as it renders the whole dress 'ombroso' ('[...] l'implicate fronde / de le due viti, d'onde / il leggiadro vestir tutto era ombroso', ll. 105-107). The theme of the black dress paradoxically generating light, which Ariosto underscores in these lines, was already backed by a lyric tradition, as testified by its having been also employed by Tebaldeo:

Per mostrar quanta forza i soi lumi hanno
e che non men splendor di Phebo rende,
costei, che di beltà col ciel contende,
coperta stassi sotto oscuro panno.
Ché, come da le nubi che vi vanno
intorno per ombrarlo ei si diffende,
così la donna mia luce e risplende
in veste che assai più tenebra fanno.
(Tebaldeo, *Rime extravaganti*, 394,1-8)

While here, however, the woman's super-human beauty stands out *in spite of* the black, in Ariosto the black adds something to it: clearly, the adjectives 'puro' and 'schietto' again highlight moderation, a quality that, from his perspective, might outmatch extreme luxury (l. 110: 'le porpore

60 As commentaries note, however, this simile also has a Homeric antecedent (Ariosto 2012, p. 810).

61 In the earlier version of the poem, testified by **Vb**, ll. 102-103 contain a further reference to the woman's tailoring skills: 'a cui la industria havea sì dato aiuto / che ivi fê ogn'altro rimaner negletto'.

et l'oro il nero vinse'). This general ideal leads us back to Ariosto's classical vision, a famous example being Propertius's poem I 2, in which the poet protests against his beloved's excessive use of cosmetics, arguing that 'love is naked, and loves not beauty gained by artifice' ('nudus Amor formam non amat artificem', l. 8).

This value is also at the core of the description of Alessandra that we find in the *Furioso*. In canto XLII Rinaldo is led by a mysterious knight to admire a marble fountain, supported by eight female statues. In a sort of prophecy, the knight reveals that they are illustrious ladies that will live at later times. Among them, occupying the place between Lucrezia Borgia and Beatrice d'Este, is Alessandra. Her description is fairly similar to that in the canzone, and here too, her actual name is not mentioned. Her outfit is once again defined as 'puro' and 'schietto', and as at l. 102 of the canzone, the effect of this absence of embellishment is likened to that of a star more luminous than all the others:

Tra questo loco e quel de la colonna
che fu sculpita in Borgia, com'è detto,
formata in alabastro una gran donna
era di tanto e sì sublime aspetto,
che sotto puro velo, in nera gonna,
senza oro e gemme, in un vestire schietto,
tra le più adorne non parea men bella,
che sia tra l'altre la ciprigna stella.
(*Fur.*, XXXVIII 90 A; XXXVIII 93 B; XLII 93 C)

The possibility, sometimes put forward by critics, that here Ariosto should refer to a mourning dress[62] is not an impediment to linking the two descriptions, which cooperate towards the expression of a precise idea of beauty. The portrayal offered by Alessandra's statue is even more interesting if one tries to understand the point of view of a contemporary reader. Beatrice and Lucrezia were famous – even among their peers – for the lavishness of their clothes: in that, they could compete (and indeed did, as documents testify) only with Isabella d'Este, whose elegance was almost legendary.[63] If we return to the second section of Trissino's *I ritratti*,

---

[62] See Catalano 1930-1931, I, pp. 421-422, who especially places the woman's white ('puro') veil in relation to mourning attires of the time. From this hypothesis (which is shared by Dorigatti 2011, pp. 43-44), the conclusion should be drawn that the octave was composed after Tito Strozzi's death in October 1515: it would be, therefore, one of the last additions to the poem, just before it went to press.

[63] Luzio – Renier 1896 examine in detail the sources attesting Isabella's look, including her purchases.

we find a realistic account of Isabella's outfit, which so greatly adds to her natural beauty that it prompts Macro to refer to the *topos* of *ars simia naturae*. Another black dress is here described, decorated with awe-inspiring embroideries and even solid gold buckles:

indosso aveva una bella, e ricca robba di velluto nero, carica di alcune fibie d'oro tanto ben poste, e tanto ogni cosa, che aveva d'intorno, era mirabilmente lavorata, che pareva gli artefici, per ornar costei, aver voluto con la natura istessa contendere.[64]

Rich, laden: such adjectives, which seem to precisely contrast Alessandra's dress – unadorned, without any gold or gems –, may undoubtedly also be applied to the gowns of Beatrice and Lucrezia.[65] Ariosto does not give this kind of detail, but the courtier reader would undoubtedly have visualised them in this manner, and the overall effect of this octave must have been that of a luxurious frame out of which the central figure of Alessandra shone in all her purity. Her dress was probably made of a plain silk cloth; we may read 'schietto' as signifying the opposite of the uneven surface of the brocade (or its more expensive variety, fashionable in the early Cinquecento, the *riccio sopra riccio*).[66] As for the dark grapevine decoration that is described in the canzone, it would appear to be very different from the luxurious *imprese* – interwoven or embroidered in gold and silver – in executing which the noblest ladies would compete. Finally, Alessandra did not resort to any 'artèfici', such as those mentioned by Trissino for Isabella, but only to her own skills.

The black of Alessandra's gown – which appears in both descriptions – deserves attention. Traditionally associated with mourning, this colour (as my previous argument implies) enjoyed a parallel popularity as a colour denoting elegance and refinement,[67] a popularity which moreover stemmed from classical literature. It is especially useful to recall Ovid's *Ars amatoria*, which was highly influential throughout the early Renaissance, and was also explicitly paraphrased in works by Calmeta, Equicola, and Castiglione.[68] Its third book offers advice to women in the art of seduction, engag-

---

64 Trissino 1729, p. 273.

65 As documented by Catalano 1930-1931, I, p. 402, Lucrezia 'compariva nelle feste di corte con magnifici abiti di velluto nero e indossava ricche vesti di broccato, coperte di raso nero'.

66 Luzio – Renier 1896, p. 16.

67 A history of colours in clothing is Luzzatto – Pompas 1997; specifically on black, see Pastoureau 2008.

68 See Kolsky 1991, pp. 268-269.

ing in a discussion on hairstyles, clothes, and cosmetics: when it comes to dress, dark hues are explicitly prescribed for women with pale skin ('Pulla decent niveas', l. 189). It is not just this passage, however, but the whole of Ovid's argument that is relevant here, as the poet begins by observing that as most women have not received from the gods the gift of perfect beauty, they must resort to stratagems to enhance their look – but should, however, as in the argument of Propertius's I 2, avoid excessive luxury.[69]

Some texts from Ariosto's time should also be taken into consideration. Castiglione's *Cortegiano*, whose fundamental concept of *sprezzatura* was in turn probably influenced by Ovid – this definition implied, in this specific case, that the lady should give what aid she could to her own natural attractiveness, but avoid showing affectation –,[70] does not give any prescription for the colours of women's dresses; it does, however, recommend black for the male courtier's everyday clothing,[71] whereas bright colours are allowed for festive occasions. A similar point is made by Equicola in his *Libro de natura de amore*; that is to say, he quotes Ovid's passage about colour choices for women, and extends its validity to men,[72] but does so within an erudite dissertation on the symbolic meaning of colours.[73] Equicola's concern is that men might appear effeminate if they dress too elegantly: therefore, he prescribes that they should 'in nesciuna parte imitare femine' but that their

69 *Ars amatoria*, III 103-106: 'Forma dei munus: forma quota quaeque superbit? / Pars vestrum tali munere magna caret. / Cura dabit faciem; facies neglecta peribit, / Idaliae similis sit licet illa deae'; ll. 169-172: 'Quid de veste loquar? Nec vos, segmenta, requiro / nec te, quae Tyrio murica, lana, rubes. / Cum tot prodierint pretio leviore colores, / quis furor est census corpore ferre suos!'.

70 *Ibid.*, III.VIII: '[...] deve questa donna aver iudicio di conoscer quai sono quegli abiti che le accrescon grazia [...] ma dissimulatamente più che sia possibile; e [...] mostrar sempre di non mettervi studio o diligenzia alcuna'.

71 *Ibid.*, II.XXVII: 'però parmi che maggior grazia abbia nei vestimenti il color nero, che alcun altro; e se pur non è nero, che almen tenda al scuro'.

72 *Libro de natura de amore*, *Libro quinto*, f. 260 (Equicola 1999, p. 502): 'Ovidio nel terzo libro dela *Arte amatoria*, dando precepti alle domne de qual colore debiano vestire, dice alle fusce convenire il bianco, alle bianche il pullo, donde si po asseverare alli bruni tucti quelli colori convenire che hanno col bianco propinquità, et alli bianchi quelli li quali hanno col negro affinità'.

73 As is well known, deciphering the meaning of colours was a popular entertainment in early Cinquecento courts. A famous example in literature is sonnet 299 by Correggio (*Sì como el verde importa speme e amore*). In this context, however, black was always interpreted as a sign of sadness/melancholy, and as such was worn by unrequited lovers in the poems belonging to this tradition. Ariosto himself features this motif in the *Furioso* when Orlando fears for Angelica's life (*Fur.*, VIII 85,5-6 ABC: 'Ma portar vòlse un ornamento nero, / e forse acciò ch'al suo dolor simigli'); see also Correggio, *Rime*, 348,43-45: 'La veste scura, e parte più che oscura, / che mostra affanno, sopra affanno vesto, / perché mia vita è più che morte dura'. An examination of lyric and especially theoretical sources of the time related to the interpretation of colours (which takes the *Furioso* as a starting point, but also includes later texts), is in Salza 1914, pp. 144-174.

outfit should be 'puro, necto et elegante' (*Libro quinto*). Simplicity thus appears as a typically manly feature. For Equicola, moreover, clothes must reflect the man's social status, and his interiority must in turn conform to them. See again from *Libro quinto*: 'Non exceda nostra conditione nostro habito; al'exteriore lo interiore responda; sia nel nostro vestire concento, l'uno habito al'altro responda'.[74]

Read against this background, Ariosto's passages on his beloved dressed in black appear to be something more than a simple imitative description of a refinedly elegant woman. The fact that they focus on the sobriety of her sartorial choices makes them very different from many coeval poems that underscore details of of female attire – such as Trissino's sonnet VIII, in which the woman described wears a golden coloured dress and veil and is adorned with gemstones, thus exhuding what appears to the poet to be a divine quality.[75] But most intriguingly, in these passages the woman is linked to a particular look in which a set of traditionally 'manly' traits are embedded. Indeed, their textual tailoring suggests that her most outstanding features are not to be sought in her external appearance, but in her interiority: it is here that the most distinctive feature of Ariosto's portraits is found. This subject will be further explored in the following section.

3. The intellectual canon

To retrace the history of the verbal depiction of women in terms of their non-physical qualities is indeed a hard task. The scope of the present study does not permit an exhaustive overview, but it should be pointed out that this type of characterisation seems to be more relevant in the classical than in the vernacular tradition – while physical description, on the other hand, is generally less sophisticated in the classical canon.[76] This may be seen, for instance, in Propertius' poems II 1 and II 3, which capture the woman in the act of dancing, singing, and composing poetry (I will quote from II 3 further on; for II 1, see above). In early Italian lyric poetry, when interior attributes were highlighted they either were subordinated to

---

[74] Quotations are from f. 243 (Equicola 1999, pp. 490-491).

[75] Trissino, *Rime*, VIII 1-2: 'Sωtt'un vel d'or cωn leggiadretti nodi / εranω insiεme i bε' capelli avolti'; ll. 9-11: 'A la nuova belleza, ε l'ωrnamentω / di pεrle ε d'ambre al collω ε vεsta d'orω, / facean parer cωstεi dal ciεl diſcεſa'.

[76] On this point, see Muñiz Muñiz 2018, p. 53. Among the exceptions should be mentioned Catullus's poem XLIII, where Lesbia's physical features can be inferred *e contrario* from the description of an ugly woman (this is, therefore, in fact a counter-canon): 'Salve, nec minimo puella naso / nec bello pede nec nigris ocellis / nec longis digitis nec ore sicco' (ll. 1-3).

physical beauty, or functioned synergetically with beauty to trace a portrait that appeared to eschew the terrestrial: medieval lyric representations of women mostly include moral attributes, related to modesty, nobility of soul, and 'divine' wisdom.[77] As a reflex of this, her actions – the immediate manifestations of the *animo* – tend to fall into the category of beautiful gestures or movements: glancing, smiling, speaking gently and wisely, walking with a graceful poise. All of these elements are frequently observable in Boccaccio and in Petrarch. The latter's sonnet CCLXI can be regarded in fact as an interior portrait of Laura. Here her exceptional eloquence is also praised (l. 9), within the context of an entirely spiritualised nature of the representation:

Qual donna attende a gloriosa fama
di senno, di valor, di cortesia,
miri fiso negli occhi a quella mia
nemica, che mia donna il mondo chiama.
Come s'acquista honor, come Dio s'ama,
come è giunta honestà con leggiadria,
ivi s'impara, et qual è dritta via
di gir al ciel, che lei aspetta et brama.
Ivi 'l parlar che nullo stile aguaglia,
e 'l bel tacere, et quei cari costumi,
che 'ngegno human non po' spiegar in carte;
l'infinita belleza ch'altrui abbaglia,
non vi s'impara: ché quei dolci lumi
s'acquistan per ventura et non per arte.

(*Rvf*, CCLXI)

Between the fifteenth and sixteenth centuries, as was anticipated in the Preamble, other features related to 'inner beauty' are gradually integrated in literary descriptions of women, in the context of an increasing interest in female nature. This interest led to the composition of a number of proto-feminist treatises both in Latin and in the vernacular, especially following the models of Petrarch's *Triumphi* and Boccaccio's *De claris mulieribus* (the latter was translated for the first time into Italian in 1506), which recalled examples of illustrious female figures of the past. In these works, authors undertook to argue for the dignity of woman and to convey positive views of women's nature, and women's position in society. The background for this growing trend for writings on the *questione femminile* is multifaceted.

[77] On this point, but with a focus on the Renaissance, see Sanson 2003, pp. 209-210.

There were at least two processes at play: the increasing literacy of women at the turn of the century (a development that paves the way for the spread of female poetry writing in the following decades),[78] and the evolution of courts, where with growing frequency power was allocated to women. In her role as patron, the court lady would encourage the production of writings in the defence of women as a means to legitimise her position. The Mantua-Ferrara nexus, with the key figures of Eleonora d'Aragona and Isabella d'Este, played a major role in this process.[79]

In this type of literature, a place of relevance is awarded to the description and praise of the woman's social behaviour. A significant example is offered by Castiglione's *Cortegiano* – in whose third book the characters verbally fashion an ideal *donna di palazzo*, engaging in a debate that in the words of Stephen Kolsky can be regarded as 'a critical *summa* of the discourse on women in Renaissance Italy'.[80] The discussion, led by Giuliano de' Medici, gives primary importance to female sociability. It is asserted that the *donna di palazzo* has to be graceful in her deportment, witty and entertaining in her conversation (but never in a dissolute manner), and insightful as regards the personality of her interlocutors. While culture also features as a fundamental element in this kind of portrait (and Francesco Sberlati highlights the absolute novelty of this),[81] it remains, however, both subordinate to and in the service of social expression:

> [...] a quella che vive in corte parmi convenirsi sopra ogni altra cosa una certa affabilità piacevole, per la quale sappia gentilmente intertenere ogni sorte d'omo con ragionamenti grati e onesti, ed accommodati al tempo e loco ed alla qualità di quella persona con cui parlerà, accompagnando coi costumi placidi e modesti e con quella onestà che sempre ha da componer tutte le sue azioni una pronta vivacità d'ingegno, [...]. Non deve adunque questa donna, per volersi far estimar bona ed onesta, esser tanto ritrosa e mostrar tanto d'aborrire e le compagnie e i ragionamenti ancor un poco lascivi, che ritrovandovisi se ne levi; [...]. (*Cortegiano*, III.V)

---

78 Studies on all these aspects are numerous and a selection must be made. An exhaustive historical overview of proto-feminist treatises is provided by Doglio 1988; see, moreover, Kolsky 2005 and its bibliography. On women's literacy in the Renaissance, see Sberlati 1997; Vecchi Galli 2006 (and the bibliography quoted at pp. 191-192); Cox 2008. An updated list of Anglophone bibliography on several subjects related to 'women and learning' (including the *querelle des femmes* and women's writing) is in King 2010.

79 On this point, see Kolsky 2005, pp. 10-16; see also the essays gathered in Panizza 2000.

80 Kolsky 2005, p. 11. Note that the discussion on women constituted the original nucleus of Castiglione's work, the *Lettera al Frisia in difesa delle donne*. On the phases of elaboration of the female theme see Romagnoli 2009 and the works cited in Chapter II, footnote 68.

81 Sberlati 1997, p. 122.

Similarly, Equicola's *De mulieribus* gives a description of Cornelia Cantelmo that is characterised, according to Kolsky, solely 'in terms of her social graces':[82]

> Cuius ut taceam suavissimae vocis leporem et formosissimi vultus decentiam quam mira gestuum dignitas convenustat. Sermo nunquam inanis, grata semper urbanitas, temperata severitas, maximum in verbis pondus et sine superstitione religio, cui non sunt admirationi? (*De mulieribus*, f. b3*r*)[83]

In lyric poetry, this model of sociability emerges, for instance, from the poems by Correggio and Boiardo that I have illustrated in section 2. To these we may add another poem by Correggio, capitolo 376 (*Cosa non è tanto secreta o rara*), also, as the one seen before, in praise of Lucrezia Borgia. After describing her physical beauty according to the *canone lungo*, the poet gives, at ll. 85-120, a detailed account of Lucrezia's social conduct, which touches on her dancing (renownedly one of her favourite entertainments), her skill in dressing her hair, and in games, alongside the more traditional 'parlar modesti' (l. 93) and 'pudicizia' (l. 97).

In addition to this type of portrait, authors may have occasionally also lingered on the cultural accomplishments of the woman they were praising. It is worth returning to Trissino's *I ritratti*. Here the speaker, Bembo, highlights Isabella's literary and philosophic culture and carefully distinguishes it from all her other virtues (mainly social and moral), which precede it in the text:

> Adunque tutti i beni di Castalia, e di Parnaso facciamola avere, [...] e di tutte quelle cose, che i Poeti ornano in versi, gl'Istorici scrivono in prosa, et i Filosofi ne l'uno, e ne l'altro ammoniscono; di queste adorno il nostro ritratto si truova [...] e sopra il tutto di Poetica si diletta, e molto in quella si dimora; [...].[84]

Bembo himself, throughout his oeuvre, often praises the inner qualities of women, almost to the point of equating their importance with their physical features. In his sonnet 5 (*Crin d'oro crespo et d'ambra tersa et pura*) he exalts the precocious wisdom of Lucrezia Borgia,[85] while Elisabetta Quirini

---

82 Kolsky 1991, p. 76.

83 Quoted *ibid.*

84 Trissino 1729, pp. 274-275. Depth of culture is an attribute that belongs to the 'official' representation of Isabella d'Este, and also features in Ariosto's praise included in the *Furioso* (*Fur.*, XI 59,1-2 AB; XIII C: '[...] quella / d'opere illustri e di bei studii amica').

85 Bembo, *Le rime*, 5,10: 'senno maturo et la più verde etade'. This concept is borrowed by Tebaldeo at l. 9 ('senno maturo in non matura etate') of his sonnet *Dui vivi soli, or fino, hebeno raro* (see above, section 1).

is defined 'Donna, cui nulla è par bella né saggia' in the opening line of sonnet 150. But besides wisdom – which is in fact often referred to women in poetry –, special attention seems to be paid to the intellect. Indeed, it should be noted that the word *ingegno*, applied to various ladies, occurs in his poetry more frequently than among his contemporaries. In the poems addressed to Veronica Gambara, this word openly refers to poetic accomplishment. See *Le rime*, 140, l. 12: 'e 'l vostro ingegno, a cui lodar son roco' (this sonnet may probably be dated to 1530); and see, from 1504, the following sonnet, in which the poet wonders if he will ever be able to meet her personally:

> di quella chiara fronte che m'invola
> già pur pensando, e 'n parte è 'l mio sostegno,
> di quel bel ragionar pien d'alto ingegno
> vedrò mai raggio, udirò mai parola?
>
> (Bembo, *Le rime*, 69,5-8)

The word 'ingegno', here highlighted by its final position to rhyme with the preceding line, returns in sonnet 151, where Bembo strives for an adequate description of Elisabetta Quirini's 'beltà sí ricca e 'ngegno sí sublime' (l. 11), and in sonnet 76.[86] In the latter it occurs within a more general celebration of *la Morosina*, mainly structured in terms of her inner qualities: only in the first tercet is a mention of her outward appearance added.[87] Alongside her ingenuity, the sonnet mentions the traditional virtues – see 'pudico' and 'honeste' –, as well as eloquence (in accordance with Petrarch) and sociability:

> Poi che 'l vostr'alto ingegno et quel celeste
> ragionar et tacer pudico et saggio
> da far cortese un huom fero et selvaggio,
> e i leggiadri atti et l'accoglienze honeste
> vi rendon tanto spatio [...]
>
> (Bembo, *Le rime*, 76,1-5)

In the dedicatory epistle of the *Asolani* (1505), Lucrezia Borgia is depicted as an aspiring erudite, and the poet himself as her guide, who always encourages her to cultivate her education, preferring it to all care she may bestow on her outward appearance:

---

86 The composition of the latter probably took place close to the first edition of the *Rime* (1530), while that of 151 must be placed at a later date, between 1537 and 1539 (see the introduction and commentary to both poems in Bembo 2008).

87 Bembo, *Le rime*, 76,9-11: 'se vi s'arroge il corpo, in cui beltade / poser, quanta pon dar, benigne stelle, / con quali rime assai potrò lodarvi?'.

Il che farete voi per aventura volentieri, sì come quella che, vie più vaga di ornare l'animo delle belle virtù che di care vestimenta il corpo, quanto più tempo per voi si può ponete sempre o leggendo alcuna cosa o scrivendo, forse acciò che di quanto con le bellezze del corpo quelle dell'altre donne soprastate, di tanto con queste dell'animo sormontiate le vostre [...].[88]

In the previous tradition, the word *ingegno* would normally have been associated to the intellect of the writer, and, following an established *topos* – an example being *Rvf*, CCLXI –, would be inadequate to celebrate the lady's beauty and/or her super-human moral qualities. Bembo slightly modifies this scheme, openly acknowledging his intellectual failure when measured against that of the woman herself (see the aforementioned poem *Le rime*, 76,6-7: 'ch'io non haggio / stile'). This theme, i.e. the more or less explicit comparison between the two lovers on the intellectual plane, is adopted regardless of the actual level of culture of the woman who is celebrated: if this corresponded to reality in the case of Veronica Gambara, whose intellectual achievement was truly great, it did not necessarily apply to Lucrezia Borgia, whose learning was definitely not outstanding. This may be a sign that Bembo was pursuing an ideal rather than a faithful description of reality. In doing this he would be following the previous or contemporary tradition, where, in the rare cases when the word *ingegno* was referred to a woman, it was normally in the context of the description of a 'divine' lady.[89] Alternatively, it may be supposed that *ingegno*, in these cases, might stand not for ingenuity or creative (e.g. poetical) intelligence, but rather for a combination of social skills. Such uncertainty in the definition of this word characterises much literary praise of women, an example being Castiglione's description of Emilia Pia, who 'per esser dotata di così vivo ingegno e giudicio, come sapete, pareva la maestra di tutti' (*Cortegiano*, I.IV).

If we now return to Lucrezia Borgia, it is interesting to note that Ariosto, too, in his eclogue, makes a point of stating that the beauty of her *ingegno* is even superior to her physical beauty:

Tutti la singular grazia del volto,
le liggiadre fattezze, il bel simbiante
e quel celeste andar laudavan molto.

---

[88] Quoted in DILEMMI 2006, p. 35.

[89] See e.g. GIUSTO DE' CONTI, *La bella mano*, 39,7: 'un singular costume, un sacro ingegno'; POLIZIANO, *Rispetti*, XXIX 6: 'piena di grazia, piena d'alto ingegno'; SANNAZARO, *Sonetti et canzoni*, XVI 10: 'li divini costumi e 'l sacro ingegno'; FILENIO GALLO, *Varie*, 39,7-8: 'le virtù, la facundia, el divo ingegno / trapassan de' mortali ogni misura'.

Ma chi noticia avea di lei più inante,
estollea più l'angelica beltade
de l'altissimo ingegno e l'opre sante.
(*Rime*, eclogue I ed. Fatini, ll. 262-267)[90]

The convergence between Ariosto and Bembo on this point may be taken as a confirmation of Lucrezia's desire for her intellectual qualities to be extolled; but most importantly, it reveals that Ariosto was himself keen on exploring this theme. And indeed the fact that he, too, privileges intellect over beauty is evident from the application of the word *ingegno* to his beloved (whether or not this was Alessandra) also in other lyric poems. While, in the opening of sonnet 51, 'beato ingegno' suggests a practical skill (that of designing and sewing a gown),[91] in other cases it seems to be adopted with the meaning of 'knowledge'. An example is sonnet XIII (*Altri lodan il viso, altri le chiome*); here the poet declares his intention of eschewing praise of transitory physical features, and proposes an alternative catalogue of qualities that refer exclusively to the woman's *animo*:[92]

Altri lodan il viso, altri le chiome
de la sua Donna, altri l'avorio bianco
di che formò natura il petto e il fianco,
altri dan a' begl'occhi eterno nome.
Me non mortal fragil bellezza, come
un ingegno divino ha mosso unquanco,
un animo così libero et franco
come non senta le corporee some,
una chiara eloquentia che deriva
da un fonte di saper, una honestade
di cortese atto et leggiadria non schiva.
(*Rime del canzoniere*, XIII 1-11)

The list includes traditional virtues such as 'onestade' and 'cortese atto', but also intelligence, frankness, and property of speech. The latter is par-

90 In the following lines, Ariosto also praises traditional womanly virtues: 'inclita onestade [...] grande animo [...] femenil contegno [...] virtù' (ll. 268-277). Note that 'celeste andar' at l. 264 may recall Poliziano's description of Simonetta in *Stanze per la giostra*, I 56,7: 'fra sé lodando il dolce andar celeste'.

91 The use of this term with this meaning also occurs in Trissino's canzone dedicated to Isabella d'Este (*Rime*, LIX). At ll. 76-78, he praises her ability in weaving: 'La dilicata manω / dimωstra anchωr ne l'opre di Minεrva / quantω sia rarω il suω leggiadrω ingegnω'.

92 It is uncertain whether Alessandra was the dedicatee of this sonnet, too. The date of its composition is unknown; given the presence of multiple versions it could have originally written by Ariosto as a young poet (Finazzi 2002-2003, p. 218). The metapoetic contents of this poem are dwelt on in Chapter II, 4.

ticularly outstanding: while eloquence features, just like *ingegno*, in entirely idealised female poetical portraits – being also included among the attributes of Laura in *Rvf*, 261 –,[93] Ariosto's engagement with this idea is rooted in 'realism'. Indeed, he highlights, and marks through the *enjambement*, that the lady's eloquence derives from culture, and is therefore not simply an effect of her superior nature.[94] The 'leggiadria non schiva' is another important point: it reminds us of Castiglione, who, too, prescribes that the *donna di palazzo* should avoid being bashful (*Cortegiano*, III.V; see above).

Note that in this case too, Ariosto makes a point of linking this perspective with its classical background. As I mentioned in Chapter II, 4, the sonnet opens with what is clearly a *priamel*, reminiscent of Horace (*Carm.*, I 7,1), and also harks back to Propertius, II 3. The latter is similarly structured around the idea of indifference towards physical beauty (identified by the same attributes we find in the modern canon) and preference for a cultural view that includes dance, song, and poetic composition:

> nec me tam facies, quamvis sit candida, cepit
> (lilia non domina sunt magis alba mea),
> nec de more comae per levia colla fluentes,
> non oculi, geminae, sidera nostra, faces, [...]
> quantum quod posito formose saltat Iaccho,
> egit ut euhantis dux Ariadna choros,
> et quantum, Aeolio cum temptat carmina plectro,
> par Aganippeae ludere docta lyrae,
> et sua cum antiquae committit scripta Corinnae
> carminaque Erinnae non putat aequa suis.
>
> (Propertius, II 3,9-22)

Another example of this perspective is sonnet XXXVI, in which the speaker is uncertain whether it is the woman's beauty or her 'chiaro ingegno' that should be regarded as more excellent, and concludes by declaring the contest essentially a draw:

> pensai che magior fosse la bellezza
> di quanti pregi il ciel, Donna, in voi pose, [...]
> Ma poi con sì gran prova il chiaro ingegno
> mi si mostrò, che rimanere in forse

[93] I shall also mention a canzone by Angelo Galli in praise of one Francesca (*Parlamo a ragione* – for which see Bartolomeo 2012, pp. 48-49), where the lady is 'magnanima, gentil, saggia, eloquente' (l. 37), and Bernardo Pulci, *Poesie*, CIII 18: 'ogni eloquenzia a lei [= Simonetta Vespucci] concessa avea'.

[94] It should be noted that Renaissance treatises rarely classified eloquence as a womanly attribute, as pointed out by Sanson 2003, pp. 214-218.

mi fe' che suo non fusse il primo loco.
Che sia maggior non so, so ben che poco
son disuguali, et so che a questo segno
altro ingegno o belezza unqua non sorse.
(*Rime del canzoniere*, XXXVI 5-6; 9-14)

It should be observed that the final syntagm of this sonnet occurs unmodified in a proem added to the third *Furioso*, where the virtues of 'donne illustri' are praised: if it were not for the envy of writers – the narrator argues –, who are often silent on the subject of their merits, 'tanto il lor nome sorgeria, che forse / viril fama a tal grado *unqua non sorse*' (*Fur.*, XXXVII 2,7-8 C). The proem goes on to praise the writing skills displayed by contemporary women and develops into an encomium of Vittoria Colonna (octaves 16-21). In this context, the occurrence of the same syntagm in the sonnet acquires a new weight. Although we have no information as to the identity of the dedicatee nor the chronology of the poem, it is possible that, as in the *Furioso*, it is a female poet that is praised – although, as we have seen, the theme seems to have been the object of a more general interest on Ariosto's part.

It should be noted that Ariosto also juxtaposes his praises of the lady, including his commendation of her intellect, with frequent laments of his own inadequacy, which often assume metapoetic nuances. In the opening of canzone 50 we find an implicit reflection on the roles of poetry and prose. The latter is preferable to illustrate extraordinary concepts, Ariosto states, but to undertake to recall an event such as his falling in love would be laborious for him regardless of the chosen medium ('Non so s'io potrò ben chiudere in rima / quel che in parole sciolte / fatica havrei di ricontarvi a pieno', ll. 1-3).[95] Later he insists again on how difficult his chosen enterprise of celebrating Alessandra has turned out to be: 'Senza fine io lavoro, / se quanto havrei da dir vuo' por in carte', ll. 117-118, lines that again recall his praise of Vittoria Colonna in the *Furioso*: 'Se quanto dir se ne potrebbe, o quanto / io n'ho desir, volessi porre in carte, / ne direi lungamente; ma non tanto, / ch'a dir non ne restasse anco gran parte' (*Fur.*, XXXVII 21,1-4 C). In sonnet XIII, after listing his beloved's skills, he regrets not being able to immortalise her by making a living statue ('viva / statua', ll. 13-14). A veiled allusion to the myth of Pygmalion, whose archetype may be found in the *Fragmenta*,[96] is detectable here. At the same time, we see a refash-

[95] Cp. *Inf.*, XXVIII 1-2: 'Chi poria mai pur con parole sciolte / dicer [...]?'.

[96] *Rvf*, LXXVIII 9-14: 'Ma poi ch'i' vengo a ragionar co ·llei, / benignamente assai par che m'ascolte, / se risponder savesse a' detti miei. / Pigmalïon, quanto lodar ti dêi / de l'imagine

ioning of the tradition of *ut pictura poesis*, with poetry and the visual arts competing in the difficult task of trying to represent the *animo*, something that would truly occur only if the image could move and speak.

The idea of a living image of the beloved woman is in fact put to use in Ariosto's poetic works. It is found in the *ekphrasis* on the fountain in the *Furioso*. Here, the alabaster statue of Alessandra is endowed with a special expressiveness, and indeed looks down on the figure placed below – the poet – with a reproachful attitude, as if, blessed with intellectual virtues in addition to her beauty and grace, she disdained his weaker intellect:

> Non si potea, ben contemplando fiso,
> conoscer se più grazia o più beltade,
> o maggior maestà fosse nel viso,
> o più indizio d'*ingegno* o d'onestade.[97]
> '– Chi vorrà di costei – dicea l'inciso
> marmo – parlar, quanto parlar n'accade,
> ben torrà impresa più d'ogn'altra degna;
> ma non però ch'a fin mai se ne vegna. –
>
> Dolce quantunque e pien di grazia tanto
> fosse il suo bello e ben formato segno,
> parea sdegnarsi che con umil canto
> ardisse lei lodar sì *rozzo ingegno*,
> com'era quel che sol, senz'altri a canto
> (non so perché), le fu fatto sostegno.
> (*Fur.*, XXXVIII 91-92, 1-6 A; XXXVIII 94-95 B;
> XLII 94-95 C – emphasis mine)

This is one of the most important points of contact between the world of the lyrics and that of the *Furioso*: as noted by Cabani, here 'il narratore si autorappresenta come poeta d'amore oltre che come amante'.[98] His statue, which acts as a physical support to that of Alessandra, is part of a set

tua, se mille volte / n'avesti quel ch'i' sol una vorrei'. This is one of the two famous sonnets on Laura's portrait by Simone Martini, which are considered the forebears of lyric poetry on portraits (see PICH 2010, pp. 52-56).

97 The scheme of this praise resembles the excerpt about Isabella d'Este in *Fur.*, XI 59,3-5 AB; XIII C: 'ch'io non so ben se più leggiadra e bella / mi debba dire, o più saggia e pudica, / liberale e magnanima Isabella'.

98 CABANI 2016, p. 94. This aspect has also been noted by PICH 2015, according to whom in the *ekphrasis* we find 'a '*mise en abyme*' of the author inside the discourse of the Narrator' (p. 344); and, what is more relevant to the present argument, 'the poetry to which the 'rozzo ingegno' is connected in canto 42 seems to be amorous poetry devoted to the woman […]. Significantly, then, […] Ariosto stages himself as a lyric poet' (p. 345).

of statues of lyric poets that similarly support those of famous Estense ladies: the poets all belong to the court milieu, thereby signifying Ariosto's sense of his own belonging to this circle (among them are Correggio, Bembo, Castiglione, Tebaldeo and Ercole Strozzi). While the other ladies are each supported by two poets, Alessandra stands above Ariosto alone, and neither of them is named. This self-portrait, however, does not simply represent fidelity: it also symbolises the almost unattainable aim of Ariosto's poetic (note that the inscription placed below the statue at 94,5-7 recalls his statements on the difficulty of expressing suitable praise both in the canzone and in the verses dedicated to Colonna). Through this theme, Ariosto goes beyond the elaboration of the *topos modestiae* which we find at the very beginning of the *Furioso*. While here, as is well known, he expressed his hopes that his own insanity 'che 'l poco ingegno ad or ad or mi lima' (*Fur.*, I 2,6 ABC) would not prevent him from concluding his work, in the *ekphrasis* of the fountain he goes one step further and juxtaposes his intellectual inadequacy to Alessandra's *ingegno*, thus representing himself as inferior to her.[99]

What specific meaning should be assigned to the word *ingegno* in this case? It is hard to imagine that Ariosto might be referring to cultural skills and ingenuity. Although little is known of Alessandra's biography, nothing supports the hypothesis that she might have been a woman of letters, and Catalano, judging from her epistolary correspondence, even infers a 'deficienza di cultura'.[100] As in the case of Bembo, two solutions are possible: either Ariosto painted an idealised portrait of her, or the description aims to reflect reality; in the latter case the poet wishes to praise a combination of qualities through which Alessandra distinguishes herself in her environ-

---

[99] An ostensibly similar concept may be found in Bembo's poems 76 (quoted above) and 77. They are connected to each other by close links: both are dedicated to *la Morosina* and foreground the poet's inability to express adequate praise. While in 76 the celebration of her *ingegno* and of other interior qualities precedes that of her physical beauty, in 77 the opposite happens: praise of her physical qualities acts as a prelude of that of her *animo*, which is thus valorised. Here, however, what Bembo mentions are unspecified virtues of the soul, and *ingegno* does not appear (unlike in 76). See *Le rime*, 77,1-8: 'Se 'n dir la vostra angelica bellezza, / neve, or, perle, rubin', due stelle, un sole, / subietto abonda et mancano parole / a chi sua fama et veritate apprezza, / quai versi agguaglieran l'alta dolcezza / ch'ogni avaro intelletto appagar sòle / di chi v'ascolta, et l'altre tante et sole / doti de l'alma, et sua santa ricchezza?'. Furthermore, the closing of the sonnet sets Bembo apart from Ariosto in terms of how the theme is developed: in Donnini's words, 'l'impossibilità del poeta [= Bembo] alla lode è dovuto al rifiuto della donna, che, pare di capire, amandolo, lo doterebbe delle qualità necessarie' (Bembo 2008, I, p. 176). See ll. 12-14: 'Per che se questo stile solo accenna, / non compie l'opra et ne fa prova indarno, / il mio diffetto vèn, donna, da voi'.

[100] Catalano 1930-1931, I, pp. 424-425.

ment and in social relations. An amalgam of the two solutions is also possible and is perhaps the most plausible answer to our question. In any case, the picture of Alessandra that emerges from canzone 50 resembles, as was already noted, the typical *donna di palazzo* foregrounded by Castiglione, but is additionally endowed – because Alessandra did not live at court –[101] with a 'universal' character that gives it validity even outside of the courtly context.

4. Female wisdom and social behaviour

Let us now return to garments, and re-examine two further details of Alessandra's outfit. The first is the laurel-leaf crown ('gemmato alloro', l. 113). Laurel is an evident symbol of poetry and intellectual work in general; it is possible that Alessandra, too, may have cared about fashioning herself according to this ideal. The second detail worth noting is the *impresa* embroidered on her dress, consisting, as mentioned above, in a pattern of two intertwined grapevines. It is precisely this motif which triggers Ariosto's declaration of inadequacy, as he says that the meaning of this design escapes him, and implores the woman to decipher it for him:

> Deh, se lece il pensiero
> vostro spiar, de l'implicate fronde
> de le due viti, donde
> il leggiadro vestir tutto era ombroso,
> ditemi il senso ascoso.
>
> (*Rime del canzoniere*, 50,104-108)

> Senza misterio non fu già trapunto
> il drappo nero, [...]
>
> (*ibid.*, ll. 111-112)

In the *Furioso*, the grapevine is present with a symbolic meaning in the description of the love grotto of Angelica and Medoro: 'Aveano in su l'entrata il luogo adorno / coi piedi storti edere e viti erranti' (*Fur.*, XXI 106,1-2 AB; XXIII C). It is paired with the similar image of the ivy, and both also recur elsewhere in the poem as a term of comparison for the sexual act (see for instance *Fur.*, VII 29,1-4 ABC: 'Non così strettamente edera preme / pianta ove intorno abbarbicata s'abbia, / come si stringon li dui amanti insieme, / cogliendo de lo spirto in su le labbia'; or *Fur.*, XXVI 34,6

---

[101] On her life as wife of Tito Strozzi, see *ibid.*, I, pp. 403-415.

AB; XXVIII C: 'ch'un nano aviticchiato era con quella').[102] In the capitolo on the happy night of love (XXI), again, this meaning is associated with the ivy, which is here paired with the acanthus: 'O complessi iterati, che con tanti / nodi cingeste [...] / che non ne fan più l'edere o li acanti!' (ll. 19-21). Such vegetal images were often made to symbolise love in the classical tradition. One may for example recall a similar use of both the grapevine and the ivy in Catullus's epithalamion for the nuptials of Manlius Torquatus and Vinia Aurunculeia:

mentem amore revinciens,
ut tenax hedera huc et huc
arborem implicat errans.

(Catullus, LXI 33-35)

lenta sed velut adsitas
vitis implicat arbores,
implicabitur in tuum
complexum [...]

(*ibid.*, ll. 106-109)

The ivy is also associated with a vow of fidelity in Horace's fifteenth epode,

in verba iurabas mea,
artius atque hedera procera adstringitur ilex,
lentis adhaerens bracchiis,
[...]
fore hunc amorem mutuum.

(Horace, *Epodes*, XV 4-10)

while grapevines appear in poem II 16 from Ovid's *Amores*, in the context of the speaker's complaint about the distance that separates him from his beloved: 'Ulmus amat vitem, vitis non deserit ulmum; / separor a domina cur ego saepe mea?' (ll. 41-42). The grapevine *impresa* in canzone 50 clearly carries a similar meaning – if not openly sexual, at least related to mutual love and fidelity. It should be noted that Ariosto also deploys this image in relation to the Alfonso-Lucrezia couple in his eclogue, when he writes: 'come ben confan le viti e gli olmi, / confanno i dui consorti' (eclogue I ed. Fatini, ll. 289-290).

---

102 Note that the verbs featured in these examples occur together in a simile by Dante, where the ivy image is also adopted (*Inf.*, XXV 58-60: 'Ellera abbarbicata mai non fue / ad alber sì, come l'orribil fiera / per l'altrui membra avviticchiò le sue').

Although this meaning lies within the grasp of any careful reader of the canzone, in the poetic fiction the symbol is described as 'mysterious'. It is the woman who has devised and probably embroidered it. In doing so she fashions herself as an enigma, implicitly inviting a solution from those who are watching her. Not only were *imprese* very dear to Ariosto (who employs them numerous times in his *Furioso*): they were, in general, extremely popular in courts, where, as I anticipated in Chapter I, 3 regarding Ippolito d'Este's passion for them, they often took on the character of an actual game, involving intelligence and intuition.[103] Aristocrats liked to be portrayed with their favourite emblems, as can be seen in Raphael's portrait of Elisabetta Gonzaga, whose forehead is decorated by a mysterious jewel in the shape of a scorpion. Another ornament belonging to the duchess of Urbino, an 'S'-shaped brooch, prompts a discussion between the interlocutors of Castiglione's *Cortegiano* and the improvisation of a sonnet by Bernardo Accolti (I.IX).[104] Indeed, Castiglione regards the *impresa* as a symbol of intelligence, and explicitly prescribes it to the courtier as a way of attracting attention.[105] It is also interesting to recall the letter (for which see again Chapter I, 3) in which Equicola promises Cardinal Ippolito that he will refrain from trying to interpret his *imprese*. This promise must be viewed as an example of courtly rhetoric, in which the superiority of the interlocutor may be glimpsed: nevertheless, it also testifies to the importance of 'enigmaticity' as a fundamental characteristic of the *imprese*. In this respect also, Alessandra qualifies as a worthy follower of the modern model of court lady, and it is interesting to note that garments, in this view, constitute the meeting point of inner and outer beauty, and are therefore a crucial element in social and intellectual characterisation – something that had already partly been seen in the analysis of the portrayal of Isabella d'Este in Trissino's *I ritratti*.

Clothing and *imprese* exhibit the same function as a threshold between the public and the private in capitolo XXVII (*De la mia negra penna in fregio d'oro*). In this poem, a female speaker refuses to reveal the meaning of the symbol embroidered in her dress, a black pen in a golden frame:

> De la mia negra penna in fregio d'oro
> molti mi sono a dimandar molesti
> l'occulto senso, et io nol vuo' dir loro.

---

[103] An exhaustive introduction to the subject of Renaissance *imprese* is LIPPINCOTT 1990. On the *imprese* that feature in Ariosto's works, see SALZA 1914, pp. 174-218.

[104] On this point, see BOLZONI 2010, pp. 200-208.

[105] *Cortegiano*, II.VIII: 'porrà cura d'aver [...] abiti ben intesi, motti appropriati, invenzioni ingeniose, che a sé tirino gli occhi de' circonstanti, come calamita il ferro'.

Vuo' che sempre nel cor chiuso mi resti,
né per pregare o stimular d'altrui
già mai mi potrò indur ch'io 'l manifesti.

(*Rime del canzoniere*, XXVII 1-6)

Se voi direte ostination la nostra,
io dirò che immodesti et importuni
voi sete, et gran discortesia la vostra.

(*ibid.*, ll. 19-21)

It is in my opinion likely that Ariosto wrote this capitolo specifically for a lady's *impresa*. The possibility that it may have originally been an 'occasional' poem,[106] if accepted, foregrounds its marked similarity to XXV, the poem on Ippolito d'Este's camel device (see Chapter I, 3). Moreover, the two capitoli resemble each other closely in terms of length – XXV consists of 43 lines, XXVII of 46 – and of structure. The latter is strictly non-narrative: both poems 'embroider on' a single image, without truly developing it, and XXVII even adopts a circular structure as its last line is almost identical to its first. One may suppose that, as with capitoli XXI-XXII, in this case also, Ariosto imagined them as a diptych.[107] One may even go as far as to hypothesise that, while XXV was written for Ippolito, XXVII may have been dedicated to one of the cardinal's mistresses (perhaps Dalida de' Putti, a musician much appreciated at the Este court, who gave Ippolito two sons). It should furthermore be pointed out that the female speaker's attitude exactly mirrors that of Ippolito – as recorded in the letter by Equicola, mentioned in Chapter I, 3 –, displaying on the one hand great pride in the *impresa*, and on the other an almost contradictory stance of opposition to the courtly game of interpretation. This ambiguous attitude on the part of the 'clients' of both poems is respected and in a way echoed by the poet himself, who offers a detailed description of the two *imprese* but avoids entering into any form of deciphering. Given the lack of evidence, the speaker of XXVII cannot with any degree of certainty be identified as the cardinal's lover. However, while this must remain simply a hypothesis, it is just as valid as the more commonly-held assumption that the female voice is in fact that of Alessandra Benucci.

This poem is significant not only in that it further testifies to Ariosto's attention for the contemporary fashion of *imprese*, but especially be-

---

106 Note that the poem features in **L3**, on which see Chapter I, footnote 27.

107 The parallel is, however, imperfect: in XXV it is the camel depicted in the *impresa* that talks; here the speaker is the woman whose emblem is the pen.

cause it shows his interest in a theme that was equally important in contemporary literature and society, i.e. the correct use of silence, of which this poem constitutes an endorsement. 'Silence' is here the choice of the speaker, who stubbornly refuses to reveal her secret; at the same time, 'silence' is not the choice of her audience, who asks her insistent questions. The woman's attitude is not exclusively one of personal restraint. In fact, she here gives a moral lesson proper: 'Ciò ch'altri asconder vol, spiar non lice' (l. 28) – the act of peeking ('spiar') recalling that of Ariosto himself as he tries to interpret Alessandra's *impresa* in canzone 50 (ll. 104-105).

The reflection on the necessity of silence, and its association with prudence, was crucial in the Cinquecento, achieving even fuller complexity in the second half of the century, and lending itself to various kinds of elaborations. This trend proved particularly fruitful in courtly contexts, where it inevitably became intertwined and compromised with the ambiguous art of simulation and dissimulation.[108] The humanist formulations of this topic hark back to an age-long tradition, intermingling popular proverbs, Biblical wisdom, and stimuli from ancient philosophers such as Plutarch, Cicero, and Seneca.[109] Among many possible texts which were popular in Ariosto's environment (and which include Erasmus's *Adagia*),[110] Calcagnini's *Descriptio silentii* deserves particular mention.[111] A detailed *ekphrasis* is developed in this pamphlet on the Egyptian god of silence Harpocrates, following a taste for allegory that complies with the Lucianic tradition: the god, allegedly encountered by the speaker in the Temple of Fortune in Preneste, is accompanied by Prudence and Faithfulness, and each attribute belonging to these gods is illustrated and explained with great display of erudition. As mentioned in Introduction, 4, this pamphlet probably influenced Ariosto's personification of Silence in *Fur.*, XII 94-97 AB; XIV C. Furthermore, its moral precept is also in line with the underlying concept of capitolo XXVII: 'Nam cui parum exploratum est in humanis silentio nihil salubrius, nihil etiam optabilius? Loquacitate nihil turpius, nihil periculosius?'.[112]

---

108 On dissimulation in early modern court culture, see SNYDER 2009 (and see below). Specifically on silence, see BURKE 1993; PATRIZI 1998; BISELLO 2003. Several inputs are also found in Salvatore Silvano Nigro's introduction to CALCAGNINI 1990, pp. 9-24.

109 On this point, see RINALDI 2000, pp. 337-338.

110 See, for example, *Adagia*, 2403 (*Silentium tutum praemium*); 2966 (*Qui continet arcanum*).

111 This can be read in CALCAGNINI 1544, pp. 490-494 (see also Nigro's Italian translation in CALCAGNINI 1990, pp. 31-50).

112 CALCAGNINI 1544, p. 491.

That Ariosto's penchant for the theme of silence may have been boosted by his knowledge of the *Descriptio silentii* is suggested, among others,[113] by Rinaldi in his overview of this theme in the poet's works, where he also touches on this capitolo. The scholar interprets the pen *impresa* as a symbol for silence itself, his belief being that Ariosto sought to set up a paradoxal dynamic: the more the female speaker refuses to explain the meaning, the more she is in fact revealing it, 'in un vertiginoso rinvio dalla parola al silenzio'.[114] Rinaldi's interpretation prompts us to recall a somewhat similar symbol, that is Isabella d'Este's so-called *impresa delle pause*. This was embroidered on the dress she wore during her brother's wedding to Lucrezia Borgia (1502) and is also depicted in the ceiling of her grotto in the Corte Vecchia of Mantua's Palazzo Ducale: it consists in a piece of stave featuring a clef, four mensuration signs and several signs of rest. This *impresa*, which testifies to Isabella's keenness on music, lends itself – as devices regularly do – to multiple interpretations. Clearly, however, an allusion to silence and to prudence can be recognised in it,[115] and it is no coincidence that Equicola should refer to this symbol within a discourse on courtly conversation, while he touches on silence and also mentions Harpocrates:

> Sia il ragionare facile, non pertinace; use più le orecchie che la lingua; recordesi li antiqui havere adorato un simulacro il quale col dito sopra le labia admoniva silentio (il nominavano Harpocrate). [...] Questo in figure ingeniosamente ha significato la prudentissima Isabella da Este di Mantua marchesa, con tucte le pause della musica pratica, le quali ne admoniscono et quasi ad viva voce ne dicono: «Ad tempo taci». (*Libro de natura de amore, libro quinto*, f. 240r)[116]

Ariosto's *negra penna*, too, seems consistent with this framework, though some additional observations may be made on it. The 'golden

---

113 See Prandi 2006 and Genovese 2012. Both especially focus on the *Furioso*: the former tackles this aspect from a humanist perspective, while the latter analyses the role of silence in the narrative development of the poem.

114 Rinaldi 2000, pp. 339-351, esp. pp. 347-349 (quotation at p. 348). To bolster this interpretation, Rinaldi recalls the traditional association between silence and black – it is no coincidence that Silence wears a 'mantel bruno' in *Fur.*, XII 94,6 AB; XIV C –, while the pen in his opinion alludes at the same time to the activity of writing, and to the raven, which according to the myth (to which I shall return shortly) was punished for talking too much. Rinaldi supports his reading by recalling a sententious passage of the *Furioso*, where the pen (black from ink) also appears as the narrator's instrument to write in favour of silence and against slanderers: 'Io farò sì con penna e con inchiostro, / ch'ognun vedrà che gli era utile e buono / aver taciuto, e mordersi anco poi, / prima la lingua, che dir mal di voi' (*Fur.*, XXVII 2,5-8 AB; XXIX C).

115 A recent overview of the meanings attributed to this device is Shephard 2014, pp. 90-96.

116 Equicola 1999, pp. 487-488.

frame' of the pen, in particular, deserves some attention: indeed, the contrast between gold and black determines the ambiguity of the symbol, which may stand equally well for happiness or for sadness – as the speaker herself says, significantly, at the exact midpoint of the capitolo ('et non vuo' dir se mostra / l'anima lieta o di dolor compunta', ll. 17-18). It is precisely this ambiguity, and the tension thus created between opposites, that may constitute the ultimate meaning of the *impresa*. In turn, the concept of opposition may evoke the *serio ludere*, or, alternatively, the ambivalence of the amorous sentiment, and the poetic expression of such contrasts through Petrarchan oxymorons (to which the pen in this case alludes). Finally, one must recall Segre's suggestion to consider, in interpreting the symbol, the meaning associated with these colours in Coronato Occolti's *Stanze intorno il significato dei colori* (1568): '[Mostra] fermezza eterna il ner, l'oro gran fede' (l. 2).[117] If we accept this reading, this device also foregrounds the concept of fidelity; in this it is like the one worn by Alessandra in the canzone. It moreover displays a similarity with another *impresa* which Ariosto took as the subject of a poem: two flowers, a lily and an amaranth, which embellish the dress of a 'vergine illustre' (the meaning, in this case, is explained by the author).[118]

Several interpretations of the black pen are therefore possible: the lady, however, discourages them all. In doing so she playfully threatens her audience with mythological examples of excessive curiosity. She recalls, in particular, Tyresias and Actaeon, who were guilty of seeing Minerva and Artemis bathing:

> Se d'esser sopragionte a la fontana,
> nude il bel corpo, così increbbe ad esse
> che vendetta ne fero acerba et strana,
> non fora oltra ragion che mi dolesse
> che voi molto più adentro che alle gonne
> veder cercasse come il cor mi stesse.
>
> (*Rime del canzoniere*, XXVII 34-39)

If the two goddesses raged at being seen naked, then the lady has all the right to be upset by those who attempt to look into her heart, which, while

---

117 Ariosto 1954, p. 173. On Occolti's work, see Salza 1914, pp. 165-168.

118 *Rime del canzoniere*, XLVII 1-8: 'Non senza causa il giglio e l'amaranto, / l'uno di fede e l'altro fior d'amore, / di bel liggiadro lor vago colore, / vergine illustre, v'orna il sacro manto. / Candido e puro l'un mostra altro tanto / in voi candore et purità di core; / all'animo sublime l'altro fiore / di constantia real dà il pregio e il vanto'. On this poem, whose dedicatee is unknown, see also Introduction, 3.

being 'trasparente [...] più che cristallo' (to quote from *Rime del canzoniere*, XXXI 15) to God, should not be entirely accessible to people. Indeed,

> Dio, come in l'altri magisterii sui,
> providentia hebbe assai quando il cor pose
> ne la più ascosa parte che era in nui;
> ch'ivi i pensieri et le secrete cose
> volse riporre, e chiuderne la via
> a queste avide menti et curiose.
>
> (*Rime del canzoniere*, XXVII 7-12)

In addition to the theme of silence Ariosto is here exploring the threshold between what is exhibited and what is secret: a point that, as noted by Bolzoni,[119] links this poem to canzone 50. By implicitly rejecting the *topos* of the *homo fenestratus*, namely the model – imposed by moral literature – of complete transparency of thoughts and feelings, the woman complies with the courtly code and aligns with the position of court humanists such as Calcagnini, who, too, seems to have disowned this *topos*.[120] Intriguingly, however, despite Ariosto's apparent adoption of this perspective, in the following tercet there emerges a subtle criticism of that very same humanist circle and its excessive exegetical effort:

> quilli che 'l studio et tutto il pensier loro
> sol per volere interpretar post'hanno
> questa mia negra penna in fregio d'oro.
>
> (*Rime del canzoniere*, XXVII 44-46)

Here perhaps may be detected a subtle thrust at Calcagnini himself, who embraces precisely this attitude in his erudite *Descriptio silentii*, and may be read as a proof that Ariosto, far from passively conforming to the cultural milieu he aspired to belong to, engaged in a lively dialogue with its topics and themes.[121]

---

119 Bolzoni 2010, p. 187. The scholar also underlines that in the capitolo emerges, even more than in the canzone (thanks to the mythological references), 'la dimensione erotica, la carica sensuale che si nasconde dietro la curiosità intellettuale'.

120 See D'Ascia 2004, p. 318 and Prandi 2006.

121 There is no shortage of this kind of criticism in the *Furioso* – where the humanist models sometimes constitute, according to Prandi, 'un'occasione di conflitto' (Prandi 2006, p. 5): a significant case in this respect is precisely the episode involving Silence. The Archangel Michael, who is following his tracks, fails to find him where he would expect, in the monasteries and in the midst of philosophers: indeed Silence has long left such company, and prefers now to associate with the worst vices (*Fur.*, XII 88-90 AB; XIV C). From this episode we gather the author's skeptical stance towards the virtuosity of silence and a critique of what it had become in his times. Such a clear-cut divide from humanist positions is not to be found in the

We shall now look at the most notable aspect of this capitolo, namely, its being spoken in female voice. According to a long-established tradition, silence was seen as the most appropriate condition – if not the only possible one – for a woman, and a natural correlate of her subordinate position, though (according to the same misogynistic prejudice) it was often breached on account of women's natural tendency to *garrulitas*.[122] Here, however, the silence the lady keeps is not the traditional 'womanly' submissive silence, but rather its 'manly' version, associated with prudence and wisdom exerted in social contexts. This makes her similar to Castiglione's *donna di palazzo*, who constituted another exception to the misogynistic commonplace – indeed the *Cortegiano* prescribes that the lady should be actively involved in courtly conversation and, just like the man, know not only *how* but also *when* to speak.[123] Most of all, in Ariosto's capitolo the lady not only stays silent, but also prescribes silence to an audience that arguably include men (as suggested by their being likened to two male mythological figures, namely Tyresias and Actaeon): it is here implied that men, too, can be guilty of *garrulitas*.

The choice of a female speaker links the capitolo we have just examined with the poem that immediately follows it in **Vr**, capitolo XXVIII, in which again we find a moral lesson conveyed in the form of an invective against *multiloquium*.[124] Another common feature is the recourse to mythological examples. Indeed, XXVIII opens (ll. 1-9) with the stories of Corvus, the raven – who was originally white but was turned black by Apollo for having revealed the betrayal of his beloved Coronis –[125] and of Ascalaphus, metamorphosed by Ceres into an owl for telling the other gods that Persephone had eaten pomegranate seeds in the Underworld (and who was therefore responsible for her being permanently bound to that world):[126]

---

capitolo, where a critical note may, if anything, be perceived with regard to its methodology, not to its concepts.

122 This network of *topoi* has been analysed, with a focus on the Cinquecento, by Sanson 2003.

123 See Sanson 2003, pp. 219-222. It should be noted, however, that Castiglione's prescriptions in this sense are contradicted by the female speakers' overall limited contribution to the dialogue, and moreover, contradictions may be found within the set of virtues required of the *donna di palazzo*. Sanson blames this situation on Castiglione's dual aim: on the one hand, to furnish a female equivalent to the courtier, and on the other to endow her with those virtues that traditionally guaranteed woman's honour and respectability (discretion, virtuous motherhood, etc.).

124 Also according to Volta's reconstruction of the antigraph of **Vr**, the two poems should be placed next to each other, as numbers 21 and 22 (Volta 2019, p. 34).

125 *Met.*, II 544-632.

126 *Ibid.*, V 533-550.

Era candido il corvo, et fatto nero
meritamente fu, perché troppo hebbe
expedita la lingua a dire il vero.
Haver tacciuto Ascalapho vorebbe
el testimonio che sul stigio fiume
alla matre e alla figlia udire increbbe:
ché di funeste et d'infelici piume
si ricoverse et restò augello obsceno,
danato sempre ad abborrire il lume.

(*Rime del canzoniere*, XXVIII 1-9)

A possible direct source for this opening (whose sententiousness is nevertheless typical of the capitolo form) may be identified in a Latin poem by Tito Vespasiano Strozzi, *In maledicum*, which is also structured as an invective, featuring the former of the two myths.[127] But even without this specific reference, it should be pointed out that Ariosto's adoption of ornithological imagery complies with a tradition that saw birds as a symbol for poets and courtiers, with either a positive or a negative connotation depending on the context. This tradition is also recalled in the lunar episode of the *Furioso* – where swans and ravens symbolise 'true' poets and adulators respectively – as well as in the *Satire*, where several symbolic birds are to be found.[128] What especially matters here is that Ariosto also follows it in the above-examined capitolo XXVII, where the myth of Cornix – the crow – appears, just before those of Tyresias and Actaeon, once again to symbolise an excess of curiosity. The crow enraged Athena by telling her that Aglaurus had opened the basket containing the infant Erichthonius: this story is found in the same book of Ovid's *Metamorphoses* that contains the myth of the raven and is, in addition, embedded in the latter as a second-degree story (*Met.*, II 551-595). Incidentally, the fact that the two myths should be interlinked further enhances the connection – also on a macrotextual level – between the two capitoli.[129]

---

[127] See ll. 15-16: 'Albus erat quondam volucris Phoebeia Corvus, / nunc importunae praemia vocis habet' (Strozzi 1513, II, f. 26*v*).

[128] On ravens and swans in Ariosto, see Chapter II, 4 (and footnote 149). Specifically on the ornithological imagery of the *Satire*, see Bucchi 2019, esp. pp. 338-339 and p. 341. Here I shall at least recall the *apologo della gazza* of *Sat.*, III 109-150: during a drought, a farmer succeeds in finding water by digging a well; he allows only the members of his family and the most useful animals to drink of it, excluding a magpie, whom he greatly loved but was of no use to him. The apologue symbolises the exclusion of Ariosto from Pope Leo X's favour. As noted by Campeggiani (Ariosto 2019, p. 112 footnote 45), the choice of the magpie may derive from one of Persius's *Choliambi*, which also uses it to symbolise those poets who are spurred on to write only by poverty.

[129] See *Rime del canzoniere*, XXVII 25-27: 'L'uccel c'ha bigio il petto et l'ale nere / fu prima

While the target of XXVII is the garrulousness that is the outcome of excessive curiosity, that of XXVIII is slander. We gather that the speaker is a victim of gossip mongers, who have spread false rumours that stain her honour. The topic of calumny was often raised in contemporary treatises linked to a courtly environment and constituted a legacy of the humanist tradition. Besides recalling Alberti's *Calumnia* – a translation of Lucian carried out in competition with Guarino's –[130] it will be useful to return, once again, to Calcagnini, who, besides making slander the primary subject of a pamphlet, *De calumnia* (dedicated to Ercole I),[131] also lingers on it in his treatise on court life *De patientia, seu vita aulica commentatio*, in which he suggests patience as the best 'correction' to this widespread vice.[132] These topics are also found in contemporary anti-court poetical satire, which voices a critique of envy and calumny drawing on *topoi* which originate in Juvenal and at the same time reflect the authors' personal experience (this tradition also, of course, contained the seedlings of Ariosto's *Satire*). Among the authors geographically close to Ariosto, these themes are developed with particular insistence by Correggio, of whose work I shall mention only one example:

L'un foco ha in gli occhi, e l'altro ha in bocca fele,
la invidia a' pecti lor dà più tormenti
che supplicio che sia, benché crudele;
calumnie puoi gli iubilan fra' denti
con false detractioni, accuse e fraude,
e gemiti e suspir continuo senti.

(Correggio, *Rime*, 368,58-63)[133]

---

donna, et diventò cornice / per esser troppo vaga di vedere'. Ariosto here makes two mistakes, which have so far escaped all commentators of the lyrics. First of all, in the myth, Aglaurus – whose fault was that she was 'vaga di vedere' (namely, eager to see Erichthonius) – was not the crow: this was, instead, Cornix, who was guilty of telling Minerva of Aglaurus's curiosity (Ariosto therefore conflates the two characters). Secondly, the fact that Cornix became a bird is not a consequence of this episode: she was already a crow when she made her report to Minerva (her metamorphosis, which had allowed her to escape Neptune's pursuit, had taken place earlier), and it was on account of this that the goddess punished her by excluding her from her retinue. Ariosto's confusion probably derived from the interference of the myth of Ascalaphus from *Met.*, V, which involves a human-to-bird metamorphosis and which features at the beginning of capitolo XXVIII. This might suggest that the two poems were written in parallel.

130 D'Ascia 1998, p. 309.

131 Calcagnini 1544, pp. 415-422.

132 *Ibid.*, pp. 400-404. It is unlikely, however, that Ariosto could be inspired by this pamphlet; indeed, Cherchi 2016, p. 183 hypothesises that it was written in the 1530-1540 decade. On this work, which was plagiarised by Lucio Paolo Rosello in the second of his *Due dialoghi*, see Snyder 2009, pp. 81-85; Ugolini 2020, p. 183 and their bibliography.

133 Other examples of Renaissance anti-court satire are provided by Ugolini 2020, pp. 84-144.

Slander is also mentioned in the *Cortegiano*, where it is specified that women are more often exposed to it.[134] Poetical applications of this concept may be found in Tebaldeo's oeuvre; for instance, in *Rime extravaganti*, 419 (quoted in Chapter II, 2), whose female addressee worries precisely about her reputation, and *Rime della vulgata*, 71, where the poet invites his addressee – again most probably a woman – to ignore her slanderers: 'Per questo l'honor tuo non verrà meno, / ché sempre al fin convien che 'l ver stia sopra' (ll. 3-4). The common trait of all these works is that exposure to calumny is the primary risk for anybody involved in social relationships: accordingly, the implicit prescription of capitolo XXVIII is that all should refrain from it as much as they can, if they do not wish to entirely pervert the system in which they live. Ariosto here expresses the need for honesty/truthfulness as a regulator of social relationships, and describes it in a manner that closely recalls his description of *fides* in his love lyrics, namely as a normative bond. While this bond is entirely human, the gods are expected to watch over it, and their carelessness is lamented by the speaker, who in fact comes close to questioning their existence:

> O di noi più non curano [the gods], o non hanno
> qua giù più forza, o de li nostri casi
> quei che regono il ciel più poco sanno.
> Che non vi sieno anchor crederei quasi,
> se non ch'io veggio pur per camin certo
> le stati e i verni andar, li orti et li occasi.
> Ma se vi son, come è da lor soferto
> che lode e oltraggi et che premii et suplici
> non sien secondo il bono e il tristo merto?
> Lor debito saria da le radici
> le malediche lingue sveller tosto
> che di falsi rumor sono inventrici.
>
> (*Rime del canzoniere*, XXVIII 22-33)

This theme is probably borrowed by Ariosto from the classics. A particularly relevant reference seems to be a poem from the *Amores*, in which Ovid laments the gods' passivity in the face of Corinna's perjury:

> Esse deos, credamne? [...]
>
> (*Amores*, III 3,1)

---

134 *Cortegiano*, II.XC: 'dico ben che esse possono con più licenzia morder gli omini di poca onestà, che non possono gli omini mordere esse; e questo perché noi stessi avemo fatta una legge, che in noi non sia vicio né mancamento né infamia alcuna la vita dissoluta e nelle donne sia tanto estremo obbrobrio e vergogna, che quella di chi una volta si parla male, o falsa o vera che sia la calunnia che se le dà, sia per sempre vituperata'.

Non satis est, quod vos habui sine pondere testes,
et mecum lusos ridet inulta deos?
Ut sua per nostram redimat periuria poenam,
victima deceptus decipientis ero?
Aut sine re nomen deus est frustraque timetur
et stulta populos credulitate movet,
aut, si quis deus est, teneras amat ille puellas:
nimirum solas omnia posse iubet.

(*ibid.*, ll. 19-26)

The relatively clear-cut ideology of capitolo XXVIII would appear to cast Ariosto as a partisan of absolute truthfulness. This picture is complicated, however, by the mythological opening of the capitolo, as the two characters evoked, Corvus and Ascalaphus, were not punished for lying, but for speaking the truth. Although they are quoted by the lady to demonstrate *a fortiori* the justness of punishing liars – that is: if they were punished for being 'del vero garuli et loquaci' (l. 19), all the more should those guilty of actual falsehood be punished –, nevertheless the moral we glimpse through this argument, which is ancillary to the main subject of the capitolo, is that truthfulness is not always the best mode of social interaction if its measure is exceeded. If one tries to harmonise the two concepts of the poem, therefore, the prescribed social rule that emerges is not truthfulness for its own sake, but rather, self-restraint and moderation:

Porsi devrian tutte le lingue freno
e in li altrui fatti apprender da costoro
di spiar poco, et di parlarne meno.

(*Rime del canzoniere*, XXVIII 10-12)

As in capitolo XXVII, here too, we may see looming Ariosto's interest in the themes of dissimulation and prudence, which are closely linked to the 'norm' of silence. These in turn remind us of a proem of the *Furioso*, where simulation is recommended as a bitter if necessary choice that stems from a pessimistic conception of human relations:

Quantunque il simular sia le più volte
ripreso, e dia di mala mente indici,
si truova pur in molte cose e molte
aver fatti evidenti benefici,
e danni e biasmi e morti aver già tolte;
che non conversiam sempre con gli amici
in questa assai più oscura che serena
vita mortal, tutta d'invidia piena.

(*Fur.*, IV 1 ABC)

It seems natural to think here of Giovanni Pontano's treatise *De prudentia* (1498), which among various other themes deals precisely with the legitimacy of simulation, and also of Machiavelli's 'political realism'.[135] Moreover, once again on this point we should recall the ideas expressed by Calcagnini, whose endorsement of such attitude constitutes a fundamental aspect in his ethical and political reflection. In *De patientia*, his description of courtly dynamics paves the way for a broader discussion, which touches upon the themes of simulation and dissimulation, and his advocacy of silence in *Descriptio silentii* is also clearly related to the concept of dissimulation.[136] A more explicit endorsement of simulation is provided by Calcagnini in a Latin poem, *Simulatae virtutis defensio*, where it is recommended as a means to live honourably: 'Qui probus esse cupit, simulet: sic iudicat omnis, / ut videt, atque animi nunquam discludere nodos / nititur' (ll. 4-6).[137] While Prandi argues that on the subjects of truthfulness and appearance Ariosto's beliefs substantially differed from those of Calcagnini, and although the *Satire* and several passages of the *Furioso* may bear out this assumption,[138] I believe these capitoli point to a more complex position. Such nuances certainly depend partly on the poetic convention adopted (indeed, speaking the truth is a prominent feature of Ariosto's satiric persona, as shown in Chapter I, 3) but at the same time are the result of Ariosto's engagement with, and vital absorption of, a vast and varied landscape of humanist sources.

5. Conclusion

As shown in this chapter, Ariosto's portrayal of women, whose relevance in the *Furioso* is universally recognised, proves to be of great significance also in the lyrics. It seems to have been, for Ariosto, an opportunity to confront a long-established *topos* of the vernacular tradition, and to inject it with various innovations. The presence of a significant classicising vein,

---

135 In the commentary to this proem, Bigi refers to *Principe*, XV and XVIII and to *Discorsi*, III.XL (Ariosto 2012, p. 173). The closeness of the position put forward in this proem with those of Pontano and Machiavelli is also underscored by Santoro 1989, pp. 62-63.

136 See Snyder 2009, p. 51.

137 This poem was published for the first time, with an English translation, by Bacchelli 1998, pp. 350-351. Note that Calcagnini's interest in these themes was certainly prompted by his heterodox religious beliefs and has, therefore, links with the notion of Nicodemism (see *ibid.*, pp. 338-343).

138 Prandi 2006, esp. pp. 29-32. For the whole discussion, see also Ugolini 2017.

which interacts with the Petrarchan canon, is clear, and makes Ariosto's fashioning of this theme consistent with the general tendency described in the previous two chapters. At the same time, however, the poet makes a point of 'placing' his lady in his own time, reverberating through his lyrics the contemporary discourse on women and featuring details of the actual physical appearance (e.g. clothes) and social dynamics that defined the early sixteenth-century lady, thereby making her the subject of a new and not merely topic type of interest. This confirms another propensity displayed by Ariosto-the-lyric poet which emerged in the previous chapters, that is to reflect in his poems his power of observation, anchoring them to a dimension that maintains a firm hold on reality.

CONCLUSION

The most fascinating aspect of Ariosto's engagement with lyric poetry is constituted by the strong relationship it entertains with its 'context', or rather, with a plurality of contexts. The internal variety of the corpus, as well as the fact that it functioned as an extremely open and receptive workshop, means that each poem may be understood in relation to its individual background, even before and without its being necessarily placed in relation to other elements in the 'system'. The opposite is also true – that is, the observations that may be made on each individual text allow us to progressively nuance our understanding of the cultural constellation of which it is part.

At the same time, the critical recognition of such relationships also pushes to the fore those elements that most deeply sustain Ariosto's poetic production, in a manner which may be termed transversal, which is independent, in other words, from the poems' actual chronology and from the Petrarchan 'maturity' achieved by the poet. This book has repeatedly stressed two specific points: a close imitation of the classics and a search for verisimilitude. While both these aspects were already in some way part of the landscape of critical studies on the *rime,* a more thorough and systematic study seemed timely. Indeed, even when Latin models *were* pointed out, these tended to interest critics less than a comparison of Ariosto with Petrarch and Petrarchism (or rather the different varieties of Petrarchism).[1] I have tried to show how deeply the classical models influence the process of 'construction' of his poems, functioning both as stylistic and ideological tools. As regards the quality of verisimilitude, this has already for some time been part of the accepted critical view of Ariosto-the-lyric poet:[2] it is now however possible to further clarify this aspect of his work, by viewing it as part of a system of subtle continuation and variations of

---

[1] Carrai 2000 is, among the general overviews of Ariosto's lyrics, that which has most highlighted the significance of the classical tradition.

[2] See for instance Binni 1947.

the Quattrocento 'Lombard' tradition,[3] which is today much better known to us than before.

Ariosto's poems, however, enjoy a special status even when viewed against the backdrop of his entire oeuvre. The poems span a significant chronological arc, progressing in step with his other works and coinciding largely with the writing of the *Furioso*. But while the *Furioso*, even in its 1516 version, is (to pick up the architectural metaphor used by Cabani)[4] a finished edifice, the *rime* remain an open building site. Therefore, although it may be fascinating to search for elements of continuity between the epic-chivalric poem and his lyrics (which indeed are frequently highlighted in this work), it is at the same time indispensable not to forget that the latter are, by their very nature, a 'privato controcanto'[5]. When Ariosto's discourse on love is conjugated in the first person, it does not achieve organic wholeness – a fact that it is tempting to interpret as Ariosto's inclination towards an analytical observation of the complexity of life, rather than as a drive towards self-reflection. Nevertheless, while the *Furioso* may prompt seemingly inexhaustible critical work on its 'structure', the intriguing element of Ariosto's lyric project is precisely its 'unfinished' nature, an aspect that leaves this area of his work still open to new philological and interpretative possibilities. The exploration of Ariosto's *rime* is therefore far from exhausted.

[3] See Malinverni 2000, p. 513: 'Ma questo atteggiamento è appunto difficilmente spiegabile al di fuori di una precisa [...] tradizione 'lombarda' [...] dall'intonazione discretamente ma pur chiaramente avvertibile. Ed è l'intenzione che si suole un po' genericamente definire 'realistica': [...] nel senso di un realismo inteso come rifiuto di qualsiasi forma di idealizzazione del reale, dunque con l'accettazione di ogni suo aspetto e la sua conseguente abilitazione, per così dire 'etica', alla rappresentazione poetica di tono alto e sublime'.

[4] Cabani 2016, p. 103.

[5] Fedi 1990, p. 85.

Appendix

CONVERSION BETWEEN THE NUMBERING OF FATINI'S EDITION OF THE *RIME* AND THAT OF FINAZZI'S EDITION

Finazzi	Fatini	Opening line
I	Son. XXIV	*O messaggi del cor, sospiri ardenti*
II	Son. VIII	*Del mio pensier, che così veggio audace*
III	Son. XXII	*Quando muovo le luci a mirar voi*
IV	Mad. II	*Quando vostra beltà, vostro valore*
V	**Mad. V	*Oh, se quanto è l'ardore*
VI	Canz. II	*Quante fiate io miro*
VII	Son. IX	*La rete fu di queste fila d'oro*
VIII	**Mad. III	*Amor, io non potrei*
IX	Son. XXV	*Madonna sète bella et bella tanto*
X	**Mad. VI	*Se voi così mirasse alla mia fede*
XI	Son. X	*Com'esser può che degnamente io lodi*
XII	Son. VII	*Uno arbuscel che 'n le solinghe rive*
XIII	Son. XV	*Altri lodan il viso, altri le chiome*
XIV	Son. XVIII	*Quel capriol che, con invidia et sdegno*
XV	Son. XII	*Non fu qui dove Amor tra riso et giuoco*
XVI	**Mad. IV	*Per gran vento che spire*
XVII	Son. XX	*Chiuso era il sol da un tenebroso velo*
XVIII	Son. III	*O sicuro, secreto et fidel porto*
XIX	Son. XIII	*Aventuroso carcere soave*
XX	Cap. VII	*Forza è ch'al fine scopra et che si veggia*
XXI	Cap. VIII	*O più che 'l giorno a me lucida et chiara*
XXII	Cap. IX	*O ne' miei danni più che 'l giorno chiara*
XXIII	Cap. XII	*O lieta piaggia, o solitaria valle*

XXIV	Cap. XIII	*Qual son, qual sempre fui, tal esser voglio*
XXV	Cap. XIV	*De sì calloso dosso et sì robusto*
XXVI	Cap. III	*Ne la stagion che 'l bel tempo rimena*
XXVII	Cap. IV	*De la mia negra penna in fregio d'oro*
XXVIII	Cap. VI	*Era candido il corvo, et fatto nero*
XXIX	Cap. V	*Meritamente hora punir mi veggio*
XXX	Cap. XI	*Gentil città, che con felici auguri*
XXXI	Cap. XV	*Ben è dura et crudel, se non si piega*
XXXII	Son. II	*Mal si compensa, ahi lasso, un breve sguardo*
XXXIII	Son. XVI	*Deh, voless'io quel che voler devrei!*
XXXIV	Son. XVII	*Occhi miei belli, mentre ch'i' vi miro*
XXXV	Son. IV	*Perché simil' le siano et de li artigli*
XXXVI	Son. XIV	*Quando prima i crin d'oro et la dolcezza*
XXXVII	**Mad. VII	*A che più strali, Amor, s'io mi ti rendo?*
XXXVIII	Son. XIX	*Madonna, io mi pensai che 'l stare absente*
XXXIX	Son. XXXI	*Se con speranza di mercé perduti*
XL	Son. I	*Perché, Fortuna, quel che Amor mi ha dato*
XLI	Canz. IV	*Spirto gentil, che sei nel terzo giro*
XLII	Cap. XVII	*O qual tu sia nel cielo, a chi concesso*
XLIII	Cap. X	*Del bel numero vostro havrete un manco*
XLIV	Cap. XIX	*Piaccia a cui piace, et chi lodar vuol lodi*
XLV	Cap. XVI	*O vera o falsa che la fama suone*
XLVI	Cap. XVIII	*Chi pensa quanto il bel disio d'amore*
XLVII	Son. VI	*Non senza causa il giglio e l'amaranto*
XLVIII	Son. XXIII	*Come creder debbo io che tu in ciel oda*
49	Canz. V	*Anima eletta, che nel mondo folle*
50	Canz. I	*Non so s'io potrò ben chiudere in rima*
51	Son. XXVI	*Aventurosa man, beato ingegno*
52	Son. XXVIII	*Qual avorio di Gange, o qual di Paro*
53	Son. XXVII	*Son questi i nodi d'or, questi i capelli*
54	Son. XXIX	*Qual volta io penso a quelle fila d'oro*
55	Son. XXX	*Giorno a me sol più che la notte oscuro*
56	Son. XXI	*Qui fu dove il bel crin già con sì stretti*
57	Mad. I	*Se mai cortese fusti*

58*	Son. V	*Felice stella, sotto ch'il sol nacque*
59*	Son. XI	*Benché 'l martir sia periglioso et grave*
60*	Son. XXXII	*Lasso, i miei giorni lieti e le tranquille*

** These are in fact ballate.

Rime extravaganti newly discovered by Finazzi:[1]

(1) – *"Amor"! "Che vòi?" "Ragion." "Da cui la vòi?"* (capitolo)
(2) – *Benignio Serristor, dolce Guidetto* (sonnet)
(3) – *Deh, perché non è in voi tanta pietade* (ballata)
(4) – *Se questa parte ch'hanno i miei pensieri* (ballata)
(5) – *Spinto da quel disio* (ballata)

1 Finazzi 2002-2003, p. 319.

BIBLIOGRAPHY

Abbreviations

The text of Ariosto's *rime* is quoted from Finazzi 2002-2003 and from Ariosto 1954. See Introduction, section 6 for details. Other abbreviations are as follows:

A	= Ariosto 2016
Amorosa visione	= Boccaccio 1964-1998
Amorum libri tres	= Boiardo 2012
Ars amatoria	= Ovid 2016
Asolani	= Bembo 1991
B	= Ariosto 1521
Barignano, *Rime*	= Vecchio 1972-1973
Bembo, *Carmina*	= Bembo 2005
Bembo, *Le rime*	= Bembo 2008
Bernardo Pulci, *Poesie*	= Lanza 1975
Boccaccio, *Comedia delle ninfe fiorentine*	= Boccaccio 1964-1998
Boccaccio, *Genealogie deorum gentilium*	= Boccaccio 1964-1998
Boccaccio, *Filostrato*	= Boccaccio 1964-1998
C	= Ariosto 2012
Carm.	= Ariosto 2017
Catullus	= Catullus 1983
Cino, *Poesie*	= Marti 1969
Colonna, *Rime*	= Colonna 1982
Correggio, *Rime*	= da Correggio 1969
Cortegiano	= Castiglione 1981
Dante, *Rime*	= Alighieri 1939
Decameron	= Boccaccio 1982
De rerum natura	= Lucretius 1982
Erasmus, *Adagia*	= Erasmus 2013
Filenio Gallo, *Rime*	= Gallo 1973
Fórnari, *Spositione*	= Fórnari 1549

Heroides	= Ovid 1977
Horace, *Carm.*	= Horace 1959
Horace, *Epist.*	= Horace 1959
Horace, *Epodes*	= Horace 1959
Horace, *Serm.*	= Horace 1959
Inf., *Purg.*, *Par.*	= Alighieri 1966-1967
Inn.	= Boiardo 1963
Isidore of Seville, *Etymologiae*	= Isidore of Seville 2006
Laudatio	= Bruni 2000
Lettere	= Ariosto 1965
Libro de natura de amore	= Equicola 1999
Lorenzo de' Medici, *Selve*	= de' Medici 1992
Met.	= Ovid 1977-1984
Nature of Man	= Hippocrates 1943
Ovid, *Amores*	= Ovid 1977
Piccolomini, *Historia de duobus amantibus*	= Piccolomini 2001
Poliziano, *Rispetti*	= Poliziano 1986
Propertius	= Propertius 1990
Prose della volgar lingua	= Bembo 1960
Rem. am.	= Ovid 1979
Rvf	= Petrarch 2005
Sannazaro, *Rime*	= Sannazaro 1961
Sasso	= Sasso 1501
Sat.	= Ariosto 2019
Serafino Aquilano, *Sonetti*	= Serafino Aquilano 1894
Serafino Aquilano, *Strambotti*	= Serafino Aquilano 1967
Stampa, *Rime*	= Stampa 1913
Stanze per la giostra	= Poliziano 1992
Statius, *Theb.*	= Statius 1983
Strozzi, *Sonetti*	= Vagni 2011
Tarocchi	= Boiardo 1993
Tebaldeo, *Rime*	= Tebaldeo 1989-1992
Tibullus	= Tibullus 1971
Trissino, *Rime*	= Trissino 1981
Triumphi	= Petrarch 1988
Virgil, *Georg.*	= Virgil 2014
Visconti, *I canzonieri*	= Visconti 1979
Vita nuova	= Alighieri 2015

Works by Ariosto

Ariosto 1521 = Ludovico Ariosto, *Orlando furioso*, Ferrara, Giovanni Battista della Pigna, 1521.

— 1730 = *Opere di M. Lodovico Ariosto*, 2 vols, Venice, Stefano Orlandini, 1730.

— 1924 = Ludovico Ariosto, *Lirica*, ed. Giuseppe Fatini, Bari, Laterza, 1924.

— 1954 = Ludovico Ariosto, *Rime*, in *Opere minori*, ed. Cesare Segre, Milan-Naples, Ricciardi, 1954.

— 1965 = Ludovico Ariosto, *Lettere*, ed. Angelo Stella, in *Tutte le opere*, 3. *Satire, Erbolato, Lettere*, Milan, Mondadori, 1965.

— 1989 = Ludovico Ariosto, *Rime*, in *Opere di Ludovico Ariosto*, ed. Mario Santoro, *Volume terzo. Carmina, Rime, Satire, Erbolato, Lettere*, Turin, UTET, 1989.

— 1992 = Ludovico Ariosto, *Rime*, ed. Stefano Bianchi, Milan, Rizzoli, 1992.

— 2006 = Ludovico Ariosto, *Orlando furioso, secondo la* princeps *del 1516*, ed. Marco Dorigatti, Florence, Olschki, 2006.

— 2012 = Ludovico Ariosto, *Orlando furioso*, introduction and commentary by Emilio Bigi, ed. Cristina Zampese, Milan, Rizzoli, 2012.

— 2016 = Ludovico Ariosto, *Orlando furioso secondo l'editio princeps del 1516*, ed. Tina Matarrese & Marco Praloran, Turin, Einaudi, 2016.

— 2017 = Ludovico Ariosto, *Latin Poetry*, ed. Dennis Looney & D. Mark Possanza, Cambridge (MA), Harvard University Press (I Tatti Renaissance Library 84), 2017.

— 2018 = Ludovico Ariosto, *Cinque canti*, ed. Valentina Gritti, Padua, libreriauniversitaria.it, 2018.

— 2019 = Ludovico Ariosto, *Le Satire*, ed. Emilio Russo, Rome, Edizioni di Storia e Letteratura, 2019.

Primary sources

Achillini 1513 = *Viridario de Gioanne Philoteo Achillino Bolognese*, Bologna, Girolamo di Plato, 1513.

Alighieri 1939 = Dante Alighieri, *Rime*, ed. Gianfranco Contini, Turin, Einaudi, 1939.

— 1966-1967 = Dante Alighieri, *La Commedia secondo l'antica vulgata*, ed. Giorgio Petrocchi, Milan, Mondadori, 1966-1967.

— 2015 = Dante Alighieri, *Vita nuova – Rime*, ed. Donato Pirovano & Marco Grimaldi, Rome, Salerno, 2015.

Bembo 1960 = Pietro Bembo, *Prose e rime*, ed. Carlo Dionisotti, Turin, UTET, 1960.

— 1991 = Pietro Bembo, *Gli Asolani*, ed. Giorgio Dilemmi, Florence, Accademia della Crusca, 1991.

— 2005 = Pietro Bembo, *Lyric Poetry, Etna*, ed. and trans. Mary P. Chatfield, Cambridge (MA), Harvard University Press (I Tatti Renaissance Library 18), 2005.

— 2008 = Pietro Bembo, *Le rime*, ed. Andrea Donnini, 2 vols, Rome, Salerno, 2008.

Boccaccio 1964-1998 = Giovanni Boccaccio, *Tutte le opere*, ed. Vittore Branca, 10 vols, Milan, Mondadori, 1964-1998.

— 1980 = Giovanni Boccaccio, *Decameron*, ed. Vittore Branca, Turin, Einaudi, 1980.

Boiardo 1963 = Matteo Maria Boiardo, *Orlando innamorato, Amorum libri*, ed. Aldo Scaglione, 2 vols, 2nd ed., Turin, UTET, 1963.

— 1993 = Matteo Maria Boiardo, *Tarocchi*, ed. Simona Foà, Rome, Salerno, 1993.

— 2012 = Matteo Maria Boiardo, *Amorum libri tres*, ed. Tiziano Zanato, Novara, Interlinea, 2012.

Bruni 2000 = Leonardo Bruni, *Laudatio Florentine Urbis*, ed. Stefano Ugo Baldassarri, Florence, SISMEL-Edizioni del Galluzzo, 2000.

Calcagnini 1544 = Celio Calcagnini, *Opera aliquot*, Basel, Froben, 1544.

— 1990 = Celio Calcagnini, *Descriptio silentii*, in Celio Calcagnini and others, *Elogio della menzogna*, ed. Salvatore Silvano Nigro, Palermo, Sellerio, 1990.

Calmeta 1959 = Vincenzo Calmeta, *Prose e lettere inedite*, ed. Cecil Grayson, Bologna, Commissione per i testi di lingua, 1959.

Castiglione 1968 = *La seconda redazione del "Cortegiano" di Baldassarre Castiglione*, ed. Ghino Ghinassi, Florence, Sansoni, 1968.

— 1981 = Baldassarre Castiglione, *Il Libro del Cortegiano*, ed. Nicola Longo & Amedeo Quondam, Milan, Garzanti, 1981.

Catullus 1983 = *Catullus*, ed. G. P. Goold, London, Duckworth, 1983.

Colonna 1982 = Vittoria Colonna, *Rime*, ed. Alan Bullock, Rome-Bari, Laterza, 1982.

Cornazano 1502 = *Sonetti e canzone del preclarissimo poeta messere Antonio Cornazano Placentino*, Venice, Manfredo Bonelli, 1502.

da Correggio 1969 = Niccolò da Correggio, *Opere: Cefalo. Psiche. Silva. Rime*, ed. Antonia Tissoni Benvenuti, Bari, Laterza, 1969.

de' Medici 1992 = Lorenzo de' Medici, *Tutte le opere*, ed. Paolo Orvieto, Rome, Salerno, 1992.

Equicola 1999 = *La redazione manoscritta del* Libro de natura de amore *di Mario Equicola*, ed. Laura Ricci, Rome, Bulzoni, 1999.

Erasmus 1508 = *Erasmi Roterodami Adagiorum chiliades tres, ac centuriae fere totidem*, Venice, Aldus Manutius, 1508.

— 1514 = *Erasmi Rotherodami Prouerbiorum chiliades tres, et totidem centuriae, additis quibusdam rebus optimis nouiter excussae plurimisque in locis diligentissime castigatae*, Ferrara, Giovanni Mazzocchi, 1514.

— 2013 = Erasmus of Rotterdam, *Adagi*, ed. Emanuele Lelli, Milan, Bompiani, 2013.

Fórnari 1549 = Simone Fórnari, *La spositione sopra l'Orlando Furioso*, Florence, Lorenzo Torrentino, 1549.

Gallo 1973 = Filenio Gallo, *Rime*, ed. Maria Antonietta Grignani, Florence, Olschki, 1973.

Giovio 1559 = Paolo Giovio, *Dialogo dell'imprese militari et amorose di monsignor Giovio vescovo di Nocera; con un Ragionamento di Messer Lodovico Domenichi, nel medesimo soggetto*, Lyon, Guillaume Rouillé, 1559.

Guicciardini 1988 = Francesco Guicciardini, *Storia d'Italia*, ed. Ettore Mazzali, Milan, Garzanti, 1988.

HIPPOCRATES 1943 = HIPPOCRATES, *Volume IV. Nature of man. Regimen in health. Humours. Aphorisms. Regimen 1-3. Dreams. Heracleitus: On the Universe*, trans. W. H. S. Jones, Cambridge (MA) – London, Cambridge University Press, 1943.

HORACE 1959 = *Q. Horati Flacci Opera*, ed. F. Klingner, Leipzig, Teubner, 1959.

ISIDORE OF SEVILLE 2006 = ISIDORO DI SIVIGLIA, *Etimologie o origini*, ed. Angelo Valastro Canale, 2 vols, Turin, UTET, 2006.

LANZA 1975 = *Lirici toscani del Quattrocento*, ed. Antonio Lanza, Rome, Bulzoni, 1975.

LUCRETIUS 1982 = LUCRETIUS, *De rerum natura*, ed. W. H. D. Rouse & Martin Ferguson Smith, 2nd ed., Cambridge (MA) – London, Harvard University Press – Heinemann, 1982.

MARTI 1969 = *Poeti del Dolce Stil Nuovo*, ed. Mario Marti, Florence, Le Monnier, 1969.

OVID 1977 = OVID, *Heroides – Amores*, ed. Grant Showerman & G. P. Goold, 2nd ed., Cambridge (MA) – London, Harvard University Press – Heinemann, 1977.

— 1977-1984 = OVID, *Metamorphoses*, ed. F. J. Miller & G. P. Goold, 2 vols, 3rd ed., Cambridge (MA) – London, Harvard University Press – Heinemann, 1977-1984.

— 1979 = OVID, *The Art of Love, and Other Poems*, ed. J. H. Mozley & G. P. Goold, 2nd ed., Cambridge (MA) – London, Harvard University Press-Heinemann, 1979.

PETRARCH 1988 = FRANCESCO PETRARCA, *Triumphi*, ed. Marco Ariani, Milan, Mursia, 1988.

— 2004 = FRANCESCO PETRARCA, *Canzoniere*, ed. Marco Santagata, Milan, Mondadori, 2004.

— 2005 = FRANCESCO PETRARCA, *Rerum vulgarium fragmenta*, ed. Rosanna Bettarini, Turin, Einaudi, 2005.

PICCOLOMINI 2001 = ENEA SILVIO PICCOLOMINI, *Historia de duobus amantibus*, ed. Donato Pirovano, Alessandria, Edizioni dell'Orso, 2001.

PIGNA 1553 = GIOVANNI BATTISTA PIGNA, *Carminum libri quatuor, ad Alphonsum Ferrariae principem, his adiunximus C. Calcagnini carmina libri III, L. Areosti carmina libri II*, Venice, Vincenzo Valgrisi, 1553.

— 1554 = GIOVANNI BATTISTA PIGNA, *I romanzi*, Venice, Vincenzo Valgrisi, 1554.

POLIZIANO 1986 = ANGELO POLIZIANO, *Rime*, ed. Daniela Delcorno Branca, Florence, Accademia della Crusca, 1986.

— 1992 = ANGELO POLIZIANO, *Stanze per la giostra*, ed. Davide Puccini, Milan, Garzanti, 1992.

PROPERTIUS 1990 = PROPERTIUS, *Elegies*, ed. and trans. G. P. Goold, Cambridge (MA), Harvard University Press, 1990.

SANNAZARO 1961 = IACOBO SANNAZARO, *Opere volgari*, ed. Alfredo Mauro, Bari, Laterza, 1961.

SASSO 1501 = *Opera del praeclarissimo miser Pamphilo Sasso Modenese*, Venice, Bernardino Vercellense, 1501.

SAVONAROLA 1486 = MICHELE SAVONAROLA, *Practica medicinae, sive de aegritudinibus*, Venice, Andrea Bonetti, 1486.

SERAFINO AQUILANO 1894 = SERAFINO AQUILANO (Serafino de' Ciminelli), *Le rime*, ed. Mario Menghini, Bologna, Romagnoli, 1894.

— 1967 = *Die Strambotti des Serafino dell'Aquila*, ed. Barbara Bauer-Formiconi, München, W. Fink, 1967.

Stampa 1913 = Gaspara Stampa, *Rime*, ed. Abdelkader Salza, Bari, Laterza, 1913.

Statius 1983 = *P. Papini Statii Thebaidos Libri XII*, ed. D. E. Hill, Leiden, Brill, 1983.

Strozzi 1513 = Tito Vespasiano and Ercole Strozzi, *Strozii poetae pater et filius*, Venice, Aldus Manutius, 1513 [1514].

Tebaldeo 1989-1992 = Antonio Tebaldeo, *Rime*, ed. Tania Basile & Jean-Jacques Marchand, Modena, Panini, 1989-1992.

Tibullus 1971 = *Albii Tibulli aliorumque carminum libri tres*, ed. Friedrich Walther Lenz & Karl Galinsky, Leiden, Brill, 1971.

Trissino 1729 = Gian Giorgio Trissino, *I ritratti*, in *Tutte le opere di Giovan Giorgio Trissino gentiluomo vicentino non più raccolte. Tomo secondo contenente le prose*, Verona, Jacopo Vallarsi, 1729, pp. 266-277.

— 1981 = Gian Giorgio Trissino, *Rime*, ed. Amedeo Quondam, Vicenza, Neri Pozza, 1981.

Virgil 2014 = Virgil, *Eclogues, Georgics, Aeneid, Appendix Virgiliana*, rev. G. P. Goold, 2 vols, Cambridge (MA), Harvard University Press, 2014.

Visconti 1979 = Gasparo Visconti, *I canzonieri per Beatrice d'Este e per Bianca Maria Sforza*, ed. Paolo Bongrani, Milan, Il Saggiatore, 1979.

Secondary sources

Agamben 1977 = Giorgio Agamben, *Stanze. La parola e il fantasma nella cultura occidentale*, Turin, Einaudi, 1977.

Albonico 2006 = Simone Albonico, *Ordine e numero: studi sul libro di poesia e le raccolte poetiche del Cinquecento*, Alessandria, Edizioni dell'Orso, 2006.

— 2017 = Simone Albonico, 'Appunti su "forma" e "materia" nella poesia di Pietro Bembo e del suo tempo', in Motta – Vagni 2017, pp. 73-100.

Anconetani 2009 = Raffaella Anconetani, 'Il lessico della follia nell'*Orlando Furioso*', *Bollettino di Italianistica*, VI, 2009, pp. 15-58.

Ascoli 1987 = Albert Russell Ascoli, *Ariosto's Bitter Harmony: Crisis and Evasion in the Italian Renaissance*, Princeton, Princeton University Press, 1987.

— 1997 = Albert Russell Ascoli, *'Faith' as Cover-Up: An Ethical Fable from Early Modern Italy*, Berkeley, UC Berkeley Library, 1997.

— 2003 = Albert Russell Ascoli, 'Fede e riscrittura: Il *Furioso* del 1532', *Rinascimento*, XLIII, 2003, pp. 93-130.

Bacchelli 1998 = Franco Bacchelli, 'Science, Cosmology and Religion in Ferrara, 1520-1550', in Ciammitti – Ostrow – Settis 1998, pp. 333-354.

Bacchelli 1931 = Riccardo Bacchelli, *La congiura di don Giulio d'Este*, 2 vols, Milan, Treves, 1931.

Baillet 1982 = Roger Baillet, 'L'Arioste et les princes d'Este: poésie et politique', in *Le pouvoir et la plume. Incitation, contrôle et répression dans l'Italie du XVI*[e] *siècle*, Paris, Université de la Sorbonne Nouvelle, 1982, pp. 85-95.

Baja Guarienti 2018 = Carlo Baja Guarienti, 'Non sono omo da governare altri omini: Ludovico Ariosto commissario estense in Garfagnana', *Schifanoia*, 54-55, 2018, pp. 83-98.

Bakhtin 1984 = Mikhail Bakhtin, *Problems of Dostoevsky's Poetics* [1963], ed. and trans. Caryl Emerson, Minneapolis, University of Minnesota Press, 1984.

Bàrberi Squarotti 1988 = *Prospettive sul* Furioso, ed. Giorgio Bàrberi Squarotti, Turin, Tirrenia Stampatori, 1988.

Bartolomeo 2012 = Beatrice Bartolomeo, 'Linee tematiche sensuali nella lirica di ispirazione petrarchesca del Quattrocento: alcuni esempi', in *Le forme della tradizione lirica*, ed. Guido Baldassarri & Patrizia Zambon, Padua, Il Poligrafo, 2012, pp. 37-60.

Beecher – Ciavolella – Fedi 2003 = *Ariosto Today. Contemporary Perspectives*, ed. Donald Beecher, Massimo Ciavolella & Roberto Fedi, Toronto, University of Toronto Press, 2003.

Beer 1987 = Marina Beer, *Romanzi di cavalleria. Il* Furioso *e il romanzo italiano del primo Cinquecento*, Rome, Bulzoni, 1987.

— 1990 = Marina Beer, 'Idea del ritratto femminile e retorica del Classicismo: I *Ritratti* di Isabella d'Este di Gian Giorgio Trissino', *Schifanoia*, 10, 1990, pp. 161-173.

Berra 1996 = Claudia Berra, *La scrittura degli* Asolani *di Pietro Bembo*, Florence, La Nuova Italia, 1996.

— 2000 = *Fra satire e rime ariostesche* ed. Claudia Berra, Milan, Cisalpino, 2000.

— 2000*bis* = Claudia Berra, 'La "sciocca speme" e la "ragion pazza": la conclusione delle Satire', in Berra 2000, pp. 165-181.

Bigi 1953 = Emilio Bigi, 'Petrarchismo ariostesco', *Giornale storico della letteratura italiana*, 130, 1953, pp. 31-62.

— 1968 = Emilio Bigi, 'Vita e letteratura nella poesia giovanile dell'Ariosto', *Giornale storico della letteratura italiana*, 145, 1968, pp. 1-37.

— 1975 = Emilio Bigi, 'Le liriche volgari dell'Ariosto', in *Ludovico Ariosto*, atti del Convegno internazionale, Rome, Accademia Nazionale dei Lincei, 1975, pp. 49-71.

Binni 1947 = Walter Binni, *Metodo e poesia di Ludovico Ariosto*, Messina, G. D'Anna, 1947.

Bisello 2003 = Linda Bisello, *Sotto il "manto" del silenzio. Storia e forme del tacere (secoli XVI-XVII)*, Florence, Olschki, 2003.

Bologna 1998 = Corrado Bologna, *La macchina del «Furioso»*, Turin, Einaudi, 1998.

Bolzoni 2010 = Lina Bolzoni, *Il cuore di cristallo. Ragionamenti d'amore, poesia e ritratto nel Rinascimento*, Turin, Einaudi, 2010.

Bonoldi 2002-2003 = Lorenzo Bonoldi, *Equalmente et in ogni parte bella. Isabella d'Este: ritratti e immagini*, MA thesis, Venice, Università Ca' Foscari, a.y. 2002-2003.

Bozzetti 1985 = Cesare Bozzetti, 'Notizie sulle rime dell'Ariosto', in *Studi di filologia e critica offerti dagli allievi a Lanfranco Caretti*, 2 vols, Rome, Salerno, 1985, I, pp. 83-118.

Bozzetti – Vela 2000 = 'Le rime di Ludovico Ariosto secondo il codice Rossiano (Vat. Ross. 639) nell'edizione e col commento ai testi I-XX di Cesare Bozzetti', ed. Claudio Vela, in Berra 2000, pp. 223-290.

Bruscagli 2003 = Riccardo Bruscagli, 'Ariosto morale dal «Furioso» del '16 alle «Satire»', in *Studi cavallereschi*, Florence, Società Editrice Fiorentina, 2003, pp. 103-117.

Bucchi 2016 = Gabriele Bucchi, 'Morale', in Izzo 2016, pp. 261-282.

— 2019 = Gabriele Bucchi, '«Come augel che muta gabbia»: immaginario zoomorfo e mondo morale nelle *Satire*', in Ariosto 2019, pp. 329-348.

Burke 1993 = Peter Burke, *The Art of Conversation*, Cambridge, Polity Press, 1993.

CABANI 1990 = MARIA CRISTINA CABANI, *Fra omaggio e parodia: Petrarca e petrarchismo nel* Furioso, Pisa, Nistri-Lischi, 1990.

— 2016 = MARIA CRISTINA CABANI, 'Le *Rime* e il *Furioso*', in BERRA 2000, later revised and reissued as 'Dalle *Rime* al *Furioso*', in *Ariosto, i volgari e i latini suoi*, Lucca, Pacini Fazzi, 2016, pp. 93-139.

— 2016*bis* = MARIA CRISTINA CABANI, *«Qui vanno gli assassini in sì gran schiera». Ariosto in Garfagnana*, Lucca, Pacini Fazzi, 2016.

CANNATA SALAMONE 1989 = NADIA CANNATA SALAMONE, 'Per un catalogo di libri di rime 1470-1530: considerazioni sul canzoniere', in SANTAGATA – QUONDAM 1989, pp. 83-89.

CARLINI 1958 = ANNA CARLINI, 'Progetto di edizione critica delle liriche di Ludovico Ariosto', *Giornale storico della letteratura italiana*, 135, 1958, pp. 1-40.

CARRAI 2000 = STEFANO CARRAI, 'Classicismo dell'Ariosto lirico', in BERRA 2000, pp. 379-392.

CASADEI 1993 = ALBERTO CASADEI, *Il percorso del "Furioso". Ricerche intorno alle redazioni del 1516 e del 1521*, Bologna, il Mulino, 1993.

— 1992 = ALBERTO CASADEI, '*Sulle prime edizioni a stampa delle «Rime» ariostesche*', *La Bibliofilia*, 94, 1992, pp. 187-195.

— 2004 = ALBERTO CASADEI, 'Note ariostesche', now in CASADEI 2016, pp. 141-151.

— 2016 = ALBERTO CASADEI, *Ariosto: i metodi e i mondi possibili*, Venice, Marsilio, 2016.

CASTOLDI 1993 = MASSIMO CASTOLDI, 'Un caso di interferenza tra madrigale e ballata. Da «Quando viveva in pene» di Niccolò Amanio al coro finale del «Re Torrismondo» di Torquato Tasso', *Lettere italiane*, XLV, 1993, pp. 252-266.

CATALANO 1930-1931 = MICHELE CATALANO, *Vita di Ludovico Ariosto ricostruita su nuovi documenti*, 2 vols, Geneva, Olschki, 1930-1931.

CAVICCHI 2011 = CAMILLA CAVICCHI, '*Musici, cantori e 'cantimbanchi' a corte al tempo dell'Orlando furioso*', in VENTURI 2011, pp. 263-289.

CESERANI 1985 = REMO CESERANI, 'Ludovico Ariosto e la cultura figurativa del suo tempo', in *Studies in the Italian Renaissance. Essays in Memory of Arnolfo B. Ferruolo*, ed. Gian Paolo Biasin, Albert N. Mancini & Nicolas J. Perella, Naples, Società Editrice Napoletana, 1985, pp. 145-166.

CHERCHI 2016 = PAOLO CHERCHI, *Il tramonto dell'onestade*, Rome, Edizioni di Storia e Letteratura, 2016.

CHITTOLINA 1967 = ROBERTO CHITTOLINA, 'Sulle rime dell'Ariosto. Problemi di attribuzione', *Studia Ghisleriana*, s. II, III, 1967, pp. 296-311.

CIAMMITTI – OSTROW – SETTIS 1998 = *Dosso's fate: Painting and Court in Renaissance Italy*, ed. Luisa Ciammitti, Steven F. Ostrow & Salvatore Settis, Los Angeles, Getty Research Institute for the History of Art and the Humanities, 1998.

CIAVOLELLA 1976 = MASSIMO CIAVOLELLA, *La malattia d'amore dall'antichità al Medioevo*, Rome, Bulzoni, 1976.

COGOTTI – FARINELLA – PRETI 2016 = *I voli dell'Ariosto. L'Orlando Furioso e le arti*, ed. Marina Cogotti, Vincenzo Farinella & Monica Preti, Milan, Officina Libraria, 2016.

COMBONI 2000 = ANDREA COMBONI, 'Il canzoniere ariostesco e la poesia delle corti padane: alcune annotazioni', in BERRA 2000, pp. 291-310.

— 2000*bis* = ANDREA COMBONI, 'Eros e Anteros nella poesia italiana del Rinascimento: appunti per una ricerca', *Italique*, III, 2000, pp. 9-21.

COMBONI – DI RICCO 2003 = *L'elegia nella tradizione poetica italiana*, ed. Andrea Comboni & Alessandra Di Ricco, Trento, Dipartimento di scienze filologiche e storiche, 2003.

COMBONI – ZANATO 2017 = *Atlante dei canzonieri in volgare del Quattrocento*, ed. Andrea Comboni & Tiziano Zanato, Florence, SISMEL Edizioni del Galluzzo, 2017.

CONTE 2000 = FLORIANA CONTE, 'Ispirazione figurativa e lessico ecfrastico nell'Orlando furioso', *Annali della Scuola Normale Superiore di Pisa. Classe di Lettere e Filosofia*, s. IV, IX, 2004, pp. 139-165.

CORSARO 1999 = ANTONIO CORSARO, 'Fortuna e imitazione nel Cinquecento', in *I* Triumphi *di Francesco Petrarca*, ed. Claudia Berra, Bologna, Cisalpino, 1999, pp. 429-485.

COX 2008 = VIRGINIA COX, *Women's Writing in Italy, 1400-1650*, Baltimore, Johns Hopkins University Press, 2008.

CRACOLICI 2001 = STEFANO CRACOLICI, 'Remedia amoris sive elegiae: appunti sul dialogo antierotico del Quattrocento', in *Il sapere delle parole. Studî sul dialogo latino e italiano del Rinascimento*, ed. Walter Geerts, Annick Paternoster & Franco Pignatti, Rome, Bulzoni, 2001, pp. 23-35.

— 2011 = STEFANO CRACOLICI, 'Michele Savonarola e le bizzarrie di corte', in CRISCIANI – ZUCCOLIN 2011, pp. 23-58.

CRISCIANI – ZUCCOLIN 2011 = *Michele Savonarola. Medicina e cultura di corte*, ed. Chiara Crisciani & Gabriella Zuccolin, Florence, SISMEL Edizioni del Galluzzo, 2011.

CUCCHIARELLI 2019 = ANDREA CUCCHIARELLI, *Ariosto, Orazio e la tradizione satirica latina*, in ARIOSTO 2019, pp. 265-288.

CURTI 2016 = ELISA CURTI, *Una cavalcata con l'Ariosto. L'Equitatio di Celio Calcagnini*, Ferrara, Fondazione FerraraArte, 2016.

CURTIUS 2013 = ERNST ROBERT CURTIUS, *European Literature and the Latin Middle Ages* [1948], trans. Willard R. Trask, Princeton, Princeton University Press, 2013.

DANZI 2017 = MASSIMO DANZI, 'Gli alberi e il «libro». Percorsi dell'*Arcadia* di Sannazaro', *Italique*, XX, 2017, pp. 119-148.

— 2018 = MASSIMO DANZI, 'Primi elementi per una 'grammatica' dell'egloga volgare', in FAVARO – HUSS 2018, pp. 199-219.

D'ASCIA 1998 = LUCA D'ASCIA, 'Humanistic Culture and Literary Invention in Ferrara at the Time of the Dossi', in CIAMMITTI – OSTROW – SETTIS 1998, pp. 309-332.

D'ASCIA 2000 = LUCA D'ASCIA, 'La biblioteca di Celio Calcagnini umanista ferrarese', in *Storia di Ferrara*, VI, *Il Rinascimento: situazioni e personaggi*, ed. Adriano Prosperi, Ferrara, Corbo, 2000, pp. 396-407.

DAVOLI 2017-2018 = FRANCESCO DAVOLI, *Le Rime (1529) di G. G. Trissino: Commento alle Canzoni*, MA thesis, Padua, Università degli Studi di Padova, a.y. 2017-2018.

DEGL'INNOCENTI PIERINI 2012 = RITA DEGL'INNOCENTI PIERINI, 'Nei cieli di Icaro e Fetonte, fra antico e moderno', in *Aspetti della Fortuna dell'Antico nella Cultura Europea*, ed. Sergio Audano & Giovanni Cipriani, Foggia, Edizioni Il Castello, 2012, pp. 103-127.

DELCORNO 1989 = CARLO DELCORNO, *Exemplum e letteratura. Tra Medioevo e Rinascimento*, Bologna, il Mulino, 1989.

DELCORNO BRANCA 2019 = DANIELA DELCORNO BRANCA, 'L'*Orlando furioso* e la tradizione romanzesca arturiana', in DORIGATTI – PAVLOVA 2019, pp. 3-30.

DELL'AIA 2013 = LUCIA DELL'AIA, 'Il platonismo di Ariosto', *Enthymema*, IX, 2013, pp. 241-256.

— 2017 = Lucia Dell'Aia, *L'antico incantatore. Ariosto e Plutarco*, Rome, Carocci, 2017.

Dilemmi 2000 = Giorgio Dilemmi, 'Una scheda per i "sospiri" dell'Ariosto (Sonetti XXIV)', in Berra 2000, pp. 479-498.

— 2000*bis* = Giorgio Dilemmi, *Dalle corti al Bembo*, Bologna, CLUEB, 2000.

— 2006 = Giorgio Dilemmi, *«Giovin pianta in morbido terreno». Lucrezia Borgia nella Ferrara dei poeti*, in *Lucrezia Borgia. Storia e mito*, ed. Michele Bordin & Paolo Trovato, Florence, Olschki, 2006, pp. 23-42.

Dionisotti 1937 = Carlo Dionisotti, 'Documenti letterari di una congiura estense', *Civiltà moderna*, IX, 1937, pp. 327-340.

— 1974 = Carlo Dionisotti, 'Fortuna di Petrarca nel Quattrocento', *Italia medievale e umanistica*, XVII, 1974, pp. 61-113.

Doglio 1988 = Maria Luisa Doglio, *Introduzione*, in Galeazzo Flavio Capra, *Della eccellenza e dignità delle donne*, ed. Maria Luisa Doglio, Rome, Bulzoni, 1988, pp. 5-57.

Dorigatti 2011 = Marco Dorigatti, 'Il manoscritto dell'*Orlando furioso* (1505-1515)', in Venturi 2011, pp. 1-44.

— 2017 = Marco Dorigatti, 'La raffigurazione del potere nell'*Orlando furioso*', in *Cultural Reception, Translation and Transformation from Medieval to Modern Italy. Essays in Honour of Martin McLaughlin*, ed. Guido Bonsaver, Brian Richardson & Giuseppe Stellardi, Cambridge, Legenda, 2017, pp. 69-83.

— 2018 = Marco Dorigatti, '«Donno Hippolyto da Este». Il vero volto del dedicatario del «Furioso»', in Zampese 2018, pp. 17-48.

Dorigatti – Pavlova 2019 = *'Dreaming again on things already dreamed'. 500 years of* Orlando furioso *(1516-2016)*, Oxford, Peter Lang, 2019.

Drinkwater 2013 = Megan O. Drinkwater, '*Militia amoris*. Fighting in love's army', in *The Cambridge Companion to Latin Love Elegy*, Cambridge, Cambridge University Press, 2013, pp. 194-208.

Durling 1965 = Robert M. Durling, *The Figure of the Poet in Renaissance Epic*, Cambridge (MA), Harvard University Press, 1965.

Einstein 1951 = Alfred Einstein, 'Andrea Antico's *Canzoni nove* of 1510', *The Musical Quarterly*, XXXVII, 1951, pp. 330-339.

Erspamer 1987 = Francesco Erspamer, 'Il canzoniere rinascimentale come testo o come macrotesto: il sonetto proemiale', *Schifanoia*, 4, 1987, pp. 109-114.

Farinella 2016 = Vincenzo Farinella, 'Su Ludovico Ariosto e le arti: premesse figurative al *Furioso* 1516', in Cogotti – Farinella – Preti 2016, pp. 41-61.

Fatini 1924 = Giuseppe Fatini, 'Su la fortuna e l'autenticità delle liriche di Ludovico Ariosto', *Giornale storico della letteratura italiana*, suppl. 22-23, 1924, pp. 133-297.

— 1934 = Giuseppe Fatini, 'Le "Rime" di Ludovico Ariosto', *Giornale storico della letteratura italiana*, suppl. 25, 1934.

Favaro 2010 = Maiko Favaro, 'Giochi di prospettive: le Rime dell'Ariosto fra petrarchismo e classicismo', *Hvmanistica*, V, 2, 2010, pp. 123-131.

— 2011 = Maiko Favaro, 'Sotto il segno della 'fede' d'amore: lettura di Orlando Furioso XXIV', *Studi Rinascimentali*, IX, 2011, pp. 99-106.

— 2012 = Maiko Favaro, *«L'ospite preziosa». Presenze della lirica nei trattati d'amore del Cinquecento e del primo Seicento*, Lucca, Pacini Fazzi, 2012.

FAVARO – HUSS 2018 = *Interdisciplinarità del petrarchismo. Prospettive di ricerca fra Italia e Germania*, ed. Maiko Favaro & Bernhard Huss, Florence, Olschki, 2018.

FEDI 1990 = ROBERTO FEDI, 'Petrarchismo prebembesco in alcuni testi lirici dell'Ariosto', in SEGRE 1976, later revised and reissued as 'Preistoria di un canzoniere: le *Rime* di Ludovico Ariosto', in *La memoria della poesia. Canzonieri, lirici e libri di rime nel Rinascimento*, Rome, Salerno, 1990, pp. 83-115.

— 2007 = ROBERTO FEDI, *I poeti preferiscono le bionde. Chiome d'oro e letteratura*, Florence, Le Càriti, 2007.

FENZI 2006 = ENRICO FENZI, 'Isabella o Lucrezia? Una proposta per le rime di Niccolò da Correggio', *Hvmanistica*, 1 / 2, 2006, pp. 145-160.

FERRETTI 2008 = FRANCESCO FERRETTI, 'Bradamante elegiaca. Costruzione del personaggio e intersezione di generi nell'"Orlando Furioso"', *Italianistica*, XXXVII, 3, 2008, pp. 63-75.

FERRONI 1975 = GIULIO FERRONI, 'L'Ariosto e la concezione umanistica della follia', in *Ludovico Ariosto*, atti del Convegno internazionale, Rome, Accademia Nazionale dei Lincei, 1975, pp. 73-92.

— 1986 = GIULIO FERRONI, 'Lecteur ou lectrice: l'Ariosto et les images du public', in *L'écrivain face à son public en France et en Italie à la Renaissance*, ed. Charles Adelin Fiorato & Jean-Claude Margolin, Paris, Vrin, 1986, pp. 321-335.

— 2008 = GIULIO FERRONI, *Ariosto*, Rome, Salerno, 2008.

FINAZZI 2002-2003 = MARIA FINAZZI, *Edizione critica delle rime del canzoniere di Ludovico Ariosto*, doctoral thesis, Università degli studi di Pavia, a.y. 2002-2003.

FINUCCI 1992 = VALERIA FINUCCI, *The Lady Vanishes: Subjectivity and Representation in Castiglione and Ariosto*, Redwood City, Stanford University Press, 1992.

FLORIANI 1976 = PIERO FLORIANI, 'Dall'amore cortese all'amor divino', in *Bembo e Castiglione. Studi sul classicismo del Cinquecento*, Rome, Bulzoni, 1976, pp. 169-186.

— 1988 = PIERO FLORIANI, *Il modello ariostesco. La satira classicistica nel Cinquecento*, Rome, Bulzoni, 1988.

— 1988*bis* = PIERO FLORIANI, 'Il classicismo primo-cinquecentesco e il modello 'augusteo'', in *L'età augustea vista dai contemporanei e nel giudizio dei posteri*, ed. Alessandro Barchiesi & Eros Benedini, Mantua, Accademia Nazionale Virgiliana, 1988, pp. 237-264.

FRAGNITO 1992 = GIGLIOLA FRAGNITO, 'Intorno alla "religione" dell'Ariosto: i dubbi del Bembo e le credenze ereticali del fratello Galasso', *Lettere italiane*, XLIV, 1992, pp. 208-239.

FULKERSON 2013 = LAUREL FULKERSON, '*Seruitium amoris*. The interplay of dominance, gender and poetry', in *The Cambridge Companion to Latin Love Elegy*, Cambridge, Cambridge University Press, 2013, pp. 180-193.

GAISSER 1993 = JULIA HAIG GAISSER, *Catullus and His Renaissance Readers*, Oxford, Clarendon Press, 1993.

— 2007 = JULIA HAIG GAISSER, 'Catullus in the Renaissance', in SKINNER 2007, pp. 439-460.

GALBIATI 1987 = GIUSEPPINA MARIA STELLA GALBIATI, 'Per una teoria della satira fra Quattro e Cinquecento', *Italianistica*, XVI, 1987, pp. 9-37.

GALLINARO 1999 = ILARIA GALLINARO, *I castelli dell'anima: architetture della ragione e del cuore nella letteratura italiana*, Florence, Olschki, 1999.

Gardini 2017 = Nicola Gardini, 'Introduzione', in Celio Calcagnini, *L'ombra o sul cammino della virtù*, ed. Nicola Gardini, Lucca, Pacini Fazzi, 2017, pp. 5-36.

Genovese 2012 = Gianluca Genovese, '«Quel c'ha detto, non può far non detto». Il silenzio nell'*Orlando furioso*', in *Silenzio*, ed. Silvia Zoppi Garampi, Rome, Salerno, 2012, pp. 145-165.

Gentili 2003 = Gaia Gentili, *Il capitolo in terza rima in Niccolò da Correggio: non solo elegia*, in Comboni – Di Ricco 2003, pp. 115-146.

Ghinassi 1967 = Ghino Ghinassi, 'Fasi dell'elaborazione del «Cortegiano»', *Studi di filologia italiana*, XXV, 1967, pp. 155-196.

— 1968 = Ghino Ghinassi, *La seconda redazione del «Cortegiano» di Baldassarre Castiglione*, Florence, Sansoni, 1968.

Gigliucci 1990 = Roberto Gigliucci, *Oxymoron amoris. Retorica dell'amore irrazionale nella lirica italiana antica*, Rome, De Rubeis, 1990.

— 2000 = *La lirica rinascimentale*, ed. Roberto Gigliucci, Rome, Istituto poligrafico e Zecca dello Stato, 2000.

— 2001 = Roberto Gigliucci, 'Contro la luna. Appunti sul motivo antilunare nella lirica d'amore da Serafino Aquilano al Marino', *Italique*, IV, 2001, pp. 19-29.

— 2004 = Roberto Gigliucci, *Contraposti. Petrarchismo e ossimoro d'amore nel Rinascimento*, Rome, Bulzoni, 2004.

— 2009 = *La melanconia. Dal monaco medievale al poeta crepuscolare*, ed. Roberto Gigliucci, Milan, Rizzoli, 2009.

Giusti 2013 = Francesco Giusti, 'Il complesso di Icaro e il canto del cigno, ovvero due miti del soggetto lirico', *Strumenti critici*, XXXVIII, 1, 2013, pp. 93-118.

Gnocchi 1999 = Alessandro Gnocchi, 'Tommaso Giustiniani, Ludovico Ariosto e la Compagnia degli Amici', *Studi di filologia italiana*, LVII, 1999, pp. 277-293.

Gnudi 1975 = Cesare Gnudi, 'L'Ariosto e le arti figurative', in *Ludovico Ariosto*, atti del Convegno internazionale, Rome, Accademia Nazionale dei Lincei, 1975, pp. 332-401.

Godioli 2010 = Alberto Godioli, 'La prima satira di Ariosto e la poesia delle corti padane', *Italianistica*, XXXIX, 2, 2010, pp. 115-127.

Gorni 1989 = Guglielmo Gorni, 'Il libro di poesia cinquecentesco: principio e fine', in Santagata – Quondam 1989, pp. 35-41.

— 1993 = 'Le forme primarie del testo poetico' [1984], now in Guglielmo Gorni, *Metrica e analisi letteraria*, Bologna, il Mulino, 1993, pp. 15-134.

Greenblatt 1980 = Stephen Greenblatt, *Renaissance Self-Fashioning: From More to Shakespeare*, Chicago, University of Chicago Press, 1980.

Guassardo 2018 = Giada Guassardo, 'Ludovico Ariosto ed Ercole Strozzi: appunti su un rapporto dimenticato', *Schifanoia*, 54-55, 2018, pp. 343-358.

— 2019 = Giada Guassardo, 'Strozzi, Ercole', in *Dizionario Biografico degli Italiani*, XCIV, Rome, Treccani, 2019, pp. 392-394.

— 2020 = Giada Guassardo, 'Ne la stagion che 'l bel tempo rimena: a 'Medicean' Poem by Ludovico Ariosto', *Italianistica*, XLIX, 1, 2020, pp. 83-98.

Güntert 1971 = Georges Güntert, 'Per una rivalutazione dell'Ariosto minore: le Rime', *Lettere italiane*, XXIII, 1971, pp. 29-42.

Izzo 2016 = *Lessico critico dell'*Orlando furioso, ed. Annalisa Izzo, Rome, Carocci, 2016.

JOSSA 2003 = STEFANO JOSSA, 'Ariosto, Alfonso I e la rappresentazione del potere. Nota sull'ideologia del *Furioso*', *Filologia e critica*, XXVIII, 1, 2003, pp. 114-124.

— 2008 = STEFANO JOSSA, 'La penna e il pennello. Retoriche a confronto', in *Officine del nuovo. Sodalizi fra letterati, artisti ed editori nella cultura italiana fra Riforma e Controriforma*, ed. Harald Hendrix & Paolo Procaccioli, Manziana, Vecchiarelli, 2008, pp. 245-256.

— 2009 = STEFANO JOSSA, *Ariosto*, Bologna, il Mulino, 2009.

— 2013 = STEFANO JOSSA, 'The Lies of Poets: Literature as Fiction in the Italian Renaissance', in *Renaissance Studies in Honor of Joseph Connors*, ed. Machtelt Israëls & Louis A. Waldman, 2 vols, Harvard, Harvard University Press, 2013, II, pp. 565-574.

— 2016 = STEFANO JOSSA, 'Ironia', in IZZO 2016, pp. 177-197.

— 2019 = STEFANO JOSSA, 'L'*Orlando furioso* nel suo contesto editoriale', in DORIGATTI – PAVLOVA 2019, pp. 147-171.

KING 2010 = MARGARET KING, 'Women and Learning', *Oxford Bibliographies in Renaissance and Reformation*, New York, Oxford University Press, 2010-.

KLIBANSKY – PANOFSKY – SAXL 1964 = RAYMOND KLIBANSKY – ERWIN PANOFSKY – FRITZ SAXL, *Saturn and Melancholy: Studies in the History of Natural Philosophy, Religion, and Art*, London, Nelson, 1964.

KOLSKY 1986 = STEPHEN KOLSKY, '"The Good Servant": Mario Equicola. Court and Courtier in Early Sixteenth-Century Italy', *The Italianist*, 6, 1986, pp. 34-60.

— 1990 = STEPHEN KOLSKY, 'The Courtier as Critic: Vincenzo Calmeta's *Vita del facondo poeta vulgare Serafino Aquilano*', *Italica*, LXVII, 2, 1990, pp. 161-172.

— 1991 = STEPHEN KOLSKY, *Mario Equicola: The Real Courtier*, Geneva, Droz, 1991.

— 2005 = STEPHEN KOLSKY, *The Ghost of Boccaccio: Writing on Famous Women in Renaissance Italy*, Turnhout, Brepols, 2005.

LARIVAILLE 1990 = PAUL LARIVAILLE, 'Poeta, principe, pubblico dall''Orlando Innamorato' all''Orlando Furioso'', in *La corte di Ferrara e il suo mecenatismo (1441-1598) – The Court of Ferrara and its Patronage*, ed. Marianne Pade, Waage Petersen & Daniela Quarta, Paris, Vrin, 1990, pp. 9-32.

LEE 1940 = RENSSELAER WRIGHT LEE, 'Ut Pictura Poesis: the Humanistic Theory of Painting', *The Art Bulletin*, XXII, 4, 1940, pp. 197-269.

LENTZEN 1985 = MANFRED LENTZEN, 'Le lodi di Firenze di Cristoforo Landino: l'esaltazione del primato politico, culturale e linguistico della città sull'Arno del Quattrocento', *Romanische Forschungen*, XCVII, 1, 1985, pp. 36-46.

LIBONI 2018 = GIONATA LIBONI, 'Dal palco della ragione al palco del ciarlatano: l'Herbolato di Ariosto e la cultura medica ferrarese del Cinquecento', *Schifanoia*, 54-55, 2018, pp. 113-139.

LIPPINCOTT 1990 = KRISTEN LIPPINCOTT, 'The Genesis and Significance of the Fifteenth-Century Italian Impresa', in *Chivalry in the Renaissance*, ed. Sydney Anglo, Woodbridge SF, Boydell Press, 1990, pp. 49-76.

LONGHI 1979 = SILVIA LONGHI, 'Il tutto e le parti nel sistema di un canzoniere', *Strumenti critici*, XIII, 39-40, 1979, pp. 265-300.

— 1989 = SILVIA LONGHI, 'Lettere a Ippolito e a Teseo: la voce femminile nell'elegia', in *Veronica Gambara e la poesia del suo tempo nell'Italia settentrionale: Atti del convegno, Brescia-Correggio, 17-19 ottobre 1985*, ed. Cesare Bozzetti, Pietro Gibellini & Ennio Sandal, Florence, Olschki, 1989, pp. 385-398.

Looney 2003 = Dennis Looney, 'Ariosto and the Classics in Ferrara', in Beecher – Ciavolella – Fedi 2003, pp. 18-31.

— 2005 = Dennis Looney, 'Introduction', in *Phaeton's Children: The Este Court and Its Culture in Early Modern Ferrara*, ed. Dennis Looney & Deanna Shemek, Tempe, Arizona Center for Medieval and Renaissance Studies, 2005, pp. 1-23.

— 2013 = Dennis Looney, 'Ariosto's Dialogue with Authority in the *Erbolato*', *Modern Language Notes*, 128, 1, 2013, pp. 20-39.

— 2016 = Dennis Looney, 'Corte', in Izzo 2016, pp. 41-60.

Lucioli 2010 = Francesco Lucioli, '«D'ogni cortese amor nimico vero». Della (s)fortuna di Anteros nel Rinascimento', *Lettere italiane*, LXII, 3, 2010, pp. 395-422.

Luzio – Renier 1896 = Alessandro Luzio & Rodolfo Renier, *Il lusso di Isabella d'Este marchesa di Mantova*, Rome, Forzani, 1896.

Luzzatto – Pompas 1997 = Lia Luzzatto & Renata Pompas, *I colori del vestire. Variazioni, ritorni, persistenze*, Milan, Hoepli, 1997.

Mac Carthy 2007 = Ita Mac Carthy, *Women and the Making of Poetry in Ariosto's* Orlando Furioso, Leicester, Troubador, 2007.

— 2009 = Ita Mac Carthy, 'Ariosto the Lunar Traveller', *The Modern Language Review*, 104, 1, 2009, pp. 71-82.

Macinante 2011 = Alessandra Paola Macinante, *Erano i capei d'oro a l'aura sparsi». Metamorfosi delle chiome femminili tra Petrarca e Tasso*, Rome, Salerno Editrice, 2011.

Maffia Scariati 2008 = Irene Maffia Scariati, 'La *descriptio puellae* dalla tradizione mediolatina a quella umanistica: Elena, Isotta e le altre', in *A scuola con ser Brunetto. La ricezione di Brunetto Latini dal Medioevo al Rinascimento*, ed. Irene Maffia Scariati, Florence, SISMEL Edizioni del Galluzzo, 2008, pp. 437-490.

Maldina 2016 = Nicolò Maldina, *Ariosto e la battaglia della Polesella. Guerra e poesia nella Ferrara di inizio Cinquecento*, Bologna, il Mulino, 2016.

Malinverni 1998 = Massimo Malinverni, 'La lirica volgare padana tra Boiardo e Ariosto: appunti su una transizione rimossa', in *Il Boiardo e il mondo estense nel Quattrocento*, ed. Giuseppe Anceschi & Tina Matarrese, Padua, Antenore, 1998, pp. 695-722.

— 2000 = Massimo Malinverni, 'Per una notte luminosa: fortuna di un *topos* da Properzio ad Ariosto', in Berra 2000, pp. 499-513.

Marchand 1997 = Jean-Jacques Marchand, 'Le *disperate* di Antonio Tebaldeo dall'elegia al racconto dell'io', in *Feconde venner le carte. Studi in onore di Ottavio Besomi*, ed. Tatiana Crivelli, 2 vols, Bellinzona, Edizioni Casagrande, 1997, I, pp. 160-172.

Marini 2008 = Paolo Marini, 'Ariosto magnanimo. Sulla figura dell'io poetico nelle *Satire*', *Lettere italiane*, LX, 1, 2008, pp. 84-101.

— 2018 = Paolo Marini, 'L'inferno in Garfagnana. Per una lettura della satira IV di Ludovico Ariosto', *Giornale storico della letteratura italiana*, CXCV, 1, 2018, pp. 1-21.

Martelli 1964 = Mario Martelli, 'Una delle *Intercenali* di Leon Battista Alberti fonte sconosciuta del *Furioso*', *La Bibliofilia*, LXVI, 1964, pp. 163-170.

Martinez 1993 = Roland Martinez, 'Dante's Bear: A Note on "Così nel mio parlar"', *Dante Studies, with the Annual Report of the Dante Society*, 111, 1993, pp. 213-222.

Masi 1996 = Giorgio Masi, 'La lirica e i trattati d'amore', in *Storia della letteratura italiana*, ed. Enrico Malato, Rome, Salerno, 1996, IV, pp. 595-679.

— 2002 = Giorgio Masi, 'I segni dell'ingratitudine. Ascendenze classiche e medioevali delle imprese ariostesche nel *Furioso*', *Albertiana*, V, 2002, pp. 141-164.

— 2003 = Giorgio Masi, 'The Nightingale in a Cage: Ariosto and the Este Court', in Beecher – Ciavolella – Fedi 2003, pp. 71-92.

Menegatti 2016 = Marialucia Menegatti, 'Ippolito I d'Este, dedicatario della prima edizione del *Furioso*', in Cogotti – Farinella – Preti 2016, pp. 27-39.

— 2017 = Marialucia Menegatti, 'Le *Satire* tra Ippolito I d'Este e Alfonso d'Este', *L'ellisse. Studi storici di letteratura italiana*, XII, 2, 2017, pp. 49-59.

Mengaldo 1960 = Pier Vincenzo Mengaldo, 'Appunti su Vincenzo Calmeta e la teoria cortigiana', *La rassegna della letteratura italiana*, LXIV, 3, 1960, pp. 446-469.

— 1963 = Pier Vincenzo Mengaldo, *La lingua del Boiardo lirico*, Florence, Olschki, 1963.

Merrill 1944 = Robert V. Merrill, 'Eros and Anteros', *Speculum*, 19, 1944, pp. 265-284.

Miller 2007 = Paul Allen Miller, 'Catullus and Roman Love Elegy', in Skinner 2007, pp. 399-417.

Motta 2003 = Uberto Motta, *Castiglione e il mito di Urbino: studi sulla elaborazione del 'Cortegiano'*, Milan, Vita e Pensiero, 2003.

— 2018 = Uberto Motta, '«Capei d'oro». Fortuna rinascimentale di un *topos* petrarchesco', in Favaro – Huss 2018, pp. 77-105.

Motta – Vagni 2017 = *Lirica in Italia 1494-1530: esperienze ecdotiche e profili storiografici*, ed. Uberto Motta & Giacomo Vagni, Bologna, I Libri di Emil, 2017.

Muñiz Muñiz 2018 = María de las Nieves Muñiz Muñiz, *La* descriptio puellae *nel Rinascimento. Percorsi del* topos *fra Italia e Spagna con un'appendice sul* locus amoenus, Florence, Cesati, 2018.

Musarra 2013 = Franco Musarra, *«L'antiqua damigella». Dell'ironia nell'«Orlando furioso»*, Florence, Cesati, 2013.

Ossola 1976 = Carlo Ossola, 'Métaphore et inventaire de la folie dans la littérature italienne du XVIe siècle', in *Folie et déraison à la Renaissance*, Brussels, Ed. De l'Université de Bruxelles, 1976, pp. 171-196.

Padoan 1978 = Giorgio Padoan, ''Ut pictura poesis': le «pitture» di Ariosto, le «poesie» di Tiziano', in *Momenti del Rinascimento veneto*, Padua, Antenore, 1978, pp. 347-370.

Panizza 2000 = *Women in Italian Renaissance Culture and Society*, ed. Letizia Panizza, Oxford, Legenda, 2000.

Panofsky 1939 = Erwin Panofsky, *Studies in Iconology: Humanistic Themes in the Art of the Renaissance*, New York, Oxford University Press, 1939.

Pantani 2002 = Italo Pantani, *«La fonte d'ogni eloquenzia». Il canzoniere petrarchesco nella cultura poetica del Quattrocento ferrarese*, Rome, Bulzoni, 2002.

Pasquazi 1966 = *Poeti estensi del Rinascimento, con due appendici*, ed. Silvio Pasquazi, Florence, Le Monnier, 1966.

Pastoureau 2008 = Michel Pastoureau, *Black: the History of a Color*, trans. Jody Gladding, Princeton-Oxford, Princeton University Press, 2008.

Patrizi 1998 = Giorgio Patrizi, 'Pedagogie del silenzio: tacere e ascoltare come fondamenti dell'apprendere', in *Educare il corpo, educare la parola nella trattatistica del Rinascimento*, ed. Giorgio Patrizi & Amedeo Quondam, Rome, Bulzoni, 1998, pp. 415-424.

Pattanaro 2007 = Alessandra Pattanaro, *Garofalo e la corte negli anni di Alfonso I (1505-1534)*, in *Il camerino delle pitture di Alfonso I*, ed. Alessandro Ballarin, 6 vols, Padua, Cittadella, 2007, t. VI, pp. 77-101.

PEIRONE 1988 = CLAUDIA PEIRONE, 'Il mito di Angelica. Paesaggi e percorsi d'amore nell'universo femminile del Furioso', in BÀRBERI SQUAROTTI 1988, pp. 87-115.

— 1990 = CLAUDIA PEIRONE, *Storia e tradizione della terza rima. Politica e cultura nella Firenze del Quattrocento*, Genoa, Tirrenia Stampatori, 1990.

PICH 2008 = FEDERICA PICH, '«Qual sempre fui, tal esser voglio» (*O.F.* XLIV, 61-66). Bradamante e la fede 'sognata' di Ruggiero', *Schifanoia*, 34-35, 2008, pp. 259-267.

— 2010 = FEDERICA PICH, *I poeti davanti al ritratto. Da Petrarca a Marino*, Lucca, Pacini Fazzi, 2010.

— 2015 = FEDERICA PICH, 'Beyond the story of storytelling: the narrator as lover in Ariosto's *Orlando Furioso*', *The Italianist*, 35, 3 , 2015, pp. 334-352.

POZZI 1974 = GIOVANNI POZZI, *La rosa in mano al professore*, Fribourg, Edizioni Universitarie, 1974.

— 1979 = GIOVANNI POZZI, 'Il ritratto della donna nella poesia d'inizio Cinquecento e la pittura di Giorgione', *Lettere italiane*, XXXI, 1, 1979, pp. 3-30.

— 1993 = GIOVANNI POZZI, 'Nota additiva alla descriptio puellae', in *Sull'orlo del visibile parlare*, Milan, Adelphi, 1993, pp. 173-184.

PRALORAN 2005 = MARCO PRALORAN, 'Petrarca in Ariosto: il "principium constructionis"', in *I territori del petrarchismo: frontiere e sconfinamenti*, ed. Cristina Montagnani, Rome, Bulzoni, 2005, pp. 51-74.

PRANDI 2004 = STEFANO PRANDI, 'Il volo, il desiderio, la caduta: Icaro nella lirica italiana e francese del XVI secolo', *Italique*, VII, 2004, pp. 103-135.

— 2006 = STEFANO PRANDI, 'Premesse umanistiche del *Furioso*: Ariosto, Calcagnini e il silenzio (*O.F.* XIV, 78-97)', *Lettere italiane*, LVIII, 1, 2006, pp. 3-32.

PRAZ 1970 = MARIO PRAZ, *Mnemosyne: The Parallel between Literature and the Visual Arts*, Princeton, Princeton University Press, 1970.

PRIZER 1998 = WILLIAM F. PRIZER, 'Music in Ferrara and Mantua at the Time of Dosso Dossi: Interrelations and Influences', in CIAMMITTI – OSTROW – SETTIS 1998, pp. 290-308.

PROCACCIOLI 2016 = PAOLO PROCACCIOLI, 'Ancora sui silenzi di Bembo. Il caso Ariosto', in *Dentro il Cinquecento. Per Danilo Romei*, Manziana, Vecchiarelli, 2016, pp. 313-331.

QUINT 1977 = DAVID QUINT, 'Astolfo's Voyage to the Moon', *Yale Italian Studies*, 1, 1977, pp. 398-409.

QUONDAM 1991 = AMEDEO QUONDAM, *Il naso di Laura. Lingua e poesia lirica nella tradizione del classicismo*, Modena, Panini, 1991.

— 1995 = AMEDEO QUONDAM, 'Sull'orlo della bella fontana. Tipologie del discorso erotico nel primo Cinquecento', in *Tiziano: Amor sacro e Amor profano*, ed. Maria Grazia Bernardini & others, Milan, Electa, 1995, pp. 65-81.

— 2000 = AMEDEO QUONDAM, *Questo povero Cortegiano. Castiglione, il libro, la storia*, Rome, Bulzoni, 2000.

RABITTI 2000 = GIOVANNA RABITTI, 'Forme del petrarchismo ariostesco', in BERRA 2000, pp. 429-456.

RENIER 1885 = RODOLFO RENIER, *Il tipo estetico della donna nel Medioevo*, Ancona, Stab. Sarzani, 1885.

RESIDORI 2018 = MATTEO RESIDORI, 'Sur l'ingratitude dans le *Roland furieux*', in *Il* Furioso *del 1516 tra rottura e continuità*, ed. Alessandra Villa, Toulouse, Collection de l'E.C.R.I.T., 2018, pp. 157-182.

RIGO 2014 = PAOLO RIGO, '*Pugna spiritualis, pugna amoris*: la metafora bellica nei *Rerum vulgarium fragmenta*', *Petrarchesca*, 2, 2014, pp. 49-67.

RINALDI 1988 = RINALDO RINALDI, '«Mai senza finzion non si favella». Lettura di Orlando furioso', in BÀRBERI SQUAROTTI 1988, pp. 51-86.

— 2000 = RINALDO RINALDI, 'Maghe e silenzi dell'Ariosto, fra i capitoli e il "Furioso"', in BERRA 2000, pp. 311-354.

RIVOLETTI 2014 = CHRISTIAN RIVOLETTI, *Ariosto e l'ironia della finzione. La ricezione letteraria e figurativa dell'«Orlando furioso» in Francia, Germania e Italia*, Venice, Marsilio, 2014.

ROMAGNOLI 2009 = ANNA ROMAGNOLI, *La donna del Cortegiano nel contesto della tradizione*, 2 vols, doctoral thesis, Universitat de Barcelona, 2009.

RONCACCIA 2012 = ALBERTO RONCACCIA, 'Ariosto petrarchista: appunti sul sonetto «Aventuroso carcere soave»', *Italique*, XV, 2012, pp. 151-161.

ROSCHER 1993 = H. ROSCHER, 'La nostalgie, maladie mélancolique dans la littérature de médecine ancienne, et les poètes latins dans l'Europe de la Renaissance', *Journal of the Institute of Romance Studies*, 2, 1993, pp. 141-149.

ROSSI 1980 = ANTONIO ROSSI, *Serafino Aquilano e la poesia cortigiana*, Brescia, Morcelliana, 1980.

ROTONDI SECCHI TARUGI 1999 = *Malinconia ed allegrezza nel Rinascimento*, ed. Luisa Rotondi Secchi Tarugi, Milan, Nuovi Orizzonti, 1999.

SACCONE 1968 = EDUARDO SACCONE, 'Cloridano e Medoro, con alcuni argomenti per una lettura del primo *Furioso*', *Modern Language Notes*, 83, 1, 1968, pp. 67-99.

— 1974 = EDUARDO SACCONE, *Il soggetto del «Furioso» e altri saggi tra Quattro e Cinquecento*, Naples, Liguori, 1974.

SALZA 1914 = ABDELKADER SALZA, *Studi su Ludovico Ariosto*, Città di Castello, Lapi, 1914.

SANDROLINI 2004 = ALESSANDRA SANDROLINI, 'Celio Calcagnini, *Epitoma super Prometheo et Epimetheo*. Un inedito umanistico sul mito di Prometeo, con traduzione e saggio introduttivo', *engramma*, 30, 2004, online at http://originale.engramma.it/engramma_v4/rivista/saggio/30/030_sandrolini_celio.html.

SANGIRARDI 2006 = GIUSEPPE SANGIRARDI, *Ludovico Ariosto*, Florence, Le Monnier, 2006.

— 2014 = GIUSEPPE SANGIRARDI, 'Trame e genealogie dell'ironia ariostesca', *Italian Studies*, 69, 2, 2014, pp. 189-203.

SANSON 2003 = HELENA SANSON, '*Ornamentum mulieri breviloquentia*: donne, silenzi, parole nell'Italia del Cinquecento', *The Italianist*, 23, 2, 2003, pp. 194-244.

SANTAGATA 1975 = MARCO SANTAGATA, 'Connessioni intertestuali nel «Canzoniere» del Petrarca', *Strumenti critici*, IX, 26, 1975, pp. 80-112.

SANTAGATA – CARRAI 1993 = MARCO SANTAGATA & STEFANO CARRAI, *La lirica di corte nell'Italia del Quattrocento*, Milan, FrancoAngeli, 1993.

SANTAGATA – QUONDAM 1989 = *Il libro di poesia dal copista al tipografo*, ed. Marco Santagata & Amedeo Quondam, Modena, Panini, 1989.

SANTORO 1989 = MARIO SANTORO, *Ariosto e il Rinascimento*, Naples, Liguori, 1989.

SAVARESE 1984 = GENNARO SAVARESE, *Il Furioso e la cultura del Rinascimento*, Rome, Bulzoni, 1984.

SBERLATI 1997 = FRANCESCO SBERLATI, 'Dalla donna di palazzo alla donna di famiglia: pedagogia e cultura femminile tra Rinascimento e Controriforma', *I Tatti Studies in the Italian Renaissance*, 7, 1997, pp. 119-174.

Schirg 2015 = Bernhard Schirg, 'Decoding Da Vinci's *impresa*: Leonardo's Gift to Cardinal Ippolito d'Este and Mario Equicola's *De opportunitate* (1507)', *Journal of the Warburg and Courtauld Institutes*, 78, 2015, pp. 135-155.

Scianatico 2014 = Giovanna Scianatico, *Storia e follia nel «Furioso»*, Bari, Progedit, 2014.

Segre 1966 = Cesare Segre, *Esperienze ariostesche*, Pisa, Nistri-Lischi, 1966.

— 1976 = *Ludovico Ariosto: lingua, stile e tradizione*, ed. Cesare Segre, Milan, Feltrinelli, 1976.

Severi 2018 = Andrea Severi, 'Ab inutile pigraque mole gratiorem in speciem hanc. L'apprendistato letterario di Ludovico Ariosto tra i "contemporanei suoi"', *Schifanoia*, 54-55, 2018, pp. 33-46.

Shemek 1989 = Deanna Shemek, 'Of Women, Knights, Arms, and Love: The Querelle des femmes in Ariosto's Poem', *Modern Language Notes*, 104, 1989, pp. 68-97.

Shephard 2014 = Tim Shephard, *Echoing Helicon: Music, Art and Identity in the Este Studioli, 1440-1530*, Oxford, Oxford University Press, 2014.

Skinner 2007 = *A Companion to Catullus*, ed. Marilyn B. Skinner, Oxford, Blackwell, 2007.

Snyder 2009 = Jon R. Snyder, *Dissimulation and the Culture of Secrecy in Early Modern Europe*, Berkeley-Los Angeles-London, University of California Press, 2009.

Stimato 2009 = Gerarda Stimato, 'Il ritratto di «Hippolyto da Este» nel primo «Furioso»: un'ecfrasi problematica', in *Gli dèi a corte. Letteratura e immagini nella Ferrara estense*, ed. Gianni Venturi & Francesca Cappelletti, Florence, Olschki, 2009, pp. 209-225.

— 2011 = Gerarda Stimato, 'Identità o omonimia? Il problema della doppia Melissa nell'*Orlando furioso*', in Venturi 2011, pp. 45-57.

Stoppino 2012 = Eleonora Stoppino, *Genealogies of Fiction: Women Warriors and the Dynastic Imagination in the Orlando furioso*, New York, Fordham University Press, 2012.

Tateo 1990 = Francesco Tateo, *I miti della storiografia umanistica*, Rome, Bulzoni, 1990.

— 1990*bis* = Francesco Tateo, 'La disputa dell'amore: retorica e poetica del contrario', in *Il dialogo filosofico nel Cinquecento europeo*, ed. Davide Bigalli & Guido Canziani, Milan, FrancoAngeli, 1990, pp. 209-228.

— 2002 = Francesco Tateo, 'Urbanesimo e cultura umanistica nella latinità germanica', online at http://www.phil-hum-ren.uni-muenchen.de/GermLat/Acta/Tateo.htm.

Tissoni Benvenuti 1976 = Antonia Tissoni Benvenuti, 'La tradizione della terza rima e l'Ariosto', in Segre 1976, pp. 303-313.

— 1980 = Antonia Tissoni Benvenuti, *Quattrocento settentrionale*, Rome-Bari, Laterza, 1980.

— 1989 = Antonia Tissoni Benvenuti, 'La tipologia del libro di rime manoscritto e a stampa nel Quattrocento', in Santagata – Quondam 1989, pp. 25-33.

— 2003 = Antonia Tissoni Benvenuti, 'Boiardo elegiaco e Tito Vespasiano Strozzi', in Comboni – Di Ricco 2003, pp. 81-102.

— 2004 = Antonia Tissoni Benvenuti, 'Alfonso I e i letterati del suo tempo', in *L'età di Alfonso I e la pittura del Dosso*, ed. Gianni Venturi, Ferrara, Istituto di Studi Rinascimentali – Modena, Franco Cosimo Panini, 2004, pp. 15-27.

— 2007 = Antonia Tissoni Benvenuti, 'Alberti a Ferrara', in *Alberti e la cultura del Quattrocento*, ed. Roberto Cardini, & Mariangela Regoliosi, Florence, Polistampa, 2007, pp. 267-291.

Tomalin 1976 = Margaret Tomalin, 'Bradamante and Marfisa: An Analysis of the 'Guerriere' of the 'Orlando Furioso', *The Modern Language Review*, 71, 2, 1976, pp. 540-552.

TONELLI 1998 = NATASCIA TONELLI, 'Petrarca, Properzio e la struttura del canzoniere', *Rinascimento*, XXXVIII, 1998, pp. 249-315.

— 2003 = NATASCIA TONELLI, 'I *Rerum vulgarium fragmenta* e il codice elegiaco', in COMBONI – DI RICCO 2003, pp. 17-35.

TORRACA 1888 = FRANCESCO TORRACA, 'Donne reali e donne ideali', in *Discussioni e ricerche letterarie*, Livorno, Vigo, 1888, pp. 291-347.

UGOLINI 2017 = PAOLA UGOLINI, 'Self-Portraits of a Truthful Liar: Satire, Truth-Telling, and Courtliness in Ludovico Ariosto's *Satire* and *Orlando Furioso*', *Renaissance and Reformation / Renaissance et Réforme*, 40, 1, 2017, pp. 141-159.

— 2020 = PAOLA UGOLINI, *The Court and its Critics. Anti-Court Sentiments in Early Modern Italy*, Toronto-Buffalo-London, University of Toronto Press, 2020.

VAGNI 2011 = GIACOMO VAGNI, 'Su un sonetto di Ercole Strozzi già attribuito a Baldassar Castiglione', *Aevum*, LXXXV, 3, 2011, pp. 751-775.

— 2017 = GIACOMO VAGNI, 'Intorno alle 'Rime' di Giuliano di Lorenzo de' Medici', in MOTTA-VAGNI 2017, pp. 125-150.

— 2019 = GIACOMO VAGNI, 'Tenzoni liriche intorno a Pietro Bembo all'inizio del Cinquecento', in *Memoria poetica: questioni filologiche e problemi di metodo*, ed. Giuseppe Alvino, Marco Berisso & Irene Falini, Genoa, Genova University Press, 2019, pp. 207-219.

VECCHI GALLI 1982 = PAOLA VECCHI GALLI, 'La poesia cortigiana tra XV e XVI secolo. Rassegna di testi e studi (1969-1981)', *Lettere italiane*, XXXIV, 1982, pp. 95-141.

— 1994 = PAOLA VECCHI GALLI, 'Poeti e libri di poesia alla corte degli Estensi. Nuovi accertamenti', in *Alla corte degli Estensi. Filosofia, arte e cultura a Ferrara nei secoli XV e XVI*, ed. Marco Bertozzi, Ferrara, Università degli Studi, 1994, pp. 405-424.

— 2000 = PAOLA VECCHI GALLI, 'Fra Ariosto e Tebaldeo: a proposito del capitolo XXVI, *Or che la terra di bei fiori è piena*', in BERRA 2000, pp. 355-378.

— 2003 = PAOLA VECCHI GALLI, 'Percorsi dell'elegia quattrocentesca in volgare', in COMBONI – DI RICCO 2003, pp. 37-79.

— 2006 = PAOLA VECCHI GALLI, 'Donna e poeta. Metamorfosi cinquecentesche', in *Il Petrarchismo. Un modello di poesia per l'Europa*, ed. Loredana Chines, 2 vols, Rome, Bulzoni, 2006, I, pp. 189-216.

VECCHIO 1972-1973 = M. G. VECCHIO, *Rime di Pietro Barignano*, MA thesis (Università degli Studi di Pavia).

VELA 1988 = CLAUDIO VELA, 'Il primo canzoniere del Bembo (ms. Marc. It. IX. 143)', *Studi di filologia italiana*, XLXI, 1988, pp. 163-251.

— 1989 = CLAUDIO VELA, 'Poesia in musica: rime della Gambara e di altri poeti settentrionali in tradizione musicale', in *Veronica Gambara e la poesia del suo tempo nell'Italia settentrionale. Atti del convegno (Brescia-Correggio, 17-19 ottobre 1985)*, ed. Cesare Bozzetti, Pietro Gibellini & Ennio Sandal, Florence, Olschki, 1989, pp. 399-414.

— 2018 = CLAUDIO VELA, 'Ariosto e Bembo all'altezza del primo Furioso', in ZAMPESE 2018, pp. 49-69.

VELLI 1983 = GIUSEPPE VELLI, 'Un sonetto del Sannazaro', in *Tra letteratura e creazione. Sannazaro, Alfieri, Foscolo*, Padua, Antenore, 1983, pp. 57-72.

VENTURI 2011 = *L'uno e l'altro Ariosto in Corte e nelle Delizie*, ed. Gianni Venturi, Florence, Olschki, 2011.

VILLA 2000 = ALESSANDRA VILLA, 'Gli apologhi delle *Satire*', in BERRA 2000, pp. 183-205.

— 2008 = ALESSANDRA VILLA, 'Ludovico Ariosto e la «famiglia d'allegrezza piena», con una riflessione sul progetto delle *Satire*', *Giornale storico della letteratura italiana*, CLXXXV, 2008, pp. 510-535.

VOLTA 2019 = NICOLE VOLTA, 'Sull'ordinamento dei capitoli ariosteschi nel manoscritto Rossiano 639: alcuni emendamenti necessari', *Filologia italiana*, 16, 2019, pp. 23-38.

WATTEL 2018 = ARVI WATTEL, 'Good Vibrations. Mutual Love in Garofalo's Frescoes for Antonio Costabili', *Artibus et historiae*, 78, 2018, pp. 39-58.

WEAVER 2003 = ELISSA B. WEAVER, 'A Reading of the Interlaced Plot of the Orlando Furioso: The Three Cases of Love Madness', in BEECHER – CIAVOLELLA – FEDI 2003, pp. 126-153.

— 2016 = ELISSA B. WEAVER, 'Filoginia e misoginia', in Izzo 2016, pp. 81-97.

ZACCHETTI 2018 = CARLO ZACCHETTI, 'L'*arx rationis* nei *Rerum vulgarium fragmenta*', *Petrarchesca*, 6, 2018, pp. 11-34.

ZAMPESE 2000 = CRISTINA ZAMPESE, 'Presenze intertestuali nelle *Rime* dell'Ariosto', in BERRA 2000, pp. 457-478.

— 2001 = CRISTINA ZAMPESE, 'Connessioni di tipo petrarchesco nella lirica di Quattro e Cinquecento', *Lectura Petrarce*, 21, 2001, pp. 231-252.

— 2018 = *Di donne e cavallier. Intorno al primo* Furioso, ed. Cristina Zampese, Milan, Ledizioni, 2018.

— 2018*bis* = CRISTINA ZAMPESE, 'Prefazione. Donne, cavalieri, libri', in ZAMPESE 2018, pp. 5-16.

ZANATO 2014 = TIZIANO ZANATO, 'Provare «l'ultimo valor» di amore. Sensualità ed erotismo negli *Amorum libri* di Boiardo', *Italique*, XVII, 2014, pp. 21-42.

ZANCAN 1998 = MARINA ZANCAN, *Il doppio itinerario della scrittura. La donna nella tradizione letteraria italiana*, Turin, Einaudi, 1998.

ZANCANI 2007 = DIEGO ZANCANI, 'Antonio Cornazzano: *De laudibus urbis Florentiae* (1464)', *Letteratura italiana antica*, VIII, 2007, pp. 169-177.

ZATTI 1990 = SERGIO ZATTI, *Il* Furioso *fra epos e romanzo*, Lucca, Pacini Fazzi, 1990.

CONTENTS

Preface by Lina Bolzoni . . . . Pag. V
Acknowledgements . . . . » VII

Preliminary note . . . . » 1

Introduction . . . . » 3

Preamble . . . . » 3
1. *The history of Ariosto's 'canzoniere'* . . . . » 5
2. *The* rime extravaganti . . . . » 9
3. *General features of the lyric corpus* . . . . » 11
4. *Between Latin and Italian: the cultural context* . . . . » 18
5. *Ariosto as court poet?* . . . . » 22
6. *Methodology* . . . . » 29

Chapter I – Between Love and Duty: Ariosto's Elegiac Self-Fashioning . . . . » 31

Preamble . . . . » 31
1. *Ariosto and the tradition of the 'parting between two lovers'* » 34
2. *Love and warfare* . . . . » 36
3. *A poem addressed to Ippolito d'Este* . . . . » 42
4. *A mission to Florence* . . . . » 52
5. *The journey to the Garfagnana: style and sources* . . . . » 57
6. *Portrait of the lyric speaker as a lover* . . . . » 66
7. *Conclusion* . . . . » 83

Chapter II – Ariosto, the Lyric Lover . . . . » 85

Preamble . . . . » 85
1. *Love encounters: a classical theme* . . . . » 92
2. Fides *and constancy* . . . . » 103
3. *Another path of the love discourse: the 'courtly-Petrarchan' celebration of woman* . . . . » 126

4. *The flight of the poet: cases of metapoetry* . . . . Pag. 137
5. *Between realism and myth* . . . . » 144
6. *The conclusion of* **Vr** . . . . » 155
7. *Final note: Ariosto's 'Catullian' lyric poetry* . . . . » 160

Chapter III – The Portrayal of Women . . . . » 163

Preamble. . . . . » 163
1. *Experiments on the canon* . . . . » 165
2. *The 'dressed beauty' and her social context* . . . . » 175
3. *The intellectual canon*. . . . . » 190
4. *Female wisdom and social behaviour*. . . . . » 201
5. *Conclusion* . . . . » 214

Conclusion . . . . » 217

Appendix – Conversion Between the Numbering of Fatini's Edition of the Rime and That of Finazzi's Edition . . . . . » 219

Bibliography . . . . » 223

FINITO DI STAMPARE
PER CONTO DI LEO S. OLSCHKI EDITORE
PRESSO ABC TIPOGRAFIA • CALENZANO (FI)
NEL MESE DI MARZO 2021

BIBLIOTECA DELL'«ARCHIVUM ROMANICUM»

Serie I: Storia - Letteratura - Paleografia

. Bertoni, G. *Guarino da Verona fra letterati e cortigiani a Ferra (1429-1460)*. 1921. (esaurito)

. — — *Programma di filologia romanza come scienza idealistica*. 922. (esaurito)

. Verrua, P. *Umanisti ed altri «studiosi viri» italiani e stranieri qua e di là dalle Alpi e dal mare*. 1924, 234 pp., 2 tavv.

. Cino da Pistoia, *Le rime*. 1925. (esaurito)

. Zaccagnini, G. *La vita dei maestri e degli scolari nello Studio Bologna nei secoli XIII e XIV*. 1926. (esaurito)

. Jordan, L. *Les idées, leurs rapports et le jugement de l'homme*. 926, X-234 pp.

. Pellegrini, C. *Il Sismondi e la storia della letteratura dell'Eupa meridionale*. 1926, 168 pp.

. Restori, A. *Saggi di bibliografia teatrale spagnola*. 1927, 122 p., 3 cc.

. Santangelo, S. *Le tenzoni poetiche nella letteratura italiana alle origini*. 1928. (esaurito)

0. Bertoni, G. *Spunti, scorci e commenti*. 1928, VIII-198 pp.

1. Ermini, F. *Il «dies irae»*. 1928, VIII-158 pp.

2. Filippini, F. *Dante scolaro e maestro. (Bologna - Parigi - Ravenna)*. 1929, VIII-224 pp.

3. Lazzarini, L. *Paolo de Bernardo e i primordi dell'Umanesimo Venezia*. 1930. (esaurito)

4. Zaccagnini, G. *Storia dello Studio di Bologna durante il Rinascimento*. 1930, X-348 pp., 42 ill.

5. Catalano, M. *Vita di Ludovico Ariosto*. 2 voll. 1931. (esaurito)

6. Ruggieri, J. *Il canzoniere di Resende*. 1931, 238 pp.

7. Döhner, K. *Zeit und Ewigkeit bei Chateaubriand*. 1931. (esaurito)

8. Troilo, S. *Andrea Giuliano politico e letterato veneziano del uattrocento*. 1932. (esaurito)

9. Ugolini, F. A. *I Cantari d'argomento classico*. 1933. (esaurito)

0. Berni, F. *Poesie e prose*. 1934. (esaurito)

1. Blasi, F. *Le poesie di Guilhem de la Tor*. 1934, XIV-78 pp.

2. Cavaliere, A. *Le poesie di Peire Raimond de Tolosa*. 1935. (esaurito)

3. Toschi, P. *La poesia popolare religiosa in Italia*. 1935. (esaurito)

4. Blasi, F. *Le poesie del trovatore Arnaut Catalan*. 1937. (esaurito)

5. Gugenheim, S. *Madame d'Agoult et la pensée européenne de n époque*. 1937. (esaurito)

6. Lewent, K. *Zum Text der Lieder des Giraut de Bornelh*. 1938. (esaurito)

7. Kolsen, A. *Beiträge zur Altprovenzalischen Lyrik*. 1938. (esaurito)

8. Niedermann, J. *Kultur. Werden und Wandlungen des Breiffs und seiner Ersatzbegriffe von Cicero bis Herder*. 1941. (esaurito)

9. Altamura, A. *L'Umanesimo nel mezzogiorno d'Italia*. 1941. (esaurito)

0. Nordmann, P. *Gabriel Seigneux de Correvon, ein schweizescher Kosmopolit. 1695-1775*. 1947. (esaurito)

31. Rosa, S. *Poesie e lettere inedite*. 1959. (esaurito)

32. Panvini, B. *La leggenda di Tristano e Isotta*. 1952. (esaurito)

33. Messina, M. *Domenico di Giovanni detto il Burchiello. Sonetti inediti*. 1952. (esaurito)

34. Panvini, B. *Le biografie provenzali. Valore e attendibilità*. 1952. (esaurito)

35. Moncallero, G. L. *Il Cardinale Bernardo Dovizi da Bibbiena umanista e diplomatico*. 1953. (esaurito)

36. D'Aronco, G. *Indice delle fiabe toscane*. 1953, 236 pp.

37. Branciforti, F. *Il canzoniere di Lanfranco Cigala*. 1954. (esaurito)

38. Moncallero, G. L. *L'Arcadia*. Vol. I: *Teorica d'Arcadia*. 1953. (esaurito)

39. Galanti, B. M. *Le villanelle alla napolitana*. 1954. (esaurito)

40. Crocioni, G. *Folklore e letteratura*. 1954. (esaurito)

41. Vecchi, G. *Uffici drammatici padovani*. 1954, XII-258 pp., 73 tavv. esempi mus.

42. Vallone, A. *Studi sulla Divina Commedia*. 1955. (esaurito)

43. Panvini, B. *La scuola poetica siciliana*. 1955. (esaurito)

44. Dovizi, B. *Epistolario di Bernardo Dovizi da Bibbiena*. Vol. I (1490-1513). 1955. (esaurito)

45. Collina, M. D. *Il carteggio letterario di uno scienziato del Settecento (Janus Plancus)*. 1957, VIII-174 pp., 5 tavv. f.t.

46. Spaziani, M. *Il canzoniere francese di Siena (Biblioteca Comunale HX 36)*. 1957. (esaurito)

47. Vallone, A. *Linea della poesia foscoliana*. 1957. (esaurito)

48. Crinò, A. M. *Fatti e figure del Seicento anglo-toscano. (Documenti inediti sui rapporti letterari, diplomatici e culturali fra Toscana e Inghilterra)*. 1957. (esaurito)

49. Panvini, B. *La scuola poetica siciliana. Le canzoni dei rimatori non siciliani*. Vol. I. 1957. (esaurito)

50. Crinò, A. M. *John Dryden*. 1957, 406 pp., 1 tav. f.t.

51. Lo Nigro, S. *Racconti popolari siciliani. (Classificazione e Bibliografia)*. 1958. (esaurito)

52. Musumarra, C. *La sacra rappresentazione della Natività nella tradizione italiana*. 1957. (esaurito)

53. Panvini, B. *La scuola poetica siciliana. Le canzoni dei rimatori non siciliani*. Vol. II. 1958. (esaurito)

54. Vallone, A. *La critica dantesca nell'Ottocento*. 1958, 240 pp. Ristampa 1975.

55. Crinò, A. M. *Dryden, poeta satirico*. 1958. (esaurito)

56. Coppola, D. *Sacre rappresentazioni aversane del sec. XVI, la prima volta edite*. 1959, XII-270 pp., ill.

57. Piramus et Tisbè. *Introduzione - Testo critico - Traduzione e note a cura di F. Branciforti*. 1959. (esaurito)

58. Gallina, A. M. *Contributi alla storia della lessicografia italo-spagnola dei secoli XVI e XVII*. 1959, 336 pp.

59. Piromalli, A. *Aurelio Bertola nella letteratura del Settecento. Con testi e documenti inediti*. 1959. Ristampa 1998.

60. Gamberini, S. *Poeti metafisici e cavalieri in Inghilterra*. 1959, 270 pp.

61. Berselli Ambri, P. *L'opera di Montesquieu nel Settecento italiano*. 1960. (esaurito)

62. *Studi secenteschi*, vol. I (1960). 1961, 220 pp.

63. Vallone, A. *La critica dantesca del '700*. 1961. (esaurito)

64. *Studi secenteschi*, vol. II (1961). 1962, 334 pp., 7 tavv. f.t.

65. Panvini, B. *Le rime della scuola siciliana*. Vol. I: Introduzione - Edizione critica - Note. 1962, LII-676 pp. Rilegato.

66. Balmas, E. *Un poeta francese del Rinascimento: Etienne Jodelle, la sua vita - il suo tempo*. 1962, XII-876 pp., 12 tavv. f.t.

67. *Studi secenteschi*, vol. III (1962). 1963, IV-238 pp. 4 tavv. f.t.

68. Coppola, D. *La poesia religiosa del sec. XV*. 1963, VIII-150 pp.

69. Tetel, M. *Étude sur la comique de Rabelais*. 1963. (esaurito)

70. *Studi secenteschi*, vol. IV (1963). 1964, VI-238 pp., 5 tavv.

71. Bigongiari, D. *Essays on Dante and Medieval Culture*. 1964. (esaurito)

72. Panvini, B. *Le rime della scuola siciliana* - Vol. II: Glossario. 1964, XVI-180 pp. Rilegato.

73. Bax, G. *«Nniccu Furcedda», farsa pastorale del XVIII sec. in vernacolo salentino*, a cura di Rosario Jurlaro. 1964, VIII-108 pp., 12 tavv.

74. *Studi di letteratura, storia e filosofia in onore di Bruno Revel*. 1965, XXII-666 pp., 3 tavv.

75. Berselli Ambri, P. *Poemi inediti di Arthur de Gobineau*. 1965, 232 pp., 3 tavv. f.t.

76. Piromalli, A. *Dal Quattrocento al Novecento. Saggi critici*. 1965, VI-190 pp.

77. Bascapè, A. *Arte e religione nei poeti lombardi del Duecento*. 1964, 96 pp.

78. Guidubaldi, E. *Dante Europeo, I. Premesse metodologiche e cornice culturale*. 1965. (esaurito)

79. *Studi secenteschi*, vol. V (1964). 1965, 192 pp., 2 tavv. f.t.

80. Vallone, A. *Studi su Dante medioevale*. 1965, 276 pp.

81. Dovizi, B. *Epistolario di Bernardo Dovizi da Bibbiena*. Vol. II (1513-1520). 1965. (esaurito)

82. *La Mandragola* di Niccolò Machiavelli per la prima volta restituita alla sua integrità. 1965. (esaurito)
Edizione di lusso numerata da 1 a 370, su carta grave, con 2 tavv. f.t.

83. Guidubaldi, E. *Dante Europeo, II. Il paradiso come universo di luce (la lezione platonico-bonaventuriana)*. 1966, VIII-462 pp., 2 tavv. f.t.

84. Lorenzo de' Medici Il Magnifico, *Simposio*, a cura di Mario Martelli. 1966, 176 pp., 2 riproduzioni.

85. *Studi secenteschi*, vol. VI (1965). 1966, IV-310 pp., 1 tav. f.t.

86. *Studi in onore di Italo Siciliano*. 1966, 2 voll. di XII-1240 pp. compless. e 6 tavv. f.t.

87. Rossetti, G. *Commento analitico al "Purgatorio" di Dante Alighieri*. Opera inedita a cura di Pompeo Giannantonio. 1966, CIV-524 pp.

88. Piromalli, A. *Saggi critici di storia letteraria*. 1967. (esaurito)

89. *Studi di letteratura francese*, vol. I. 1967, XVI-176 pp.

90. *Studi secenteschi*, vol. VII (1966). 1967, VI-166 pp., 6 tavv. f.t.

91. Personè, L. M. *Scrittori italiani moderni e contemporanei. Saggi critici*. 1968, IV-340 pp.

92. *Studi secenteschi*, vol. VIII (1967). 1968, VI-230 pp., 1 tav. f.t.

93. Toso Rodinis, G. *Galeazzo Gualdo Priorato, un moralista veneto alla corte di Luigi XIV*. 1968, VI-226 pp., 9 tavv. f.t.

94. Guidubaldi, E. *Dante Europeo, III. Poema sacro come esperienza mistica*. 1968, VIII-736 pp., 24 tavv. f.t. di cui 1 a colori.

95. Distante, C. *Giovanni Pascoli poeta inquieto tra '800 e '900*. 1968, 212 pp.

96. Renzi, L. *Canti narrativi tradizionali romeni. Studi e testi*. 1969, IV-170 pp.

97. Vallone, A. *L'interpretazione di Dante nel Cinquecento. Studi e ricerche*. 1969, 306 pp.

98. Piromalli, A. *Studi sul Novecento*. 1969. (esaurito

99. Caccia, E. *Tecniche e valori dal Manzoni al Verga*, 1969 X-286 pp.

100. Giannantonio, P. *Dante e l'allegorismo*. 1969. (esaurito

101. *Studi secenteschi*, vol. IX (1968). 1969, IV-384 pp., 9 tavv. f.t

102. Tetel, M. *Rabelais et l'Italie*. 1969, IV-314 pp.

103. Reggio, G. *Le egloghe di Dante*. 1969, X-88 pp.

104. Moloney, B. *Florence and England. Essays on cultural relations in the second half of the eighteenth century*. 1969, VI-20 pp., 4 tavv. f.t.

105. *Studi di letteratura francese*, vol. II (1969). 1970, VI-36 pp., 11 tavv. f.t.

106. *Studi secenteschi*, vol. X (1969). 1970, VI-312 pp.

107. *Il Boiardo e la critica contemporanea* a cura di G. Anceschi 1970, VIII-544 pp.

108. Personè, L. M. *Pensatori liberi nell'Italia contemporanea Testimonianze critiche*. 1970, IV-290 pp.

109. Gazzola Stacchini, V. *La narrativa di Vitaliano Brancati* 1970, VIII-160 pp.

110. *Studi secenteschi*, vol. XI (1970). 1971, IV-292 pp. con tavv. f.t.

111. Bargagli, G. (1537-1587), *La Pellegrina*. Edizione critic con introduzione e note di F. Cerreta. 1971, 228 pp. con ill. f.t.

112. Sarolli, G. R. *Prolegomena alla Divina Commedia*, 1971 LXXII-454 pp. con 9 tavv. f.t. Ristampa 2002.

113. Musumarra, C. *La poesia tragica italiana nel Rinascimento*. 1972, IV-172 pp. Ristampa 1977.

114. Personè, L. M. *Il teatro italiano della «Belle Époque». Saggi e studi*. 1972, 410 pp.

115. *Studi secenteschi*, vol. XII (1971). 1972, IV-516 pp. con tavv. f.t.

116. Lomazzi, A. *Rainaldo e Lesengrino*. 1972, XIV-222 pp. con 2 tavv. f.t.

117. Perella, R. *The critical fortune of Battista Guarini's «Il Pastor Fido»*. 1973, 248 pp.

118. *Studi secenteschi*, vol. XIII (1972). 1973, IV-372 pp. con 1 tavv. f.t.

119. De Gaetano, A. *Giambattista Gelli and the Florentine Academy: the rebellion against Latin*. 1976, VIII-436 pp. e 1 ill.

120. *Studi secenteschi*, vol. XIV (1973). 1974, IV-300 pp. con tavv. f.t.

121. Da Pozzo, G. *La prosa di Luigi Russo*. 1975, 208 pp.

122. Paparelli, G. *Ideologia e poesia di Dante*. 1975, XII- 332 pp

123. *Studi di letteratura francese*, vol. III (1974). 1975, 220 pp.

124. Comes, S. *Scrittori in cattedra*. 1976, XXXII-212 pp. con un ritratto e 1 tav. f.t.

125. Tavani, G. *Dante nel Seicento. Saggi su A. Guarini, N. Villani, L. Magalotti*. 1976, 176 pp.

126. *Studi secenteschi*, vol. XV (1974). *Indice generale dei voll. I-X(1960-1969)*. 1976, 188 pp.

127. Personè, L. M. *Grandi scrittori nuovamente interpretati: Petrarca, Boccaccio, Parini, Leopardi, Manzoni*. 1976, 256 pp.

128. *Innovazioni tematiche, espressive e linguistiche della letteratura italiana del novecento* - Atti dell'VIII Congresso dell'Associazione internazionale per gli studi di lingua e letteratura italiana. 1976, XII-300 pp.

129. *Studi di letteratura francese*, vol. IV (1975). 1976, 180 pp. con 2 ill.

130. *Studi secenteschi*, vol. XVI (1975). 1976, IV-244 pp.

131. Caserta, E. G. *Manzoni's Christian Realism*. 1977, 260 pp.

132. Toso Rodinis, S. *Dominique Vivant Denon. I fiordalisi, Il berretto frigio, La sfinge*. 1977, 232 pp. con 10 ill. f.t.

133. Vallone, A. *La critica dantesca nel '900*. 1976, 480 pp.

134. Fratangelo, A. e M. *Guy De Maupassant scrittore moderno*. 1976, 180 pp.

135. Cocco, M. *La tradizione cortese e il petrarchismo nella poesia di Clément Marot*. 1978, 320 pp.

136. Mastrobuono, A. C. *Essays on Dante's Philosophy of History*. 1979, 196 pp.

137. *Primo centenario della morte di Niccolò Tommaseo (1874-1974)*. 1977, 224 pp.

138. Siciliano, I. *Saggi di letteratura francese*. 1977, 316 pp.

139. Schizzerotto, G. *Cultura e vita civile a Mantova fra '300 e '500*. 1977, 148 pp. con 9 ill. f.t.

140. *Studi secenteschi*, vol. XVII (1976). 1977, 184 pp., con 5 tavv. f.t.

141. Gazzola Stacchini, V. - Bianchini, G. *Le Accademie dell'Aretino nel XVII e XVIII secolo*. 1978, XVIII-598 pp. con 18 ill. n.t. e 24 f.t.

142. Friggieri, O. *La cultura italiana a Malta. Storia e influenza letteraria e stilistica attraverso l'opera di Dun Karm*. 1978, 172 pp. con 5 ill. f.t.

143. *Studi secenteschi*, vol. XVIII (1977). 1978, 276 pp.

144. Vanossi, L. *Dante e il «Roman de la Rose» Saggio sul «Fiore»*. 1979, 380 pp.

145. Ridolfi, R. *Studi Guicciardiniani*. 1978, 344 pp.

146. Allegretto, M. *Il luogo dell'Amore. Studio su Jaufre Rudel*. 1979, 104 pp.

147. Misan, J. *L'Italie des doctrinaires (1817-1830). Une image en élaboration*. 1978, 204 pp.

148. Toaff, A. *The Jews in medieval Assisi 1305-1487. A social and economic history of a small Jewish community in Italy*. 1979, 240 pp. con 14 ill. f.t.

149. Trovato, P. *Dante in Petrarca. Per un inventario dei dantismi nei «Rerum vulgarium Fragmenta»*. 1979, X-174 pp.

150. Fiorato, A. C. *Bandello entre l'histoire et l'écriture. La vie, l'expérience sociale, l'évolution culturelle d'un conteur de la Renaissance*. 1979, XXII-686 pp.

151. *Studi secenteschi*, vol. XIX (1978). 1979, 260 pp.

152. Bosisio, P. *Carlo Gozzi e Goldoni. Una polemica letteraria con versi inediti e rari*. 1979, 444 pp.

153. Zanato, T. *Saggio sul «Comento» di Lorenzo de' Medici*. 1979, 340 pp.

154. *Studi di letteratura francese*, vol. V. 1979, 204 pp.

155. Piromalli, A. *Società, cultura e letteratura in Emilia Romagna*. 1980, 180 pp.

156. Accademici Intronati di Siena, *La Commedia degli Ingannati*. 1980, 248 pp.

157. *Studi di letteratura francese*, vol. VI. 1980, 176 pp.

158. Harran, D. *«Maniera» e il Madrigale - Una raccolta di poesie musicali del Cinquecento*. 1980, 124 pp.

159. *Studi secenteschi*, vol. XX (1979). 1980, VI-214 pp.

160. Ussia, S. *Carteggio Magliabechi. Lettere di Borde, Arnaud e associati lionesi ad A. Magliabechi*. 1980, 244 pp.

161. Da Col, I. *Un romanzo del Seicento. La Stratonica di Luca Assarino*. 1981, 244 pp. con 24 tavv. f.t.

162. *Studi secenteschi*, vol. XXI (1980). 1981, 294 pp.

163. *Studi di letteratura francese*, vol. VII. 1981, 224 pp.

164. Castelletti, C. *Stravaganze d'amore. «Comedia»*. 1981, 172 pp.

165. *Carteggio inedito fra N. Tommaseo e G. P. Vieusseux*. I: (1835-1839). A cura di V. Missori. 1981, 688 pp.

166. *Studi secenteschi*, vol. XXII (1981). *Indice generale dei voll. XI-XX (1970-1979)*. 1981, 184 pp.

167. *Il Rinascimento. Aspetti e problemi attuali*. Atti del X Congresso dell'Associazione internazionale per gli studi della lingua e letteratura italiana. 1982, VI-700 pp.

168. *Stendhal e Milano*. Atti del XIV Congresso internazionale Stendhaliano. 1982, 2 tomi di complessive XXVI-972 pp. e 2 tavv. a colori.

169. *Studi secenteschi*, vol. XXIII (1982). 1982, 328 pp. con 1 tav. f.t.

170. *Studi di letteratura francese*, vol. VIII. 1982, 208 pp.

171. *Studi di letteratura francese*, vol. IX. 1983, 274 pp.

172. Aonio Paleario, *Dell'economia o vero del governo della casa*. 1983, 120 pp. con 4 tavv. f.t.

173. Dalla Palma, G. *Le strutture narrative dell'«Orlando Furioso»*. 1984, 228 pp.

174. *Studi secenteschi*, vol. XXIV (1983). 1983, 324 pp.

175. Raugei, A. M. *Bestiario valdese*. 1984, 362 pp. con ill. n.t.

176. Da Pozzo, G. *L'ambigua armonia. Studio sull'«Aminta» del Tasso*. 1983, 336 pp.

177. *Studi di letteratura francese*, vol. X. 1983, 208 pp.

178. *Miscellanea di studi in onore di V. Branca*. Vol. I: *Dal Medioevo al Petrarca*. 1983, XII-492 pp. con 1 tav. f.t.

179. —— Vol. II: *Boccaccio e dintorni*. 1983, VI-450 pp.

180. —— Vol. III: *Umanesimo e Rinascimento a Firenze e Venezia*. 1983, 2 tomi di complessive XII-848 pp.

181. —— Vol. IV: *Tra Illuminismo e Romanticismo*. 1983, 2 tomi di complessive XII-900 pp.

182. ——Vol. V: *Indagini Otto-Novecentesche*. 1983, VI-390 pp.

183. Rizzo, G. *Tommaso Briganti. Inedito poeta romantico*. 1984, 274 pp.

184. Poliaghi, N. F. *Stendhal e Trieste*. 1984, VI-202 pp. con 22 ill.

185. Michelangelo Buonarroti il giovane, *La Fiera. Redazione originaria (1619)*. 1984, 162 pp. con 4 tavv. f.t.

186. *I cantari. Struttura e tradizione*. 1984, 200 pp.

187. Bianchini, G. *Federico Nomi. Un letterato del '600. Profilo e fonti manoscritte*. 1984, XVI-338 pp. con 11 tavv. f.t.

188. *Studi secenteschi*, vol. XXV (1984). 1984, 304 pp.

189. Zambon, F. *Robert De Boron e i segreti del Graal*. 1984, 132 pp.

190. *Fenoglio a Lecce*. 1984, 248 pp.

191. Schettini Piazza, E. *Giuseppe Chiarini. Saggio biobibliografico di un letterato dell'Ottocento*. 1984, X-158 pp. con 1 tav. f.t.

192. *Studi di letteratura francese*, vol. XI. 1985, 362 pp. con 9 tavv. f.t.

193. Misan, J. *Les lettres italiennes dans la presse française (1815-1824)*. 1985, 210 pp.

194. Cairns, C. *Pietro Aretino and the Republic of Venice. Researches on Aretino and his circle in Venice, 1527-1556*. 1985, 272 pp.

195. Bertelà , M. *Stendhal et l'Autre. L'homme et l'oeuvre à travers l'idée de féminité*. 1985, 352 pp.

196. Piglionica, A. M. *Dalla realtà all'illusione*: The Tempest *o la parola preclusa*. 1985, 146 pp.

197. *Studi secenteschi*, vol. XXVI (1985), 1985, 352 pp.

198. Cervigni, D. S. *Dante's poetry of dreams*. 1986, 230 pp.

199. *Studi di letteratura francese*, vol. XII. 1986, II-282 pp. con 4 tavv. f.t.

200. Marco Polo, *Il milione*. Edizione del testo toscano («ottimo»). 1986, XII-418 pp.

201. Delmay, B. *I personaggi della «Divina Commedia». Classificazione e regesto*. 1986, LVI-414 pp.

202. *Patronage and Public in the Trecento*. 1986, 180 pp. con 36 ill. f.t.

203. Mitchell, B. *The Majesty of the State. Triumphal Progresses of Foreign Sovereigns in Renaissance Italy, 1494-1600*. 1986, VIII-240 pp. con 8 ill. f.t.

204. *Ugo Angelo Canello e gli inizi della filologia romanza in Italia*. 1987, 276 pp. con 4 tavv. f.t.

205 *Studi secenteschi*, vol. XXVII (1986). 1986, IV-348 pp.

206. Dé dé yan, C. *Diderot et la pensée anglaise*. 1986, IV-366 pp.

207. *La letteratura e i giardini*. 1987, 436 pp. con 9 tavv. f.t.

208. *Letteratura italiana e arti figurative*. 1988, 3 voll. di complessive VIII-1438 pp. con 60 ill. f.t.

209. *Studi secenteschi*, vol. XXVIII (1987). 1987, IV-332 pp. con 2 ill. f.t.

210. *Dante e la Bibbia*. Atti del convegno internazionale. 1988, 372 pp.

211. *Veronica Gàmbara e la poesia del suo tempo nell'Italia Settentrionale*. Atti del convegno. 1989, 442 pp.

212. *Studi di letteratura francese*, vol. XIII. 1987, 194 pp.

213. Colombo, A. *I «Riposi di Pindo». Studi su Claudio Achillini (1574-1640)*, 1988, 228 pp.

214. *Letteratura e storia meridionale. Studi offerti a Aldo Vallone*. 1989, 2 tomi di complessive XVI-960 pp. con 7 tavv. f.t.

215. Sabbatino, P. *La «Scienza» della scrittura. Dal progetto del Bembo al manuale*. 1988, 256 pp.

216. *Studi di letteratura francese*, vol. XIV. 1988, 144 pp.

217. Pirro Schettino, *Opere edite e inedite*. Edizione critica. 1989, 410 pp. con 4 tavv. f.t.

218. *Giorgio Pasquali e la filologia classica del '900*. Atti del convegno. 1988, VI-278 pp.

219. *Studi secenteschi*, vol. XXIX (1988). 1988, IV-328 pp.

220. Landoni, E. *La teoria letteraria dei provenzali*. 1989, XXXIV-168 pp.

221. *Il meraviglioso, il verosimile tra antichità e medioevo*. 1989, 360 pp. con 5 tavv. f.t.

222. Procaccioli, P. *Filologia ed esegesi dantesca nel Quattrocento. L'«Inferno» nel «Comento sopra la Comedia» di Cristoforo Landino*. 1989, 266 pp.

223. Santarcangeli, P. *Homo Ridens. Estetica, filologia, psicologia, storia del comico*. 1989, VI-452 pp.

224. *Filologia e critica dantesca. Studi offerti a Aldo Vallone*. 1989, XVI-660 pp. con 2 tavv. f.t.

225. *Dantismo russo e cornice europea*. 1989, 2 voll. indivisibili di XXXVI-880 pp. complessive.

226. *Studi di letteratura francese*, vol. XV. 1989, 284 pp. con 1 tav. f.t.

227. *Studi secenteschi*, vol. XXX (1989). 1989, IV-316 pp.

228. *Il tema della fortuna nella letteratura francese e italiana del Rinascimento. Studi in memoria di Enzo Giudici*. 1990, XX-550 pp. con 1 tav. f.t.

229. Sebastio, L. *Strutture narrative e dinamiche culturali in Dante e nel «Fiore»*. 1990, 320 pp.

230. *Studi di letteratura francese*, vol. XVI. 1990, 248 pp. con 1 tav. f.t.

231. *Studi di letteratura francese*, vol. XVII. 1990, 156 pp.

232. *Studi di letteratura francese*, vol. XVIII. 1990, 332 pp. con 1 tav. f.t.

233. Dozon, M. *Mythe et symbol dans la «Divine Comédie»*. 1991, XVI-634 pp.

234. Vallone, A. *Strutture e modulazioni nei canti della «Divina Commedia»*. 1990, 226 pp.

235. Comollo, A. *Il dissenso religioso in Dante*. 1990, 154 pp.

236. Bendinelli Predelli, M. *Alle origini del «Bel Gherardino»*. 1990, 362 pp.

237. Guerin Dalle Mese, J. *Egypte: La mémoire et le rêve. Itineraires d'un voyage, 1320-1601*. 1990, 656 pp. con 7 tavv. f.t.

238. Sorella, A. *Magia, lingua e commedia nel Machiavelli*. 1990, 264 pp.

239. *Studi secenteschi*, vol. XXXI (1990). 1990, XXVIII-296 pp. con 6 tavv. f.t.

240. *Miscellanea di studi in onore di Marco Pecoraro*. 1991. Vol. I: *Da Dante al Manzoni*, X-398 pp. con 7 tavv. f.t.; Vol. II: *Dal Tommaseo ai contemporanei*, IV-414 pp.

241. *Lingua e letteratura italiana nel mondo oggi*. 1991, 2 tomi di XVI-732 pp. complessive.

242. Sabbatino, P. *L'Eden della nuova poesia. Saggi sulla «Divina Commedia»*. 1991, 232 pp.

243. *Alfonso M. De Liguori e la società civile del suo tempo*. 1990, 2 tomi di VIII-682 pp. complessive.

244. *Famiglia e società nell'opera di Giovanni Verga*. 1991, VI-494 pp.

245. *Studi secenteschi*, vol. XXXII (1991). 1991, IV-332 pp. con 4 tavv. f.t.

246. Hein, J. *Enigmaticité et messianisme dans la «Divine Comédie»*. 1992, II-654 pp.

247. Sanguineti White, L. *Dal detto alla figura. Le tragedie di Federico Della Valle*. 1992, 162 pp.

248. Grossvogel, S. *Ambiguity and allusion in Boccaccio's* Filocolo. 1992, 254 pp.

249. *Studi di letteratura francese*, vol. XIX. 1992, 526 pp. con 4 ill. f.t. e figg. n.t.

250. Padoan, G. *Il lungo cammino del «Poema sacro». Studi danteschi*. 1992, IV-310 pp.

251. *Studi secenteschi*, vol. XXXIII (1992). 1992, IV-210 pp. con 4 tavv. f.t.

252. Ankli, R. *Morgante iperbolico. L'iperbole nel* Morgante *di Luigi Pulci*. 1993, 422 pp.

253. *Studi secenteschi*, vol. XXXIV (1993). 1993, IV-476 pp. con 1 tav. ripiegata f.t.

254. Sabbatino, P. *Giordano Bruno e la "mutazione" del Rinascimento*. 1993, 230 pp. con 6 figg. f.t. Ristampa 1998.

255. *Studi secenteschi*, vol. XXXV (1994). 1994, IV-286 pp. con 4 tavv. f.t.

256. *Studi di letteratura francese*, vol. XX. 1994, 294 pp. con 1 tav. f.t.

257. Sabbatino, P. - Scorrano, L. - Sebastio, L. - Stefanelli, R. *Dante e il Rinascimento. Rassegna bibliografica e studi in onore di Aldo Vallone*. 1994, 212 pp.

258. *Italo Svevo scrittore europeo*. A cura di N. Cacciaglia e L. Fava Guzzetta. 1994, VIII-574 pp.

259. Sebastio, L. *Il poeta e la storia. Una dinamica dantesca*. 1994, 264 pp.

260. *Le feste dei pastori del Rubicone per Napoleone I Re d'Italia*. Opera inedita a cura di A. Piromalli e T. Iermano. 1994, 152 pp.

261. *Studi secenteschi*. Vol. XXXVI (1995). 1995, IV-302 pp. con 5 tavv. f.t.

262. *Geografia, storia e poetiche del fantastico*. A cura di M. Farnetti. 1995, 244 pp. con 4 ill. f.t.

263. *Studi secenteschi*. Vol. XXXVII (1996). 1996, IV-406 pp.

264. Iermano, T. *Il melanconico in dormiveglia. Salvatore Di Giacomo*. 1995, 270 pp.

265. Ardissino, E. *L'«aspra tragedia». Poesia e sacro in Torquato Tasso*. 1996, 236 pp.

266. Zangheri, L. *Feste e apparati nella Toscana dei Lorena (1737-1859)*. 1996, 332 pp. con 115 ill. f.t.

267. *Letteratura e industria*. Atti del XV Congresso dell'Associazione internazionale per gli studi di lingua e letteratura italiana. 1997, 2 tomi di XVIII-1288 pp. complessive con 76 ill. f.t.

268. Angiolillo, G. *La nuova frontiera della tanatologia. Le biografie della Commedia*. Vol. I: *Inferno*. 1996, 182 pp.

269. Angiolillo, G. *La nuova frontiera della tanatologia. Le biografie della Commedia*. Vol. II: *Purgatorio*. 1996, 308 pp.

270. Angiolillo, G. *La nuova frontiera della tanatologia. Le biografie della Commedia*. Vol. III: *Paradiso*. 1996, 270 pp.

271. *Studi secenteschi*. Vol. XXXVIII (1997). 1997, IV-444 pp.

272. Benporat, C. *Cucina italiana del Quattrocento*. 1996, 306 pp. con 4 figg. f.t. in b. e n. e 8 tavv. f.t. a colori. Ristampa 2001.

273. *Studi di letteratura francese. Rivista europea*, vol. XXI (1996). 1996, 238 pp. con 2 figg. n.t.

274. Fratnik, M. *Enrico Pea et l'écriture du moi*. 1997, 402 pp.

275. Montevecchi, F. *Il potere marittimo e le civiltà del Mediterraneo antico*. 1997, 596 pp. con 85 figg. n.t.

276. Rossetto, S. *Per la storia del giornalismo. Treviso dal XVII secolo all'unità*. 1996, 222 pp. con 10 tavv. f.t.

277. Girardi, R. *Incipitario della lirica meridionale e repertorio generale degli autori di lirica nati nel Mezzogiorno d'Italia (secolo XVI)*. 1996, 458 pp.

278. Sabbatino, P. *La bellezza di Elena. L'imitazione nella letteratura e nelle arti figurative del Rinascimento*. 1997, 270 pp. con 1 grafico n.t. e 12 tavv. f.t. Ristampa 2001.

279. Panicara, V. *La nuova poesia di Giacomo Leopardi. Una lettura critica della* Ginestra. 1997, 148 pp.

280. *Torquato Tasso e la cultura estense*. A cura di G. Venturi, indice dei nomi e bibliografia generale a cura di A. Ghinato e R. Ziosi. 1999, 3 tomi di VIII-1462 pp. complessive con 101 ill. f.t.

281. Gavioli, E. *Filologia e nazione: l'«Archivum romanicum» nel carteggio inedito di Giulio Bertoni*. 1997, 202 pp. con 4 ill. f.t.

282. *Studi di letteratura francese. Rivista europea*, vol. XXII (1997). 1997, 330 pp.

283. *Studi secenteschi*. Vol. XXXIX (1998). 1998, IV-368 pp. con 4 tavv. f.t.

284. *Studi secenteschi*. Vol. XL (1999). 1999, IV-390 pp.

285. *Studi di letteratura francese. Rivista europea*, vol. XXIII (1998). «Lire le roman». 1998, 270 pp.

286. *Alfonso M. de Liguori e la civiltà letteraria del Settecento*. Atti del Convegno internazionale per il tricentenario della nascita del Santo (1696-1996). Napoli 20-23 ottobre 1997. A cura di P. Giannantonio. 1999, XX-476 pp.

287. *Leopardi e Bologna*. Atti del Convegno di studi per il Secondo Centenario Leopardiano (Bologna 18-19 maggio 1998). A cura di M. A. Bazzocchi. 1999, XVI-316 pp. con 4 tavv. f.t.

288. *Studi secenteschi*. Vol. XLI (2000). 2000, IV-502 pp.

289. *Studi di letteratura francese. Rivista europea*, vol. XXIV (1999). «L'estranéité». 1999, 246 pp.

290. Smith, G. *The Stone of Dante and later florentine celebrations of the Poet*. 2000, X-72 pp. con 16 ill. f.t.

291. *L'immaginario contemporaneo*. Atti del Convegno letterario internazionale, Ferrara, 21-23 maggio 1999. A cura di R. Pazzi. 2000, XII-198 pp.

292. *The Poetics of Place. Florence Imagined*. Edited by I. Marchegiani Jones and T. Haeussler. 2001, XIV-220 pp.

293. Lawson Lucas, A. *La ricerca dell'ignoto. I romanzi d'avventura di Emilio Salgari*. Traduzione di S. Rizzardi e F. Rusciadelli. 2000, XVI-208 pp. con 1 tav. f.t.

294. *Il castello, il convento, il palazzo e altri scenari dell'ambientazione letteraria*. A cura di M. Cantelmo. 2000, VI-326 pp.

295. *Studi secenteschi*. Vol. XLII (2001). 2001, IV-472 pp. con 20 ill. f.t.

296. *Studi di letteratura francese. Rivista europea*, vol. XXV (2000). 2001, 192 pp.

297. *La lingua e le lingue di Machiavelli*. Atti del Convegno internazionale di studi, Torino 2-4 dicembre 1999. 2001, 352 pp.

298. *Studi secenteschi*. Vol. XLIII (2002). 2002, IV-372 pp. con 9 ill. f.t.

299. *Umanisti bellunesi fra Quattro e Cinquecento*. Atti del Convegno di Belluno, 5 novembre 1999. A cura di P. Pellegrini. 2001, XIV-296 pp. con 24 tavv. f.t.

300. Sodini, C. *L'Ercole tirreno. Guerra e dinastia medicea nella prima metà del '600*. 2001, VI-326 pp. con 16 tavv. f.t. in b. e n. e 9 a colori.

301. *Il tragico e il sacro dal Cinquecento a Racine*. Atti del Convegno internazionale, Torino e Vercelli, 14-16 ottobre 1999. A cura di D. Cecchetti e D. Dalla Valle. 2001, X-330 pp.

302. Benporat, C. *Feste e banchetti. Convivialità italiana fra Tree Quattrocento*. 2001, 290 pp. con 12 tavv. f.t. a colori.

303. *Studi di letteratura francese. Rivista europea*, vol. XXVI (2001). «Théâtre et société au XVIIe siècle». 2002, 254 pp.

304. *La «liquida vertigine»*. Atti delle giornate di studio su Tommaso Landolfi. Prato, Convitto Nazionale Cicognini, 5-6 febbraio 1999. A cura di I. Landolfi. 2002, XXVI-266 pp.

305. *Studi secenteschi*. Vol. XLIV (2003). 2002, IV-340 pp. con 3 tavv. f.t.

306. Leushuis, R. *Le Mariage et l'"amitié courtoise' dans le dialogue et le récit bref de la Renaissance*. 2003, XIV-286 pp.

307. Fratnik, M. *Paysages. Essai sur la description de Federico Tozzi*. 2002, XVI-182 pp.

308. *Alfieri e il suo tempo*. Atti del Convegno internazionale, Torino - Asti, 29 novembre - 1 dicembre 2001. A cura di M. Cerruti, M. Corsi, B. Danna. 2003, XII-488 pp. con 3 figg. n.t. e 5 tavv. f.t. di cui 4 a colori.

309. *Robert Davidsohn (1853-1937). Uno spirito libero tra cronacae storia*. Tomo I: *Atti della giornata di studio*. Tomo II: *Gli scritti inediti*. Tomo III: *Catalogo della biblioteca*. A cura di W. Fastenrath Vinattieri e M. Ingendaay Rodio. 2003, XXX-812 pp. complessive con 1 fig. n.t. e 30 tavv. f.t.

310. *Studi di letteratura francese. Rivista europea*, vol. XXVII (2002). 2003, 286 pp.

311. *Il volto e gli affetti. Fisiognomica ed espressione nelle arti del Rinascimento*. Atti del Convegno di studi, Torino, 28-29 novembre 2001. A cura di A. Pontremoli. 2003, 314 pp. con 14 tavv. f.t.

312. Sica, P. *Modernist Forms of Rejuvenation. Eugenio Montale and T.S. Eliot*. 2003, X-156 pp.

313. *Studi secenteschi*. Vol. XLV (2004). 2004, IV-484 pp. con 6 tavv. f.t.

314. *Sabba da Castiglione (1480-1554). Dalle corti rinascimentali alla Commenda di Faenza*. Atti del Convegno, Faenza, 19-20 maggio 2000. A cura di A.R. Gentilini. 2004, X-496 pp. con 16 figg. n.t. e 54 tavv. f.t. di cui 6 a colori.

315. Sabbatino, P. A l'infinito m'ergo. *Giordano Bruno e il volo del moderno Ulisse*. 2003, XVI-212 pp. con 15 tavv. f.t.

316. Mastroianni, M. *Le* Antigoni *sofoclee del Cinquecento francese*. 2004, 264 pp.

317. *Francesco di Giorgio alla corte di Federico da Montefeltro*. Atti del Convegno internazionale di studi, Urbino, monastero di Santa Chiara, 11-13 ottobre 2001. A cura di F.P. Fiore. 2004, 2 tomi di complessive XXIV-710 pp. con 296 figg. n.t.

318. *Relazioni letterarie tra Italia e Penisola Iberica nell'epoca rinascimentale e barocca*. Atti del primo Colloquio Internazionale, Pisa, 4-5 ottobre 2002. A cura di S. Vuelta Garcı´a. 2004, X-178 pp. con 2 figg. n.t.

319. Bozzola, S. *Tra Cinque e Seicento. Tradizione e anticlassicismo nella sintassi della prosa letteraria*. 2004, VIII-168 pp.

320. Balmas, E. *Studi sul Cinquecento*. 2004, XXX-666 pp. con 11 figg. n.t. e 11 tavv. f.t.

321. *Studi di letteratura francese. Rivista europea*, vol. XXVIII (2003). 2004, 138 pp.

322. Furlan, F. *La donna, la famiglia, l'amore tra Medioevo e Rinascimento*. 2004, 122 pp.

323. Alfieri, V. *Esquisse du Jugement Universel*. A cura di G. Santato. 2004, 128 pp. con 2 figg. n.t.

324. *Studi secenteschi*. Vol. XLVI (2005). 2005, IV-386 pp. con 13 tavv. f.t.

325. *Il Capitolo di San Lorenzo nel Quattrocento*. Convegno di studi, Firenze, 28-29 marzo 2003. A cura di P. Viti. 2006, XII-360 pp. con 8 tavv. f.t.

326. Martellotti, A. *I ricettari di Federico II. Dal «Meridionale» al «Liber de coquina»*. 2005, 284 pp. Ristampa 2011.

327. Foscolo, U. *Dell'origine e dell'ufficio della letteratura. Orazione*. 2005, 172 pp.

328. Ruggiero, R. *«Il ricco edificio». Arte allusiva nella* Gerusalemme Liberata. 2005, XXII-194 pp.

329. *Studi secenteschi*. Vol. XLVII (2006). 2006, IV-368 pp.

330. Pozzi, M. - Mattioda, E. *Giorgio Vasari storico e critico*. 2006, XXII-438 pp.

331. *Leonis Baptistae Alberti Descriptio Vrbis Romae*. Edizione critica di Jean-Yves Boriaud e Francesco Furlan. 2005, 164 pp. con 10 tavv. f.t.

332. *Resultanze in merito alla vita e all'opera di Piero Jahier. Saggi e materiali inediti*. A cura di F. Giacone. 2007, XII-368 pp. con 4 tavv. f.t.

333. Cevolini, A. *De arte excerpendi. Imparare a dimenticare nella modernita`*. 2006, 460 pp. con 9 figg. n.t.

334. *Studi secenteschi*. Vol. XLVIII (2007). 2007, IV-432 pp.

335. Montinaro, G. *L'epistolario di Ludovico Agostini. Riforma e utopia*. 2006, 294 pp.

336. *Il mito d'Arcadia. Pastori e amori nelle arti del Rinascimento*. Atti del Convegno internazionale di studi, Torino, 14-15 marzo 2005. A cura di D. Boillet e A. Pontremoli. 2007, XXII-266 pp. con 8 figg. n.t. e 14 tavv. f.t.

337. Sebastio, L. *Il Poeta tra Chiesa ed Impero. Una storia del pensiero dantesco*. 2007, 214 pp.

338. *Studi di letteratura francese. Rivista europea*, voll. XXIXXXX (2004-2005). «Il viaggio francese in Italia». 2007, 226 pp. con 1 fig. n.t.

339. *I linguaggi dell'Altro. Forme dell'alterità nel testo letterario*. Atti del Convegno *I Linguaggi dell'Altro/altro*, Università di Lecce, 21-22 aprile 2005. A cura di A.M. Piglionica, C. Bacile di Castiglione, M.S. Marchesi. 2007, XXIV-228 pp. con 2 figg. n.t.

340. Benporat, C. *Cucina e convivialita` italiana del Cinquecento*. 2007, 344 pp. con 16 tavv. f.t.

341. *Il cantare italiano fra folklore e letteratura*. Atti del Convegno internazionale di Zurigo, Landesmuseum, 23-25 giugno 2005. A cura di M. Picone e L. Rubini. 2007, XIV-528 pp. con 6 figg. n.t.

342. Covino, S. *Giacomo e Monaldo Leopardi falsari trecenteschi. Contraffazione dell'antico, cultura e storia linguistica nell'Ottocento italiano*. 2009, I tomo XVI-328 pp. II tomo VI-392 pp. con 2 tavv. f.t.

343. *Studi secenteschi*. Vol. XLIX (2008). 2008, IV-434 pp. con 8 tavv. f.t.

344. *Traduzioni, imitazioni, scambi tra Italia e Portogallo nei secoli*. Atti del primo Colloquio internazionale, Pisa, 15-16 ottobre 2004. A cura di M. Lupetti. 2008, X-172 pp. con 2 figg. n.t. e 15 tavv. f.t. di cui 12 a colori.

345. *L'identità italiana ed europea tra Sette e Ottocento*. A cura di A. Ascenzi e L. Melosi. 2008, XIV-184 pp. con 5 figg. n.t.

346. Wilson, R. *Prophecies and prophecy in Dante's* Commedia. 2007, X-228 pp.

347. *Writing Relations: American Scholars in Italian Archives. Essays for Franca Petrucci Nardelli and Armando Petrucci*. Edited by D. Shemek and M. Wyatt. 2008, XII-242 pp. con 13 figg. n.t. e 2 tavv. f.t.

348. Ioly Zorattini, P. *I nomi degli altri. Conversioni a Venezia e nel Friuli Veneto in età moderna*. Con prefazione di M. Massenzio. 2008, XX-388 pp. con 4 tavv. f.t.

349. Urraro, R. *Giacomo Leopardi: le donne, gli amori*. 2008, VIII-378 pp.

350. Rabboni, R. *Speculare sodo, ragionar sostanzioso. Studi sull'abate Conti*. 2008, X-336 pp.

351. Tiozzo, E. *La letteratura italiana e il premio Nobel. Storia critica e documenti*. 2008, VIII-358 pp. con 29 tavv. f.t.

352. Capecchi, G. - Marzi, M. G. - Saladino, V. *I granduchi di Toscana e l'antico. Acquisti, restauri, allestimenti*. 2008, VIII-342 pp. con 78 tavv. f.t. di cui 16 a colori.

353. *Studi secenteschi*. Vol. L (2009). 2008, IV-346 pp. con 2 figg. n.t. e 13 tavv. f.t.

354. *In assenza del re. Le reggenti dal secolo XIV al secolo XVII (Piemonte ed Europa)*. A cura di F. Varallo. 2008, XXXII-610 pp. con es. mus. n.t. e 7 tavv. f.t.

355. Celli, C. *Il carnevale di Machiavelli*. 2009, IV-218 pp.

356. *Iacopo Sannazaro. La cultura napoletana nell'Europa del Rinascimento*. Convegno internazionale di studi, Napoli, 27-28 marzo 2006. A cura di P. Sabbatino. 2009, VIII-430 pp. con 5 figg. n.t. e 14 tavv. f.t.

357. *«La bourse des idées du monde». Malaparte e la Francia*. Atti del Convegno internazionale di studi su Curzio Malaparte, Prato-Firenze, 8-9 novembre 2007. A cura di M. Grassi. 2008, XII-234 pp.

358. *La metafora in Dante*. A cura di M. Ariani. 2009, VI-286 pp.

359. Coen, P. *Il mercato dei quadri a Roma nel diciottesimo secolo. La domanda, l'offerta e la circolazione delle opere in un grande centro artistico europeo*. I. Con una prefazione di E. Castelnuovo. II. Appendice documentaria. 2010, LX-816 pp. con 32 tavv. f.t. a colori.

360. *Saggi di letteratura architettonica, da Vitruvio a Winckelmann*. I. A cura di F.P. Di Teodoro. 2009, VI-372 pp. con 67 figg. n.t. e 21 tavv. f.t.

361. *Don Giovanni nelle riscritture francesi e francofone del Novecento*. Atti del Convegno internazionale di Vercelli, 16-17 ottobre 2008. A cura di M. Mastroianni. 2009, XIII-330 pp.

362. Marchesi, M.S. *Eliot's Perpetual Struggle. The Language of Evil in* Murder in the Cathedral. 2009, XXXVIII-144 pp.

363. *Studi di letteratura francese. Rivista europea*, voll. XXXIXXXII (2006-2007). «Dictionnaires et écrivains». 2009, 130 pp.

364. *Studi secenteschi*. Vol. LI (2010). 2010, IV-394 pp.

365. *Saggi di letteratura architettonica, da Vitruvio a Winckelmann*. II. A cura di L. Bertolini. 2009, VI-254 pp. con 66 figg. n.t. e 5 tavv. f.t. a colori.

366. Frenquellucci, C. *Dalla Mancha a Siena al Nuovo Mondo. Don Chisciotte nel teatro di Girolamo Gigli*. 2010, XVI-334 pp.

367. *Giuseppe Ungaretti - Jean Lescure. Carteggio (1951-1966)*. A cura di R. Gennaro. 2010, XXVI-252 pp.

368. Testa, F. *Winckelmann e l'architettura antica*. In preparazione.

369. *Saggi di letteratura architettonica, da Vitruvio a Winckelmann*. III. A cura di H. Burns, F.P. Di Teodoro e G. Bacci. 2010, VI-392 pp. con 126 figg. n.t.

370. Barsella, S. *In the Light of the Angels: Angelology and Cosmology in Dante's* Divina Commedia. 2010, XVI-214 pp.

371. Durante, E. - Martellotti, A. *«Giovinetta peregrina». La vera storia di Laura Peperara e Torquato Tasso*. 2010, VI-352 pp. con 2 tavv. f.t. a colori, con CD contenente "Madrigali per Laura Peperara".

372. Squillace, G. *Il profumo nel mondo antico. Con la prima traduzione italiana del «Sugli odori» di Teofrasto*. Prefazione di L. Villoresi. 2010, XX-282 pp. con 8 tavv. f.t. a colori. Esaurito.

373. Cerocchi, M. *Funzioni semantiche e metatestuali della musica in Dante, Petrarca e Boccaccio*. 2010, XII-160 pp. con 6 es. mus. n.t.

374. *La Ronde. Giostre, esercizi cavallereschi e* loisir *in Francia e Piemonte fra Medioevo e Ottocento*. Atti del Convegno internazionale di Studi, Museo storico dell'Arma di Cavalleria di Pinerolo, 15-17 giugno 2006. A cura di F. Varallo. 2010, XIV-276 pp. con 37 figg. n.t. e 19 tavv. f.t. a colori.

375. *La parola e l'immagine. Studi in onore di Gianni Venturi*. A cura di M. Ariani, A. Bruni, A. Dolfi, A. Gareffi. 2010, 2 tomi di complessive VIII-892 pp. con 42 figg. n.t. e 35 tav. f.t. di cui 10 a colori.

376. Bertelli, S. *La tradizione della «Commedia»: dai manoscritti al testo. I. I codici trecenteschi (entro l'antica vulgata) conservati a Firenze*. Presentazione di P. Trovato. 2011, XVI-446 pp. con 68 figg. n.t. e 32 tavv. f.t. a colori.

377. *Nascita della storiografia e organizzazione dei saperi*. Atti del Convegno internazionale di studi, Torino, 20-22 maggio 2009. A cura di E. Mattioda. 2010, XII-346 pp. con 1 tav. f.t. a colori.

378. *Studi secenteschi*. Vol. LII (2011). 2011, VI-446 pp. con 6 figg. n.t.

379. Ardizzone, M.L. *Dante: il paradigma intellettuale. Un'*inventio *degli anni fiorentini*. 2011, XXVI-264 pp.

380. Fenech Kroke, A. *Giorgio Vasari. La culture de l'allégorie*. Préface de P. Morel. 2011, XXII-556 pp. con 24 figg. n.t. e 16 tavv. f.t. a colori.

381. *Gabriele d'Annunzio. Inediti 1922-1936. Carteggio con Maria Lombardi e altri scritti*. A cura di F. Caburlotto, prefazione di P. Gibellini. 2011, XLVI-80 pp. con 3 figg. n.t. e 8 tavv. f.t.

382. Bertozzi, R. *L'immagine dell'Italia nei diari e nell'autobiografia di Paul Heyse*. 2011, XVI-822 pp. con 4 figg. n.t. e 1 tavv. f.t. a colori.

383. Leonardi, M. *L'Età del Vespro siciliano nella storiografia tedesca (dal XIX secolo ai nostri giorni)*. 2011, X-148 pp.

384. *Un trattato universale dei colori. Il ms. 2861 della Biblioteca Universitaria di Bologna*. Edizione del testo, traduzione e commento a cura di Francesca Muzio. 2012, XXIV-300 pp.

385. *Beniamino Dal Fabbro, scrittore*. Atti della giornata di studi, Belluno, 29 ottobre 2010. A cura di R. Zucco. 2011, X-164 pp. con 20 tavv. f.t. a colori.

386. Carnevale Schianca, E. *La cucina medievale. Lessico, storia, preparazioni*. 2011, XLVI-758 pp.

387. Remigi, G. *Cesare Pavese e la letteratura americana: «una splendida monotonia»*. 2012, XVIII-226 pp.

388. Segatori, S. *Forme, temi e motivi della narrativa di Ippolito Nievo*. 2011, VIII-188 pp.

389. *I Marmi di Anton Francesco Doni: la storia, i generi e le arti*. A cura di G. Rizzarelli. 2012, XVIII-430 pp. con 35 figg. n.t.

390. *Paesaggio ligure e paesaggi interiori nella poesia di Eugenio Montale*. Atti del Convegno internazionale, «Credo non esista nulla di simile al mondo», Parco Nazionale delle Cinque Terre, Riomaggiore-Monterosso, 11-13 dicembre 2009. A cura di P. Polito e A. Zollino. 2011, VIII-284 pp. con 7 figg. n.t.

391. Fumagalli, E. *Il giusto Enea e il pio Rifeo. Pagine dantesche*. 2012, VIII-266 pp.

392. *Dialogo & conversazione. I luoghi di una socialità ideale dal Rinascimento all'Illuminismo*. A cura di M. Høxbro Andersen e A. Toftgaard. 2012, IV, 264 pp.

393. Payne, A. *The Telescope and the Compass. Teofilo Gallaccini and the Dialogue between Architecture and Science in the Age of Galileo*. 2012, XX-242 pp. con 96 figg. n.t.

394. *Teofilo Gallaccini. Selected Writings and Library*. Edited by A. Payne, with the Contribution of G.M. Fara. 2012, X-414 pp. con 102 figg. n.t.

395. Buccini, S. *Francesco Pona. L'ozio lecito della scrittura*. 2013, XIV-228 pp. con 37 figg. n.t.

396. *Studi di letteratura francese. Rivista europea*, voll. XXXII-IXXXIV (2008-2009). «La poésie de langue française contemporaine». 2011, 154 pp.

397. D'Elia, A. *La* peregrinatio *poietica di David Maria Turoldo*. Prefazione di D. Della Terza. 2012, XIV-182 pp.

398. Battisti, E. *Michelangelo: fortuna di un mito. Cinquecento anni di critica letteraria e artistica*. A cura di G. Saccaro Del Buffa. 2012, XVIII-248 pp. con 19 tavv. f.t. di cui 15 a colori.

399. *Studi secenteschi*. Vol. LIII (2012). 2012, IV-404 pp. con 4 figg. n.t.

400. Addesso, C.A. *Teatro e festività nella Napoli aragonese*. 2012, X-172 pp.

401. Bellorini, G. *Il magnifico Signor Cavallier Luigi Cassola Piacentino. Edizione critica dei* madrigali. *Censimento e indice dei capoversi di tutte le rime*. 2012, XVI-222 pp.

402. Martellotti, A. *Linguistica e cucina*. 2012, XIV-172 pp.

403. Marselli, N. *L'architettura in relazione alla storia del mondo*. A cura di D. Iacobone. 2012, IV-90 pp.

404. *«Legato con amore in un volume». Essays in honour of John A. Scott*. Edited by John J. Kinder and Diana Glenn. 2013, XX-350 pp. con 6 figg. n.t. e 3 tavv. f.t.

405. Buckstone, J.B. *Robert Macaire, or, the Exploits of a Gentleman at Large*. Edited and with an introduction by M.S. Marchesi. 2012, LII-64 pp.

406. Capecchi, G. - Pegazzano, D. - Faralli, S. *Visitare Boboli all'epoca dei Lumi. Il giardino e le sue sculture nelle incisioni delle 'Statue di Firenze'*. 2013, VI-244 pp. con 228 ill. n.t. e 1 pieghevole.

407. *Studi di letteratura francese. Rivista europea*, voll. XXXVXXXVI (2010-2011). «Henri Meschonnic entre langue et poésie». 2012, 210 pp. con 12 figg. n.t. e 8 tavv. f.t.

408. Doni, A.F. *I Marmi*. A cura di G. Rizzarelli e C.A. Girotto.In preparazione.

409. Del Gatto, A. Quel punto acerbo. *Temporalità e conoscenza metaforica in Leopardi*. 2012, X-116 pp.

410. Giambonini, F. *Bernardino Lanino ritrattista e l'ambiente artistico politico del suo tempo*. 2013, VI-334 pp. con 9 tavv. f.t. a colori.

411. *Studi secenteschi*. Vol. LIV (2013). 2013, X-372 pp. con 5 figg. n.t.

412. Butti de Lima, P. *Il piacere delle immagini. Un tema aristotelico nella riflessione moderna sull'arte*. 2012, VIII-202 pp. con 3 tavv. f.t. a colori.

413. Mocca, C. *Discorsi Preservativi e curativi delle peste Col modo di purgare le Case, & Robbe Appestate*. A cura di R. Scarpa. 2012, XXX-54 pp.

414. Tordella, P.G. *Il disegno nell'Europa del Settecento. Regioni teoriche ragioni critiche*. 2012, XIV-284 pp. con 16 tavv. f.t.

415. *Regionis forma pvlcherrima. Percezioni, lessico, categorie del paesaggio nella letteratura latina*. Atti del Convegno di studio, Palazzo Bo, Università degli studi di Padova, 15-16 marzo 2011. A cura di G. Baldo e E. Cazzuffi. 2013, VIII-278 pp. con 6 figg. n.t.

416. *Lo «Zibaldone» di Leopardi come ipertesto*. Atti del Convegno internazionale, Barcellona, 26-27 ottobre 2012. A cura di M. de las Nieves Muñiz Muñiz. 2013, X-506 pp. con 5 figg. n.t e 9 tavv. f.t. a colori.

417. Viglione, M. *Le insorgenze controrivoluzionarie nella storiografia italiana. Dibattito scientifico e scontro ideologico (1799-2012)*. 2013, XII-132 pp.

418. Burlamacchi, M. *Nobility, Honour and Glory. A brief Military History of the Order of Malta*. Translated from the Italian by M. Roberts. 2013, X-76 pp. con 13 tavv. f.t. di cui 9 a colori

419. Petrioli Tofani, A. *L'inventario settecentesco dei disegni degli Uffizi di Giuseppe Pelli Bencivenni*. 2014, 4 tomi di complessive XXX-1826 pp.

420. Marzi, M.G. *Il Gabinetto delle Terre di Luigi Lanzi nella Galleria degli Uffizi. Vasi, terrecotte, lucerne e vetri dalle Collezioni medicee-lorenesi al Museo Archeologico Nazionale di Firenze*. In preparazione.

421. *L'*Iconologia *di Cesare Ripa. Fonti letterarie e figurative dall'antichità al Rinascimento*. Atti del Convegno internazionale di studi, Certosa di Pontignano, 3-4 maggio 2012. A cura di M. Gabriele, C. Galassi, R. Guerrini. 2013, XXVIII-236 pp con 58 figg. n.t.

422. Aricò, N. *Architettura del tardo Rinascimento in Sicilia Giovannangelo Montorsoli a Messina (1547-57)*. 2013, XIV-226 pp. con 60 figg. n.t. e 16 tavv. f.t. a colori.

423. Modesti, P. *Le delizie ritrovate. Poggioreale e la villa del Rinascimento nella Napoli aragonese*. 2014, X-272 pp. con 1 fig. n.t e 64 tavv. f.t. di cui 15 a colori.

424. *Architettura e identità locali*. Vol. I. A cura di L. Corrain e F.P. Di Teodoro. 2013, X-586 pp. con 161 figg. n.t. e 3 tavv f.t. a colori.

425. *Architettura e identità locali*. Vol. II. A cura di H. Burns e M. Mussolin. Con la collaborazione di Clara Altavista. 2015 X-718 pp. con 163 figg. n.t. e 4 tavv. f.t. a colori.

426. Fara, G.M. *Albrecht Dürer nelle fonti italiane antiche: 1508-1686*. 2014, XII-590 pp.

427. *Studi secenteschi*. Vol. LV (2014). 2014, IV-330 pp. con 4 figg. n.t.

428. Fara, A. *L'arte della scienza. Architettura e cultura militare a Torino e nello stato sabaudo 1673-1859*. 2014, XII-272 pp. con 1 fig. n.t. e 64 tavv. f.t.

429. *Studi di letteratura francese. Rivista europea*, voll. XXXVI-IXXXVIII (2012-2013). «La langue de la poésie française contemporaine». 2014, 168 pp.

430. Felici, A. *Michelangelo a San Lorenzo (1515-1534). Il linguaggio architettonico del Cinquecento fiorentino*. Premessa di G. Frosini. 2015, X-378 pp. con 64 figg. n.t.

431. Ceccherini, I. *Sozomeno da Pistoia (1387-1458). Scrittura e libri di un umanista*. Premessa di S. Zamponi, con un saggio di D. Speranzi. 2016, XX-468 pp. con 12 figg. n.t. e 120 tavv. f.t.

432. *Traiano Boccalini tra satira e politica*. Atti del Convegno, Macerata-Loreto, ottobre 2013. A cura di Laura Melosi, Paolo Procaccioli. 2015, XII-482 con 3 figg. n.t.

433. Durante E. - Martellotti, A. *"Amorosa fenice". La vita, le rime e la fortuna in musica di Girolamo Casone da Oderzo (c. 1528-1592)*. 2015, VI-482 pp. con 4 figg. n.t.

434. *Incontri di civiltà nel Mediterraneo. L'Impero Ottomano e l'Italia del Rinascimento. Storia, arte e architettura*. A cura di

Alireza Naser Eslami. 2014, 184 pp. con 75 figg. n.t. di cui 56 a colori.

435. Rossi, M., *Unione e diversità. L'Italia di Vasari nello specchio della Sistina*. 2014, 184 pp. con 48 figg. n.t. e 16 tavv. f.t. a colori.

436. *L'architettura militare di Venezia in terraferma e in Adriatico fra XVI e XVII secolo*. A cura di Francesco Paolo Fiore. 2014, XXVIII-462 pp. con 185 figg. n.t. e 16 tavv. f.t. di cui 8 a colori.

437. *Studi di Letteratura Francese. Rivista europea*, vol. XXXIX (2014). 2015, 172 pp.

438. *Studi secenteschi*. Vol. LVI (2015). 2015, 458 pp.

439. Urraro, R. *Questa maledetta vita. Il "romanzo autobiografico" di Giacomo Leopardi*. 2015, X-446 pp.

440. Platina, B. De honesta voluptate et valitudine. *Un trattato sui piaceri della tavola e la buona salute*. Nuova edizione commentata con testo latino a fronte a cura di Enrico Carnevale Schianca. 2015, VI-590 pp.

441. Morabito, R. *L'Evo e il tempo del* Canzoniere. 2015, IV-72 pp.

442. *Studi linguistici e letterari tra Italia e mondo iberico in età moderna*. A cura di M. Graziani e S. Vuelta García. 2015, VI-140 pp.

443. Lia, P. *Poetica dell'amore e conversione. Considerazioni teologiche sulla lingua della* Commedia *di Dante*. 2015, XIV-324 pp.

444. Gabriele, M. *La* Porta Magica *di Roma simbolo dell'alchimia occidentale*. 2015. (esaurito)

445. Blanco, M. *Edipo non deve nascere. Lettura delle* Poésies *di Mallarmé*. 2016, XII-248 pp. con 4 tavv. f.t.

446. *Studi di letteratura francese. Rivista europea*, vol. XL (2015). 2016, 126 pp.

447. McLaughlin, M. *Leon Battista Alberti. La vita, l'umanesimo, le opere*. 2016, XXII-174 pp. con 9 tavv. f.t.

448. Bertelli, S. *La tradizione della «Commedia» dai manoscritti al testo*. II. *I codici trecenteschi (oltre l'antica vulgata) conservati a Firenze*. 2016, VIII-610 pp. con 89 figg. n.t. e 64 tavv. f.t. a colori.

449. Villani, G. *Il convitato di pietra. Apoteosi e tramonto della linea curva nel Settecento*. 2016, X-120 pp. con 8 tavv. f.t. a colori.

450. Valignano, A. *Dialogo sulla Missione degli ambasciatori giapponesi alla curia romana e sulle cose osservate in Europa e durante tutto il viaggio basato sul diario degli ambasciatori e tradotto in latino da Duarte de Sande, sacerdote della Compagnia di Gesù*. A cura di M. Di Russo, traduzione di P.A. Airoldi, presentazione di D. Maraini. 2016, XVI-670 pp. con 79 figg. n.t., 3 cartine e 32 tavv. f.t. a colori.

451. Tordella, P.G. *Hugo von Hofmannsthal e la poetica del disegno tra Otto e Novecento*. 2016, VIII-256 pp. con 8 tavv. f.t. a colori.

452. *Studi secenteschi*. Vol. LVII (2016). 2016, IV-362 pp. con 13 figg. n.t.

453. Aricò, N. *La fondazione di Carlentini nella Sicilia di Juan de Vega*. 2016, XII-280 pp. con 37 figg. n.t. e 16 tavv. f.t. a colori.

454. *Traduzioni, riscritture, ibridazioni: prosa e teatro fra Italia, Spagna e Portogallo*. A cura di M. Graziani e S. Vuelta García. 2016, VI-142 pp.

455. Caputo, G. *L'aurora del Giappone tra mito e storiografia. Nascita ed evoluzione dell'alterità nipponica nella cultura italiana, 1300-1600*. 2016, XX-352 pp. con 19 figg. n.t.

456. Lawson Lucas, A. *Emilio Salgari. Una mitologia moderna tra letteratura, politica, società*. Vol. I. 2017, XVI-444 pp. con 83 figg. b/n n.t. e 32 tavv. f.t. a colori.

457. Lawson Lucas, A. *Emilio Salgari. Una mitologia moderna tra letteratura, politica, società*. Vol. II. 2018. X-506 pp. con 72 figg. b/n n.t. e 25 tavv. f.t. a colori.

458. Lawson Lucas, A. *Emilio Salgari. Una mitologia moderna tra letteratura, politica, società*. Vol. III. 2019. X-514 pp. con 48 figg. b/n n.t. e 38 tavv. f.t. a colori.

459. Lawson Lucas, A. *Emilio Salgari. Una mitologia moderna tra letteratura, politica, società*. Vol. IV. In preparazione.

460. *Ius Leopardi. Legge, natura, civiltà*. A cura di L. Melosi. 2016, VI-114 pp.

461. *La* Comedia Nueva *e le scene italiane nel Seicento*. A cura di F. Antonucci e A. Tedesco. 2016, 340 pp.

462. Morabito, R. *Le virtù di Griselda. Storia di una storia*. 2017, IV-144 pp. con 8 tavv. f.t.

463. *Studi di letteratura francese. Rivista europea*, vol. XLI (2016). 2016, 302 pp. con 8 tavv. f.t.

464. Gazzola, G. *Montale, the modernist*. 2016, VIII-234 pp. con 4 figg. n.t.

465. Celio Secondo Curione, Pasquillus extaticus *e* Pasquino in estasi. Edizione storico-critica commentata. A cura di G. Cordibella e S. Prandi. 2018, IV-316 pp. con 7 figg. n.t.

466. Cappozzo, V. *Dizionario dei sogni nel Medioevo. Il* Somniale Danielis *in manoscritti letterari*. In preparazione.

467. Zamuner, I. – Ruzza, E. *I ricettari del codice 52 della Historical Medical Library di New Haven (XIII sec. u.q.)*. 2017, XXVIII-72 pp. con 1 fig. n.t. a colori.

468. Fenu Barbera, R. *Dante's Tears. The Poetics of Weeping from* Vita Nuova *to the* Commedia. 2017, XVIII-206 pp.

469. Fabbri, L. *Il papavero da oppio nella cultura e nella religione romana*. 2017, XII-400 pp. con 16 tavv. f.t. a colori.

470. Pierguidi, S. *Pittura di marmo. Storia e fortuna delle pale d'altare a rilievo nella Roma di Bernini*. 2017, XX-294 pp. con 95 figg. n.t.

471. Ruggiero, R. *Baldassarre Castiglione diplomatico. La missione del cortegiano*. 2017, XVI-154 pp.

472. *A Portuguese Abbot in Renaissance Florence. The letter collection of Gomes Eanes (1415-1463)*. A cura di R. Costa-Gomes. 2017, XLVIII-580 pp. con 1 fig. b/n n.t.

473. Coco, E. *Dal cosmo al mare. La naturalizzazione del mito e la funzione filosofica*. 2017, IV-132 pp.

474. *Studi secenteschi*. Vol. LVIII (2017). 2017, IV-344 pp. con 4 tavv. b/n f.t.

475. «M'exalta el nou i m'enamora el vell». *J.V. Foix e Joan Mirò tra arte e letteratura*. A cura di Ilaria Zamuner. Premessa di Enric Bou. 2017, XII-110 pp. con 2 figg. b/n n.t. e 24 tavv. f.t. a colori.

476. *Incontri poetici e teatrali fra Italia e penisola iberica*. A cura di Michela Graziani e Salomé Vuelta Garcìa. 2017, VI-138 pp.

477. Fara, A. *Buontalenti e Le Nôtre. Geometria del giardino da Pratolino a Versailles*. 2017, VIII-132 pp. con 48 tavv. a colori f.t. e 12 tavv. b/n f.t.

478. *Saperi per la Nazione. Storia e geografia nella costruzione dell'Italia unita*. A cura di Paola Pressenda e Paola Sereno. 2017, VIII-504 pp.

479. Bartoli, S. *La felicità di una donna. Émilie du Châtelet tra Voltaire e Newton*. 2017, 252 pp.

480. Bragagnolo, M., *Lodovico Antonio Muratori e l'eredità del Cinquecento nell'Europa del XVIII secolo*. 2018, XX-168 pp.

481. Minutelli, M. *L'arca di Saba: «i sereni animali / che avvicinano a Dio»*. 2018, XXIV-330 pp. con 3 figg. b/n n.t.

482. *Studi di letteratura francese. Rivista europea*, vol. XLII (2017). 2017, 120 pp.

483. Villani, G., *Un atlante della cultura europea. Vittorio Pica: il metodo e le fonti*. 2018, VIII-140 pp.

484. Waddington, R., *Titian's Aretino: a contextual study of all the portraits*. 2018, X-154 pp. con 32 tavv. f.t. a colori.

485. Fadda, E., *Come in un rebus. Correggio e la Camera di San Paolo*. 2018, IV-108 pp. con 56 tavv. f.t.

486. *Approcci interdisciplinari al petrarchismo. Prospettive di ricerca tra Italia e Germania*. A cura di Bernard Huss e Maiko Favaro. 2018, X-270 pp. con 6 figg. n.t. e 23 tavv. f.t. a colori.

487. *Studi secenteschi*. Vol. LIX (2018). 2018, IV-344 pp. con 4 figg. b/n n.t. e 16 tavv. f.t. a colori.

488. Mirabile, A., *Ezra Pound e l'arte italiana. Fra le Avanguardie e D'Annunzio*. 2018, VI-138 pp.

489. Mastrobuono, Antonio C. *Il viaggio dantesco della santificazione*. 2018, XVIII-280 pp. con 4 tavv. f.t. a colori.

490. *Incroci teatrali italo-iberici*. A cura di M. Graziani e S. Vuelta García. 2018, VIII-154 pp.

491. Reuter-Mayring, U., *Giuseppe Baretti: sugo, sostanza e qualità. La critica letteraria italiana moderna a metà del* xviii *secolo*. 2019, VIII-164 pp. con 4 tavv. f.t. a colori.

492. Fabbri, L., *Mater florum. Flora e il suo culto a Roma*. 2019, XIV-280 pp. con 11 figg. f.t. a colori.

493. *Albrecht Dürer e Venezia*. A cura di G.M. Fara. 2018, VIII-196 pp. con 47 figg. n.t. e 8 tavv. f.t. a colori.

494. *Studi di letteratura francese. Rivista europea*, vol. XLIII (2018). 2018, 122 pp.

495. *Studi secenteschi*. Vol. LX (2019). 2019, IV-306 pp. con 3 figg. b/n n.t.

496. *Storiografia e teatro tra Italia e penisola iberica*. A cura di M. Graziani e S. Vuelta García. 2019, VIII-160 pp.

497. Parasiliti, Andrea G.G., *All'ombra del vulcano. Il Futurismo in Sicilia e l'Etna di Marinetti*. 2020, XX-288 pp. con 74 figg. b/n n.t. e 4 tavv. a colori f.t.

498. *Un trésor de textes. Images, présences et métaphores du trésor dans la langue et la littérature françaises*. Textes réunis par Anna Bettoni et Marika Piva. 2020, VIII-288 pp. con 11 figg. b/n n.t. e 4 tavv. f.t. a colori.

499. Squillace, G., *Il profumo nel mondo antico. Con la traduzione italiana del «Sugli odori» di Teofrasto*. Prefazione di L. Villoresi. 2020, XX-282 pp. con 8 tavv. f.t. a colori.

500. Signorini, M., *Sulle tracce di Petrarca. Storia e significato di una prassi scrittoria*. 2020, XII-224 pp. con 41 figg. b/n n.t.

501. *Luigi Lanzi a Udine (1796-1801). Storiografia artistica, cultura antiquaria e letteraria nel cuore d'Europa tra Sette e Ottocento*. A cura di Paolo Pastres. 2020, XII-280 pp. con 32 tavv. b/n f.t.

502. *Studi di letteratura francese. Rivista europea*. vol. XLIV (2019). 2019, 120 pp.

503. Di Teodoro, F.P., *Lettera a Leone X di Raffaello e Baldassarre Castiglione*. 2020, XII-72 pp. con 32 tavv. f.t. a colori.

504. Gandolfi, R., *Le Vite degli artisti di Gaspare Celio. Compendio delle* Vite *di Vasari con alcune altre aggiunte*. XII-392 pp. con 45 tavv. f.t. a colori.

505. *Studi secenteschi*. Vol. LXI (2020). 2020, VI-312 pp. con 34 figg. b/n n.t.

506. *Comunicare l'infinito: orizzonti leopardiani*. A cura di F. Berardi, A. Lombardinilo, P. Ortolano. 2020, X-186 pp.

507. Urraro, R., *Il romanzo familiare di Pierfrancesco Leopardi*. 2020, X-260 pp.

508. Guassardo, G., *The italian love poetry of ludovico ariosto: court culture and classicism*. Preface di L. Bolzoni. 2021, VIII-246 pp.

509. *Variazioni sull'autore in epoca moderna*. A cura di S. Vuelta García e M. Graziani. 2020, VIII-90 pp.

510. *Studi di letteratura francese*. Vol. XLV (2020). 2020, 152 pp.

511. Gabriele, M. *La* Porta Magica *di Roma simbolo dell'alchimia occidentale*. Nuova edizione ampliata e riveduta. In preparazione.

Serie II: Linguistica

1. Spitzer, L. *Lexikalisches aus dem Katalanischen und den übrigen ibero-romanischen Sprachen*. 1921. VIII-162 pp.

2. Gamillscheg, E. und Spitzer, L. *Beiträge zur romanischen Wortbildungslehre*. 1921, 230 pp., 3 cc.

3. [Schuchardt, U.]. *Miscellanea linguistica dedic. a Ugo Schuchardt per il suo 80° anniv*. 1922, 121 pp., 2 cc.

4. Bertoldi, V. *Un ribelle nel regno dei fiori (I nomi romanzi del «colchicum autunnale L.» attraverso il tempo e lo spazio)*. 1923, VIII-224 pp. con ill.

5. Bottiglioni, G. *Leggende e tradizioni di Sardegna*. (Testi dialettali in grafia fonetica). 1922. (esaurito)

6. Onomastica - I. Paul Aebischer, *Sur la formation des noms de famille dans le canton de Fribourg (Suisse)*. - II. Dante Olivieri, *I cognomi della Venezia Euganea*. Saggio di uno studio storico-etimologico. 1924, 272 pp.

7. Rohlfs, G. *Grichen und Romanen in Unteritalien* Ein Beitrag zur Geschichte der unteritalienischen Gräzität. 1923. (esaurito)

8. *Studi di dialettologia alto italiana*. - I. Gualzata, M. *Di alcuni nomi locali del Bellinzonese e Locarnese*. - II. Bläuer-Rini, A. *Giunte al «vocabolario di Bormio»*. 1924, 166 pp.

9. Pascu, G. *Romänische elemente in den Balkansprachen*. 1924, IV-112 pp.

10. Farinelli, A. *Marrano* (Storia di un vituperio). 1925, X-80 pp.

11. Bertoni, G. *Profilo storico del dialetto di Modena. (Con appendice di «Giunte al Vocabolario Modenese»)*. 1925, 88 pp.

12. Bartoli, M. *Introduzione alla neolinguistica* (Principi - Scopi - Metodi), 1926. (esaurito)

13. Migliorini, B. *Dal nome proprio al nome comune*. 1927, VI-358 pp. con LXXVIII pp. di supplemento. Seconda ristampa 1999.

14. Keller, O. *La flexion du verbe dans le patois genevois*. 1928, XXVIII-216 pp., 1 c. ripiegata.

15. Spotti, L. *Vocabolarietto anconitano-italiano*. 1929. (esaurito)

16. Wagner, M. L. *Studien über den sardischen Wortschatz. (I. Die Familie - II. Der menschliche Körper)*. 1930, XVI-156 pp., 15 cc.

17. Soukup, R. *Les causes et l'évolution de l'abreviation des pronoms personnels régimes en ancien français*. 1932, 130 pp.

18. Rheinfelder, H. *Kultsprache und Profansprache in den romanischen Ländern*. 1933. (esaurito)

19. Flagge, L. *Provenzalisches Alpenleben in den Hochtälern des Verdon und der Bléone*. Ein Beitrag zur Volkskunde des Basses-Alpes. 1935. (esaurito)

20. Sainéan, L. *Autour des sources indigènes*. Etudes d'étymologie française et romaine. 1935. (esaurito)

21. Seifert, E. *Tenere «Haben» im Romanischen*. 1935, 122 pp., 4 tavv.

22. Tagliavini, C. *L'Albanese di Dalmazia*. 1937. (esaurito)

23. Bosshard, H. *Saggio di un glossario dell'antico Lombardo*. 1938. (esaurito)

24. Vidos, B. E. *Storia delle parole marinaresche italiane passate in francese*. 1939. (esaurito)

25. Alessio, G. *Saggio di Toponomastica calabrese*. 1939. (esaurito)

26. Folena, G. *La crisi linguistica del 400 e l'«Arcadia» di I. Sanazaro*. 1952. (esaurito)

27. *Miscellanea di studi linguistici in ricordo di Ettore Tolomei*. 1953. (esaurito)

28. Vidos, B. E. *Manuale di linguistica romanza*. Prima edizione italiana completamente aggiornata dall'Autore. 1959, XXIV-440 pp. Terza ristampa 1975.

29. Ruggieri, R. *Saggi di linguistica italiana e italo-romanza*. 1962, 242 pp.

30. Mengaldo, P. V. *La lingua del Boiardo lirico*. 1963, VIII-380 pp.

31. Vidos, B. E. *Prestito espansione e migrazione dei termini tecnici nelle lingue romanze e non romanze*. 1965, VIII-424 pp., 3 ill.

32. Altieri Biagi, M. L. *Galileo e la terminologia tecnico-scientifica*. 1965. (esaurito)

33. Polloni, A. *Toponomastica romagnola*, Prefazione di Carlo Tagliavini. 1966. Ristampa 2002.

34. Ghiglieri, P. *La grafia del Machiavelli studiata negli autografi*. 1969, IV-364 pp.

35. *Linguistica matematica e calcolatori*. A cura di A. Zampolli. 1973, XX-670 pp.

36. *Computational and mathematical linguistics*. Vol. I. A cura di A. Zampolli e N. Calzolari. 1977, 2 voll. di XLVI-796 pp. complessive.

37. *Computational and mathematical linguistics*. Vol. II. A cura di A. Zampolli e N. Calzolari. 1980, 2 voll. di VIII-906 pp. complessive.

38. Semerano, G. *Le origini della cultura europea. Rivelazioni della linguistica storica*. 1984, 2 voll. di LXX-956 pp. complessive. Ristampa 2010.

39. *Fonologia etrusca, fonetica toscana. Il problema del sostrato*. 1983, 204 pp. con 1 tav. f.t.

40. La Stella, T. E. *Dizionario storico di deonomastica*. 1984, 236 pp.

41. Rando, G. *Dizionario degli anglicismi nell'italiano contemporaneo*. 1987, XLII-256 pp.

42. *Lessicografia, filologia e critica*. 1986, 204 pp.

43. Semerano, G. *Le origini della cultura europea*. Vol. II. *Dizionari etimologici. Basi semitiche delle lingue Indeuropee*. I tomo: *Dizionario della lingua greca*. II tomo: *Dizionario della lingua latina*. 1994, 2 voll. di C-726 pp. complessive. III ristampa 2007.

44. Scavuzzo, C. *Studi sulla lingua dei quotidiani messinesi di fine Ottocento*. 1988, 208 pp.

45. Agostiniani, L. - Hjordt-Vetlesen, O. *Lessico etrusco cronologico e topografico dai materiali del «Thesaurus Linguae Etruscae»*. 1988, XXXVI-224 pp.

46. O'Connor, D. *A history of Italian and English bilingual dictionaries*. 1990, 188 pp.

47. Boselli, P. *Dizionario di toponomastica bergamasca e cremonese*. 1990, 346 pp.

48. Delmay, B. *Usi e difese della lingua*. 1990, 154 pp. con 1 tav. f.t.

49. Catenazzi, F. *L'italiano di Svevo. Fra scrittura pubblica e scrittura privata*. 1994, 202 pp.

50. Facchetti, G. M. *Frammenti di diritto privato etrusco*. 2000, 116 pp.

51. *La scrittura professionale: ricerca, prassi, insegnamento*. Atti del I Convegno di studi, Perugia, Università per Stranieri, 23-25 ottobre 2000. A cura di S. Covino. 2001, XXIV-454 pp. con 29 figg. n.t. e 1 pieghevole.

52. Leone, A. *Conversazioni sulla lingua italiana*. 2002, 160 pp.

53. Natella, P. *La parola 'Mafia'*. 2002, 172 pp.

54. Facchetti, G. M. *Appunti di morfologia etrusca. Con un'appendice sulla questione delle identità genetiche dell'etrusco*. 2002, 160 pp.

55. Facchetti, G. M. - Negri, M. *Creta minoica. Sulle tracce delle più antiche scritture d'Europa*. 2003, 200 pp. con 21 figg. n.t. e 2 tavv. f.t.

56. Prandi, M. - Gross, G. - De Santis, C. *La finalità. Strutture concettuali e forme d'espressione in italiano*. 2005, 366 pp.

57. Ferguson, R. *A Linguistic History of Venice*. 2007, 322 pp. con 3 figg. n.t.

58. *L'italiano parlato di Firenze, Perugia e Roma*. A cura di L. Agostiniani e P. Bonucci. 2011, 206 pp. con 8 figg. n.t.

59. Medina Montero, J.F. *El verbo, el participio y las clases de palabras "invariables" en las gramáticas de español para extranjeros de los siglos XVI y XVII*. 2015, VIII-192 pp.

60. *Digital Texts, translations, lexicons in a multi-modular web application: methods and samples*. A cura di A. Bozzi. 2015, X-146 pp. con 38 figg. n.t.

61. Parenti, A. *Parole strane. Etimologie e altra linguistica*. 2015, VI-158 pp. con 2 figg. n.t.

62. Arcaini, E. *L'indeterminatezza del segno e il trasferimento delle culture*. 2018, X-254 pp. con 8 tavv. f.t. a colori.

63. Guida, A. *Lexicon Vindobonense*, 2018, LXIV-350 pp.